Henry David Thoreau
and the Moral Agency of Knowing

Henry David Thoreau, 1856. (Archives of the Gray
Herbarium, Harvard University; reproduced by permission)

Henry David Thoreau and the Moral Agency of Knowing

ALFRED I. TAUBER

University of California Press

BERKELEY   LOS ANGELES   LONDON

University of California Press
Berkeley and Los Angeles, California

University of California Press, Ltd.
London, England

First paperback printing 2003

© 2001 by
The Regents of the University of California

Library of Congress Cataloging-in-Publication Data

Tauber, Alfred I.
  Henry David Thoreau and the moral agency of knowing /
Alfred I. Tauber
    p. cm.
  Includes bibliographical references and index.
  ISBN 0-520-23915-6 (pbk: alk. paper)
    1. Thoreau, Henry David, 1817–1862—Philosophy. 2. Thoreau,
Henry David, 1817–1862—Ethics. 3. Knowledge, theory of, in
literature. 4. Romanticism—United States. 5. Positivism. I. Title.

PS3057.P4T38   2001
818'.309—dc21

                                        00-068283

Printed in the United States of America

10 09 08 07 06 05 04 03
10 9 8 7 6 5 4 3 2 1

The paper used in this publication is both acid-free and totally
chlorine-free (TCF). It meets the minimum requirements of
ANSI/NISO Z39.48-1992 (R 1997) (*Permanence of Paper*). ∞

For Paula, again

Contents

Acknowledgments

This study addresses Thoreau from an unusual vantage point. As a historian and philosopher of science, I note that my own discipline has paid scant attention to him, but here I wish to claim Thoreau—or, better, to "borrow" him. He offers a rich grist for the philosopher's mill and, by extension, to those current cultural studies that begin with the philosophical questions he poses: the character of the self, the grounding of moral agency, the nature of knowledge. Thoreau was no postmodern, but he faced many of the same challenges we do, and in studying his life, I have come to value the ethical example he offered. While philosophical readings might enrich the literary approaches that have dominated Thoreauvian scholarship for a century, I believe structuring his project on a philosophical edifice also offers critical insights into certain quandaries that reach into the very mainstream of contemporary science studies.

For me, Thoreau is a fascinating "hinge" character residing between an ebbing Romanticism and a rising positivism. Stretching from early Romanticism to the contemporary molecular revolution, my own endeavor is to better understand the tension generated by science's positivist leanings against both the humane demands of its knowledge and the role of the participating scientist. In this respect, Thoreau, usually seen as a naturalist and champion of the environment, is of interest to me because of the clear fashion in which his life and work have focused the problem of the observer in this scientific setting. More generally, he exemplifies the difficulty of assigning value to our science that seeks dispassionate objectivity, yet remains firmly tied to humane understanding. We assign value to our knowledge; we require placing the self in its world; we seek to use our knowledge for humane purposes. Each requires the assignment of value and the exercise of choice.

But the roots of my interest in Thoreau reach to older issues than my professional concerns, in fact to the awakening of my intellect as an adolescent, when I first read *Walden*. It made a lasting impression on me, and I am well aware that its challenge beckoned for a thorough response. In part, this has been accomplished in the writing of this study, for I have come to articulate the meaning of that work, which had such a profound influence on how I thought of individuality and my own personhood. At about the same time I was introduced to Thoreau, I also began reading Freud and guides to his work. Of these, the most memorable was Philip Rieff's *Freud: The Mind of the Moralist* (1959), a book that impressed me in many ways, not the least of which was the intimation that a scientific project might reflect a moral attitude or program. Although I abandoned a serious interest in Freudian psychology, the interpretative point has apparently been internalized, and in my own work I find interesting parallels in reading Thoreau's life as Rieff read Freud's. Rieff's sequel, *The Triumph of the Therapeutic* (1966), was written in a similar vein but lacked, at least to my current recollection, the same moral verve exhibited by the earlier text. But there is an interesting parallel regarding Thoreau, inasmuch as I think he too exhibited a "therapeutic triumph"—for himself and for us all. Although he claimed that "I love nature partly *because* she is not man, but a retreat from him" (January 3, 1853, *Journal* 5, 1997, p. 422), he reaches out to each of us in the most intimate fashion, and we respond. Despite the all too apparent failings, Thoreau indeed did prevail in his own struggle and, in doing so, provided us with a moral example we might emulate.

My exploration freely draws on previous essays that are related to the overall themes treated here but were written in other contexts. The discussion on Romanticism, and specifically Goethe, is based on Tauber 1993; on history and memory, Tauber 1999a; on the aesthetic elements of science, Tauber 1996a; on the philosophical characterization of modern science, the introduction to Tauber 1997 and Tauber 1999b; on the relation of science and ethics, Tauber 1998a; on the historical evolution of the self concept and its philosophical standing, Tauber 1992, 1994, 1999c. There are other issues that have served as the organizing subjects of my writing—reductionism and positivism; the limits of analysis in philosophy; the ethics of history; the character of moral philosophy in our postmodern age; the subject-object relationship in science generally. In a sense, this study of Thoreau ties together what at first glance represents apparently far-flung issues that I have considered in different formats and that are drawn together here by the attempt to outline an understanding of the self and, more specifically, of how a moral voice might guide an epistemology. It is in this last context that the deepest strata of this study find their settings in the writings of Emmanuel Levinas, specifically in his notion of an "ethical metaphysics" as superseding other modes of being and knowing. I have interpreted Levinas in various guises (Tauber 1995, 1998b, 1999a), and his philosophy might be detected here as only a faint and undeclared echo if my debt were not explicitly acknowledged.[1]

Seven editors refused even to send this book out for review: "too interdisciplinary," "too unorthodox," "won't fit into our list," "won't sell" were the typical responses. Not until Stan Holwitz embraced this project did the manuscript enjoy the prospect of publication. He ensured that my efforts were realized, and I am especially grateful to him. I am also indebted to the University of California Press staff, especially Jean McAneny and Nicholas Goodhue, who so ably took my manuscript through production. Various readers have generously offered important critical comment to me, so to Rick Adler, Dan Dahlstrom, Menachem Fisch, Erazim Kohak, Leo Marx, Emanuel Papper, David Roochnik, Stanley Rosen, and Jan Zwicky, thank you. Dan Peck has been most intimate with my own project, I think largely because we regard Thoreau from several shared perspectives, and I am especially indebted to his insights and criticisms of my own work. My wife, Paula Fredriksen, has, as always, been my most enthusiastic reader. Beyond patiently teaching me Augustine's philosophy—which was to become a main pillar of this study—her editorial suggestions, critical acumen, and abiding emotional support sustain me. Naturally, I alone am responsible for the interpretation offered here, but such a work is influenced in acknowledged and in unconscious fashion by many sources that I cannot enumerate. This book has been a joy to write, one that has flowed easily, and on that basis alone, I trust, at least, that I have given fair expression to my own dialogue with Thoreau. I can only hope that this essay contributes to our understanding of him—and thereby of ourselves.

A.I.T.
Boscawen, New Hampshire
November 1999

Introduction

There is no account of the blue sky in history.
　　　　　Thoreau, January 7, 1851,
　　　　　Journal 3, 1990, p. 174

Would you see your mind–look at the sky.
　　　　　Thoreau, January 26, 1852,
　　　　　Journal 4, 1992, p. 291

Henry David Thoreau lived in an age of keen observers, and he was very much a man of his time. Both scientists and artists developed an acute self-consciousness of their respective methods and faculties of observation, and of the limits as well as the prospects of their new modes of inspection. Thus each appreciated the problems of cognition with new insight. Within this tradition, for Thoreau, *seeing*—both the world *and* himself—became his preoccupation, and his problem. The least conspicuous or most obvious were equally susceptible to his gaze, and thus he made his contribution by making the ordinary extraordinary. He believed that the secrets of nature, and of humanity's place within it, were ultimately revealed by identifying what was significant in the everyday world; and that this revelation, in turn, depended on meticulous attention to, and accounting of, the commonplace. On the other hand, he too was guilty of complacency. An amusing observation made by Henry Petroski makes the point:

> Henry David Thoreau seemed to think of everything when he made a list of essential supplies for a twelve-day excursion into the Maine woods. He included pins, needles, and thread among the items to be carried in an India-rubber knapsack, and he even gave the dimensions of an ample tent. . . . He wanted to be doubly sure to be able to start a fire and to wash up, and so he listed: "matches (some also in a small vial in the waist-coat pocket); soap, two pieces." He specified the number of old newspapers (three or four, presumably to be used for cleaning chores), the length of strong cord (twenty feet), the size of his blanket (seven feet long), and the amount of "soft hardbread" (twenty-eight pounds!). . . .
> . . . [h]e advised like-minded observers to carry a small spyglass . . . a pocket microscope . . . tape measure . . . and paper and stamps, to mail letters back to civilization.

But there is one object that Thoreau neglected to mention, one that he most certainly carried himself. For without this object Thoreau could not have sketched . . . fauna. . . . Without it he could not label his blotting paper . . . or his insect boxes . . . record measurements . . . write home . . . [nor] make his list. Without a pencil Thoreau would have been lost in the Maine woods.

According to his friend Ralph Waldo Emerson, Thoreau seems always to have carried, "in his pocket, his diary and pencil." So why did Thoreau . . . neglect to list even one among the essential things to take on an excursion? Perhaps the very object with which he may have been drafting this list was too close to him, too familiar a part of his own everyday outfit, too integral a part of his livelihood, too common a thing for him to think to mention. (1989, pp. 3–4)

This is an unusual omission and only highlights Thoreau's scrupulous care in constructing his world. It is amusing precisely because it is out of character, jarringly inconsistent with Thoreau's own meticulous attention to the seemingly obvious. Petroski was writing about the innocuous pencil as an object of historical interest. I cite the omission to emphasize a philosophical point and a psychological truism: Knowledge is selective. We know what we want to know, or at least seek knowledge in the particular context of self-interest. Each of us follows his or her unique train.

Certainly, Thoreau was aware of this adage, and in acknowledging the limits of his observations, he both appreciated the endless splendor of the world about him and his own limited ability to fully appreciate it:

As I look north westward to that summit from a Concord cornfield– how little can I realize all the life that is passing between me & it–the retired up country farm houses–the lonely mills–wooded vales–wild rocky pastures–and new clearings on stark *mt* sides–& rivers gurgling through primitive woods–! All these and much more I *overlook.* (Thoreau, September 27, 1852, *Journal* 5, 1997, p. 357)

This preoccupation with the limits of his vision is a constant Thoreauvian theme, and even as his observations of nature became more scrupulous and even "scientific" in character, a self-consciousness remained, beguiling the growing positivist efforts to objectify the world. This Janus-like vision— simultaneously observing both the world and himself—offers us an essential clue in understanding Thoreau's project.

So, as Thoreau sought to know nature, he again and again faced his own autonomy—his consciousness of that world and his capacity to comprehend it. Thus he was both fascinated with understanding his place in the world, and at the same time committed to making that world, or at least his place in it, his *own*. So there was always a bidirectional movement in Thoreau's work: he would not only develop, even create, his personal identity in the context of nature, he would also engage and *know* nature in his particular fashion and thereby uniquely identify his world. Despite his commitment to empiricism and public discourse, Thoreau understood that *what* he saw and *how* he processed that experience were characteristic of his personal vision and ultimately shaped by it. My interest in Thoreau is primarily to understand what informed this dialectical process—the development of the man and the making of his world. Consequently, on this reading, I see Thoreau asking profound philosophical questions.

Thoreau regarded himself as living a philosophically informed life. For him, philosophy was a moral guide, and in the same spirit in which he criticized the mercantile pursuits of his neighbors, he distanced himself from philosophers who, in his view, failed to rise to his standard of living the virtuous life:

> There are nowadays professors of philosophy, but not philosophers. Yet it is admirable to profess because it was once admirable to live. To be a philosopher is not merely to have subtle thoughts, nor even to found a school, but so to love wisdom as to live according to its dictates, a life of simplicity, independence, magnanimity, and trust. It is to solve some of the problems of life, not only theoretically, but practically. (*Walden,* 1971, pp. 14–15; revised from Fall-Winter 1845–46 Journal entry [*Journal 2,* 1984, p. 145])

As the passage continues, Thoreau's identification with his own definition of the true philosopher emerges clearly:

> The success of great scholars and thinkers is commonly a courtier-like success, not kingly, not manly. They make shift to live merely by conformity, practically as their fathers did, and are in no sense the progenitors of a nobler race of men. . . . The philosopher is in advance of his age even in the outward form of his life. He is not fed, sheltered, clothed, warmed, like his contemporaries. How can a man be a philosopher and not maintain his vital heat by better methods than other men? (Ibid., p. 15)

Despite certain misgivings sprinkled in the Journal, Thoreau was, at least, sympathetic to philosophy and would repeatedly assume the philosopher's voice (e.g., ibid., pp. 65 and 94; *Journal 5,* 1997, p. 470). At the end of *Walden,* he asserted Socrates' credo, "Rather than love, than money, than fame, give me truth" (1971, p. 330). Indeed, one might summarize Thoreau's life as dedicated to this proclamation.

But I will make a more radical claim: Thoreau deeply engaged the key philosophical issue of his time, one which has dominated much of modern philosophy, and he offered an original response to it. I am referring to the post-Cartesian predicament, one framed in diverse ways but all converging on exposing the fragmentation of experience and the elusive epistemological character of our identities. Beginning with Descartes, the knowing subject was irreconcilably separated from the world. In this Cartesian construction, *res cogitans* was a distinct domain, and while humans might *know* the world and act in it, the mind was not *part of* the world. Thoreau hoped to demonstrate that there was, in fact, no final divide between man and nature, and that mind and nature might be integrated. For him, to be *in* the world was to appropriate nature using all his "rationalities"—objective, aesthetic, spiritual, and moral—each contributing to some final synthesis. Inspired by his mystical states, sustained by identifying his core "wildness," Thoreau then pursued his naturalist studies as extensions of these intimate experiences of nature.

On this reading, Thoreau's imperative of seeing was ultimately an attempt to establish a full integration. But this picture of man and nature as fundamentally unified remained a poetic or spiritual aspiration. Despite the cogency of his enterprise, Thoreau was caught in the web of his own self-consciousness. His metaphysical construction was flawed, because he was unable to overcome the self-awareness imposed by his writing. Both a blessing and a curse, writing—deliberate and intellectually ordered—was Thoreau's own self-definition of *who* he was. And here we come face to face with the inherent tension (or even contradiction) of Thoreau's project: Despite all his efforts to touch, if not live, his "wildness," Thoreau remained "civilized" as a writer. After all, writing is a defining activity of civilization, and in the self-conscious act of capturing experience, it confers an acute awareness of one's distance (if not removal) from nature. The voice of interpretation is ever-present and stands out as the dominant theme of his work. In short, throughout his multifaceted enterprises, we see Thoreau's study of nature coupled with introspective inspection as he surveyed the world.

If we understand Thoreau as partaking in the general philosophical discussion about the Cartesian subject, specifically in defining the relationship of man and nature as well as in deciphering the basis of knowing the world, his endeavors, irrespective of their philosophical success or failure, take on added significance. That being asserted, Thoreau was no philosopher, at least not in any ordinary sense. His thought was not systematic, and his reference to philosophy was filtered and highly derivative. Indeed, Stanley Cavell correctly observed that *Walden* was written in a "pre-philosophical moment of its culture" (1981, p. xiii); yet Thoreau's philosophical education extended from the Stoics to American Transcendentalism, often guided by Emerson's own passion for German idealism and its English refractions.[1] So, while Thoreau would not have designated himself a philosopher, it is difficult to escape the philosophical sensibility he embraced again and again in his writings. More than a sensitivity to life's moral challenges, beyond ambitions to capture time and nature in poetic and scientific descriptions, Thoreau exhibited a sophisticated self-awareness of the epistemological limits of his various projects and the limits of rationality as *philosophical* problems. Eschewing orthodox philosophy, he nevertheless enunciated a response to the key philosophical questions of his time. I confess that there are many places in his writings where I would have appreciated a more complete development of a philosophical position or an argument for a philosophical stand; nevertheless, to read Thoreau philosophically is to enrich our appreciation of the structure of his thought and his attitudes about himself and the world he studied.

Rather than arguing about Thoreau's philosophical sophistication, it is more profitable to regard his intellectual efforts as "innocent" of the fractionation of knowledge and experience that so marks our own era. Just as he was able to understand and participate in the science of his era, he could well appreciate the philosophical issues debated at the time. Richly literate in diverse branches of knowledge, Thoreau possessed a philosopher's passion for epistemology, pursuing his quest for knowing the real relentlessly, and understanding the limitations of his knowing. Thoreau is particularly appealing to me in this last respect, for he held the key insight: seeing was ultimately dependent on the individual's *ability* to see and create, and the world as known is thus radically dependent on character. In other words, Thoreau's communing with nature, his historical pursuits of various kinds, his observations of society and people, he recognized as value-laden and thus organized around a self-image of his own ethical standing and what he wished to be. In short, Thoreau's world became a moral expression.

"Moral" is being used here—and throughout this book—not in reference to the more narrow ideas of "right and wrong" or "good and evil" but in reference to the generic understanding of "value." To comprehend "moral" in this way is to acknowledge that prior to assigning "rightness" or "wrongness," we must begin by regarding the act of judgment as following the decision that a verdict is to be made in the first place. With this broadened conception, value judgments not only include choices about one's actions typically regarded as "ethical" but encompass assigning *value* in any context. Each act—whether appreciating an apple tree, curbing one's consumerism, or refusing to pay a poll tax—then becomes a self-conscious valuation. In this regard, morality has been extended into every facet of experience, because the knowing agent is acutely self-conscious that each act is significant or not significant as determined by the attention and value that is assigned. Thus there is no neat separation between knowing the world (epistemologically) and valuing that knowledge (a moral judgment). In short, I will regard Thoreau's life as a grand moral example, where the ethics of self-integrity have assumed primacy. If he indeed regarded the world as one of his own making, one radically dependent on what he saw, understood, and thus signified, then each moment, each observation, each understanding was imbued with judgment. From this vantage we might better peer into the pupil of his world, for Thoreau profoundly appreciated that "the 'ought' is, in fact, one of the most common features of what 'is,' of what is happening" (Caputo 1993, p. 7).

I am pursuing the path of modern scholarship that has been dubbed "Thoreau's epistemology of nature" (Buell 1995, p. 364). Following Krutch's (1948) and Paul's (1958) vision of Thoreau as an intellectual quester, Thoreau has been portrayed as reacting against Emersonian idealism (Porte 1966) or exhibiting a "programmed inconsistency" in his "divided attitudes toward nature" (McIntosh 1974); more recently he has been provocatively regarded as "writing Nature" (Cameron 1985), apprehending nature's "nextness to me" (Cavell 1981), or establishing unique epistemological categories by which he might know nature (Peck 1990). Not to delve into my agreements and disputes with these various studies here, suffice it to note that none has adequately accounted for the deeper orienting force of Thoreau's moral character on his epistemology. Thus both my approach (a reliance on contemporary philosophy) and orienting theme (the epistemological orientation bestowed by Thoreau's moral philosophy) are different from previous studies.

In adopting this strategy, "the self" becomes a central concern, and in this regard two fundamental axes of Thoreau's personhood must be portrayed. The first is the self as knower, an epistemological examination, and the second is the self as a moral category. In the end, we will see that the two dimensions collapse into one, and that the world Thoreau sees and knows is the world he creates out of his moral attitude about that world and the ego which appreciates it. Personalizing knowledge of the past and of the natural world in his own terms—formulations constructed on a grid of value and meaning—the self was in danger of falling into a solipsistic hole, and so Thoreau lived with a balanced tension, where his perspectivism was constantly measured against facts. Thoreau's Romantic struggle of the self's self-definition and his pursuits to place that self within a cosmos of his own discernment reflect a dialectical struggle between engagement with the world and at the same time a retreat from it. In this sense, he truly was a Romantic Hero, for the odyssey of self-discovery—an arduous spiritual journey—was a key Romantic metaphor (Cardinal 1997), and Thoreau was truly one of the great introspective travelers of his era. Triumphing in his inward voyage, Thoreau overcame the seductions of a crippling solipsism and emerged with a freed imagination, one enacted on the primacy of his independent personhood.

This theme of fierce independence and individuality, famously enunciated in the "Conclusion" of *Walden* ("If man does not keep pace with his companions, perhaps it is because he hears a different drummer" [1971, p. 326]), became Thoreau's cardinal ethical mandate. He jealously guarded against what he perceived as the distractions of a "normal" life: "Even the wisest and best are apt to use their lives as the occasion to do something else in than to live greatly" (May 20, 1841, *Journal 1*, 1981, p. 290). And to live greatly was to live independently: "My life will wait for nobody . . . It will cut its own channel" (April 7, 1841, ibid., p. 297), and in word and deed this became his manifest credo. Indeed, the young Thoreau possessed an uncommon confidence of purpose ("I shall not mistake the direction of my life" [May 6, 1841, ibid., p. 308]) and will ("I make my own time I make my own terms" [November 13, 1841, ibid., p. 342]). In fact, Thoreau's overarching moral philosophy was deliberately to define and to establish his unique self, an act of will that linked every aspect of his intellectual and emotional personality. The present study hinges upon that theme as we explore the various modalities in which Thoreau thought and wrote.

THE FORCE OF CHARACTER

Gradually it has become clear to me what every great philosophy so far has been: namely, the personal confession of its author and a kind of involuntary and unconscious memoir; also that the moral (or immoral) intentions in every philosophy constituted the real germ of life from which the whole plant had grown.

Nietzsche [1886] 1966, p. 14

[A] man's vision is the great fact about him. Who cares for Carlyle's reasons, or Schopenhauer's, or Spencer's? A philosophy is the expression of a man's intimate character, and all definitions of the universe are but the deliberately adopted reactions of human characters upon it.

James [1909] 1987, p. 639

Nietzsche and James, in the passages set out above, were either repeating or rediscovering Johann Gottlieb Fichte's own dictum, "The kind of philosophy one chooses depends upon what kind of person one is" (*Wissenschaftslehre* [1797], quoted by Neuhouser 1990, p. 56). Whoever said it first, and there are undoubtedly ancient antecedents, the sentiment summarizes my own view. I similarly hold the reciprocity of a philosophy reflecting character and character expressed in a philosophy. In this regard, Thoreau is a particularly vivid case study, and indeed, one can barely understand his philosophy independent of his life work and the personality that lived it. But more, he also exemplifies how the entire enterprise is grounded in the moral personality. In this latter respect, Nietzsche was specifically referring to how *value*—what is chosen as important, indeed as critical, to a serious and deliberate life—must serve as the very foundation of any guiding philosophy or spirituality. And James built his *Principles of Psychology* ([1890] 1983) around the precept that our *"interest in things"* (p. 304) not only organizes our world but is the clue to understanding consciousness and the very notion of the self:

> Millions of items of the outward order are present to my senses which never properly enter into my experience. Why? Because they have no *interest* for me. *My experience is what I agree to attend to.* Only those items which I *notice* shape my mind—without selective interest, experience is an utter chaos. (Ibid., pp. 380–81; emphasis in original)

As a phenomenologist, James sought to show not only how we actively and deliberately select sensory experience but also how the philosophical consequences of such an insight frame our understanding of consciousness. What and how we see is largely informed by what we *want* to see and *can* see as determined by the structure of our knowing, a value system of the senses and their cognition. For instance, I enter a room looking for my copy of *Walden*. Of the myriad visual details available to me, I quickly fasten on a particular text, which, except for some very minor details, is almost identical with the other volumes of the Princeton edition, *The Writings of Henry D. Thoreau*. My interest, the value structure of that moment, determines not only my seeking that particular book but the very cognitive focusing required to do so. From this almost trivial example we might extrapolate to a grand vision of nature, which is, indeed, I maintain, how we should "read" Thoreau. To be sure, we have many criteria by which we select our impressions and thus mold our experience. Here, I wish to explore how an epistemology is informed by a specifically moral vision. So there is a two-pronged issue to explicate. First, for a philosopher, "nothing whatever is impersonal, and above all, his morality bears decided and decisive witness to *who he is*," that is, to the innermost nature of his character (Nietzsche [1886] 1966, p. 14); and second, the value structure of thought determines to a greater or lesser degree *what* one sees, and therefore what one *knows*. Thus I will attempt to draw such a philosophical, ultimately moral, portrait of Thoreau by looking both at the man and at his philosophy in order to achieve a composite, and thereby more complete, understanding in both of these domains, the moral and the epistemological.

It has often been remarked how philosophy reflects the philosopher, how character and personality may be articulated in various conceptual projects (e.g., Atwood and Stolorow 1993), and Thoreau has endlessly fascinated his students in their attempts to tie together the threads of his thought with the rich intensity and eccentricity of his life. While commenting on Thoreau's evolution of thought, I do not specifically follow the biographical path but instead adopt a philosopher's stance in showing how Thoreau's metaphysics of the self informs and guides each aspect of his multifarious project, where each topic must relate to the overarching questions, How did Thoreau situate himself in the cosmos? What indeed is that problematic self, and what are the metaphysics underlying it? How did the Romantic vision of the person lead to the essential problems with which Thoreau grappled?

Thoreau has a certain "plasticity." He lived multiple personae: Romantic poet, champion of rugged individualism, naturalist, American patriot and social reformer, middle-class misanthrope, mystic, Transcendentalist, prophet, and on. We have ready testaments for each of these aspects of a life which in many ways was both a failure and a heroic venture. Both in his time and in ours, Thoreau is vilified as a nonconformist ne'er-do-well or celebrated as a key member of the American pantheon, an architect of our contemporary consciousness—a physician to our discontent. His reputation as seer largely rests on *Walden*, a text more widely read in American literature courses than any other. *Walden* is a "solution" of the question of how to express nature, whether "nature" be thought of as the external natural environment or as the internal, wild, and natural self. These two poles are expressed in a myth of Thoreau's making, namely, that we each potentially possess the heroic ability to elevate our respective lives by conscious effort, by deliberate moral choice. That choice, he insists, requires the rejection of a material, money-driven economy in favor of an economy of personal renewal resting on an awakening to a greater reality: the world of the spirit found in nature. In naming the wild, celebrating nature, and identifying our true self with communal nature, humankind's deepest divinity might be discovered and released from its shackles. Thoreau's standing rests on how one regards this call to seek our deepest identity, irrespective of how we orient ourselves to environmentalism. The sanctity of nature—environmental ethics writ large—is perhaps central to Thoreau's own views, but even deeper than those concerns is the primacy of the identity of the self.

Thoreau also polarizes us, and in so doing, he reenacts in us the deep attitudes of his detractors and followers. Apparently, none is neutral. Why? Because he challenges us at the level of moral reckoning: he *demands* that we declare our own views of nature, society, and ultimately ourselves. In announcing what he values, Thoreau makes us confront our own values, for in word and deed he challenges our complacency, demanding that we respond to his summons for a new ethic. He marshals his rhetorical power so that we must respond, we cannot remain complacent; and thus he breaks our silence. In the service of that moral accounting, Thoreau marshals his epistemological project as well as the various efforts at social reform. But more than crying for a sensitivity to nature or a call for public reform, he calls us to reform ourselves. So in asking us, What indeed do we value?, Thoreau initiates a dialogue with our moral personalities. And he begins that dialogue by exposing himself to our scrutinizing his own self-inspection.

But a psychological portrait is not offered here. To what degree Thoreau suffered, or what inner dynamic might describe his inner conflicts, is indeterminate, even irrelevant to this discussion. What *is* of interest is *how* he consciously dealt with his existential state and *what* he bequeathed us as a testament of his response. Thoreau's autobiography—the Journal and his other published writings—reveals as much as we need to know: Thoreau was keenly aware of the metaphysical instability of the self, most evident in its groping for knowledge about the world, in its yearning to seek its own grounding in that world, and, perhaps most fundamentally, in the study of its own split consciousness. This must remain the focus of our interest. We have much philosophical discussion of the general epistemological and metaphysical crisis which appeared in the mid-nineteenth century. Thoreau both illustrated its outline and then offered a response to that challenge.

From at least shortly after his graduation from college, he had already set his sights on the moral work that would occupy him throughout his life. The trajectory of his thought and work seem to me clear from his earliest Journal entries at age twenty, and while there was significant development through the publication of *Walden* at age thirty-four, the philosophical project appears quite constant—a view at odds with that of other critics who have traced his literary development (e.g., Adams and Ross 1988), his science (e.g., Walls 1995), or his view of nature (e.g., McGregor 1997). That is not to say that

Thoreau's mature musings were the "same" as his youthful musings. Ironically perhaps, as Thoreau discharged Emerson, he more fully and enthusiastically embraced Transcendentalism between the springs of 1851 and 1852. In a careful textual analysis, Stephen Adams and Donald Ross (1988, pp. 155 ff.) have shown how Thoreau assumed a different vocabulary describing his attitude toward nature and poetry, a process they call a "conversion" but which might be better referred to as a crystallization, endorsement, or confirmation.[2] The difference between these latter characterizations and the first suggests that the Romantic elements were present before 1851 and only became better articulated as Thoreau more fully realized his mature philosophical attitude. After all, we have strong early evidence for his sympathy to nature, his jaundiced view of objectivity and its scientific expression (see chapter 4), his endorsement of intuition and conscience, and his strong aesthetic and spiritual sense of being. But after 1851, his style changes, shifting from references to classical sources to more contemporary citations. He uses "wild" and all of its variants much more liberally; "sympathy" (see, for example, Journal entries of July 18 and July 23, 1851; January 26, 1852) and "imagination" (see, for example, 1851 Journal entries for July 11th, August 21st, and December 20th) appear more frequently and with deepened significance; and finally, a certain exuberance about life, himself, and his connection to nature punctuate the Journal of this period. Integral to these shifts is a certain self-consciousness, also part of the Romantic temperament: "My practicalness [empiricism] is not to be trusted to the last. . . . I begin to be transcendental and show where my heart is" (June 7, 1851, *Journal* 3, 1990, p. 244).[3]

All of this attests to a Romantic sensibility coming forth—the expressiveness of the self, reaching out through spirit and poesis to an expanded vision of the cosmos and his place in it. Coincident with his renewed efforts on *Walden*, Thoreau wrote at the emergence of spring of a new vitality and hope—no less than a prayer for his own salvation:

> My life partakes of infinity. The air is as deep as our natures. . . . I go
> forth to make new demands on life. I wish to begin this summer
> well–to do something in it worthy of it & of me– To transcend my
> daily routine–& that of my townsmen to have my immortality
> now–that it be in the *quality* of my daily life. To pay the greatest
> price–the–greatest tax of any man in Concord–& enjoy the most!! I
> will give all I am for *my* nobility. I will pay all my days for *my* success.
> I pray that the life of this spring & summer may ever lie fair in my
> memory. May I dare as I have never done– may I persevere as I have
> never done. May I purify myself anew as with fire & water–soul &
> body– May my melody not be wanting to the season. May I gird
> myself to be a hunter of the beautiful that naught escape me– May I

attain to a youth never attained[.] I am eager to report the glory of the universe– may I be worthy to do it– To have got through with regarding human values so as not to be distracted from regarding divine values. It is reasonable that a man should be something worthier at the end of the year than he was at the beginning. (March 15, 1852, *Journal 4*, 1992, p. 390)

And so he began again to revise his reflections on his life at Walden Pond. Central to that reconsideration was a radical insight concerning time and his own temporality (see Peck 1990; also chapter 1 here) and, closely linked, a reassessment of his personal goals. The elliptical reference he gives in *Walden* about the reason why he went to the woods and why he left is more forthrightly addressed in the Journal, but as he himself admits, "Why I left the woods? I do not think that I can tell" (January 22, 1852, *Journal 4*, 1992, p. 275). Still, he offers an insight:

Perhaps if I lived there much longer I might live there forever– One would think twice before he accepted heaven on such terms– A ticket to Heaven must include tickets to Limbo–Purgatory–& Hell. Your ticket to the boxes admits you to the pit also. And if you take a cabin-passage you can smoke at least forward of the engine.– You have the liberty of the whole boat. But no I do not wish for a ticket to the boxes–nor to take a cabin passage. I will rather go before the mast & on the deck of the world. I have no desire to go "abaft the engine[.]" (Ibid.)

Thoreau truly was not satisfied with any permanence, reading his own "wildness" as an incessant need for "freedom." In this context it was the freedom of a perpetual search of himself, and this too is part of his abiding Romanticism.

There is, of course, a meta-theme, developed during this same period, that addresses the question of personal purpose, the agenda of living (Adams and Ross 1988, p. 172). *Walden* does offer an answer to the enigmatic question why Thoreau "left the woods." In a dialogue between a Hermit and a Poet, Thoreau thrashes out the course of his life:

Shall I go to heaven or a-fishing? If I should soon bring this meditation to an end, would another so sweet occasion be likely to offer? I was as near being resolved into the essence of things as ever I was in my life. I fear my thoughts will not come back to me. . . . There never is but one opportunity of a kind. (*Walden*, 1971, pp. 224–25)

Thoreau indeed goes "fishing" in a return to the world: "Well, then, let's be off. Shall we to Concord? There's good sport there if the water be not too high" (ibid.). He again pursues various agendas—some mundane, others of vast philosophical import. He would continue to seek the unity of the world, the arrest of time, the poetic metaphors of life, the scientific insight of nature—all in the quest to know what was real for him, both ontologically and morally. So in some sense, *Walden* crystallized a composite view which pulled each of these concerns into some coherence, and which he may well have regarded with a profound sense of completeness (Richardson 1986). Yet in another sense, reflecting the metaphysics of his own self, Thoreau could not be satisfied with any "answer," and so he continued to explore all the subjects previously approached. Although that pursuit was essentially structured by the mature completion of his magnum opus (in 1854), there is an unmistakable inward turning, exemplified by the massive expansion of his Journal, which became the central focus of his creative endeavors. His observations of nature seem to have a new intensity and clarity. This was achieved at a high personal cost.

As even early Journal entries indicate, the seeds of solitude had been sown long before Thoreau fully realized that his youthful dreams of heroic leadership were not to be fulfilled. At age twenty-four, he wrote presciently of what would become the Walden Pond experiment, and more generally, the posture of his life:

> I want to go soon and live away by the pond where I shall hear only the wind whispering among the reeds– It will be a success if I shall have left myself behind, But my friends ask what I will do when I get there? Will it not be employment enough to watch the progress of the seasons? (December 24, 1841, *Journal 1*, 1981, p. 347)

This is precisely what Thoreau eventually did, formalizing what had heretofore been intermittent excursions:

> I sit in my boat on walden–playing the flute this evening–and see the perch, which I seem to have charmed, hovering around me–and the moon travelling over the ribbed bottom–and feel that nothing but the wildest imagination can conceive of the manner of life we are living. Nature is a wizzard. The Concord nights are stranger than the Arabian nights. (May 27, 1841, ibid., p. 311)

Thoreau went to the pond and played his flute, putting a spell not only on the fish but upon himself. During this period he was extensively reading Eastern religious writings, and the solitude he sought was critical for the mystical experiences he craved. This posturing may be regarded as a push-pull phenomenon: a manifestation of his incipient misanthropy and thus a countermove against the society of men, as well as a pull toward a primary spiritual communion. In either or both cases, Thoreau recognized the dual need for privacy ("I cannot think nor utter my thought unless I have infinite room" [March 22, 1842, *Journal* 1, 1981, p. 385]) and an existential reality about himself:

> How alone must our life be lived– We dwell on the sea-shore and none between us and the sea– Men are my merry companions–my fellow pilgrims–who beguile the way, but leave me at the first turn in the road–for none are travelling *one* road so far as myself. (March 13, 1841, *Journal* 1, 1981, p. 288)

Thoreau eventually was to regard his solitude (always denying "loneliness") as a virtue, one he fully described in *Walden* (its fifth chapter) and unabashedly admitted in an early Journal entry: "Whoever has had one thought quite lonely–and could consciously digest that in solitude, knowing that none might accept it, may rise to the height of humanity–and overlook all living men as from a pinnacle" (April 10, 1841, *Journal* 1, 1981, p. 300). In solitude, Thoreau would garner himself as a leader, a hero, a prophet. The Journal is replete with such allusions (more fully discussed in chapter 6).

Thoreau's youthful self-absorption was later replaced with keen attention to the otherness of the natural world and his place in it. Following the Walden experiment, the Journal testifies to an endless search for the meaning of nature and the corresponding knowing self. I will consider that evolution of thought and sensibility in this sketch of "the mind of a moralist," for an abiding and relentlessly recursive self-evaluation undergirds this portrait of Thoreau. His was a voice that beckons us to address the apparently irresolvable dilemma of self-consciousness facing that chasm between a perceiving self and its world. Thoreau enacted a classic Romantic struggle: establishing a firm and abiding relation with nature, even a union, yet recognizing that this aspiration is dangerous, even misguided, since the self would, in its merger, be lost. Some students of the Romantics see this poetic quest as transfiguring an alienated nature to one redeemed, while others read an unreconciled, alienated nature whose pursuit is tragic. Thoreau lived with both aspects and characteristically played these themes as a complex counterpoint.[4] He was well aware of these conflicting movements, and his typically Romantic introspective cognizance reflects a deeper source of inquiry as he engaged in perplexing and oftentimes agonizing meditations on the nature of his personhood and the meaning of his life in the context of nature. Thoreau offered an original response to this Romantic imbroglio.

Much of Thoreau's writing may be heard as the turning of a creaking axle, whose linchpin, consciousness, holds the entire enterprise together. As Leo Marx wrote,

> Thoreau is clear, as Emerson seldom was, about the location of meaning
> and value. He is saying that it does not reside in the natural facts or in
> social institutions or in anything "out there," but in consciousness. It is
> a product of imaginative perception, of the analogy-perceiving,
> metaphor-making, mythopoetic power of the human mind. For
> Thoreau the realization of the golden age is, finally, a matter of private
> and, in fact, literary experience. (1964, p. 264)

Laurence Buell (perhaps ironically) aptly draws out the key implication of
this reading: "Thoreau was not really *that* interested in nature as such;
nature was a screen for something else" (1995, p. 11).[5] I would agree with
the focus on self-consciousness as the locus of Thoreau's project, but I think
we err in telescoping three different dimensions of "mind" into some single realm of consciousness: the private world consists of self-aware consciousness and another domain of unmediated experience, which is, in fact,
not conscious but rather preconscious or unconscious. A third realm, the
public world, reckons the processed word, written or spoken, to "read" or
"hear" thought. Consciousness then mediates raw experience as processed
thought, or as Thoreau put it, "the pen" is the fulcrum, or "lever" (August
4, 1841, *Journal 1*, 1981, p. 315), that allows him to lift experience, memory, and emotion from the depths of pre- and unconsciousness to the surface of the public forum. Rightly regarded as the nucleus of his *work*, consciousness must also be acknowledged in some sense as only a "solvent,"
the necessary medium through which unmediated, unselfconscious experience assumes articulated value and meaning.

Questions of consciousness aside, Thoreau also aspired to mystical
states—the suspension of self-awareness—and this aspect must also be considered.[6] He reveled in the mystical moments of pure communion—experience most genuine and authentic—but his polished literary product can
only serve as a translation or distillation of that experience. Thoreau's mystical experiences are in this sense "lost," remaining as faint echoes in his
own allusions to them, and thus we cannot confidently factor them into the
complex calculus of his project. Due to their elusive character, I have *almost*
allowed Thoreau's mystical visions to fall outside my own analysis. But
because they were an important reservoir of his experience, their influence
must be acknowledged. While Thoreau sought such mystical experiences,
he also recognized that they served principally as a well of inspiration as he
moved beyond the isolation of the mystical state to his public role as seer.
He was no starry-eyed mystic, and he exercised the full force of his critical
faculties to explore even those most intimate experiences for greater literary purposes. In short, mystical revelry was only one aspect of his self-

consciousness, one source from which he drew to write.[7] This self-conscious, split-screen image of the self—the self experiencing and the self digesting the experience—appears at various sites of this study, for what intrigues me is not only how Thoreau regarded his world but how he attempted to understand the character of his selfhood and resolve the multiple tensions of its confrontation with the world and itself.

PLAN OF THE BOOK

In chapter 1, the metaphysical foundation of Thoreau's thought is outlined by posing the question of how he understood time and how that understanding functioned to orient his epistemology and moral philosophy. When Thoreau left Walden Pond in September 1847, he had fully embraced his mature understanding of time and his "place" in nature. Specifically, Thoreau's understanding of the full immediacy of the present is the most sensitive measure of his metaphysics of nature. I contrast his understanding of "time" as restricted to the present (the Augustinian notion that past and future exist only in the mind) and serving as a human category of temporality with his notion of "eternity." Thoreau's recognition that nature's flux is immediate and ever-present, existing in an eternal now, represents a crucial metaphysical insight, and his strategies for integrating the ceaseless evolution of the cosmos and himself revolve around efforts to "capture" time either in self-conscious understanding or in the total eclipse of mystical revelry. Time's apprehension or suspension becomes the foundation of his own reckoning of his selfhood and thereby introduces the basic themes of this study.

Time not only serves to ground Thoreau's thought in a deep ontology but leads us into the study of two epistemologies—history of culture (chapter 2) and natural history (chapter 3). In both chapters I endeavor to show how Thoreau chose to attend to the world—past and present—with highly selective purpose, guided by an aesthetic sensibility and, more profoundly, by a moral attitude. The life of "doing" becomes a life of "virtue," and Thoreau was ever conscious of that ethical mandate. Chapter 2 is structured on describing different forms of history writing employed by Thoreau, ranging from his interpretative narratives of New England history to the play between private memory and public history. The reconstruction of memory and the use of semiotic clues reflect most clearly the role of a personalized history in Thoreau's writing of his own identity. He thus refracts the past through the same moral prism that illuminates his nature study. Indeed, I hope to explicate Thoreau's own admission why natural history, both more immediate and accessible, is in some sense more "real" than the history of his own culture:

> It is easier far to recover the history of the trees which stood here a century or more ago than it is to recover the history of the men who walked beneath them. How much do we know—how little more can we know—of these two centuries of Concord life? (October 19, 1860, *Journal*, [1906] 1962, 14:152)

While social history served as a vehicle for Thoreau's various messages, it was superseded by natural history, which assumed the more powerful and intimate voice. I will argue that the *immediacy of experience* that nature study afforded Thoreau largely explains the centrality of this literary genre for him.

Chapter 3 offers a general "epistemological topography" of Thoreau's modes of knowing, and thereby we obtain a manifold on which his various projects, from the mystical to the scientific, might be situated. For as important as natural history was for Thoreau, we must bear in mind that this was the subject of only one facet of his writing. In this chapter, I explore how Thoreau both was indebted to, and reacted against, several key intellectual mentors—Emerson most directly, but Goethe, Coleridge, and Humboldt also played supporting roles in posing the challenges Thoreau responded to. Placing Thoreau in the intellectual context of his era—with the European Romantics immediately preceding him and the Transcendentalists with whom he lived—allows us to appreciate his unique position. And to offer a fair intellectual portrait, we must move Thoreau beyond the Transcendentalists and explore his nature study as some unique alloy of science and the introspective sensibility typical of the Emersonian circle.

Thoreau's standing as a naturalist, both from the perspective of the growing professionalization of science in the mid-nineteenth century and from his own attempt to offer his own unique reading of nature as a nature writer, revolved around the effort to "personalize nature." My discussion of this issue falls into two parts. Chapter 4 presents a survey of the scientific culture of Thoreau's era, and in the rise of positivism we see the ethos of a worldview at odds with Thoreau's Romanticism. Against the positivists' radical divorce of the observer from his object of scrutiny, Thoreau attempted to create his own nature study, appreciating that he could not fit into a science dominated by a positivist epistemology. He used "facts" as his own currency, for his own purpose.

We must place Thoreau's attitude toward nature within the problem of objectivity and the value of knowledge more generally, specifically how his attitude toward nature is regarded within the broader discussion of the knowing subject. His was "a lovely dance between the self and nature" (Peck 1990, p. 121)—"the inner landscape . . . symbiotic with the outer" (Buell 1995, p. 101). Chapter 5 explores Thoreau's nature observations, specifically how he composed his poetic view of the world, and the difficulty he experienced in writing of that experience. My discussion is based on the nature of facts, how Thoreau discovered or created them in the crucible of "unmediated experience"—personal and valued—and how he used them to create a personalized vision of the world. I maintain that one of the key themes tying Thoreau's many projects together is the world's "pliability" for fulfilling an intuition, or as he observed much better in *A Week*, "This world is but canvass to our imaginations" (1980a, p. 292). In Thoreau's urgency to find his own place in nature (McIntosh 1974; Garber 1977, 1991), he offered us not only a portrait of nature but a means of placing ourselves *in* the world that has had an abiding influence on contemporary culture. To Thoreau we owe much of our heightened awareness of nature's sanctity, a complex fusion of Romantic sentiment and an ecological (scientific) consciousness. Nature was not thereby redeemed so much as transformed in an ongoing creative project, which positioned the scientific worldview within a broadened humanistic context. So to note Thoreau's self-consciousness is only to place him among Romantics generally. What separates Thoreau most characteristically is his discerning naturalist's eye, informed by a scientific attitude yet committed to an enchanted vision of nature. These central chapters then treat "the fact" as their common theme, specifically how Thoreau used them as a painter might use various oils to create an image. His commitment to a poetic vision composed from hard-won facts made Thoreau the seer of our own environmentalism. I wish to emphasize that this popular appreciation is an epiphenomenon of a deeper metaphysical realization of the self.

The question of how to live the good life ordered Thoreau's every activity, and he consistently pursued the attempt to actualize his life in the attainment of virtue. He was driven to live a life where he could hold meaning and value under tireless scrutiny. Again, the question of agency guides our investigation, for to ask, How should one live? already assumes the character of a moral agency—or as Bernard Williams quips, "the generality of *one* already stakes a claim" (1985, p. 4). Here Thoreau assumes his characteristic voice. As important as nature was for him, his own identity was even more intimate and crucial. Indeed, from his perspective, the self assumes its most solid standing in the moral enterprise, ordering the way one sees the world.

Chapter 6 explores Thoreau's own sense of his "heroic" venture and the construction of his moral universe using virtue ethics as the scaffold of examination. For Thoreau, virtue meant living the deliberate life, one acutely self-conscious in all domains. This was best expressed in his writing, and while he steadfastly pursued his literary art, the enactment of what he considered his virtuous calling, there is a fascinating "failure" between the attempt and its execution. The limits of writing focus much of the previous epistemological concerns and points on the central issues of Thoreau's conundrum of "writing his life" and thereby inscribing his selfhood. And then there is a second "failure," one directly derivative of his personalized vision of the world and himself within it. I am referring to Thoreau's political writings, which reveal a moral solipsism that exposes the egocentrism of his ethics. So we see not only in his epistemological strivings but also in his moral philosophy a reduction of the world, natural and moral, to his own measure.

Thoreau's moral vision arose from the Romantic "solution" to the character of the self, which is best expressed in Fichte's notion of the "self-positing I." With that idea, in chapter 7 I examine the self from two vantages: The first is a short sketch of the philosophical context in which Thoreau's own efforts might be understood. The discussion is based on exploring the evolution of the self as an isolated entity (surveying its world with Lockean detachment) to the Romantic notion of the self as *relation*. If the self was to be understood and thereby defined as fundamentally seeking relation to an Other—the natural world, society, the self itself—then the basis for such relationships became a problem. The Romantic answer was that the self was free, self-determined, and morally obligated when establishing such relationships. Thoreau expressed this aspiration in word and deed. So in the second portion of this discussion, I situate Thoreau's triumphant vision of the self. This discussion freely draws on contemporary appraisal of autobiography, for in many respects Thoreau's work is the elaboration of an autobiography, a life "self-written" both in action and in narrative form, in response to an existential trial.

From this perspective, Thoreau met two cardinal challenges. The first pertained to his "aloneness," to the irreducible solitude that he understood as a metaphysical condition of being human; the second was a Romantic grasp of destiny, which was to recognize consciously and deliberately the full expanse of his metaphysical horizon and develop an identity in response to that conscious vision of nature. As he wrote in his early Journal:

> Each one marches in the van. The weakest child is exposed to the fates henceforth as barely as its parents . . . they cannot stand between him and his destiny. This is the one bare side of every man– There is no fence–it is clear before him to the bounds of space. (March 13, 1841, *Journal* 1, 1981, p. 288)[8]

The road to Thoreau's destiny was the dual path of "self-discovery" and "self-creation." Especially in this latter regard, Thoreau truly followed Emerson's call in "Nature":

> Every spirit builds itself a house; and beyond its house a world; and beyond its world, a heaven. Know then, that the world exists for you. For you is the phenomenon perfect. What we are, that only can we see. . . . Build, therefore, your own world. (1983a, p. 48)

This was a shared vision, one that became a heroic venture for Thoreau insofar as he regarded himself as committed to a valiant though perhaps impossible task.

In our post-positivist era, we now appreciate that the radical separation of the subject from the object of examination is a false conceit. Our view of nature is always a construction, known in a particular way, in a particular context, with a particular history. But Thoreau lived in a period that witnessed the rapid rise of positivism, when human knowing was thought to be totally transparent on its object. He recognized that such an idealized objectivity would rob us of making the world our own. He struggled with a response to this challenge. He showed us why the positivist perspective was distorting, alienating, and ultimately false. He sought to preserve an enchanted world and to place the passionate observer in the center of his or her universe.

Thoreau's venture, seen either as a success or as a splendid failure, has linked him to our own moment. One tributary of his thought leads from Walden Pond to twentieth-century environmentalism, where he is justly regarded as one of those in the vanguard leading urbanized Americans back to nature. Indisputably, the aesthetic and spiritual character of that movement owes much to the model offered by Thoreau's own nature studies and writings. The other stream of thought is, I believe, a deeper contribution, for his life's example has served many more who do not share his passion for nature. So, while most would see him as the author of a new ecological consciousness, I argue that what he offers is a *moral* consciousness more radical than that required simply to green America. The Epilogue comments on how Thoreau's contributions to our own concerns are best understood as an effort to "mend the world," or what Edmund Husserl later referred to as the project of seeking a unifying Reason. For those who see a world fractured, where splintered knowledge and local beliefs are loosely coordinated in a pragmatic utilitarianism, the basis for unification of experience remains elusive. And *meaning* finds little support in a secularism that has sequestered God, and in a science that preaches materialism. We are left radically alone, bereft of a moral compass in a world devoid of meaning other than what we bestow upon it. In Thoreau's admonitions, we recognize the moral precariousness of our lives, which are uncoordinated by any great enterprise and isolated by our individual pursuits. What most see as a conundrum, he saw as a surmountable challenge (or even an opportunity), albeit one that called for heroic effort. Thoreau regarded himself as engaging a silent but ominous tyranny that had crept into his pastoral garden and, like the weeds in his bean field, must be vanquished. Now, when moral agency has lost its foundations and our confidence in our own autonomy and free will has been weakened, he confidently strides forth from the nineteenth century with a bold assertion of the primacy of the self in all of its dominions.

Thoreau charted a metaphysics of the self that sought to integrate aesthetic, spiritual, and scientific faculties in order to forge a synthesis of diverse experience and disparate knowledge. In celebrating personalized knowledge, Thoreau decried positivism not as a philosophy of science, but as a philosophy of knowing, whose objectivity was inadequate for navigating the world and making it meaningful. Radical objectivity fails because the view from nowhere leaves Man out of the picture, and with no perspective there is no significance, no meaning, no order, and ultimately no self. Thoreau's prescription: a complex amalgam of aesthetic empiricism, Eastern mysticism, poetry, and manual labor. Each was marked by deliberate purpose, self-reflection, and most important, the self-conscious effort of *doing*. Those inspired by Thoreau may not be taken by any of his particular pursuits, but they see in his life a steadfast moral commitment of seeking and affirming personalized meaning and signification. This encompassing ethics of the self resonates with the current, widely held sentiment that ultimately we are responsible for making sense of the world and our place in it.

This anthem of selfhood has become a popular moral call to arms. For those enlisted, an interest in nature may be only a passing fancy, but the necessity of finding personal meaning in an increasingly alienated world is a clear challenge. Thoreau, by offering his life as an example of such a search, has been promoted from captain of a huckleberry party (Emerson's derisive characterization [see p. 174]) to general of legions.

To a large extent, Thoreau's appeal depends on how far we regard his life and work as a triumph in asserting his will and the primacy of his personhood. Robert Milder astutely notes, regarding the writing of *Walden*, that there are two stories, not always congruent, that unfold in Thoreau's writing: the *narrated* story of discovery and renewal (which we commonly attend to) and the *enacted* story of the writer's efforts to adapt himself to the world (Milder 1995, pp. 54–55) or, as I would say, to create a moral cosmos. Indeed, using Milder's trope, I regard the two stories as converging in the various ways Thoreau attempts to create a self-mythology. This study is an examination of how Thoreau discovered, indeed constructed, his personhood, and how he did so not primarily as a literary, nor even an epistemological, project but as a moral one that reached well beyond his writings, encompassing experience he made no attempt to capture with his pencil. The mind of a moralist—a category superseding any authorial voice—is at the epicenter connecting all of Thoreau's endeavors. The pivotal issue for us is to probe the constitution of Thoreau's moral philosophy, to see how it informed his life's work, and its expression. It is this ethical dimension that brings him to the forefront of our contemporary concerns.

1   The Eternal Now

A wise man will know what game to play to-day, and play it. We must not be governed by rigid rules, as by an almanac, but let the season rule us. The moods and thoughts of man are revolving just as steadily and incessantly as nature's. Nothing must be postponed. Take time by the forelock. Now or never! You must live in the present, launch yourself on every wave, find your eternity in each moment.

> Thoreau, April 23, 1859,
> *Journal*, [1906] 1962, 12:159

1848 was a pivotal year. In Europe, conservative forces quashed democratic revolts in Paris, Vienna, Berlin, Rome, and Warsaw. Marx and Engels published the *Communist Manifesto*. American "manifest destiny" became ever more manifest as Mexico ceded its claims to Texas and California. Boston was inundated with hungry Irish—over thirty-five thousand new arrivals as compared to roughly five thousand per year a decade earlier. Harriet Tubman escaped from slavery, joining the Underground Railroad. And Henry David Thoreau, aged thirty, was again living with the Emersons, house-sitting, while his erstwhile mentor lectured in Europe.

Having come out of the woods in September of the preceding fall, Thoreau, in retrospect, said that he had left Walden Pond simply because he had "other lives to live." We gain a glimpse into what those other lives might have entailed through his remarkable correspondence with Harrison Gray Otis Blake, begun six months later, in mid-March. Blake, a minister, teacher, and liberal intellectual living in Worcester, Massachusetts, had written him in response to the powerful impression ignited by Thoreau's essay on Perseus (published eight years earlier):

> If I understand rightly the significance of your life, this is it: You would sunder yourself from society, from the spell of institutions, customs, conventionalities, that you may lead a fresh, simple life with God. Instead of breathing a new life into the old forms, you would have a new life without and within. . . . Speak to me in this hour as you are prompted. . . . I honor you because you abstain from action, and open your soul that you may *be* somewhat. Amid a world of noisy, shallow actors it is noble to stand aside and say, "I will simply *be*." (Thoreau, *Correspondence*, 1958, p. 213)

Thoreau was obviously moved to respond with extraordinary openness. Rambling over various themes which preoccupied him, Thoreau's initial letter—the first of thirty written over a period extending up to the year before Thoreau's death—contains many of his credos: the correspondence of the outward and inward life; the importance of simplicity; the challenge to *see;* the crucial connection between literature and life; the summons to break complacency; and the need to "journey to a distant country." Any one of these themes is fecund, but let us focus on another matter: Thoreau declares here, as he does throughout *Walden* and the Journal, that the ethical life necessitates living life to the fullest *in the present.* Any postponement resulted in lost authenticity. I will maintain that it is Thoreau's conception of time's flow, the metaphysical character of the present, that informs and guides his ethics. Even from this short letter we may glean this. Thoreau first observes about our finitude and the centrality of living in the present:

> Change is change. No new life occupies old bodies;—they decay. *It* is born, and grows, and flourishes. Men very pathetically inform the old, accept and wear it. Why put up with the almshouse when you may go to heaven? It is embalming,—no more. (Letter to Blake, March 27, 1848, *Correspondence,* 1958, p. 215)

Then he makes a cogent statement:

> My actual life is a fact in view of which I have no occasion to congratulate myself, but for my faith and aspiration I have respect. It is from these that I speak. Every man's position is in fact too simple to be described. I have sworn no oath. I have no designs on society—or Nature—or God. I am simply what I am, or I begin to be that. I *live* in the *present.* I only remember the past—and anticipate the future. (Ibid., p. 216)

Thoreau's existential stance closely follows from this position:

> I love to live. . . . I believe something, and there is nothing else but that. I know that I am—I know that another is who knows more than I who takes interest in me, whose creature and yet whose kindred, in one sense, am I. I know that the enterprise is worthy—I know that things work well. I have heard no bad news.
>
> As for positions—as for combinations and details—what are they? In clear weather when we look into the heavens, what do we see, but the sky and the sun?
>
> . . . When you travel to the celestial city, carry no letter of introduction. When you knock ask to see God—none of the servants. In what concerns you much do not think that you have companions—know that you are alone in the world. (Ibid., pp. 216–17)

And from this steadfast embrace of his independence, Thoreau calls upon the ancient Delphic oracle, "Know thyself," from which his ethic must emanate:

> Pursue, keep up with, circle round and round your life as a dog does his master's chaise. Do what you love. Know your own bone; gnaw at it, bury it, unearth it, and gnaw it still. Do not be too moral. You may cheat yourself out of much of life so. Aim above morality. Be not *simply* good—be good for something.—All fables indeed have their morals, but the innocent enjoy the story.
> Let nothing come between you and the light. (Ibid., p. 216)[1]

These various elements—the elusiveness of time that can only be captured in the present; the existential crux of living, alone, to the fullest in that present; the demand to live according to "what you love," namely by individual dictates and not socially sanctioned morality—served as Thoreau's guiding philosophy, informing his life's work. Overarching each component is the construction of his moral domain, which I perceive as flowing directly from his conception of time. His consciousness, the deliberate consideration of nature, economy, the world, oneself, stems from his appreciation of the present. For him, in a sense, there is no past and no future. Divine time is eternal, knowing no divisions. There is only the present moment as he wrote in *Walden:*

> Men esteem truth remote, in the outskirts of the system, behind the farthest star, before Adam and after the last man. In eternity there is indeed something true and sublime. But all these times and places and occasions are now and here. God himself culminates in the present moment, and never will be more divine in the lapse of all the ages. (1971, p. 98)

Let us unpack Thoreau's vision of the present, the only time he *knew.*

THE EVER-PRESENT PRESENT

Neither future nor past exists.

> Augustine,
> *Confessions* 11.20.26

Two different senses of time preoccupied Thoreau. The first was past time, history. Seeking ancient origins, chronicling young America's past, both native and colonial, keenly aware of recent local events and inhabitants, Thoreau wrestled with the eclipse of time, the passing of civilizations, countries, and people. History, in a conventional sense, he appreciated as the substratum of his own life, and Thoreau went to considerable effort both in his formal education and in his later reading as well as in his literary efforts to deal with this aspect of time. These themes dominate *A Week on the Concord and Merrimack Rivers* (1980a). There we witness the conventional progress of time. Proceeding through the days of the week, he presents linearized time in an orthodox fashion. Thoreau goes downriver in time and then paddles back to the present. The future is similarly constructed; that is, there is a future, and it will be ours. Furthermore, as we read his book some time in the future, we might reflect with Thoreau on the river of time, the river of history, and situate ourselves in present memory, a redemptive task: "There is something even in the lapse of time by which time recovers itself" (*A Week*, 1980a, p. 351).

The second aspect of time is more abstract and elusive. This is the notion of time alluded to in Thoreau's letter to Blake, quoted above. Specifically, Thoreau recognizes, as Augustine fourteen centuries before him, that there is indeed no such division of time as the past, present, and future. In a phenomenological sense, indeed existentially, we *are* only in the present, because, strictly speaking, only the present exists. We live in the present moment, and while the past is recalled or witnessed as artifact, that witness is experienced only in the present. The future, like the past, exists only as a mental construct only in the present moment. And then the imbroglio: the present is never held on to; it is always slipping by into the past, flowing from a future never quite here.

This vision of time is hardly unique to Thoreau, and indeed has a celebrated history, perhaps most famously in book 11 of Augustine's *Confessions*. There we find an apt description of time's passing, the nature of the past, present, and future, the illusion of temporality, and the essential character of time, unfathomable and fundamentally elusive.[2] For our purposes, it is the character of Augustine's deft development of the idea of the present that is so pertinent to Thoreau's own project—and sheds light upon it. Augustine observes that the present cannot be assigned any duration; it is so fleeting that he calls it a series of "fugitive moments. Whatever part of it has flown away is past. What remains to it is future" (11.15.20). But, though the present has no duration, we nonetheless perceive time only in the present, in our awareness. Augustine comes to the critical point: the character of time—past, present, and future—remains confined only to the present, as elusive as that might be. The past and the future only exist in our cognition of the present, and more to the point, the past and the future only exist *as* the present, in the soul:

In the soul there are three aspects of time, and I do not see them anywhere else. The present considering the past is the memory, the present considering the present is immediate awareness, the present considering the future is expectation. . . . This customary way of speaking is incorrect, but it is common usage. Let us accept the usage. I do not object . . . as long as what is said is being understood, namely that neither the future nor the past is now present. There are few usages of everyday speech which are exact, and most of our language is inexact. Yet what we mean is communicated. (11.20.26)

Augustine confesses that he still does not know "what time is," although he admits to being "conditioned by time" (11.25.32), and he goes on to discuss how time is a function of mind. "Present consciousness is what I am measuring, not the streams of past events which have caused it" (11.27.36). There are two cardinal points to be emphasized: First, "time" is a human perception, a faculty of thought or cognition found in the "soul," which in modern parlance will be translated as mind, and sometimes as self-consciousness; and second, neither past, present, nor future can be "captured." To our contemporary ears, Augustine is an astute philosopher of language, a critical epistemologist, and a profound metaphysician. Thoreau, although not documented as having read Augustine (Sattelmeyer 1988), on this issue stands upon his shoulders—as did William James fifty years later.

James, in *The Principles of Psychology* ([1890] 1983), clearly saw the elusiveness of the present as the key perplexity in understanding consciousness and the very notion of the self. What we see in Thoreau's musings, albeit in rough outline, are the key insights of this later philosophy, one that attempted to understand consciousness proto-phenomenologically. Disallowing some kind of "transcendent non-phenomenological sort of Arch-Ego," or some "representative" feature or fixture to identify the "self," James observed that "a thing cannot appropriate itself; it is itself; and still less can it disown itself" (p. 323). Thus

the Thought never is an object in its own hands, it never appropriates or disowns itself. It appropriates *to* itself, it is the actual focus of accretion, the hook from which the chain of past selves dangles, planted firmly in the Present, which alone passes for real, and thus keeping the chain from being a purely ideal thing. Anon the hook itself will drop into the past with all it carries, and then be treated as an object and appropriated by a new Thought in the new present which will serve as a hook in turn. The present moment of consciousness is thus . . . the darkest in the whole series. It may feel its own immediate existence . . . but nothing can be known about it till it be dead and gone. (Ibid.)

James sought a middle ground between the Kantian idealist notion of a unifying transcendental self and the empiricist's raw succession of perceptions with no unifying construct by positing that unity is directly experienced—the direct and intimate linkage with successive past moments. The "present" then becomes the "hook" by which the past is held in relation to the immediate experience, and the entire construct—past and present—becomes what we understand as the unity of personal identity, or the self.[3]

Russell Goodman astutely observed that "James's almost constant preoccupation in the *Principles* is to place within experience what other writers see as outside it" (1990, p. 61). James was to develop this Romantic theme in new ways, and I cite him now only to display the deep resonance of Thoreau's own endeavors with what became a central theme in later American philosophy. By these lights, Thoreau offers a treasure trove of "data," an extensive report of experience, which might be employed to support James's subsequent claims. Indeed, Thoreau's project is recast by James into a more formalistic account of perception and consciousness, and from this perspective Goodman correctly identifies James as an articulate heir of American Romanticism, particularly the strain that seeks to portray an "intimacy" with the world. Thus James builds a nondualistic account, where the self and the world coalesce, the same theme that has served as the nexus of much of Thoreauvian scholarship—ranging from his epistemology (Cameron 1985; Peck 1990) to the import of his mystical yearnings (e.g., Kopp 1963; Baym 1966; Lyons 1967; Tuerk 1975, pp. 63 ff.). Accordingly, James's investigations of ordinary experience revealed that they are already joined (ibid., p. 84), and in his late *Essays in Radical Empiricism*, James coined the term "pure experience" to capture the place where experience occurs.

In this construction, James, like Thoreau before him, focused upon the *present* not only as the nexus for consciousness and our understanding of the self but as the epistemological hinge of knowledge itself. In the present, the distinction of self and other, of subjective and objective, is yet to be made:

> As "subjective" we say that the experience represents; as "objective" it
> is represented. What represents and what is represented is here numer-
> ically the same; but we must remember that no dualism of being repre-
> sented and representing resides in the experience *per se*. In its pure
> state, or when isolated, there is no self-splitting of it into consciousness
> and what the consciousness is "of." Its subjectivity and objectivity are
> functional attributes solely, realized only when the experience is
> "taken," *i.e.*, talked-of, twice, considered along with its two differing
> contexts respectively, by a new retrospective experience, of which that

whole past complication now forms the fresh content. (James [1904] 1987, p. 1151)

According to this formulation, experience in its primary state admits no reflection, and only by "processing" that experience retrospectively can it become *known*. Perhaps paradoxically, the present only "exists" as a construction drawn from our reflection on time; and, as such, the *apprehension* of the present, its experience *qua* present, is the product of our deliberations which divide and distill experience (see James [1890] 1983, pp. 574–75). In a sense, the present is "experienced" only in memory. So in short, self-consciousness organizes experience after the fact, an epistemological precept from which we may confidently regard Thoreau's various projects, ranging from his mystical reveries to the deliberate business of "writing nature."

THE CYCLIC CHARACTER OF TIME: CONTRA AUGUSTINE

Nature never lost a day–nor a moment– As the planet in its orbit & around its axis–so do the seasons– –so does time revolve with a rapidity inconceivable.

Thoreau, September 13, 1852, *Journal* 5, p. 343

Daniel Peck's *Thoreau's Morning Work* (1990) is the most extended and careful reading of the place of time, history, and memory in Thoreau's oeuvre.[4] One of the key distinctions Peck makes is how Thoreau relates time and history:

> [H]istory obstructs an original relation to the universe by supplanting the eternal with the merely transient. At various points throughout *A Week* he demotes history (usually in favor of "myth"), because what he wants is not a relation to time, which is limited, but to timelessness. (Ibid., p. 17)

I agree with Peck that Thoreau subordinates history to time. In its preoccupation with history, "*A Week* could not open itself to the living instant of the present, the nick of time" (ibid., p. 36). *Walden*'s power lies in part in turning time's linear progression into a cycle, where time has no beginning and no end. It has been well recognized that *Walden* follows a seasonal time line, and much of Thoreau's Journal reports the cycles of seasons; but Peck has suggested a more profound reordering of Thoreau's notions of time based on how one might interpret the famous Journal entry of April 18, 1852: "For the first time I perceive this spring that the year is a circle– I see distinctly the spring arc thus far. It is drawn with a firm line" (*Journal* 4, 1992, p. 468). One school of thought, the literalists, reads this entry as simply an observation that spring had arrived. So Richard Lebeaux writes, "more likely, he was indicating that this was the first time this spring that he had seen the year as a circle" (1984, p. 159). Robert Sattelmeyer concurs: "For a naturalist to observe for the first time at age thirty-five that the year is a circle is equivalent to a hydrologist's discovery that water runs downhill" (1990, p. 64). In general, these critics see nature's seasonal time as metaphors of life's changes which thus served Thoreau as an appropriate correspondence to his personal time, a relationship he energetically sought to capture. On this reading, the year's cycle is an important literary vehicle, representing a powerful transcendental correspondence, and a critical catalyst for Thoreau's completion of *Walden*.

Peck assumes another stance altogether, one which I find compelling and more interesting as it leads to a deeper interpretation:

> That he should at this late date have reacted profoundly to his perception of an age-old truth, the cyclical nature of seasonal change, may be difficult to comprehend.
>
> Yet this, I believe, was an entirely authentic discovery for Thoreau— indeed, the most important and determinative in his imaginative life. To understand its full importance, we need to place strong emphasis on his use of the word *see* in the entry's second sentence: "I *see* distinctly the spring arc thus far." What Thoreau announces here is that he has, for the first time, apprehended the temporal flow of nature's change in clearly spatial terms; he has set temporality on a plane, on an "arc," along whose rim rides the flow of time. In this way, time is "contained" and given a boundary, one that coincides with consciousness itself. The "line" that describes the circle, "drawn" by the divine artist from whom all time flows, is "firm." Unlike the porous, multiple figures of Emerson's essay "Circles" (1841), expanding ever outward "wheel without wheel" (*Collected Works*, 2:180 [1983d, p. 404]), Thoreau's circle is unitary. Like Walden Pond, it characteristically looks inward from its perimeter toward its own deep and complex interior. . . .
> . . . When time is conceptualized as a circle, memory and anticipation come together as a single timeless dimension of experience.
> (1990, pp. 46–47)

Peck observes that much of Thoreau's effort to define a microcosm whose unity would mirror the cosmos was stabilized by this apprehension of the circle of time.[5] To capture time, Thoreau would have to live in an ever-present present. As he moves along an arc of time, only the present exists. He, of all people, admits to being surprised by the passage of seasons, which reflects both his excitement and the novelty of experience as well as the freshness of nature's ever-changing visage. So as the seasons shift, Thoreau urges us to marvel at nature's rhythms, but at the same time he advises that the quintessential character of this flux is only experienced in the present and that accordingly the present *qua* presence must be savored and "held."

> This is June, the month of grass and leaves. . . . Already the aspens are trembling again, and a new summer is offered me. I feel a little fluttered in my thoughts, as I might be too late. Each season is but an infinitesimal point. It no sooner comes than it is gone. It has no duration. It simply gives a tone and hue to my thought. . . . Our thoughts and sentiments answer to revolutions of the seasons, as two cog-wheels fit into each other. We are conversant with only one point of contact at a time, from which we receive a prompting and impulse and instantly pass to a new season or point of contact. (June 6, 1857, *Journal*, [1906] 1962, 9:406–7)

Peck calls the arc image the "spatialization of time" and pursues this matter as an epistemological problem. I would not disagree, but will beat another path. I believe time in this formulation assumes a *moral* character in at least two ways: The first concerns Thoreau's constant reiteration of using time wisely, of not working for false ends, whether frankly materialistic, or more subtly in answer to social pressures. But there is a deeper existential sense of morality here, and again it builds from an Augustinian construction of how we perceive time.[6] So, having introduced the notion of the ever-present present in the previous section, let us follow its metaphysical implications.

In his philosophical discussion of consciousness and self, Augustine dwells at length on that aspect of soul which serves as its keystone: memory. More than a repository of images of recollected experience, memory is the seat of self-transcendence, despite being exactly that part of the soul where the individual is most deeply his or her individual self (Augustine, *Confessions* 10.8.15). But with memory comes paradox: its only temporal location is the present. When we are not thinking about something, we are not remembering it: only when we think of it is it present before us. Memory then is what gives the soul some purchase on consciousness, and on reality. But by existing, by definition, only in the present, memory encounters other complications, because of the persistent elusiveness of time, which itself is properly said to exist in the present. But what does this mean?

> Not even one day is ever entirely present. All the hours of the day add up to twenty-four. The first of them has others in the future, the last has them in the past. . . . A single hour is itself constituted of fugitive moments. If we can think of some bit of time which cannot be divided up into even the smallest instantaneous moments, that alone is what we should call "the present." And this time flies so quickly from the

future into the past that it is an interval with no duration. Any duration is divisible into past and future. The present occupies no space.
(Ibid. 11.15.23)

As discussed, Thoreau would spatialize time in a powerful metaphor, but
the essential Augustinian insight was uncontested. Human consciousness
and human selfhood, argues Augustine, are caught in an endless linear succession of infinitesimally small present moments: it is in this atomized
dimension that consciousness exists, "distended in time." This distention
constitutes the great measure of difference and distance between human
modes of consciousness and God's, for whom in eternity all time, instanta-
neously and without mediation, is present. Humans, mediating time
through memory, live trapped in the relentless succession of present
moments. The present is itself never securely present, because each moment
runs immediately into the next.

How can human consciousness escape this entrapment in time? For
Augustine the fourth-century Catholic bishop, the answer is eschatological, and austerely theistic: At the End, at the final redemption, God will bring
his saints to rest in Him, so that they will have an unmediated apprehension
of the divine: in eternity, they will have escaped the multiplicity and distention of life in time which is the consequence of Adam's fall (11.29. 39).
In this life, only in mystical experience—rare, fleeting, and temporary—can
the mind glimpse this future reality (9.10.24–25), which Augustine desig-
nates as redemption. After all, only God sees nature as whole, in all perspectives and in all times. Augustine recognized that time could not, in fact,
be captured, for only in redemption would human time turn into salvaged
eternity. Thoreau the nineteenth-century naturalist, on the other hand, does
strive to achieve this transcendence, this suppression of time's successive-
ness, but in this life, "in the bloom of the present moment" (*Walden*, 1971,
p. 111). Thoreau thus sought no eschatological redemption, but he too recognized that nature, from the divine vantage, experiences no change. So in
his study of nature, he is thrown back on a kind of personal redemption of
his own sovereign consciousness. This leads us to an important characteristic of Thoreau's metaphysics.

The critical difference with Augustine is that Thoreau attempts to capture time in the present, in this world, in nature. So while Augustine
entrusts himself to God's grace, Thoreau, self-reliant, pursues time—
nature—on his own. This is a useful contrast, inasmuch as we perceive
Thoreau's spirituality as independent of theism and, more to the point, as
radically self-reliant. In claiming that "all the change is in me" (*Walden*,

1971, p. 193), Thoreau not only affirms the centrality of his own person-hood but adopts a position which is reasserted in every facet of his project. In seeking to capture time by some resolution of nature's apparent change and the discovery of its permanence within himself, Thoreau must bridge a philosophical gulf separating himself from the world. The metaphysical question of reality's standing is articulated by Thoreau in a Kantian voice: "We think that that *is* which *appears* to be" (ibid., p. 96). And Thoreau, after accepting his crucial role of mediating reality, is both baffled and awed by the order of nature's presence: "Why do precisely these objects which we behold make a world?" (ibid., p. 225). A rich voice beckons, resonant with the metaphysical wonder of *being*. Returning to the Journal "arc" passage, we see the deep connection of Thoreau's vision of time (the arc) and his abil-ity to see the order of nature:

> It [the arc] is drawn with a firm line. Every incident is a parable of the great teacher. The cranberries washed up in the meadows & into the road on the causeways now yields a pleasant acid.
>
> Why should just these sights & sounds accompany our life? Why should I hear the chattering of blackbirds–why smell the skunk each year? I would fain explore the mysterious relation between myself & these things. I would at least know what these things unavoidably are– –make a chart of our life–know how its shores trend–that butter-flies reappear & when–know why just this circle of creatures completes the world. (April 18, 1852, *Journal* 4, 1992, p. 468)

Gazing at the intricate pattern of nature, Thoreau perceives and appreciates those changes and occurrences that lead him to ponder his own cognitive faculty. The world as the object of primary interest recedes, giving way to the self's own need to be scrutinized. While metaphysics frames the issue, the epistemological project becomes the means of navigating those deep waters: the inexorable flux of nature might be known, and perhaps his life could be charted on that grid of change, not only to "capture time" but to order nature.

Thoreau the naturalist, the consummate observer, becomes the reporter of his own thought as he asks: How do we perceive, and what is the per-ceiving faculty? But let me quickly add that Thoreau was aware, albeit in an era less psychologically self-conscious than our own, that he had access to only part of his mind and soul. Nevertheless he sought insight, and he pursued that truth within himself as best he could and to good purpose: after all, "the unconsciousness of man is the consciousness of God" (*A Week*, 1980a, p. 329). This construction is readily exposed in the "Thursday" chap-

ter of *A Week,* where Thoreau provides us with a vivid example of his egocentrism which is extended in the later Journal entry just cited:

> Let us wander where we will, the universe is built round about us, and
> we are central still. If we look into the heavens they are concave. . . . The
> sky is curved downward to the earth. . . . I draw down its skirts. The
> stars so low there seem loth to depart, but by a circuitous path to be
> remembering me, and returning on their steps. (*A Week,* 1980a, p. 331)

In "Friday," Thoreau describes the shifting perspective of local scenes but
asserts, "the universe is a sphere whose center is wherever there is intelligence. The sun is not so central as a man" (ibid., p. 349). And indeed Thoreau
in effect creates landscapes. Unlike most travelers, who do not "make objects
and events stand around them as the centre" (ibid., p. 326), "Thoreau in a
very real sense makes the heavenly spheres revolve around him, he and his
earth are more important" (Teurk 1975, p. 45). In the private Journal entry
cited above, Thoreau went one step further.

To search for some order, rhythm, placement of the seasons and creatures, is an expected activity of a Romantic naturalist, but then Thoreau
makes an extraordinary statement: "*Can I not by expectation affect the revolutions of nature–make a day to bring forth something new?*" (April 18,
1852, *Journal 4,* 1992, p. 468; emphasis added). This is remarkable metaphysics: he seems to be moving from an observer to an actor. Thoreau sees
God's presence ("every incident is a parable of the great teacher"), but he
further ponders not only His presence but Being itself. Asking the ancient
metaphysical question, Why is there this very world—why indeed is there
existence and why is that existence coupled to an individual life, namely
Thoreau's? To observe that the quality of that relationship is "mysterious"
is commonplace; to opine that he might "affect the revolutions of nature"
is bewildering. Could Thoreau be suggesting that if he could effect a perfect union of his intelligence with nature, then his imagination might share
some correspondence with divine Intelligence? Certainly, other critics have
noted such aspirations for union (e.g., Kopp 1963; Baym 1966; Lyons 1967;
Tuerk 1975, pp. 63 ff.), but I want to suggest an extension of that notion. If
Thoreau were in such harmony with nature as to *anticipate* change, in such
close identification as to effect union and thus *affect* change, has he not
indeed become a Mover, or at least striven to be? A transcendental agency
may be his goal. We cannot be certain from this passage, but it seems a small
step to go from ordering the cosmos, constructing landscapes, measuring
time, and finding union with nature to invoking transcendental agency. How
far, indeed, did his radicalism take him?

THOREAU'S GRAPPLING WITH TIME

There on that illustrated sandbank was revealed an antiquity
beside which Ninevah is young. Such a light as sufficed for the
earliest ages. From what star has it arrived on this planet?

Thoreau, July 6, 1851, *Journal 3*, 1990, p. 286

Thoreau dealt with his appreciation of the nature of time with three powerful insights, each developed in *Walden*, each of which is an important
aspect of his understanding of the limits of epistemology. The first was to
recognize the ultimate subjectivity of time. This appreciation is well caught
in such pithy statements as, "Things do not change; we change" (*Walden*,
1971, p. 328) and "all the change is in me" (ibid., p. 193). But the profun-
dity of Thoreau's insight drives to the deepest strata of his metaphysics.
Nature *knows* no time. As we chronicle, parse, divide, assign, and categorize, time is subjected to some human translation to become a human construction. As he confided in his Journal, "Why does not God make some
mistake to show to us that time is a delusion. Why did I invent Time but to
destroy it" (March 26, 1842, *Journal 1*, 1981, p. 392). Time in a fundamental sense cannot be comprehended or grasped in human terms; when it is,
temporality emerges as a profound distortion. There are critical moral reflections on such a conceptualization: Most importantly, our plasticizing time
reflects the trivialization of our lives, working in time for artificial, if not
self-destructive, goals. For *Walden*'s artist of Kouroo, time was irrelevant
as he sought perfection in making his staff: "As he made no compromise
with Time, Time kept out of his way" (*Walden*, 1971, p. 326). Because time
was so problematic, Thoreau would attempt to regard it as a function of the
soul, serving both as his deepest ontology and as the source of divine truth.

The second aspect of time, related to the subjectivity of temporal experience, is Thoreau's frank wonder at change, nature's flux that must be
appreciated constantly *in* the present. As he wrote in "Economy," "All
change is a miracle to contemplate; but it is a miracle which is taking place
every instant" (*Walden*, 1971, p. 11). The world is forever new, a world of
process, of becoming, and only by deliberate attention, expectation, and
appreciation do we fully savor nature's fruits. Any other activity, even seemingly "necessary" work, must be measured against the splendor of contemplating nature in the present moment. And this leads to the third aspect
of time's character, specifically our slavery to temporality.

Probably the most famous line of *Walden*, "The mass of men lead lives
of quiet desperation" (1971, p. 8), is immediately preceded by the critical

philosophical insight: "As if you could kill time without injuring eternity" (ibid., p. 8). This is a key phrase, for eternity, the infinite, knows no time, and by trivializing time, by wasting one's time, one does "injury" to eternity, which is as close to divine as Thoreau will approach. Injury connotes hurt and injustice, so time becomes frankly moral in this calculation. So how is time tempered and "protected"?

Time for Thoreau is the present, and to live in the present—as opposed to being directed by some uncapturable past or living for some anticipated (and thus false) future—was the key deliberate act:

> In any weather, at any hour of the day or night, I have been anxious to improve the nick of time, and notch it on my stick too; to stand on the meeting of two eternities, the past and the future, which is precisely the present moment; to toe that line. (*Walden*, 1971, p. 17)

Indeed, one might even say that *Walden* is dedicated to that endeavor, to alert the reader of the ethical imperative to live fully in the present. Then he embarks on his elusive query:

> You will pardon some obscurities, for there are more secrets to my trade than in most men's, and yet not voluntarily kept, but inseparable from its very nature. I would gladly tell all that I know about it, and never paint "No Admittance" on my gate. (Ibid.)

But he in fact can reveal little despite his open invitation, and, playing with us, Thoreau delivers the celebrated obscure passage, "I long ago lost a hound, a bay horse, and a turtle-dove, and am still on their trail" (Ibid.). Considering the wealth of critical comment on this sentence, there is a certain irony to Thoreau's juxtaposing this symbolic construction immediately next to his invitation to follow him so that he might reveal his secrets. While not attempting to adjudicate Thoreau's designs in constructing his exposition in this manner, I will simply observe that the mere sense of loss is fundamentally loss in time, and it is precisely Thoreau's inability to capture those losses that reveals the basic moral nature of time. By this reading, Thoreau is emphasizing the character of the past as lost and, in contradistinction, the present as capturable. For Thoreau, to capture time in the present is to live with integrity. Indeed, it informs his entire Walden experience, which he explicitly describes as an experiment of the present (*Walden*, 1971, p. 84). As Stanley Cavell observes,

> Of course he means that the building of his habitation (which is to say, the writing of his book) is his present experiment. He also means what the words say: that the present is his experiment, the discovery of the

present, the meeting of two eternities. ("God himself culminates in the present moment" [*Walden*, 1971, p. 97].) (Cavell 1981, p. 10)

Our enslavement to conventional time, whether posed philosophically (as the exclusiveness of the present) or socially (as the superfluous labor of man, the frivolous social dictates, and the like), concerns Thoreau because it obscures two cardinal human projects. The first is epistemological, to see the real. The imperative of appreciating nature requires living in the current moment, to observe and luxuriate in the bounty of the natural as immediately experienced. As he wrote in "Walking," this is a moral mandate: "Above all, we cannot afford not to live in the present" (1980b, p. 133) as the vehicle of capturing reality. And what is that reality? Time—both in its presence and in its present. This is time as ontology.

> Time is but the stream I go a-fishing in. I drink at it; but while I drink I see the sandy bottom and detect how shallow it is. Its thin current slides away, but eternity remains. I would drink deeper; fish in the sky, whose bottom is pebbly with stars. I cannot count one. (*Walden*, 1971, p. 98)[7]

Time is elusive, but it serves as Thoreau's fundamental ontology, the stream of experience, the substrate of nature, the fabric of eternity, the fundamental woof and warp of the divine. He realizes that this is not time as conventionally understood but a metaphysical category we call "eternity": "That time which we really improve, or which is improvable, is neither past, present, nor future" (*Walden*, 1971, p. 99).

Thoreau is swimming in deep metaphysical waters, and he knows that the faculty of imagination intuits this reality and guides him in his epistemological project. But his effort is doomed to failure, because the intellect will not release him from self-consciousness. Peering into the stream of time, Thoreau continues, "I know not the first letter of the alphabet. I have always been regretting that I was not as wise as the day I was born" (ibid.). He admits the limitation imposed by eclipsed infancy, the period after which immediate experience, unselfconscious life in the world, is forever lost. But Thoreau will make do as best he can by attempting to recapture this lost immediacy by using other tools. Integrated experience—unreflexively complete and thus authentic—must now be replaced with the mediating intellect, the ability to discern and contemplate. "The intellect is a cleaver; it discerns and rifts its way into the secret of things"; he will thus use it to "mine and burrow my way" for "the richest vein" (ibid.). Keen observation, patient looking, spiritual contemplation—Thoreau celebrates his ability to rationally know and meticulously record the natural, and thus he deliberately seeks to recapture the immediacy of experience which he now appreciates as the union with nature. This insight retains a certain irony, however, because Thoreau must be self-consciously aware of his intelligence, and it is this self-conscious awareness that apprehends time's passing, the fleeting present, the elusive basis of experience. This self-awareness is the source of Thoreau's moral understanding of time.

There were, indeed, two modes by which Thoreau grappled with time. The first, and the one for which we have the most evidence, was his self-conscious effort to live "deliberately" in the present. The second, in a sense its opposite, was to lose the self completely so that the awareness of time vanishes altogether. This is the mystical state, and Thoreau actively sought the dissolution it offered him. For instance, on a "cold and dark afternoon" in the autumn of 1851, Thoreau lamented being "yoked to Matter & to Time," and plaintively asks, "Does not each thought become a vulture to gnaw your vitals?" (November 13, 1851, *Journal* 4, 1992, pp. 180–81). One stratagem is to delight in the world, in the sensuous appreciation of nature; the other is mystical union, what Joel Porte calls "the epiphanic moment" (1966, p. 157).[8] As Thoreau wrote to Harrison Blake about his self-imposed solitude,

> It is not that we love to be alone, but that we love to soar, and when we do soar, the company grows thinner & thinner till there is none at all. It is either the Tribune on the plain, a sermon on the mount, or a very private *extacy* [sic] still higher up. We are not the less to aim at the summits, though the multitude does not ascend them. (May 21, 1856, *Correspondence*, 1958, p. 424)

To ascend to the peak of ecstasy was of paramount importance to Thoreau:

> My desire for knowledge is intermittent but my desire to commune with the spirit of the universe–to be intoxicated with the fumes, call it, of that divine nectar–to bear my head through atmospheres and over heights unknown to my feet–is perennial and constant. (February 9, 1851, *Journal* 3, 1990, p. 185)

The Journal records many of Thoreau's recollection of such states. Consider the following entries, separated by almost thirteen years:

> In the sunshine and the crowing of cocks I feel an illimitable holiness, which makes me bless God and myself. . . .
> . . . What shall I do with this hour so like time and yet so fit for eternity? . . . I lie out indistinct as a heath at noon-day– I am evaporating airs ascending into the sun. (February 7, 1841, *Journal* 1, 1981, pp. 255–56)

> The strains of the aeolian harp and of the wood thrush are the truest and loftiest preachers that I know now left on this earth. . . . They, as it

were, lift us up in spite of ourselves. They intoxicate, they charm us. Where was that strain mixed into which this world was dropped but as a lump of sugar to sweeten the draught? I would be drunk, drunk, drunk, dead drunk to this world with it forever. (December 30, 1853, *Journal*, [1906] 1962, 6:39)

The first passage explicitly contrasts time and eternity. Thoreau knows he is in time, but he also recognizes that the mystical moment suspends time and substitutes eternity, the feeling of limitless expansion of the self to "evaporate" in mystical union. In the second passage, Thoreau brings the sensuous experience of nature to a drunken state of ecstasy and delight. A few months earlier he had commented on the language that must capture these experiences:

transport–rapture ravishment, ecstasy–these are the words I want. This is the effect of music– I am rapt away by it–out of myself– These are truly poetical words. I am inspired–elevated–expanded– I am on the mount. (January 15, 1853, *Journal* 5, 1997, p. 444)

Thoreau was ever prepared to climb the mount, and it was couched in terms of time: "In all my travels I never came to the abode of the present" (October 17, 1850, *Journal* 3, 1990, p. 122). We witness the effort, the ecstasy of the vision when it happens to fall upon him, and the frustration of his solitude. But he would continue his endeavor.[9]

The mystical experience was couched and even defined in the question of temporality that informs and guides Thoreau's deepest psychological and philosophical efforts. The suspension of time, the glimpse of eternity, were transforming moments of aesthetic and spiritual insight, ones he sought in his youth (e.g., April 3, 1842, *Journal* 1, 1981, pp. 400–401) as well as in his full maturity.[10] Thoreau warranted in a letter to Blake that he only had one "*spiritual* birth,"[11] but it sufficed to sustain his spiritual quest and, indeed, allow him to have other analogous experiences. The question was, "[H]ow can I communicate with the gods who am a pencil-maker on the earth, and not be insane?" (*A Week*, 1980a, p. 140). How to walk the tightrope between acute self-consciousness and mystical ecstasy, that indeed was the question.

THE SELF IN TIME

[M]odern man . . . does not yet have an experience of time adequate to his idea of history, and is therefore painfully split between his being-in-time . . . and his being-in-history.

Agamben 1993, p. 100

For Thoreau, nature's deepest ontology is the present, which is pulled out of time to be perceived as part of eternity. Thus the notion of time's passing has been radically altered in an irresolvable paradox: each moment—only existing as a fleeting present—is concurrently "not" in any real sense and yet *ethically* immutable and precious. This acute awareness of our "presentness"—and its intransigent elusiveness—is both the product and the source of an intense self-consciousness. And in that supreme self-awareness, Thoreau perceived his place in the universe, claiming for himself—to whatever limited extent—a niche in the infinite. With this act of valuation, Thoreau entered into a stream of time that knows neither beginning nor end, and yet it served to orient his multifaceted project. The famous aphorism of living in the nick of time becomes a moral activity.[12] The attempts to live deliberately revolve about a twofold project: the demand to live fully in the present, acutely aware of nature's flux, and the attempt to capture that present in acts of recollection. For Thoreau, each assumes a moral imperative. I will close with comments on each endeavor.

Thoreau's memory assumed various expressions, ranging from social history to natural history to situate the self. Collective memory and individual interpretation are evident modes of writing cultural history, but even the naturalist writings are recollections, reconstructions of his experience, and thus must build from memory and, more fundamentally, are fashioned around the core issue of his own experience. From this perspective, the nature writing and the cultural history are all of one piece, public discourses as distillations of Thoreau's most intimate thoughts of himself in the domains of nature and the past. In each case, Thoreau's vision of time and history was understood as reconstructed memory, fashioning the past into the present. Time, actually only the present, dominates Thoreau's self-conscious endeavors at world-making. But this "time-present" is, of course, never fully captured or replayed, and by 1857 Thoreau was resigned to accepting the poetics of his memory—incomplete and thus, in some sense, inadequate, but at the same time the more salient and "truer" report:

> I would fain make two reports in my Journal, first the incidents and observations of to-day; and by to-morrow I review the same and record what was omitted before, which will often be the most significant and poetic part. I do not know at first what it is that charms me. The men and things of to-day are wont to lie fairer and truer in to-morrow's memory. (March 27, 1857, *Journal*, [1906] 1962, 9:306)

The writing of natural history and cultural history each required exercise of creative memory—imaginative, aesthetically driven, and thus deeply personal. But even more revealing are those open declarations of Thoreau's own discovery, and enunciation, of himself. Indeed, autobiography as the expression of such introspection is a critical component of the very notion of a developing self, one that not only changes but remains elusive in its evolution. Just as in his natural and cultural histories, Thoreau's view of the self emerges out of a complex understanding of the response to ceaseless change. In his view the self is ultimately posed by the problem of time in the metaphysics of change. So both in his self-appraisal and in his rendering a world which is "fixed" from that tenuous position of self-knowledge, Thoreau emerges as a self-conscious artisan, constructing a mind's "portrait" of nature ever mindful of the elusiveness of the present. Each of his reconstructions then is drawn with a wary eye on time, either as an epistemological "marker" or as an existential challenge. In either case, time must be frozen and in a sense replayed, but only as "written" under his own signature.

As we turn to the specifics of Thoreau's history writing—both cultural and natural—this precept must be borne in mind. He was perhaps most cognizant of this issue as he pondered the moral dimension of his poesis. In *A Week,* he makes a remarkable testament regarding his own vision of the poet-historian:

> The true poem is not that which the public read. There is always a poem not printed on paper, coincident with the production of this, stereotyped in the poet's life. It is *what he has become through his work.* Not how is the idea expressed in stone, or on canvass or paper, is the question, but how far it has obtained form and expression in the life of the artist. His true work will not stand in any prince's gallery.
> (1980a, p. 343; emphasis in original)

This is the definition of a life of virtue. His morning work, his dance with mythic heroes, his dreams—awake or slumbering—are unified by a vision of moral rectitude which must be achieved in doing, in reverie, in memory. Each would serve a larger purpose, and Thoreau might integrate them because of their epistemological overlap. Dreams are recalled, brought into consciousness by memory; and memory, a faculty of knowledge—albeit highly subjective, private, and untestable without extraordinary effort—blends into history. At the end of this cascade, a public record is presented, configured by the imperative of portraying a vision of the self—one seen in the doing, but only perceived as the tip of an iceberg of experience. Thus the literary project, whether presented as cultural history, natural history, or poetry, was a distillation of a deeper consciousness, one self-consciously and deliberately "fixing" time into a frozen portrait.

The precepts undergirding this construction are, first, that humans have choice and can determine to create their lives within a finite period, and second, directly leading from this, that humans are given the ethical insight to fulfill this opportunity. For Thoreau, this moral mandate was one of self-responsibility.

> I know of no more encouraging fact than the unquestionable ability of man to elevate his life by a conscious endeavor. It is something to be able to paint a particular picture, or to carve a statue, and so to make a few objects beautiful; but it is far more glorious to carve and paint the very atmosphere and medium through which we look, which morally we can do. To affect the quality of the day, that is the highest of arts. (*Walden*, 1971, p. 90)

The primacy of individual agency, the character of self-determination, and the moral demand of free action are the underlying precepts of Thoreau's vision of selfhood, and in many respects we might structure his notions of time as the keystone holding together the entire edifice of moral identity.[13]

Thoreau was caught in a deep metaphysical quandary: intellectually and emotionally committed to searching for some kind of order in nature, he recognized the irretrievability of time's passing within Heraclitean change. Change is not only apparent, it is ontologically *real*. And in a world of change, what Archimedean point might we use to survey and know that world? Indeed, can the self assume such a stance? And if so, what are its bearings? If not known, how are they to be sought? Thoreau grasped the realm of change as an arena of opportunity, and rather than abdicate personal responsibility, he renewed the call for deliberate choice in shaping our lives towards a new ideality—self-chosen and individually pursued. Thus in asserting one's individuality and believing in one's ability to act freely—both determined with acute self-awareness—he would assert one's place in the moral universe.

Ironically the impetus for this moral avowal derives from an instability. Changes, adjustment, improvement are the responses of life to its challenges, both external and from within. The ideal, the possible, the elusive potential have replaced any sense of finitude—a world with boundaries. Awash in this uncertain cosmos is the self, whose own sense gathers tenuously within indistinct boundaries and pliable structure. In espousing freedom of choice, Thoreau wrote in the opening pages of *Walden* how the thoughtless inertia of our lives might be jolted into a constant critique of ourselves that directs its energies toward a self-defining ideal. Change is of the essence, but it must be harnessed to a self-determined goal, following a direction of choice, of self-determined *value*. Thus, deeply embedded in this vision of the self is the moral character of agency. The ethic is thus not only based on the underlying foundation of change recognized as an essential component of our being, but is transfigured into an ethical drive toward self-perfection. The self is active, not reactive, and in this formulation, the active, self-conscious life is fundamentally antinihilistic. Despite the contingency, multiperspectivism, elusive character, and loss of essence, the self endures.

Asserting continual and creative self-overcoming and self-perfection, challenging prevailing social mores, decrying complacency, all emanate from Thoreau's metaphysical understanding of time and eternity. That formulation would serve as the source of the ethical power of *Walden;* it undergirds all of Thoreau's works. An interesting contrast is offered by Nietzsche, whose own construction of the cycle of eternity (the eternal recurrence) and the philosophy of self-willed overcoming was, like Thoreau's view, heavily indebted to Emerson (Stack 1992).[14] Each affirms an ethic of the self which authenticates itself in facing the infinite universe, forced to confront human insignificance and our essential powerlessness as we face the unbridgeable gulf between ourselves and the rest of existence. This posture inevitably leads us to existential loneliness. In contrast to the Transcendentalists, Nietzsche was uninterested in nature as a source of mending this metaphysical chasm that arises from recognizing our place in the universe: The indifference of nature means that nature has no reference to ends, and thus for Nietzsche, we reside alone. Our "present" is, indeed *our* present.[15] But Thoreau, the Transcendentalist, sees an immutable being which remains accessible. This is what Hans Jonas characterizes as the

> everlasting present, in which contemplation [of nature] can share in the brief durations of the temporal present. Thus it is eternity, not time, that grants a present and gives it a status of its own in the flux of time; and it is the loss of eternity which accounts for the loss of a genuine present. . . . If values are not beheld in vision as being (like the Good and the Beautiful of Plato), but are posited by the will as projects, then indeed existence is committed to constant futurity, with death as the goal; and a merely formal resolution to be, without a *nomos* for that resolution, becomes a project from nothingness to nothingness. In the words of Nietzsche, "Who once has lost what thou hast lost stands nowhere still." (1963, p. 338)

In this sense, Nietzsche's eternal recurrence is always actualized in the "futurity" of its being, and bequeaths a deep nihilism.[16] Jonas's diagnosis is that "the disruption between man and total reality is at the bottom of nihilism" (ibid., p. 340), and it is here that we see the great divide between Thoreau and later existentialists. Heidegger's interpretation of Nietzsche, "The phrase 'God is dead' means that the supra-sensible world is without effective force" (quoted by Jonas, ibid., p. 332), is denied by Thoreau, and indeed his entire life was devoted to examining the opposite position: in nature, in our communing with nature, we would find a suitable other that puts ourselves in true relief and thus helps us confer meaning upon our respective lives. Perhaps it is this call that beckons to us most powerfully across the great divide separating Thoreau's assertion of agency and our own postmodern confusions. How Thoreau projected his vision of selfhood and agency in writing memory and history is the subject of the next chapter.

2   Three Apple Trees

Though I am old enough to have discovered that the dreams of
youth are not to be realized in this state of existence yet I think it
would be the next greatest happiness always to be allowed to look
under the eyelids of time and contemplate the perfect steadily with
the clear understanding that I do not attain to it.

Thoreau, October 24, 1843,
Journal 1, 1981, p. 480

Before *A Week on the Concord and Merrimack Rivers*, before *Walden*,
before the developed years of the Journal, key themes appear in Thoreau's
notes that assure us that the abiding concerns articulated in these more
mature works had already been framed in embryo. To be sure, Thoreau
developed, modulated, and focused upon particular theses and questions as
he evolved (e.g., Richardson 1986; Milder 1995), and these demonstrate both
his varying psychological states and his growing intellectual maturity and
insight. But beneath this movement was a foundation which grounded his
thought.[1] A key support of this conceptual edifice, perhaps its very platform,
was his search for an aesthetic or spiritual ideal. Whether we define him
within the context of a Transcendental idealism, or a less well formulated
philosophical program or poetic orientation, Thoreau was, in common parlance, a dreamer. And in dreams, time is suspended. Conversely, in consciousness, time is not only "present"; it is an obstacle to be overcome.
Thoreau's reveries, his mystical excursions, his fascination with Hinduism,
his experiences communing with nature were all expressions of an unencumbered temporality, where the swings of everyday life, the cycle of hours,
days, and seasons—the flux of time's contingency—were suspended. In the
sense of acknowledging his rootedness in time, he would seek to situate himself within time's cycle, as discussed in the preceding chapter. But there was
another agenda afoot: Thoreau would pursue some perfection, a permanence, an unchanging reality "under the eyelids of time." Time would
"dream" of itself; history would be deferred; memory would be arrested in
the present. In this respect, time must be tamed, for awareness of temporality and change, the marks of time, counterpoised the mystical ideal, the
"perfect" that knows no change. "Indeed, a consciousness of history only
strengthens Thoreau's desire to escape it" (Milder 1995, p. 32). History in

this sense was a "problem," the key manifestation of our worldly motion, and Thoreau therefore would attempt to make his peace with history, to dam time's relentless flow.

Memory and history are time's arbiters. The latter emerges from the former, on a continuum. For Thoreau, their rootedness in time bestowed a shared character that in a profound sense expressed his own sense of identity and personhood. Throughout his oeuvre, Thoreau wrote in three "keys": history proper as generally understood by nineteenth-century historians and their audience; "semiotic" history based on evocative clues; and personal memory, charged with emotion and subjectivity. The first, an ostensibly objective and even scientific record of the past, was written with certain misgivings and sublimated to what may fairly be described as "ahistorical" purposes. The second expressed the natural philosopher's *modus operandi* and thus operated as an extension of Thoreau's descriptions of nature, becoming his preferred historiographic style. And the third, the most opaque, reflecting an emotional sensibility potentially opening the psyche to view, he exercised most plainly in poetic guise. To be sure, Thoreau advocated a poesis for each of these historiographic approaches he practiced, but memory—the most amenable to the aesthetic exercise—suffered a lack of "framing" required for his historical exposition, while conventional history was also suspect because of its false conceits of objectivity and comprehensiveness. Thus, in his view, each historiographic key suited a different proposal, and he wove them all together, each playing their respective expository roles. The overarching intent was to carry both Thoreau and his reader along the river of time, which in the Augustinian temper (see preceding chapter) knows not the past, only the present. In that present, each history assumes a moral character which orients the narrative and voices the historian's deepest concerns.

In *A Week* (1980a), Thoreau expounds upon his theory of history (previously published in *The Dial*, April 1843 [Thoreau 1975c]) making explicit his views of the poetic origins of memory and history. The passage, found in the "Monday" chapter, deserves careful scrutiny and will serve as the introduction of my own characterization of Thoreau's historical method and vision. He begins with a telling aesthetic simile by drawing a parallel between a landscape's changing light and atmosphere and history's "fluctuations" (*A Week*, 1980a, p. 154). Just as Monet so evocatively showed us in his series of paintings of haystacks, Rouen's cathedral, and the rivers Seine and Thames, Thoreau saw history's "groundwork and composition" as essentially given, the historian's task being to discern the "atmospheric tints and various lights and shades which the intervening spaces create. . . . Its beauty is like the sunset . . . atmospheric and roving or free . . . What is of moment is its hue and color" (ibid.). History is thus interpreted—impressionistically so it seems. Thoreau would seek to discover the past's truth by a critical and poetic faculty. Unfazed by a murky record, the outline suffices. The historian may proceed with confidence, for the past is less to be recovered than signified in the present. The Augustinian credo is thus clearly asserted as history's relevance and meaning are exclusively situated in the now.

> Time hides no treasures; we want not its *then*, but its *now*. We do not complain that the mountains in the horizon are blue and indistinct; they are the more like the heavens.
>
> Of what moment are facts that can be lost,—which need to be commemorated? The monument of death will outlast the memory of the dead. The pyramids do not tell the tale that was confided to them; the living fact commemorates itself. Why look in the dark for light? Strictly speaking, the historical societies have not recovered one fact from oblivion, but are themselves, instead of the fact, that is lost. The researcher is more memorable than the researched. . . . Critical acumen is exerted in vain to uncover the past; the *past* cannot be *presented*; we cannot know what we are not. But one veil hangs over past, present, and future, and it is the province of the historian to find out, not what was, but what is. (Ibid., pp. 154–55)

Thoreau was a consummate observer, and whether he pursued a description of the environment or of the past, he did so with active creativity. Therefore, in his view, the historian must illuminate his subject, and he does so by creative effort arising from Romantic imagination.[2] So the darkness of the past is "not a distance of time, but a distance of relation" (ibid., pp. 156–57). By bringing the past into the present—by making a "living fact"—the past is known as personal experience. History thus assumes a character of relation—the relation of the historian to his object of inquiry—and in establishing that correspondence, Thoreau understands that he is indeed *creating* the past. I will show how this personalization of the past is accomplished in the three keys mentioned above and then discuss how the entire enterprise is girded by the moral project that dominates Thoreau's thought. My primary text for this discussion is *A Week*, a work Peck rightly has called "an exemplary case of remembrance in Thoreau's work" (1990, p. 12).[3]

HISTORY AS NARRATION

Of what manner of stuff is the web of time wove[?]

Thoreau, January 8, 1842,
Journal 1, 1981, p. 361

The more common form of historical exposition, what might be called "objective" or "scientific," is fully exercised in *A Week*. There, Thoreau explores the New England heritage through historical records and narratives, personal recollection, and oral tradition, using the river both as the conduit into that past and as the vehicle of bringing history into his present. Of the various cases we might examine, the Hannah Duston story, appearing in the "Thursday" chapter, is particularly evocative. The saga of this frontier woman's abduction by a band of Canadian Indians allied with the French in King William's War was first recorded by Cotton Mather following a personal interview with the heroine in his *Magnalia Christi Americana* (1702) and has repeatedly been celebrated over the past three hundred years.[4] Thoreau read extensively in colonial history (Johnson 1986, pp. 122 ff.), but he apparently relied most on a single source for the story, B. L. Mirick's *History of Haverhill, Massachusetts* (1832), as the basis of his own account. Duston's escape has generated extensive comment (e.g., Arner 1973; Johnson 1986; Smith 1995), and Thoreau likewise used the story to reflect on the moral tenor of Indian-colonial relations and the implications of those conflicts for the American character. This episode thus exhibits, in miniature, Thoreau's use of history and his self-conscious refashioning of it to serve certain thematic ends.

The story, in outline, has some constant elements that appear in all versions. On March 15, 1697, the frontier settlement of Haverhill, Massachusetts, was attacked by Indians (20 in number [Anderson 1973]), who killed more than a score of the settlers (27 [ibid.]) and captured at least another dozen (15 [ibid.]). One of these was Hannah Duston (1657–1737). Hannah's plight was complicated by her having given birth a week or so earlier to a daughter; her nurse, Mary Neff, was also taken into captivity with mother and child, who had been left behind as her husband fled with their seven other children. Before retreating with their captives, the Indians bashed the crying infant against an apple tree. A few days later, the war party split, and Hannah, Mary, and an adolescent boy, Samuel Lennardson (Leonardson [ibid.]), were conducted toward a rendezvous in Canada by two warriors, accompanied by three squaws, and seven children of various ages. Motivated by the murder of her baby and the fearful (and humiliating) prospect of running the gauntlet naked, Hannah devised and led a daring escape by killing all the Indians except one woman and a child. According to her own account, she tomahawked the Indians in their sleep and delivered ten scalps as testimony to their death. Massachusetts had posted a bounty of 50 pounds per Indian in 1694, but cut this reward in half the following year and then repealed it entirely in 1696. Thomas Duston, upon his wife's behalf, successfully appealed to the legislature, which voted Hannah 25 pounds, and the nurse and the boy 12 pounds, 10 shillings each, "for their service in slaying their captors" (quoted by Anderson 1973).

In the 150 years preceding Thoreau's own retelling, the Duston story evoked strong moral response, beginning with Mather's original account.[5] Mather, of course, was no neutral chronicler. As an extension of his disdain for the papacy and his own separate hatred for native Americans allied with the French, he regarded the Indian Wars, beginning with King Philip's War (1675–77), as a holy conflict with barbarism, a battle that never ended in his own lifetime.[6] The unstable nature of colonial-Indian relations, the unresolved questions concerning Indian sovereignty, and the very legitimacy of land claims nagged at colonial identity. The conflicts contested in seventeenth-century Massachusetts continued to haunt Thoreau, albeit with a different moral posture, but with the same basic question posed. Jill Lepore offers a cogent summary assessment of this predicament:

> Waging the war, writing about it, and remembering it were all part of the attempt to win it, but none of these efforts ever fully succeeded. No matter how much the colonists wrote about the war, no matter how much or how eloquently they justified their cause and conduct . . . [they] could never succeed at reconstructing themselves as "true Englishmen." The danger of degenerating into Indians continued to haunt them. (Lepore 1997, p. 175)

One of the ironies of the Duston saga is that she indeed acted with as much savagery as her captors, showing us just how narrow the divide between the "civilized" colonists and the "barbaric" Indian proved to be. Thoreau, of course, sympathized much more easily with the Indians than his forefathers could,[7] and given his extraordinary interest in chronicling their history and studying their culture, we might fairly surmise that he both admired and wished to emulate them to some degree. Certainly, his view of their integration with nature was an ideal he himself pursued. Thus the Duston story of settler revenge is replete with ambiguity that Thoreau employs for his own purpose.

Thoreau's account begins with an identification: Just as he and his brother are paddling on the Merrimack, he imagines the other paddlers 142 years earlier, awkwardly manipulating the swollen spring river, ill dressed for the climate and place. Instead of a leisurely sojourn, these individuals proceeded with "nervous energy and determination," while "at the bottom of their canoe lay the bleeding scalps of ten of the aborigines" (*A Week*, 1980a, p. 320). The harmony of the wilderness of Thoreau's present is thus rudely disrupted with the memory of alien settlers holding native bounty.

The narrative continues with the protagonists' identification and their abduction briefly recalled. Not knowing the fate of her other children and husband, witnessing the fiery destruction of her homestead, and facing the gauntlet, Hannah is dispassionately described as planning and executing the escape. The crucial difference between Mather's account and Mirick's is the embellishment offered by the latter of the Indian's frightening aspect, adding a psychological element of terror for the reader not sufficiently alarmed by the savagery of the Indian assault, and the party's return to the campsite after embarking on the river to scalp the Indians as proof of their story. Thoreau omits Mirick's obvious denigration of the native American but retains the added element of Duston's return to obtain evidence of her exploit (Mirick 1832, p. 91), thus highlighting her resolute character—one that Mirick, and most other commentators, had called "heroic" (ibid.).[8] But Thoreau holds final judgment in abeyance. It is the consequences of Duston's capture and torment that dominate Thoreau's narrative:

> Early this morning this deed was performed, and now, perchance, these tired women and this boy, their clothes stained with blood, and their minds racked with alternate resolution and fear, are making a hasty meal of parched corn and moose-meat, while their canoe glides under these pine roots whose stumps are still standing on the bank. They are thinking of the dead whom they have left behind on that solitary isle far up the stream, and of the relentless living warriors who are in pursuit. Every withered leaf which the winter has left seems to know their story, and in its rustling to repeat it and betray them. (*A Week*, 1980a, p. 322)

This is a remarkable passage. Thoreau slips into the present tense and would have us party to their escape, immediate witnesses to their terror. We are there, "this morning," and thus reenact their flight before the same trees. Time in the past is thus suspended, and dramatically the historian's voice has strangely mutated.

This grammatical turn is a striking shift in perspective by which Thoreau would attempt to bring the emotional quality of these historical events into present consciousness. Despite a distance of nearly a century and a half, he would have his reader identify with the scene as essentially his or her own. Like Hannah Duston, we are intruders in the wilderness, and while we watch her canoe drift off to a safer haven, Thoreau camps at the river's edge and recognizes the odd juxtaposition of his cultural disposition in the wild, not so different from Duston's own existential quandary:

> On either side, the primeval forest stretches away uninterrupted to Canada or to the "South Sea;" to the white man a drear and howling

wilderness, but to the Indian a home, adapted to his nature, and cheer-ful as the smile of the Great Spirit. (Ibid., p. 323)

Duston is out of place, and, in a sense, a victim of her own intrusion. A mur-dered child was the price paid for a contested imperialism, and we all share in that heritage; as Thoreau concludes, "there have been many who in later times have lived to say that they had eaten of the fruit of that apple-tree" (ibid., p. 324). Through his shifting into the present, we become parties to Hannah's deed. And while the apples from the tree of the murdered baby link us to those times, it is the ever-present river that confronts Thoreau—and us—with the immediacy of Duston's moral challenge. Instead of laud-ing her bravery and commemorating her revenge, Thoreau poses us a deeper question: In what way is her past our own?

Appropriately, Thoreau immediately follows the Duston account with a comment on history and the faculties required of a historian. First, he observes that antiquity is only seemingly out of reach, and it is our lack of historical imagination that makes such stories as Hannah Duston's osten-sibly removed from our own experience. "The age of the world is great enough for our imaginations" (ibid.), and the apparently distant past is, in fact, quite accessible. Second, that accessibility requires a poetic artistry ("A true account of the actual is the rarest poetry, for common sense always takes a hasty and superficial view" [ibid., p. 325]; Thoreau expounds on Goethe as an exemplar), and one must tap into the deepest psychic recesses to draw out the critical and pertinent insight ("The unconsciousness of man is the consciousness of God" [ibid., p. 329]). Finally, Thoreau makes an hon-est admission about his own history-making:

> Unfortunately many things have been omitted which should have been recorded in our journal, for though we made it a rule to set down all our experiences therein, yet such a resolution is very hard to keep, for the important experience rarely allows us to remember such obliga-tions, and so indifferent things get recorded, while that is frequently neglected. It is not easy to write in a journal what interests us at any time, because to write it is not what interests us. (Ibid., p. 332)

Given the way the Journal dominated Thoreau's literary life, especially after the publication of *A Week*, this entry is ironic, if not astonishing, but it may be taken at face value in at least one respect: History-keeping, the writing even of one's own biography, is incomplete and biased. The significance of events, the meaning of experience, are only assumed upon the reconstruc-tion in the present for present purpose. History remains a creative, even poetic work for Thoreau, part of a master project that has other voices to be blended in with chronicles such as the plight of Hannah Duston.

Thoreau paid a price for this eclecticism. On the one hand, his histories are vignettes, unsustained commentary. And there is a literary penalty too. One might argue that *A Week* lacks coherence because the various elements of the narration, the different kinds of descriptions, are truncated, episodic, disjointed, and thematically diverse. This is a criticism much less applicable to the polished *Walden,* but in virtually all of Thoreau's published work we witness, to varying degrees and with varying success, a complex interplay of narrative tropes. Putting aside the literary criticism that such a strategy had afforded, I would simply observe that Thoreau persistently pursued the same attempt to achieve a particular harmony of a unified personal experience that must, by its very character, be produced through different voices. As a Romantic he understood, and celebrated, the variegated nature of experience. No single voice might abide alone, and more to the point, their integration gave each fuller expression. In this sense, Thoreau willingly forsook completeness, whether in his natural, historical, or autobiographical descriptions, to display the greater whole. Again, we might say he created in the manner of later Impressionists, the blurred details subordinated to the larger project that might clearly emerge, articulate and full, when viewed at a greater distance from the canvas. History would have to play its role in that endeavor as only one component among others.

If history then loses its narrative independence in Thoreau's oeuvre, if it is simply used for a greater enterprise and becomes molded to serve another encompassing vision, we understand that for him history cannot claim epistemological autonomy, nor, more saliently, even a worldview. History becomes just another element of consciousness, to be integrated and subsumed in a deeper metaphysics of the self. In this regard, it is interesting to note Thoreau's comments on Thomas Carlyle, friend to his own mentor, Emerson. Thoreau certainly takes a critical view of Carlyle's writing and historiography, but here I want to emphasize a Romantic characteristic that Thoreau heartily endorses, namely the narrative latitude allowed in the historian's craft. Primarily, Thoreau sees history as a historian's *creation,* not the past as some entity residing alone and independent:

> No doubt, Carlyle has a propensity to *exaggerate* the heroic in history, that is, he creates you an ideal hero rather than another thing, he has most of that material. This we allow in all its senses, and in one narrower sense it is not so convenient. Yet what were history if he did not exaggerate it? How comes it that history never has to wait for facts, but for a man to write it? The ages may go on forgetting the facts. . . . The

musty records of history, like the catacombs, contain perishable remains, but only in the breast of genius are embalmed the souls of heroes. (Thoreau 1975a, p. 264)

Indeed, exaggeration is elevated to a value *sui generis:*

Exaggeration! was ever any virtue attributed to a man without exaggeration? Do we not exaggerate ourselves to ourselves, or do we recognize ourselves for the actual men we are? Are we not all great men? Yet what are we actually to speak of? We live by exaggeration, what else is it to anticipate more than we enjoy? The lightening is an exaggeration of the light. *Exaggerated history is poetry, and truth referred to a new standard.* To a small man every greater is an exaggeration. He who cannot exaggerate is not qualified to utter truth. No truth we think was ever expressed but with this sort of emphasis, so that for the time there seemed to be no other. Moreover, you must speak loud to those who are hard of hearing, and so you acquire a habit of shouting to those who are not. (Ibid., pp. 264–65; emphasis added; proclaimed again in *Walden's* "Conclusion" [1971, p. 324])

In this short passage, Thoreau has offered keen insight into the very psychology by which one knows the world in general, not to speak of history in particular. On his view, the centrality of our individual perspective empowers the selection of what is important to us and, by such interpretation, the mundane is transformed into significance. This translation succinctly captures Thoreau's own vision of the poet as historian.[9] Indeed, he explicitly acknowledges that personalized (exaggerated, interpreted) history is poetry and that in its faithful execution a new (higher) truth is attained. History is thus constructed (with how much license he leaves unspecified) by bringing only certain elements of the past into the "future," that is, the historian's present.

THE STORY OF CLUES, THE GRAMMAR OF SEMIOTIC HISTORY

What makes us think that time has lapsed is that we have relapsed.

Thoreau, September 28, 1843,
Journal 1, 1981, p. 468

A Week is highly symbolic. Its structure in time (a week's journey), its use of a narrative vehicle (the river), its juxtaposition of present and past, its use of singular symbols, all fit together in a complex semiotic interplay of signifier and signified. The reader is constantly challenged to see through layers of meaning, finding associations that point to each of these symbolic dimensions and thereby relate the symbol to its various grammars. One of these intricate plays is built around a second apple tree, referred to as Elisha's tree. This marker, serving as both a geographical and a topological sign, also marks time in a moral universe. The past is thus telescoped into the present, so that this historical signifier condenses three-dimensional time into the single plane of the immediate.

In Thoreau's discussion of time alluded to above, an important theme pertains to the brevity of our human past. The remote in fact is near; and while "wearisome," "the age of the world" might be spanned by "the lives of sixty old women . . . strung together . . . to reach over the whole ground" (A Week, 1980a, p. 325). Thoreau here poetically refers to a Bible's chronology, which designated the age of world as approximately six thousand years. Indeed, so compressed is history that "it will not take a very great granddaughter of [Eve] to be in at the death of Time" (ibid.). This cryptic reference to "the death of Time" may be seen as redemptive (and thus foreshadowing the last historical episode of A Week, the meditation on Elisha's apple tree [Johnson 1986, p. 160]). In Christian mythology, the millennial "week" ends in the year 6000 since the foundation of the world, with Christ's Second Coming. Perhaps, too, Thoreau's allusion refers to a redemption, independent of any Christian eschatology. In his case redemption is a vision of time itself, to the degree that time can be grasped or captured. If time is characterized by passing, by leaving the past in the wake of the ever preceding present and receding future, then to bring the past into the present cuts against that flux. Thus from my reading, Elisha's apple tree not only is a prophetic testament but serves as the essential clue for us, in a particular time and place, to recover a heretofore lost history. What then are the implications of "the death of Time," and what might it signify for Thoreau's vision of temporality?

Overarching the particular veracity of the Elisha tree story is Thoreau's intent to explicitly show the power of obscurity and the use of the few crucial clues available to us to poetically reconstruct the significance of the history. The source of Thoreau's information is vague, even mysterious, as he begins this section by recalling a story told him by "an old inhabitant of Tyngsboro" (A Week, 1980a, p. 355) who is not identified; no other source is available to verify the account (Johnson 1986, p. 160). Thoreau might well have fabricated it—which would be consistent with his own view of history as "poetic." Thoreau's expanded vision of history affords the latitude by means of which he arrives at a deeper truth. We understand his motive as the history of Elisha's tree unravels.

Ceaselessly peering at the relation of nature and civilization—in this case between the river's endless flow and man's brief life on its banks—Thoreau becomes interested in recounting the height to which the river has swollen in the past. His informant claims that in October 1785 someone marked the river's crest by driving a nail into an apple tree behind his house which, Thoreau claims, was "at least seventeen or eighteen feet above the level of the river at the time" (*A Week,* 1980a, p. 356). This historical record is, of course, colloquial, and when an engineer later came to the site to survey for a railway, it was ignored:

> He was conducted to the apple-tree, and as the nail was not then visible, the lady of the house placed her hand on the trunk where she said that she remembered the nail to have been from her childhood. In the meanwhile the old man put his arm inside the tree, which was hollow, and felt the point of the nail sticking through, and it was exactly opposite to her hand. The spot is now plainly marked by a notch in the bark. But as no one else remembered the river to have risen so high as this, the engineer disregarded this statement, and I learn that there has since been a freshet which rose within nine inches of the rails at Biscuit Brook, and such a freshet as that of 1785 would have covered the railroad two feet deep. (Ibid.)

Thoreau in this short passage dramatically illustrates the validity of personal remembrance, the significance of a sign or symbol for a historical event, and the unwanted skepticism of a "scientific" historical attitude toward such "flimsy" data. A single-family account is, in this case, more accurate than the collective, albeit incomplete, record of the community. It is the significance of the personal memoir, the solitary memory that establishes the facts of the case. That the engineer chose to ignore the testimony reveals his own limited understanding of history, for as Thoreau goes on to comment, the river will indeed rise again as part of nature's inevitable cycle.[10]

We have already considered Thoreau's vision of time's cycle, so here I will direct our attention to what I have referred to as the *mode* of history Thoreau is writing in this passage, specifically the use of signs by which we might situate ourselves in time. As Thoreau goes on to discuss the river's natural history, he builds on the significance of an ancient grave site:

> This apple-tree, which stands within a few rods of the river, is called "Elisha's apple-tree," from a friendly Indian, who was anciently in the service of Jonathan Tyng, and, with one other man, was killed here by his own race in one of the Indian wars,—the particulars of which affair were told us on the spot. He was buried close by, no one knew exactly where, but in the flood of 1785, so great a weight of water standing over the grave, caused the earth to settle where it had once been disturbed, and when the flood went down, a sunken spot, exactly of the form and size of the grave, revealed its locality; but this was now lost

again, and no future flood can detect it; yet, no doubt, Nature will know
how to point it out in due time, if it be necessary, by methods yet more
searching and unexpected. (*A Week*, 1980a, pp. 356–57)

To be sure, we see themes here of resurrection (the apple tree, the site of a
baby's death in the Duston story, becomes a mark of friendly Indian-settler
relations) and of natural history (nature's cycling which the apple tree
marks). But, restricting ourselves to the question of historiography proper,
the narrative hinges upon two historical clues, whose significance and meaning must be carefully scrutinized.

The hidden nail and the elusive grave site each represent complex past
events that must be linked and interpolated to cohere and signify a complex
weave of social history pertinent to the current era, whether Thoreau's or
our own. The nail marks the witnessing of the precarious balance between
homesteader and the river's perilous waters that might yet again overflow
its banks and drown a farm. The past holds information we must decipher.
(In this case, we do well to know the limits imposed on our own expectations regarding nature's boundaries.) The apple tree is also prophetic: after
all, it is Elisha's tree. Prophets also warn: Be wary; guard against hubris;
note the lessons of the past. The grave may similarly be decoded. It is a mark
of relation (violence, fragile peace), telling a heretofore forgotten story of
lost opportunity and lingering possibility. In this sense it is redemptive and
serves as an important symbol of Thoreau's preoccupation with European-
Indian history. But it is also the mark of an individual life, whose memory
has its own virtue, but whose remembrance hangs on by the thinnest of
threads in a now all-but-forgotten story, told by serendipity and recounted
by Thoreau with the barest of narrative detail. The nail in the tree and the
vanishing grave each highlight the precariousness of historical record and
its necessary dependence on happenstantial human memory. By enlisting
them into his history, Thoreau captures the merest glimmer of a vanishing
past whose irredeemable effervescence may only be glanced at by reading
clues encoded by such obscure records. This is recounting through signs, or
more formally, in a semiotic mode.

Another example, perhaps better known, and certainly more transparent in design, is the "Former Inhabitants" chapter of *Walden*. Clues of former dwellings in the Walden woods are there for those with eyes to see. Old
cellar holes fringed by new-grown pines and covered with sumac and golden-
rod testify to the homes of freed negroes—Cato Ingraham, Zilpha, Brister
Freeman and his wife Fenda—and other modest white homesteads—the
Strattons, Nutting, LeGrosse, Wyman, Quoil, and the Breeds. "These cellar

dents, like deserted fox burrows, old holes, are all that is left where once the stir and bustle of human life, and 'fate, free-will, and foreknowledge absolute' . . . were discussed" (*Walden*, 1971, p. 263). Thoreau reports on his joining a member of the Breed family who was revisiting the latter's destroyed homestead:

> He gazed into the cellar from all sides and points of view by turns . . . as if there was some treasure, which he remembered, concealed between the stones, where there was absolutely nothing but a heap of bricks and ashes. The house being gone, he looked at what there was left. He was soothed by the sympathy which my mere presence implied, and showed me, as well as the darkness permitted, where the well was covered up; which, thank Heaven, could never be burned; and he groped long about the wall to find the well-sweep which his father had cut and mounted, feeling for the iron hook or staple . . . ,–all that he could now cling to,–to convince me that it was no common "rider" [top rail of a fence]. I felt it, and still remark it almost daily in my walks, for by it hangs the history of a family. (Ibid., pp. 260–61)

There is a profound poignancy in these short lines. The entire history of a family hangs from a single hook, and as Thoreau comments shortly after this passage, "What a sorrowful act that must be,–the covering up of wells! coincident with the opening of wells of tears" (ibid., p. 263). Not only are the wellsprings of life covered, their very memory is almost lost. Who, if not Thoreau, would write a census of the former inhabitants of his neighborhood? Who would care? Even he must admit that his own knowledge of their lives and thoughts is trivial (ibid.). Nevertheless, their memory must be preserved, even if it is only in his own narrative. Why? To answer that question requires an examination of Thoreau's moral philosophy as it informs his philosophy of history, a topic I will reserve for the last section of this chapter. But suffice it to note here that in the active pursuit of memory, time does come to an end, for if memory is preserved, the past is present in the present and the march of temporality is arrested.

Thoreau brought history into the ever-present present by the same stratagem by which he searched for evidence to unlock the integration of nature in all her details. Thoreau honed his naturalist and historical skills on the whetstone of patient attention to detail and the free use of an extraordinary imagination. Much as a hunter might follow an obscure track, or a fisherman survey the surface of pond for hatching insects, or a farmer peer at the leaves of a sapling for signs of disease, Thoreau studied his surroundings looking for clues that beckoned to insight—sometimes relevant to his naturalist project, sometimes to the historical. The intellectual and poetic process was the same in either case, and in some sense we might acknowledge that the vector of his interest, seemingly for a separate purpose, in fact was part and parcel of the same overall concern: natural history and man's history, intimately tied together in one great enterprise. To regard history and nature as separate categories was to commit the same error that assigned man in "civilization" to face an alienated "nature." For Thoreau, to see history in the natural context was simply to reintegrate what indeed was always one. His reconstruction of a vivid history, immediately present to him, emerged from contemplating the same riverbank Hannah Duston saw, touching the Elisha tree, and beholding an old iron hook. In each case an emblem of an apparently irretrievable past emerged, allowing Thoreau to bring it into his own intimate experience.

Thoreau's semiotic practice, what Carlo Ginzburg has called "an evidential paradigm," became widely accepted by the late nineteenth century. "Though reality may seem to be opaque, there are privileged zones—signs, clues—which allow us to penetrate it" (Ginzburg 1989, p. 123). Searching for faint and obscure clues to detect hidden meanings and verify truth was variously applied by such diverse figures as Freud in searching the unconscious, Sherlock Holmes in apprehending criminals, and Giovanni Morelli in detecting art forgeries. Each was able to detect infinitesimally small or inconspicuous keys in order to decode a deeper, otherwise unattainable reality. This historical art of reading discreet signs Ginzburg has characterized as "semiotic." Semiotics certainly has a more venerable history than its formalization in the nineteenth century, and can be traced back through Augustine and the Greco-Roman grammarians through Mesopotamian divination to the primordial practice of hunters following their prey. What characterizes "semiotics" in this context, and gives it its definitional power for history, is not its scientific character but rather the qualitative nature of the interpretative inquiry: "the historian is like the physician who uses nosological tables to analyze the specific sickness in a patient. As with the physician's, historical knowledge is indirect, presumptive, conjectural" (ibid., p. 106).[11]

Thoreau practiced a cognitive exercise that was fundamentally interpretative and thus "personal." His unique individuality and confidence in his ability to decipher those marks characterize his methodology. But he must have proceeded being aware that his approach was suspect, which explains many of his defensive, if not polemical, justifications. Thoreau had, at best, an ambivalent attitude toward history, deeply distrusting the historian removed from an immediate and original relationship to experience: "There are secret articles in our treaties with the gods of more importance than all the rest, which the historian can never know" (*A Week*, 1980a, p. 125).

Given the growing positivism of nineteenth-century natural sciences, the specific designation of "scientist" for practitioners of what was previously called natural philosophy in the 1840s,[12] and the application of this appellation to the social sciences at about the same time, Thoreau was well aware that he was sailing against a prescriptive tide of scientism. New standards called for "objective" evidence for the natural philosophy of living forms—now called biology[13]—and for the record of human history as well. Thoreau attempted to meet such standards, but he was loath to leave the facts in abeyance without an interpretation whereby their significance and meaning would emerge within his personal context. Indeed, Thoreau approaches history as would an artist, whose creative reconstruction of the past must synthesize elements of memory, artifact, historical record, oral tradition, and moral purpose. In this last respect, Thoreau recognized history written in the "objective" mode as a conceit: history was hardly unbiased, impartial, or aperspectival.[14] His efforts may be seen as part of a Romantic reaction against the positivist attitude, which he justifiedly regarded with suspicion. He was not alone. At the same time that this positivist fervor was emerging in mid-nineteenth-century sciences and social sciences, a growing sensitivity to the interpretative character of the human sciences was also appreciated. This battle, whose lines were already clearly drawn by mid-century, framed the evolution of these disciplines into our own time and will serve as a central theme of chapter 4.

THE ART OF MEMORY

In Memory is the more reality.

Thoreau, December 30, 1841,
Journal 1, 1981, p. 352

Memory is a prelude to history, and Thoreau exercised his memory both to write his autobiography and to stimulate and orient his communal history. Narrative thus becomes a vehicle of personal exposition; biography becomes autobiography (*A Week*, 1980a, p. 156). This personalized view was perhaps appropriated from Emerson's more general adage: "There is no history; only biography" (Emerson, Journal entry, May 28, 1839 [Emerson 1969, p. 202]).[15] A particularly interesting example of this exercise of memory occurs in Thoreau's recollection of his first visit to Walden Pond, a memory that must have carried potent connotations and which undoubtedly exerted a profound influence on his choice to live there. As Thoreau attests, Walden offered him a "proper nursery," a vision he first perceived as an impressionable young boy and which served to guide him as he sat as an adult at Walden's shore. He alludes to a reverie, where the music of the flute "awakes" what he calls "echoes" (by which he must mean the echoes of memory) of that childhood revelation.

We have two records to consider. The first is from his Journal entry written at Walden Pond shortly after he established his homestead; the second from the published version that appeared in *Walden* nine years later. There are both important differences and important correspondences between the two narratives, so each will be quoted in full:

> Twenty three years since when I was 5 years old, I was brought from Boston to this pond, away in the country which was then but another name for the extended world for me—one of the most ancient scenes stamped on the tablets of my memory—the oriental asiatic valley of my world—whence so many races and inventions have gone forth in recent times. That woodland vision for a long time made the drapery of my dreams. That sweet solitude my spirit seemed so early to require that I might have room to entertain my thronging guests, and that speaking silence that my ears might distinguish the significant sounds. Some how or other it at once gave the preference to this recess among the pines where almost sunshine & shadow were the only inhabitants that varied the scene, over that tumultuous and varied city—as if it had found its proper nursery.
>
> Well now to-night my flute awakes the echoes over this very water, but one generation of pines has fallen and with their stumps I have cooked my supper, And a lusty growth of oaks and pines is rising all around its brim and preparing its wilder aspect for new infant eyes.
>
> Almost the same johnswort springs from the same perennial root in this pasture.—
>
> Even I have at length helped to clothe that fabulous landscape of my imagination— —and one result of my presence and influence is seen in the bean leaves and corn blades and potato vines.
>
> Seek to preserve the tenderness of your nature as you would the bloom upon a peach. (*Journal 2*, 1984, pp. 173–74; after August 6, 1845)

> When I was four years old, as I well remember, I was brought from Boston to this my native town, through these very woods and this field, to the pond. It is one of the oldest scenes stamped on my memory. And now to-night my flute has waked the echoes over that very water. The pines still stand here older than I; or, if some have fallen, I have cooked my supper with their stumps, and a new growth is rising all around, preparing another aspect for new infant eyes. Almost the same

johnswort springs from the same perennial root in this pasture, and even I have at length helped to clothe that fabulous landscape of my infant dreams, and one of the results of my presence and influence is seen in these bean leaves, corn blades, and potato vines.

I planted about two acres and a half of upland . . . (*Walden*, 1971, pp. 155–56)[16]

Thoreau was born in Concord in 1817. The next year the family moved to Chelmsford, and then in 1821 to Boston, returning to Concord permanently in 1823. Is Thoreau recalling that final return or an earlier visit to Walden? There is a minor but obvious discrepancy in the child's age between the Journal and *Walden*, but that is not of critical importance for our purposes, or his. Paramount is how the visit was "stamped" on Thoreau's earliest memory, and it remained highly evocative. The explicit vision of the wilderness for which the city was but a gate remained an orienting experience, and Thoreau was to meditate upon that pastoral world as the focus of his mature enterprise. So when he writes in the Journal that "that woodland vision for a long time made the drapery of my dreams," we might well take heed of the importance of this memory, for it no less served as the backdrop for his later maturity.

The passage is structured on two critical phrases found in both versions: 1) "scenes stamped on my memory" and 2) "my flute has waked the echoes over that very water," and another constant element: time has elapsed as evidenced by the new growth of trees and the John's-wort, prepared to engage another infant. Thus we move with Thoreau through his own memory to its passage in time to the next generation. Thoreau evinces his own participation in that turn of time's cycle (now measured by the eyes of another as yet unidentified child—perhaps the reader of *Walden*), through clothing "that fabulous landscape of my imagination" (namely, the planting of crops). Is that all? Hardly. The basic theme of the passage is that this early memory has informed and directed Thoreau's life, and while we might read the planting of crops as emblematic of Thoreau's project, the image is understated.

Thoreau is engaged here in an interesting subterfuge, subtle yet telling. The Journal is more revealing in several respects, and by reading it carefully, we glean important clues about the way that Thoreau himself regarded this formative memory. Each version contains this critical passage: "I have at length helped to clothe that fabulous landscape of my [infant dreams {*Walden*}] [imagination {Journal}]." Note that the earlier "imagination" has been changed to "dreams" in the final published version. We are not accountable for our dreams: they appear and we may interpret them, but they appear in the night, disappear upon awakening, and correspond only loosely to our conscious life. *Imagination* is the Romantic faculty par excellence. It is to imagination that Thoreau turns again and again as the cognitive apparatus upon which he builds his history, his science, his poetry. In the Journal, the vision of Walden Pond, first appearing to him as a child, remains scored in Thoreau's *imagination*, actively working and directing him. The memory is no longer *of* the past, but resides firmly *in* his active present. His entire life is devoted to the emancipation of that imagination, the free expression of all that this muse might hold for him, whether expressed by him as a naturalist, a historian, a philosopher, or a poet. To emphasize this point, note how Thoreau ends the memory: "Seek to preserve the tenderness of your nature as you would the bloom upon a peach." Interestingly omitted in *Walden*, this sentence not only implicitly reaffirms Wordsworth's insight that the child is father to the man, but perhaps more saliently that the purity and creative power of childhood experience and imagination must be preserved to guide and inspire the adult. Thoreau explicitly pronounced the validity of infant experience in what can only be read as a rapturous passage from the Journal:

> Heaven lies about us as in our infancy [Wordsworth, "Ode: Intimations of Immortality," line 66]. There is nothing so wild and extravagant that it does not make true. It makes a dream my only real experience, and prompts faith to such elasticity, that only the incredible can satisfy it. It tells me again to trust the remotest, and finest, as the divinest instinct. All that I have imagined of heroism, it reminds and reassures me of. It is a life unlived, a life beyond life, where at length my years will pass. *I look under the lids of Time*[.] (January 30, 1841, *Journal* 1, 1981, p. 242; emphasis added)

The "lids of time" (becoming the "eyelids of time" in October 23, 1843, ibid., p. 480) poetically pronounce Thoreau's stratagem, for as he would lift the cover from his eyes, Thoreau would "see"—understand—the deeper metaphysics of time as the ever-present present. Just as the period of infancy is brought into the presence of adulthood, so would the historical past be appropriated to the current era.

We must look for clues to further decode Thoreau's memory, just as one might explicate a dream. Note the paucity of insight Thoreau offers as to *how* the childhood memory directed him. The published memory is simply a scene, and thus the reader is left with no idea what gave this memory its potency. Again, the Journal entry helps decipher its power for Thoreau by testifying that the pond represented a gate to an exotic world. The first association is with the Orient, whose worldview would be so influential in mold-ing his mature attitudes and offering a counterpoint to the mid-nineteenth-century America he so actively criticized. This oriental allusion is a rather free association, but taking it at face value it is intriguing to observe that Thoreau linked the New England woods in some fashion with an exotic world markedly removed from any prior experience. Of course, Thoreau had no knowledge of the Orient as a child, but the point is not whether there was a linkage then but rather how the memory is being *constructed* in 1845. The connection is blatantly subjective, drawing together some emotional resonance between Asian images and the American wilderness. In this sense we might consider how perhaps the woods were to a certain degree *always* foreign, an abode that one might enter but that, despite protestations, remained alien in a deep and mysterious way, as Thoreau testified about his climb to the top of Mount Ktaadn later that fall:

> It was vast titanic & such as man never inhabits. Some part of the beholder, even some vital part seems to escape through the loose grating of his ribs as he ascends– He is more lone than one–there is less of substance less of fair calculation & intellectual fullness than in the plains where men inhabit[.] Vast Titanic inhuman nature has got him at disadvantage caught him alone–& pilfers him[.] She does not smile on him as in the plains– She seems to say sternly why come Ye here before your time– This ground is not prepared for. Is it not enough that I smile in the vallies . . . Why seek me where I have not called you and then complain that I am not your genial mother. . . .
>
> For what canst thou pray here–but to be delivered from here.– And shouldst thou freeze or starve–or shudder thy life away–here is no shrine nor altar–nor access to my ear. (Fall 1846, *Journal 2*, 1984, pp. 339–40)

This episode, so unusual among Thoreau's earlier celebrations of nature, testifies to a sense that beneath the quiet pastoral of rural Concord, Thoreau recognized at that moment a fundamental chasm between the tranquillity of Walden Pond, wild in a tamed fashion, and nature untrimmed. Here, and more extensively in his later writings, Thoreau appreciates the terrifying otherness of nature, an insight that McGregor (1997) has argued was pivotal to Thoreau's existential and literary development.[17] An anxiety, sometimes surfacing only briefly (e.g., admitting his own bestiality [*Walden*, 1971, p. 210]) and sometimes dominating an essay on nature as hostile and indifferent to human life (e.g., *Cape Cod* [1988] thematically continues Ktaadn), seems to have accompanied Thoreau throughout his life. And I believe we detect the faint pull of that undercurrent even in his fond recollection. The earliest memory of Walden Pond portrays Thoreau's mixed feelings, where the mystic experience of Walden, the allure of nature, the mystery of the Asiatic, are all fused into an associated image where myriad passions, both affirmative and negative, are given free rein. So in our reading of his childhood impressions, we should attend to the complex image of the wondrous and the strange, and even the frightening, aspects of a new world.

In *A Week*, we see memory assuming its psychic function, falling between the wild associations of dreams and the finished product of history, a distilled and so less authentic rendition of free imagination. The narrative itself swings periodically between these poles of consciousness: As a naturalist Thoreau is keenly aware of his surroundings, and the text is replete with critical commentary about the scenery, the natural history, the social history of the river's banks. This critique is contrasted with a dreamlike state, which Thoreau refers to only in a poetic guise. Indistinct as an entity, possessing no character of an object of thought that might be grasped and concretized in description, the Concord River presents him the opportunity of being "embarked on the placid current of our dreams, floating from past to future as silently as one awakes to fresh morning or evening thoughts" (*A Week*, 1980a, pp. 19–20). The river itself affords Thoreau a unique perspective, one quite different in character from his normal life on land,[18] but there is more: In a sense, the river *is* dream, perceived as a mystical entity. In an unpublished poem in the Berg manuscript of *A Week*, Thoreau declares,

> I was born upon thy banks, River,
> My blood flows in thy stream,
> And thou meanderest forever
> As the bottom of my dream.[19]

For him the river was his poetic, if not existential, source of being. No wonder it sustained his imagination so effectively.

A Week would become a poetic work, a Thoreauvian mythology, carried to future readers, just as he was carried "on its bosom and float whither it would bear me" (1980a, p. 13).[20] Floating in a dory, Thoreau also beckoned to other means of travel, a history carried by memory, poetry, myth, and dream. These so-called "flitting perspectives and demi-experiences" are faculties outside time. Thoreau can only allude to the importance of this dimension attended to by a suspended intelligence, of which dreams are in most accounts the most ephemeral. When he describes dreams (waking or sleeping) as both integral to his experience and a foundation for the reality he so earnestly attempts to capture as a naturalist and historian, he does so with a firm assertion of their *authenticity*: "In dreams we never deceive

ourselves, nor are deceived. . . . Dreams are the touchstones of our characters. . . . In dreams we see ourselves naked and acting out our real characters, even more clearly than we see others awake" (ibid., pp. 296–97). Indeed,
"our truest life is when we are in dreams awake" (ibid., p. 297), a position
he was to hold unwaveringly into his full maturity (e.g., October 29, 1857,
Journal, [1906] 1962, 10:141). Thus dreams, encoding echoes of ancient
myth and personal experience lost to consciousness, possess a truth function that Thoreau acknowledges as a wellspring for his literary efforts.

Myth also served Thoreau's personalized vision of history. In a sustained
discussion of fable and myth in the "Sunday" chapter of *A Week*, Thoreau
makes three points relevant to this discussion. First, myth is "naturally and
truly composed" (1980a, p. 58) and either transmitted to us as "music of a
thought"—that is, unintelligible to scientific or historical analysis—or as
the work of a current poet who might write "without the aid of posterity"
(ibid., p. 60). In either case, myths have their own aesthetic and cognitive
functions, which—and this is the second point—express a variety of truths
more significant than our current understanding of history. The materials
of biography and history, the more mundane labors that pass as efforts of
history writing, are but materials to serve mythology, the higher function
distilling the truth content of these lesser enterprises (ibid.). Finally, myth
transmits a divine message, which the poet perceives and serves:

> In the mythus a superhuman intelligence uses the unconscious
> thoughts and dreams of men as its hieroglyphics to address men
> unborn. In the history of the human mind, these glowing and ruddy
> fables precede the noon-day thoughts of men, as Aurora the sun's rays.
> The matutine intellect of the poet, keeping in advance of the glare of
> philosophy, always dwells in this auroral atmosphere. (Ibid., p. 61)

Again, the past is brought to the immediacy of the now, available for each
of us to partake in its light.

This idea of myth, the intermediary between conventional history and
imagination, resonates deeply throughout Thoreau's writings—perhaps most
vividly in *Walden*. The ethical imperative suggested by this passage from *A
Week*, namely those efforts evoked by the sun's (Apollo's) appearance in the
morning, is built from two temporal elements better developed in *Walden*.
The first is the morning of our respective days. As Peck (1990) has so carefully shown, the morning is the cardinal image of Thoreau's endeavor, where
he would attempt to live life "deliberately" by calling for self-conscious
wakefulness. "To be awake is to be alive" (*Walden*, 1971, p. 90), and to achieve
a meaningful life Thoreau saw the morning as the crucible of his labor, where,

indeed, "moral reform is the effort to throw off sleep" (ibid.). In a Nietz-schean mode, Thoreau knew "of no more encouraging fact than the unques-tionable ability of man to elevate his life by a conscious endeavor. . . . Every man is tasked to make his life, even in its details, worthy of contemplation of his most elevated and critical hour" (ibid.). *Walden* is a treatise on how Thoreau suggests we might respond to this challenge, and he draws a corre-lation between the morning and myth, a crucial guiding source for Thoreau's own heroic quest for a meaningful existence. Thus Thoreau introduces the second temporal element, the past as present. He baldly asserts, "Morning brings back the heroic ages" (ibid., p. 88) that inspire him. For in the heroic past described by myth are to be found eternal truths that can only be learned by acknowledging the presence of those fables.[21] Thoreau is a poet, but he is in the good company of heroes. Poets and heroes are workers of the morn-ing; each is roused and vitalized by Aurora. Here we see myth operating in the now, as the poet dredges the depths of time and the unconscious which leads him to the past.

Thus this poetic venture requires conscious effort balanced by an open-ness to "dream"—to access the unconscious. "Morning" is consciousness, and it is counterpoised to dream, to the night, which holds its own impor-tance for this poetic faculty. "Not till we are lost, in other words, not till we have lost the world, do we begin to find ourselves, and realize where we are and the infinite extent of our relations" (*Walden*, 1971, p. 171). The inter-pretative character of Thoreau's journey in time—night and day; past and present—demands access to qualitative experience. Thoreau in fact built upon these impressions. For instance, from *Walden*, he relates how his dreams oriented his "morning work":

> After a still winter night I awoke with the impression that some ques-tion had been put to me, which I had been endeavoring in vain to answer in my sleep, as what–how–when–where? But there was dawn-ing Nature, in whom all creatures live, looking in at my broad windows with serene and satisfied face, and no question on *her* lips. I awoke to an answered question, to Nature and daylight. (Ibid., p. 282)

Inspired by his nocturnal questions, the morning provides him a response, and he situates himself in a confounding cosmos by performing worldly chores: carrying water, fishing, making his fire, observing the surroundings, and so on. And again, in the evening, he is left to other devices, visiting with a divine chronicler who in turn feeds his imagination:

> I have occasional visits in the long winter evenings, when the snow falls fast and the wind howls in the wood, from an old settler and original

proprietor, who is reported to have dug Walden Pond, and stoned it, and fringed it with pine woods; who tells me stories of old time and of new eternity[.] (Ibid., p. 137)

Thoreau thus swung between night dreams and day work, each fulfilling their respective functions. Note that Thoreau also dreamt while awake, and not thus necessarily at night. He also translated immediate perceptions into the domain of dream, whereby such experience might achieve its full significance. In other words, the immediacy of experience is sometimes transformed by a poetic transposition from consciousness to a dreamlike state, so that, for instance, a landscape might be experienced as dream. For example, at the top of Saddleback Mountain, remembered as an earlier excursion narrated in the "Tuesday" chapter of *A Week*, Thoreau recounts the climb through an "ocean of mist" after which he arrives in "cloudland," a dream world:

> As the light in the east steadily increased, it revealed to me more clearly the new world into which I had risen in the night, the new terra-firma perchance of my future life. . . . All around beneath me was spread for a hundred miles on every side, as far as the eye could reach, an undulating country of clouds, answering in the varied swell of its surface the terrestrial world it veiled. *It was such a country as we might see in dreams,* with all the delights of paradise. . . . It was a favor for which to be forever silent to be shown this vision. The earth beneath had become such a flitting thing of lights and shadows as the clouds had been before. *It was not merely veiled to me, but it had passed away like the phantom of a shadow* . . . and this new platform was gained. As I had climbed above storm and cloud, so by successive days' journey I might reach the region of eternal day beyond the tapering shadow of earth[.] (*A Week*, 1980a, pp. 188–89; emphasis added)

Thoreau has gone to the mountain and had a dreamlike vision—a view of eternity that he would hold firmly in his memory, informing and inspiring his spirituality.

Of course, Thoreau did not need to climb mountains to find a catalyst by which he might peer at eternity (e.g., *Walden*, 1971, p. 98) or recover time (e.g., *A Week*, 1980a, p. 351). In whatever context contemplation was exercised, he dipped into that experience through the faculty of memory. After all, dreams are only accessible through recall, through construction by memory. Their very disorder and illogic bespeak another cognitive grammar, and memory provides the bridge between that unconscious encounter and the strictures of conscious thought. So not only does memory of the mountaintop—within the memory of the river trip—make "journeying itself archetypal and therefore the property of inward life" (Peck 1990, p. 29), but memory itself becomes the fundamental faculty of consciousness of that inner life serving to conjure the past and create a more complete present. We have adequate testimony to the veracity of such experience for Thoreau.

A final comment regarding the relation of dreams, memory, and history: In *A Week*, Thoreau observes, dreams possess "a more liberal and juster apprehension of things, unconstrained by habit, which is then in some measure put off, and divested of memory, which we call history" (1980a, p. 58). History's cognitive standing is different from that of dreams or memory. Perhaps inspired by a primordial consciousness, history remains an objective and thus depersonalized account, or at least so it claims. Memory is the province of ancient fables and personal history that hover in the indistinct past and that can be recovered only in our dreams and in the faint outline of our own recall, to be reconstructed in the full light of consciousness, as history. There is, to be sure, a continuum of dream, memory, and history; for Thoreau—as a Romantic—must believe in unmediated apprehension whereby even history might be directly experienced. But the continuum itself attests to the different forms of experience that must be integrated to produce this final public, shared experience, and it is this effort that requires a synthesis of these three forms of imagination. Memory, as meditation, is situated between dream and history, partaking of the former to inform the latter. Thus for Thoreau, memory serves as the bridge which links some inarticulate infancy of experience into mature articulation.

THE ANVIL OF MEMORY

[T]he past is not . . . preserved so much as remade in the image of the present: The past is too important to be allowed to exist. . . .
[The] narrative can reveal . . . only the retrospective moment, and the retrospective self.

Fredriksen 1986

A Week ends with a third apple tree. Rushing back to Concord under sail and oar, the brothers have made full cycle: "[W]e leaped gladly on shore, drawing it [the boat] up, and fastening it to the wild apple-tree whose stem still bore the mark which its chain had worn in the chafing of the spring freshets" (1980a, p. 393). There is, to be sure, a linear beginning and ending to the voyage, but in both spatial and spiritual senses, *A Week* follows a cycle—the cycle of the week, the cycle of the brothers' return. This cycle nevertheless inscribes a unique passing, of which the tree again serves as a mark, or even a repository of history, now of Thoreau's own making. Whereas Walden Pond might stand for permanency, the river by its very nature is ever-changing. Thoreau might only obtain closure of time in the cyclic mode of return and its encapsulation within his own memory and its concretization in the memoir he had penned. The tree serves to tether that memory.

In some sense we might regard much of Thoreau's literary corpus as a project in memory. His writings, published and unpublished, serve two functions: on the one hand, they were a repository for reflections on almost every aspect of his life—observations on nature, society, reading, and so on—and on the other hand, they were an act of capturing experience already experienced. As we will explore in the next chapter, the epistemological effort of "writing nature" was constrained by reconstruction—by recapitulating sensations, impressions, observations—limited by the inadequacy both of language itself and of recall. Thoreau's writing was very much captive to what must be only a partial rendition of experience, and in this regard, the earlier comment already quoted (p. 51 above) concerning the limit of his Journal writing (*A Week*, 1980a, p. 332) refers to this incomplete record, the never completed autobiography (in this case his trip on the Concord and Merrimack Rivers). Thoreau was well aware of these restrictions, but the limitations of history as usually conceived were not of his concern. The point of history for him was to establish moral, not epistemological, accuracy. Thus two of Thoreau's key meta-themes concern how memory might be deployed in constructing the self to fulfill a moral agenda, the pursuit of a life of virtue; and, closely connected, how memory, built from imagination, was to be fashioned into works of public art.

Pursuing his own memory, as well as the collective past, was integral to Thoreau's own view of individual and communal identity. From this perspective, virtue, at least in part, hangs on the ability to readmit experience for scrutiny in order to ascertain meaning. The past follows us, there is no escape; and just as the individual lives his life cumulatively, so does the community. Each must then examine history as it reflects on our present condition. Memory is crucial in appreciating our full selves. We retain what we value, and we know what we want to know or need to know. We forget what we do not use or somehow cannot make part of ourselves. As Emerson wrote, "memory has a fine art of sifting out the pain and keeping all the joy" (1904, p. 104). And yet some memories we want to lose remain to haunt us. Those are parts of our psyche that live in a separate locale—part of us, yet somehow different. One of the gulfs separating us from Thoreau is the obscurity of such despondent memories. His celebrated solitude was more than socially contrived, for even in his intimate Journal there is little that reveals insight as to the causes of his sadnesses and disappointments, despite his biographers' best efforts to uncover them (e.g., Krutch 1948; Harding 1965; Lebeaux 1984; Bridgman 1982; Richardson 1986; Peck 1990). Thus when we seek to understand Thoreau and search his testament of memory, we must be struck by the selective nature of his narratives, the facile character of his art of memory, perhaps hammered on the anvil of experience but appearing to us as finished products of careful craftsmanship, as works of art. Rather than as a lingering quandary, I regard such opacity as an important clue to how Thoreau himself would have us understand his memory.

We might more profitably approach Thoreau's use of memory through another portal. I have maintained that for Thoreau, memory became part of the apparatus by which he constructs his moral identity. Memory was an active process directed by a particular telos. Memory is selective and intimate, to be employed for present purpose. Recollections do not remain locked in a closet called the Past. As we act in the world, we are aware of ourselves as integrated identities by linking that past with our present. So in ways deeply personal to our innermost being, we recall our own personae formed in different contexts of time and place; and in our attempts to situate ourselves in those past worlds of childhood, adolescence, young adulthood, middle age, and on, we bring the past with us. We require a construction to enable us to establish a continuous flow of identity between the present and our ever-receding past selves. Memory is thus crafted. There is no recall that is not filtered by intervening experience, and that experience interprets and reshapes the original experience. While memory helps to maintain continuity with the past, it too is reshaped to accommodate our present persona. We know, albeit implicitly, that our memory is a faculty critical in forming our very identities. We constantly refashion ourselves to adjust to new demands, goals, ideas, relationships. Memories are modulated as we redesign our views of ourselves and our world, because memory is so intimate to our very selves. Here we see the intersection of Thoreau as historian and Thoreau as poet. If indeed history and memory are constructed to address the moral expression of the self, this must be accomplished through imagination, or the poetic faculty. But to make a memory valid in a public way, to test its authenticity in the domain of "knowledge," it must be subjected to historical analysis.

Thoreau was fundamentally a poet, not a historian. Again and again, he would choose the testimony of an informant's memory and imagination as more important, if not even more valid, than conventional historical narratives. Why? Is not history, in fact, publicly verifiable and therefore more reliable? After all, the difference between memory and history, at least most obviously, is the degree of verisimilitude. History and memory each attempt to capture the past and bring it into the present in order that we may better understand ourselves now. Each is used to interpret the past, to interpret the present and, perhaps, to better predict the future. We rely on each to situate ourselves in the confusion of our own time, and to seek the antecedents of our present predicaments and knowledge. These are critical functions, to be sure, and history in its formal abilities is more "valid" in these respects, because its knowledge is generally accessible and to a certain degree agreed upon. But memory has another function altogether, also shared by history (but less self-consciously), that is, memory's essentially moral character. Memory is moral when it is radically self-referential and self-definitional and thereby value-laden. From that understanding we employ memory in order to situate ourselves in the world and thus guide our actions.

Thoreau's use of memory is so striking precisely because he uses it to convert a personalized past into history, a subjectivized public knowledge. He thus follows a contemporary view of history, and of ourselves: "Memory is the ground of history. It is the interior state of mind from which the exterior framework of history is drawn" (Hutton 1993, p. 96). Thus history is admittedly subjectivized, and in that insight we have a picture of the psyche, which

> is not an archive but a mirror. To search the psyche for the truth about ourselves is a futile task because the psyche can only reflect the images that we have conjured up to describe ourselves. Looking into the psyche, therefore, is like looking into the mirror image of a mirror. One sees oneself in an image of infinite regress. (Ibid., p. 115)

Thoreau modulates history into a species different from a scientific practice by explicitly turning objectified history into a personalized image of himself. In the process the implicit moral standing of history becomes explicitly moral. There is no confusion as to the subjective nature of Thoreau's memory, because memory, which is clearly about *his* past, exclusively reflects his subjectivity and serves to identify himself. When he makes memory integral to history—and this is the critical turn—he forthrightly assumes a particular personal orientation which, in the sense described above, is moral. Thus historical character would assume in his practice a self-portrayal—who we are, or perhaps, who we might wish to be.

Thus Thoreau's memory is a lens less to examine his "psychology" than to decipher his, and our own, moral life. In his inquiry into the American past, he asks, Who are we? What were we? What do we hope to be? Each question falls squarely in the moral domain. These are evaluative judgments, interpretations of our national persona. From this perspective the self, individual and collective, becomes fundamentally a moral category. So memory in Thoreau's imaginative cosmos is both a faculty by which to comprehend and order the world (a part of the mental agency we refer to as "knowing") and also a moral faculty. The "isness" of history thus falls into two domains: the epistemological "isness" of facts and various kinds of social relations, and the moral "isness" of rectitude and maleficence. In general, for Thoreau, the former is in league with the latter, and usually in its service.

In the main, Thoreau used history to fulfill a moral agenda—the moral actuality as revealed by historical presentation, that is, the past's bestowal. To glean the past was to create a moral universe. What makes memory moral is that we *choose* our recollections, constructing them within a particular framework that has value to us. It is the overriding value-ladenness of memory that modulates its epistemological status, radically. Because memory need not be anything but private, it may safely reflect our most intimate personal values and serve us in living them. At least part of Thoreau's importance resides in his sharing his intimate memory for public purpose.

So Thoreauvian memory has become public. It is now history, and Thoreau might be appropriately judged by the historiographical standards of his era; in that light, he stands apart. His work is distinctive, eschewing the new positivism infecting all of the human sciences. As in his nature studies, Thoreau adopted a position in opposition to the stringent objectivity of his period, and in so doing, he attacked the hegemony of the scientific ethos. To be sure, history shares many of the same epistemological values and constraints as science, and historians, as public agents of our collective past, are committed to proceeding by objective means to recover our antecedents. But Thoreau sought a more personalized vision of the past, and while he would acknowledge that science offered a highly effective means for obtaining certain kinds of knowledge about the world, he rejected its universal application: in his own writings he presented a prescient criticism of the very pillars of positivist historical analysis.[22]

However, rather than dwell on the question of scientific objectivity here, a theme developed extensively in later chapters, we remain closer to our central concern if we explore how Thoreau emphasized history's close affinity with memory: history goes beyond its epistemological project and becomes moral just as memory is a moral activity for the individual. Again, Thoreau wrote history self-consciously recognizing this dimension of history's import. His relevance today in no small measure resides in our own ability to scrutinize his experimental approach toward establishing the moral standing of history. We regard the past through the prism of our current values, and we bring the past into the present, even projecting it into the future—for example, as our "manifest destiny" or our "burden of history." We reinterpret our social evolution from the vantage of our current understanding, and although historians deplore presentism—the prejudice of interpreting the past in terms of our own cultural moment—we nevertheless cannot totally escape the strictures of our imbibed culture with all the attendant orientation it bestows. In the acts of shared memory (and forgetting), a historical character emerges, and thus history, when viewed as a social activity, becomes a critical means by which we define ourselves as a group, analogous to how memory helps define the individual. Memory is constitutive of our personal identities; history, firmly situated in the civic domain, becomes constituent of social identity.

For Thoreau, the play between memory and history reflects the duality of the past he sought to capture—a communal history entrusted to the individual interpreter. Part poet, part explorer, part philosopher, Thoreau wrote history with multiple faculties and varied agendas. Although we currently lack the moral self-consciousness exhibited by Thoreau, historians of our era might look at him as a member of their own guild, practicing a variant of their own style. We are now critical of nineteenth-century historicism, "based upon the proposition that humankind, having created its own experience, can re-create it" (Hutton 1993, p. xxiii). We are no longer sanguine that historians are so capable of reentering the mindset of the historical actors they would examine in the hopes of understanding or even reenacting their problems. "What is remembered about the past depends on the way it is represented" (ibid., p. 6), so on this view, minimally, the historians' own tradition, but more pervasively and implicitly, culture at large, provides the very framework for inquiry. Linking the past to the present, this larger Weltanschauung, with all its attendant values and posthistorical knowledge, directs the very historical enterprise that seeks "objectivity." Thus the retrospective perspective, in some sense, confines that venture.

To acknowledge the limits of our own view is to accept a deeper comprehension of the nature of history and memory. Thoreau certainly appreciated the daunting task of the historian:

> When I remember the treachery of memory, and the manifold accidents to which tradition is liable–how soon the vista of the past closes behind–as near as night's crescent to the setting day–and the dazzling brightness of noon is reduced to the faint glimmer of the evening star, I feel as if it were by rare indulgence of the fates–that any traces of the past are left us. (June 7, 1841, *Journal 1*, 1981, p. 314)

Our image of the past then is radically fragmentary and provisional, for the past is remembered only within a given social or conceptual construction which is defined by the historian's community at large. There is no preserved "whole" of time, only that which we choose to recall and reconstruct. The past then is constantly being revised in living memory, and we draw whatever inferences and conclusions seem warranted with a wary eye— self-conscious and circumspect about the limits of our own time and place. History thus becomes our own memory: "to remember the past is to reimagine it" (Hutton 1993, p. 70). This was an art Thoreau practiced with grace and verve, in large measure because he believed that "in memory is the more reality" (December 30, 1841, *Journal* 1, 1981, p. 352).

In the sense that memory was his own, a conduit into his private ego, Thoreau was most certainly correct. To be sure, history was a civic calling, an attempt to direct public policy and inform his compatriots of the moral lessons of the past, but in the end, history, like nature, was to be personalized. No wonder it was so carefully hammered on the anvil of his writing. Thoreau is perhaps an exemplar of this casting of memory into the molds of a personal vision. Again, memory becomes an artistic material in his hands both to reveal and to create his identity. The philosopher David Krell might well have referred to Thoreau when he observed that we should "ask whether writing is a metaphor for memory or memory is a metaphor for writing" (Krell 1990, p. 4), by which he was referring to the complex and multifaceted role of inscription in memory processes, whether "passive" or "active." Indeed, the interplay of active retrieval and formulation, in writing and otherwise, and the way in which memory simply visits us, impressing the past on our present, reflect the enigmatic character of consciousness itself:

> How is it that I appear to be both slave and master with respect to
> my memory? For the most part I am fed memories, am thrown into
> them by the vicissitudes of my situation; my memory flow seems
> autonomous, almost schizophrenic, perpetually announcing to me my
> bondage to a past. At the same time, I *can* remember; that is, I am able
> to pursue a memory, fasten onto it, and interrogate it. I appear to be
> able to adopt a stance over and above the involuntary flow of memory.
> But what sort of "I" is this? What must my consciousness *be* in order
> to do such a thing? (Ibid., p. xii)

This question informs much of our inquiry regarding Thoreau's construction of the self, the reflection required for his various epistemological projects, and the acute self-awareness of himself as both poet and moralist. In this chapter we have focused upon his historiography, and in the next we will consider his scientific epistemology, but in each case this "split screen" of self-consciousness visits him in various guises and represents a persistent characteristic of his thought.

3   Another Apple Tree

Nature has looked uncommonly bare & dry to me for a day or
two. With our senses applied to the surrounding world we are
reading our own physical & corresponding moral revolutions.
Nature was so shallow all at once I did not know what had
attracted me all my life. I was therefore encouraged when going
through a field this evening, I was unexpectedly struck with the
beauty of an apple tree – The perception of beauty is a moral test.

Thoreau, June 21, 1852,
Journal 5, 1997, p. 120

The last sentence of the above-quoted passage from Thoreau's Journal
resounds with *Walden's* "Our whole life is startlingly moral" (1971, p. 218)
if one properly situates these statements on a set of coordinates defined by
several axes. Just as space is geometrically defined by three vectors in Cartesian geometry, so too might we draw a "space" by "vectors" which will analogously define the coordinates of Thoreau's writings: the first, the imperative
of attention; the second, aesthetic imagination; the third, self-consciousness,
specifically the assessment of personal value. Their meeting, at the origin
of the vectors that delineate this metaphorical space, is the Thoreauvian self,
whose metaphysics I am attempting to establish. To do so, I must now deal
with Thoreau's epistemology, where these coordinates inform and guide his
naturalist enterprise. Postponing consideration of Thoreau's status as "scientist" to later chapters, I will here offer a topography of Thoreau's epistemological endeavor. Heavily influenced by the lingering effects of High
Romanticism, his epistemology, as judged by positivist standards newly
emerging in the 1830s and 1840s, would meet with only varying success. It
swings between careful observation of all forms of nature that indeed
approaches scientific, and a form of prose poetry in the guise of nature writing. We need to understand what this epistemological spectrum meant to
Thoreau and, further, why his discrediting of science resonates so powerfully with our own twenty-first-century humanism.

   Much has been written concerning Thoreau's placement as a poet, writer,
historian, naturalist, scientist, Transcendentalist, and social reformer. He, of
course, possesses many identities, and to categorize him with one or another
is to omit dimensions of his thought and work that do not fit neatly into

any single, even dual, grouping. As Henry Seidel Canby aptly noted, "Thoreau, as I see him, was a man with a foot in each of two worlds, the idealist's and the scientist's" ([1939] 1958, p. 323). At least. His complexity requires attention to his various modalities of thought. In their composite, an intellectual portrait emerges. This chapter continues the general episte-mological description of how Thoreau enacted the subject-object relation-ship and how it assumed its character as it was informed and guided by his self-conscious sense of valuation.

This signifying process is what I have been calling Thoreau's "moral atti-tude." Here, as before, I am coupling two levels of analysis. The first is the more specific of the two, and it refers to a particular moral philosophy assumed by the moral agent. In chapter 6, I will delve into Thoreau's moral philosophy as an expression of virtue ethics, and so will not pursue that matter further here. The second level is more general and perhaps more elu-sive, as it concerns the *value* of knowledge itself. The nature of knowledge is the central concern of epistemology, and philosophers from Plato (*Pro-tagoras*) on have elevated knowledge to a key human value. Indeed, because knowledge is valuable, the valuational aspect of knowledge and of the related states of justified belief have generated numerous parallels between moral and epistemic discourses (Zagzebski 1996). I read Thoreau as exemplifying that connection. By so doing, we can clearly see the interrelatedness of knowledge and value in a general sense, and perhaps more importantly, we can hear his declaration of a particular moral philosophy in the way the world and the past are known. Thoreau pursued that agenda along a con-tinuum of knowledge stretching from the unreportable mystical, to the his-torical, to the scientific. (In the next chapter, I consider this latter mode.) The merit of this approach is that it offers us a ready means to see all of Thoreau's various writing projects, whether regarded as historical, natural-ist, or political, as a single coherent effort. In exploring the structure of Thoreau's inner world, we seek primarily to discern its order and harmony, while also appreciating his contradictions and divided attitudes (McIntosh 1974).

AN EPISTEMOLOGICAL TOPOGRAPHY

We cannot see anything until we are possessed with the idea of it, and then we can hardly see anything else.

> Thoreau, November 4, 1858, *Journal*, [1906]
> 1962, 11:285; published in modified form in
> "Autumnal Hints," 1980d, p. 174

I wish to exhibit Thoreau's epistemology as the coexistence of several modes of knowing and an overlapping of several kinds of writing. He invoked various rationalities, and we must be sensitive to the role each played in mediating his experience. Knowledge and how we gain it occur in many ways, and only by examining several layers of inquiry and report may we begin to ascertain the accomplishments and failures of Thoreau's own epistemological ventures. Some inkling of my orientation has already been outlined, so let us begin on ground well trodden, namely Thoreau's discussion of time. As discussed in chapter 1, Thoreau would capture reality by capturing time. There are, to be sure, moments when Thoreau is fully in time, oblivious to its passing—as he reports, for instance, in the opening of *Walden*'s chapter, "Sounds":

> Sometimes . . . I sat in my sunny doorway from sunrise to noon, rapt in a revery, amidst the pines and hickories and sumachs, in undisturbed solitude and stillness, while the birds sang around or flitted noiseless through the house, until by the sun falling in at my west window, or the noise of some traveller's wagon the distant highway, I was reminded of the lapse of time. I grew in those seasons like corn in the night, and they were far better than any work of the hands would have been. They were not time subtracted from my life, but so much over and above my usual allowance. (*Walden*, 1971, pp. 111–12)[1]

This is a fecund passage for my theme: Thoreau reports a reverie, a mystical state where time is suspended, only to be awakened by intrusions. He thrived in these states, achieving both a peace and deep knowledge that lent renewal to his life, the "Oriental contemplation" that the Hindu mystics taught him as laudable.[2] Time's suspension is completely confluent with nature, which knows no time, for while we understand the passing of seasons and hours, marking and dividing *time* is cognitive, a categorization of the mind. In espousing an animal's ignorance of time or even an intermediary position as exemplified by a preliterate Brazilian Indian, Thoreau celebrated his total envelopment within nature, exemplified by man's obliviousness of the hour. And finally, this reverie is true to Thoreau's highest ethical commitment of achieving total integration with nature. Although these glimpses of merger with nature's flux are only fleeting, they are sustaining. After all, to have a vision is to possess an orientation, a guidance, and, for Thoreau, a fulfillment.

The power of this passage is undeniable. As a rhetoretician, Thoreau masterfully controls the rhythm of the prose and the imagery, but as an epistemological report it sorely lacks information. Thoreau cannot reveal his consciousness—it has been relieved of its cognitive burdens. He only has a vague recollection of his trance, the obscure appreciation that time had passed, but beyond that awareness, there is nothing more to say. *Indeed, there is nothing else to report.* The reverie is unreportable, otherwise it would not have been a mystical experience! So why is the passage powerfully evocative? How does the allusion Thoreau portrays resonate with our own experience? If we too have remembrance of such reveries, even short-lived and less intense, Thoreau's description reminds us of that experience. Simply put, Thoreau's passage delivers a powerful emotional impact to the extent that it evokes recall of our own mediative life.

Thoreau also achieves the same kind of evocation with the use of fable and similar narrative devices. For instance, consider *Walden*'s mythic artist of Kouroo (discussed below), a creative fantasy that also illustrates Thoreau's own aspiration to suspending time, or perhaps to become one with time. In this regard, myth offers one recourse and history another, but Thoreau is all too aware of time's passing as he records history or makes a record of his observations. As discussed in the preceding chapter, the poignancy of noting an iron hook remnant ("Former inhabitants; and Winter Visitors," *Walden*, 1971, p. 261) as the only sign of recent neighbors emphasizes the elusive character of remembrance—and significance—of our temporal existence which rests on the partial character of memory. The passing of the seasons marks more than just nature's course, for it entails the oblivion of man's seasons on earth, the insignificance of his presence. I maintain that this is a good case of Thoreau's historical epistemology in direct service to his metaphysics of time, his abiding concern with temporality and, most saliently, its passing. We respond, as he did, emotionally, as he leads us to peer into awful eternity.

Such emotive states fall well outside any rigorous scientific epistemology, or what Thoreau calls Knowledge. Transcendental emotional experience holds paramount importance for him; indeed, we have ample evidence that he regarded such encounters with the Unknown as the highest and most refined he might have. We may be struck by his "morning work"— the multiple notebooks filled with detailed descriptions ranging from careful (if not obsessive) measurements of dispersed seeds, soundings of Walden Pond, documentation of the first appearance of plants, or the behavior of animals and birds—but these pale in comparison with his passion for contemplation, dream, memory, trance. The message Thoreau was most interested in transmitting pertained to experience outside normal discourse, indeed beyond normal cognition. As important and impressive as Thoreau's achievement might be considered to be in natural philosophy, conventional history, or social comment, these ultimately are subordinated to his most personal spiritual quest. He struggled to reconcile these divergent aspects of his intelligence, for while steeped in a scientific ethos that rewarded objective, clear description, he knew that his deepest mystical experience could not be so reported. He might refer to eternity, the celestial spheres, the ancient truths, Higher Laws, the divine, the Brahma, but in the end he relied on another convention, the encompassing Romantic ideal for all of these allusions to the Beyond, *Intelligence*, which might be "known" only through *sympathy*.

> My desire for knowledge is intermittent, but my desire to bathe my head in atmospheres unknown to my feet is perennial and constant. The highest that we can attain to is not Knowledge, but Sympathy with Intelligence. I do not know that this higher knowledge amounts to anything more definite than a novel and grand surprise on a sudden revelation of the insufficiency of all that we called Knowledge before,—a discovery that there are more things in heaven and earth than are dreamed of in our philosophy. It is the lighting up of the mist by the sun. Man cannot *know* in any higher sense than this, any more than he can look serenely and with impunity in the face of the sun. ("Walking," 1980b, p. 128)

This passage offers cardinal insight into Thoreau's mind. He declares forthrightly and with no hint of irony or qualification the premier position of Intelligence. All those activities that qualify in the hierarchy of the sciences and human sciences are decisively auxiliary to the ephemeral, elusive, "unknowing" Beyond.

Thoreau derives this position from a moral judgment, and in this sense we clearly witness how his metaphysics are in the employ of his ethics. Indeed, it is fair to say that his foundation is an ethical metaphysics.[3] Thoreau continues his testimony quite plainly:

> There is something servile in the habit of seeking after a law which we may obey. We may study the laws of matter at and for our convenience, but a successful life knows no law. It is an unfortunate discovery certainly, that of a law which binds us where we did not know before that we were bound. Live free, child of the mist,—and with respect to knowledge we are all children of the mist. The man who takes the liberty to live is superior to all the laws, by virtue of his relation to the lawmaker. (Ibid., pp. 128–29)

In short, Thoreau would be oriented and guided by his communion with Intelligence. Conventional or public knowledge is not only intellectually limiting, it is morally confining, restricting the individual from living a full life. Our true being is in the ephemeral mist, where only through sympathy do we perceive the cosmic Intelligence that permeates all things with its endowment. This might be known only through an emotional and spiritual apparatus.

Yet Thoreau was no zealous pilgrim, for he divided his work between his spiritual pursuits and more conventional labors, relying on different epistemological faculties for each. A cynic might easily say that Thoreau was a part-time mystic, one no doubt sensitive to the siren's song, but intermittent in his attention. After all, the bulk of his work consisted in exactly the opposite endeavor, making his consciousness explicit and shared publicly through his writing. How might we reconcile this conflict? We do not, nor did he. I will not delve into some psychological hypothesis to explain Thoreau's emotional and intellectual life, and simply accept the phenomenological evidence: he was a complex individual, whose active intelligence pulled him in several directions which were not reconciled. To accept each on its own standing is, from my perspective, the best we might do. If, however, we insist on seeing Thoreau's intellectual and spiritual life as one piece on a continuum, one might fairly say that Thoreau attempted to use his more formal "public" endeavors as pedestals for reaching higher consciousness.

I would stretch this project along a continuum between the two poles of observation determined by the relation of the knowing subject with her object of scrutiny. The first pole is what I will call "detached observation," characterized by objective facts of measurement and date. Such knowledge is epitomized by the Kalendar project, Thoreau's formal attempt to document nature's changes and to detect some constancy and pattern. Seeking to parse time in a "natural" fashion by culling his Journal to create a series of monthly charts, he listed various natural phenomena in a left-hand column, and the years were strung along the top of the chart. The phenomena he tracked included the height of the Concord River, rain patterns, rainbow appearances, temperature, leafing of trees, and so forth. Some of such notekeeping made its way into his published writings; for instance, in *Walden*, Thoreau lists the dates when the pond was freed from ice for the years 1845, 1846, 1847, 1851, 1852, 1853, and 1854 (*Walden*, 1971, p. 303). One might regard this exercise as an attempt to "make a comprehensive picture of time" (Peck 1990, p. 47), but no matter how well motivated such recordkeeping might be, this proved to be an essentially futile endeavor, which despite Thoreau's most earnest efforts remained partial and incomplete. Indeed, as attested by his own record, the Kalendar project failed to find constancy in change. But this detailed observation had a value in and of itself to situate

Thoreau in time. I suspect that he required some anchoring as he groped in the mists.

But there is another agenda afoot in Thoreau's minute recording, namely his legitimating his interpretation of nature. One must know a subject before one might comment, and Thoreau, in a sense, was doing his homework to good purpose. Buell observes that "the potency of the environmental text consisted not just in the reader's transaction with it but also in reanimating and redirecting the reader's transactions with nature" (1995, p. 97). True, but before that reading, the writing of the text serves to focus the writer himself. To be sure, Thoreau enjoyed the naturalist work, and by his count it was "play." But he also used his careful observations as a means to discover higher laws, to comment on the world and himself. One of the most powerful examples of this approach closely follows the listing of dates when Walden Pond thawed, namely the famous passage on the thawing sand on the railroad bank near his cabin.[4] After some descriptive detail, the passage turns to its true intent—a comment on the bank's aesthetics ("I am affected as if in a peculiar sense I stood in the laboratory of the Artist who made the world and me" [ibid., p. 306]) and its metaphysical import ("What is man but a mass of thawing clay?" [ibid., p. 307]). I will have occasion to comment on these aspects of this important text, but suffice it here to simply note that the descriptions point to a deeper message, and this is a recurrent and characteristic pattern of Thoreau's nature writing: Observation is used as a springboard for contemplation, for seeking meaning, for communing with a higher intelligence. The observation, per se, takes on its significance within those contexts, and Thoreau crafted this linkage not only in published work but also in his Journal (for this passage see *Journal 2*, 1984, pp. 382–84). The epistemology was in service to his metaphysics.

This second pole, what I will call "dissolved observation," leads to an interesting tension and may refer to Thoreau's reveries (mystical states) or what Sharon Cameron has called a "writing of nature," in which *Walden*, and, even more importantly, the Journal, strive to obliterate the subject-object divide. According to Cameron, Thoreau's recording of facts effaces his own identity and consciousness, which "does not just mediate or mirror natural phenomena; . . . the fiction of the *Journal* is that consciousness is displaced by them . . . [so that] [t]he self is not to be empowered by nature. It is rather to be converted to nature" (ibid., pp. 88–89).[5] On this reading, Thoreau has no Archimedean point where the self might rest and maintain its perspective and integrity, and the dichotomy between his epistemology of observation and his mystical experience thus dissolves.[6] Cameron regards Thoreau's fully matured position in the final Journal volume as transfiguring the perceiver who, seeing nature outside the self, does not objectify it, and seeing it inside the self, does not familiarize it, for " 'seeing' is an intimate relation, not requisite for some other goal but an end in itself" (ibid., p. 153).

Whether Thoreau indeed achieved this *epistemological* epiphany is doubtful. Perhaps we might concede that Thoreau *aspired* to unselfconscious merger, and although caught in a web of self-consciousness, he indeed experienced mystical moments. But as he *wrote*, as he functioned as a naturalist, a natural philosopher, even as a "scientist," he had to translate those mystical episodes into words, into a lexicon, albeit open, so that they might be captured. In the very self-reflection, thought displaces the immediacy of nature experienced. So Cameron's interpretation, as intrigued as I am by it, is a more radical reading than I, and most critics, would allow (see chapter 5 for a more complete discussion of Thoreau's writing). As an epistemologist, Thoreau achieves what Peck calls "a lovely dance between the self and nature" (1990, p. 121). And I maintain that, however one regards the self-object dichotomy epistemologically, Thoreau is caught on his quill. Despite his stupendous effort, he "fails" on both accounts: the objectivity of "detached observation" is always personalized and thus discounted; and by the other pole of "dissolved observation," he must translate the experience into a text. When Thoreau communicated to his readers in polished works such as *Walden*, and even in the Journal—anticipating the stream-of-consciousness writing yet to become familiar in our own century—he was aware of his distance from what Cameron calls "the second self." After all, he is *writing!* Only in reverie is the self merged with nature; then of course he is not writing and, indeed, has difficulty in *reporting* his experience, as we have seen.

My disagreement with Cameron about the character of Thoreau's writing as an epistemological project should not obscure our deeper agreement on Thoreau's metaphysics. The force of her argument derives from the insight that Thoreau asserted a *metaphysical* unity between himself and the world. But was he effective in demonstrating this assertion? Did he capture his metaphysics successfully in his writing? On this we diverge—not only on whether Thoreau was successful in his literary attempts to forge such a union, but even on whether his metaphysics was a viable formulation at all. Cameron thinks that Thoreau did overcome the Cartesian divide of *res cogitans* and *res extensa*:

> [O]nce Thoreau sees that correspondences between nature and the self are incomplete and incompletable, what he would like to do is to prohibit them entirely. So doing, he would preserve the idea that nature is alien. But my claim is a complex and an apparently contradictory one,

for the way Thoreau imagines that nature is alien is also by imagining he could impersonate the alienness—that he could voice nature or be nature's voice. When Thoreau insists that he wants to write sentences that "lie like boulders on the page" or to be "the corn & the grass & the atmosphere writing," he does not mean nature can express the human or be expressed by it—either of these claims would be conventionally indebted to metaphor or analogy. Rather he says he can abandon the human, can make himself into the alienness he was forced to confront. (Cameron 1985, p. 48)

This effacement of "the human" is the fundamental issue at hand, and hinges on Thoreau's identification of "the Wild" within him. By recognizing the source of his vitality and, further, bringing it to consciousness, Thoreau sought to overcome the divide between man and nature. The dilemma, of course, is that as humans we are ever self-conscious, and this self-reflexive attitude does not tolerate obscuring our rational contemplation of the world and of ourselves contemplating that world. Thus the very wildness he hoped to integrate would by necessity be "tamed." Thoreau's metaphysics are at odds or, at least, in tension with human faculties of knowledge, and this tension accounts for an underlying anxiety present in all of his work. Cameron identifies the problem, but where she detects a "solution," I perceive a noble "failure." I maintain that, his mystical moments notwithstanding, Thoreau is caught in the web of his own self-consciousness.

THE DEEDS OF LIGHT

I have seen where the mildew on a jar had taken the form of perfect leaves–thick–downy–and luxuriant. What an impulse was given some time or other to vegetation that now nothing can stay it. Some one has said he could write an epic to be called the leaf–and this would seem to have been the theme of the creator himself. The leaf either plain or variegated–fresh or decayed–fluid or crystalline–is nature[']s constant cypher.

Thoreau, 1842–44, *Journal 2*, 1984, p. 80

Thoreau was a consummate practitioner of the naturalist vignette, a genre inspired by careful observation, but often confused as derivative of science. Highly individualized and personal, the facts of the case are only the beginning of the narrative; and the observer, not the object, assumes primacy. In science, the exact opposite occurs. In characterizing Thoreau's mode of seeing, Buell has aptly noted that "the speaker's fascination with the process of seeing, not the objects seen, is the central subject here" (Buell 1995,

p. 74). When the observer takes on a certain primacy, the self-consciousness of seeing becomes an object of scrutiny and delight in itself. In the process, the self is implicitly asserted as a central focus of interest, albeit in the engagement of the world. This address is all part of the larger challenge of environmental interpretation, which requires "us to rethink our assumptions about the nature of representation, reference, metaphor, characterization, personae, and canonicity" (ibid., p. 2)—and, I would add, the very nature of the knowing self. This issue points to the central question of man's relation to nature, or rather to nature as a construction (Evernden 1992)[7] or man's "place" (Garber 1991) in nature, which is also a construction.[8] So we must keep in mind this complex topography of Thoreau's writing with regard to the epistemological distance he might assume from his object. But given the power of his self-projected descriptions and the propensity he had for writing them, we need to better situate the place such writing held in Thoreau's epistemology.

It is incontestable that Thoreau projected his emotional state onto these "intermediary" descriptions. Indeed, one must be struck with the utterly fantastical character marking many of his depictions of animals or landscapes, and one might dip almost at random into any of his works for examples.[9] The emotionalism of his descriptions is one mark of Thoreau's Romanticism, and even if we were to place it within a developing genre of nineteenth-century realism, such writing is "far from being a transparent rendering" inasmuch as, at least by our standards, it is highly ideologically or psychohistorically determined (Buell 1995, p. 87). Thoreau was in this regard only following the lead of Goethe a generation earlier, who self-consciously allowed his putative separation as perceiver to overlap his object of scrutiny, thus compromising his objectivity and its claims to realism. This was not a naive "error" in the usual sense. Goethe was acutely self-aware of the epistemological challenge of science, and it was precisely the conceit of complete objectification that he would not only attack, but counter with his own projected personalism. In both his biological and physical studies, Goethe would include all human faculties in the employ of his science: intuition, mathematics, accurate measurements, ardent imagination, and not least "a loving delight in the world of the senses" (Goethe [1792] 1988). As stated in his *Theory of Colors*, a bald attack on Newton, Goethe sought "the deeds of light, what it does and what it endures" ([1810] 1988). Goethe, in seeking "the deeds," was intent on discovering the full panoply of phenomena in what he considered their dynamic unity of spirit and matter. For him, and for the Romantics generally, there was only nature and man as a unified whole, one continuum of *res cogitans* and *res extensa* to be perceived together through Imagination.

Goethe's treatise on color is a multipronged study of light, both as a physical phenomenon and as psychologically perceived, and includes a rich mixture of history and philosophy of science. In this sense it conforms to the rhetorical style of the day, whose authorial voice, replete with individual impressions and opinions, blatantly ignores our own conventions of the neutral observer who presents us with "nothing but the facts." The boundaries separating the subject and object are thus blurred and even disappear, so that personal judgments, and even prejudice, are projected.[10] Goethe was reflecting a different vision of science from the one that was to prove dominant in the nineteenth century, and totally hegemonic in the twentieth, namely the idea that the observer, in a radical sense, might be removed altogether, leaving his observation, preferably generated by a mechanical device, standing alone, utterly divorced from the scientist, to report on nature. (This proved to be an unattainable goal and an epistemological conceit.[11] See chapter 4.)

At one level, we might say that early-nineteenth-century science had not developed the disciplinary structure we have today, so that by modern standards, what should have been clearly separated as different modes of study—optical mechanics and visual perception (i.e., physics and physiology or cognitive psychology)—were fused in Goethe's approach. In addition, most would agree that history and philosophy of science began as parts of science proper. Prior to the mid-twentieth century, history of science was primarily a rhetorical and theoretical tool in showing how new science was part of a progressive, and rational, process. Review of the historical development of a particular science was an integral component of the *scientific* report. When Goethe wrote on color theory, Priestley on electricity, or Lyell on geology, these natural philosophers used history to legitimate their own work. Even into our own era, history of science—when still entertained as relevant to science—was often seen as exercising a beneficial influence on practice, so that the laboratory scientist might profit from history used as an analytical tool (Kragh 1987, pp. 33–34). While the historical perspective as a value in itself governed such innovators as Giambattista Vico, confusions about historical interpretation as an important scholarly activity distinct from doing science itself were only slowly untangled.

But the issue is more deeply grounded than a methodological problem. Goethe's purpose and strategy grew from a metaphysics where individual and nature were intimately connected and could not be torn asunder without violating the "natural" relationship of man in nature. Goethe, from our vantage, was both poet and scientist, but he himself knew no such divisions as fundamental. For Goethe the "poet," science must serve a complementary role to discovering a comprehensive reality. To dissect only by mathematical logic was to disjoint the whole, to destroy true relationships, and to restrict one's appreciation of nature's full horizon. The poet's eye might better serve, still with scientific method, nature's true design. In short, the decidedly Romantic view Goethe championed accused mathematics of obscuring the color phenomenon by limiting its broadened study. But Goethe already perceived twenty years before Thoreau graduated from Harvard that the Romantic perspective was in decline, if not moribund, and his scientific methodology was soon discredited (although still stimulating much current discussion—e.g., Amrine et al. 1987; Bortoft 1996; Seamon and Zajonc 1998). Hostile critics saw (and see) Goethe as a dilettante doing science without the requisite orientation toward mathematics, disabling him from partaking in the power of mathematical abstraction and rigorous methods of physical science. Goethe's preoccupation with capturing nature in her totality, as a fully human perception, not only restricted his acceptance of the value of a more divorced approach but corrupted its meaning (Wells 1971). But the problem is not so easily reduced to a deafness to mathematics' song, and again resides at a deeper metaphysical understanding of man in nature.

For our purposes, it is important to note that Thoreau was very much influenced by Goethe and frequently referred to him in his Journal and published works. This interest dates from Thoreau's last year in college, and upon graduating, he began to read Goethe in the original (borrowing various books from Emerson's fifty-five-volume German edition [Sattelmeyer 1988, pp. 26–27]) and quoting him in his Journal (e.g., entries of November 15, 16, December 8, 18, 1837; *Journal* 1, 1981). The reasons are not difficult to fathom, given the strong correspondence in their views of nature and the self. There are two general ways Thoreau followed Goethe as a Romantic natural philosopher. The first concerns Thoreau's search for the expression of a universal organizing principle in nature, and the second, the underlying rationale that justified this epistemological approach. As discussed in chapter 5, Thoreau took pains to distance himself from Goethe, but the American's pattern of inquiry, and its telos, remain closely aligned to Goethe's own project.

In brief, Goethe aimed at establishing "new relations and discovering the manner in which Nature, with incomparable power, develops the greatest complexity from the simple" (Goethe [1786–88] 1982). His quest was the

Primal (or proto-) Plant (*Urpflanze*), the basic model from which all botany might be regarded as unified and as a variation thereof. He was searching for no less than nature's Holy Grail, and in an epiphany during a sojourn in Italy, he perceived precisely that vision at the botanical gardens of Palermo. There he fulfilled his celebrated conviction that nature indeed had such unity and that a singular model might be discerned, achieved with a powerful aesthetic sense that perceived the form of such a unifying principle. His confidence in seeking an archetypal theme and in recognizing it was the appreciation that "in organic being, first the form as a whole strikes us, then its parts and their shapes and combination" (Goethe [1790] 1989).

Thoreau, in one of his earliest Journal entries, records his own sympathetic response to this Goethian problematic,[12] and this theme was to reappear as *Walden*'s climactic conclusion in the sand-bank description, where Thoreau describes his own epiphanic insight into nature's vitality and unity (1971, pp. 304–9). Less than a year before *Walden*'s publication, the sand bank as an aesthetic and natural image appears in Thoreau's Journal (first entry, December 31, 1851 [*Journal 4*, 1992, p. 230]), and we see the full harvest of the seed planted by his reading of Goethe fourteen years earlier:

> On the outside all the life of the earth is expressed in the animal or vegetable, but make a deep cut in it and you will find in the very sands an anticipation of the vegetable leaf. No wonder, then, that plants grow and spring in it. The atoms have already learned the law. Let a vegetable sap convey it upwards and you have a vegetable leaf. No wonder that the earth expresses itself outwardly in leaves, which labors with the idea thus inwardly. The overhanging leaf sees here in its prototype. The earth is pregnant with law. (March 2, 1854, *Journal*, [1906] 1962, 6:148)

This conclusion, "the earth is pregnant with law," epitomizes Goethe's specific concern with finding a template for plant diversity and, more generally, the intimation of nature's ordered unity—indeed, of the idea that nature is lawful. This insight and the foundation upon which it rests is important evidence of Thoreau's full embrace of Romanticism (Adams and Ross 1988, pp. 143 ff.), but note that its first expression is one we detect in Thoreau's earliest musings. It is for this reason that I would prefer to regard this Romantic orientation as a maturation or crystallization of an earlier, perhaps less well articulated understanding than a conversion as some critics argue (ibid.).

Goethe was an ardent holist, an orientation formed from both his aesthetic and philosophical sensibilities, and no doubt Thoreau found in him a clear articulation of this Romantic ethos with which he held a strong affinity. But there is a second important countervailing aspect of Romantic organicism, which pertains to individuality, the unique standing of each creature, sacred and beautiful in its own right. This ethos is the foundation of the self's own discovery and expression. I briefly delve into this issue, because it so pervades the metaphysics of Thoreau's own project: insofar as he seeks the universal, he is nevertheless situating himself, the individual, in that universal setting. His individuation thus balances his cosmic surveying.

Perhaps the clearest articulation of this second point of view encountered by Thoreau was Coleridge's *Hints towards the Formation of a More Comprehensive Theory of Life* ([1848] 1970). As Sattelmeyer and Hocks (1985) have argued, Thoreau's reading of this work in late 1848 strongly influenced, or at minimum legitimated, his own work as a naturalist, offering an important epistemological and aesthetic rationale of Romantic thought to guide his own endeavors. Heavily influenced by Kant, Hegel, and the *Naturphilosophie* of Schelling, Coleridge, in the *Theory of Life* (written in 1816), characterized life according to three cardinal characteristics: First, nature manifested a creative force that had universal properties, namely vitality, but was also characterized by the individual expression of that power in the particularity of species and individuals.[13] The discerning eye would recognize the aesthetic unity of nature both in the universal elements of creative vitality and in the individuality expressed in the multifarious details of animal and plant life. Because of an underlying correspondence between the human mind and intelligence, the naturalist might discern the moving spirit of the world, the divine creative force of the universe in individuality.

Second, following Kant's third Critique (*Critique of Judgment* [1790]), Coleridge judged the integration of organisms as a reflection of an overarching telos where cause and effect are self-referential, that is, effects inevitably influence initiating causes because all parts are interconnected and related to the whole that orders each constituent relative to that whole. As Coleridge put it in his own context of individuation, "a whole composed, *ab intra*, of different parts, so far independent that each part is reciprocally means and end, is an individual" ([1848] 1970, p. 44). In this general Kantian view, organisms not only had purpose but were structured by all components incorporated under the auspices of an organizing principle, the integrity of the organism. Accordingly, a central scientific pursuit was to understand the fundamental organization of animals or plants by some regulative principle, and in this respect, Romantic naturalists and biologists may be regarded as universally committed to this pursuit. It was this principle that informed Goethe's *Urpflanze*.

The third element in Coleridge's *Theory of Life* pertains to a particularly strong sense of the Hegelian dialecticism that was so influential during this period: the most general law is that of "polarity or the essential dualism of nature. . . . Life, then, we consider as the copula, or the unity of thesis and antithesis, position and counterposition,—Life itself being the positive of both" (Coleridge [1848] 1970, pp. 50–51).[14]

For our purposes, the question of individuation is paramount, and the other two themes of *Theory* are subordinate to our immediate concerns. In passing, I note that in regard to the question of the telos of nature, Thoreau repeatedly takes delight in witnessing the great design and artistry of divine order, a Romantic sentiment that is most evident in the perceiving of nature's beauty, a topic reserved for later in this chapter. And in regard to the role of "polarity" in Thoreau's work, while for Coleridge, as well as for Goethe and Emerson, polarity was a deep characteristic of nature, expressed as properties of forces and matter (e.g., magnetism, color, light, sex), this concept was far less prominent in Thoreau's metaphysics. McIntosh (1974, pp. 38–39) observes that rhetorically Thoreau used polarity in a variety of ways: in *Walden* juxtaposing chapters "Solitude" and "Visitors" or in *A Week* prominently contrasting masculine and feminine, East and West, Hindu and Yankee, or even in a phrase, like "a wilderness domestic," and perhaps more importantly in assessing the complexity of a moral thought (e.g., "I find in myself, and still find, an instinct toward a higher, or, as it is named, spiritual life . . . and another toward a rank and savage one, and I reverence them both. I love the wild not less than the good" [*Walden*, 1971, p. 210]). But I do not regard polarity guiding Thoreau's basic presuppositions of how nature works or is designed. Perhaps he simply assumed this characteristic or subsumed it in his general understanding of perception and moral understanding. In any case, *polarity* as such does not possess the metaphysical interest for Thoreau that it seems to have held for his Romantic predecessors.

So while one would be hard-pressed to argue that Thoreau followed Coleridge in any programmatic sense, there are elements in Coleridgean themes that resonate in Thoreau's own work. Consonant with our present concerns, we will consider the issue of *individuation*. Coleridge may well have inspired Thoreau to pursue the poetic notion of individuation, *sui generis*. This project was enacted in Thoreau's Journal, where it is apparent that he regarded the recording of fine detail as legitimate in its own right, albeit toward a universal insight. And in *Walden*, Thoreau indeed makes the particulars of his world a deep metaphysical question (one already alluded to in chapter 1): "Why do precisely these objects which we behold make a world?" (*Walden*, 1971, p. 225). Peck reads this line appropriately as meaning that the world as we know it seems to correspond exactly to our needs and expectations (1990, p. 117); but the "precisely" also refers to the world in its every detail, which in each instance is found to be in place and serves some greater whole. To witness the minutiae of nature to the smallest item is to testify to that order, not only marveling at its being but inquiring whence and how it came to be. The expression of each creature's own self-fulfillment is implicit and intrinsic to that order, and Thoreau recognizes this coherence of will, diverse yet integrated, as the wonder of nature. Coleridge poetically expressed this individuality guided by the telos of the whole as a metaphysical characteristic of life, and Thoreau seems to have concurred. So in complement to Goethe's own characteristic epistemology, Thoreau may well have found important support for his own endeavors in *A Theory of Life*, and we might fairly regard Goethe and Coleridge as representing contrasting methodological exponents of a Romantic view of nature which Thoreau internalized in one form or another.

A third character must also be permitted entry to this intellectual drama, the naturalist Alexander von Humboldt. Laura Dassow Walls (1993, 1995) has made a compelling case that Thoreau was inspired by, and followed the example of, Humboldt's style of natural history. Documenting that Thoreau was both knowledgeable about Humboldt's works and sympathetic to his approach, she goes on to show how they shared what she calls "Empirical Holism," in contrast to "Rational Holism," as a guiding philosophy of discovery. The latter philosophy is based on connecting observations and facts of the natural world to some underlying Divine Law, in the Coleridgean sense of Law as Logos. Empirical Holism, on the other hand, while sharing the same commitment to holism, sees facts as connected to each other in a more modern ecological sense, rather than to some preexisting Truth. This is best seen as a Baconian, inductive philosophy, where

> out of the sum total of all the interconnections the observer determines the laws, or inherent properties of matter that appear to govern the phenomena observed. This method of connection does not rely on a central axis but on an understanding of the "network" of interacting factors. (Walls 1993, p. 57)

This Humboldtian approach, like those of Goethe and Coleridge, regarded nature as a unified and harmonious whole, but advanced an empirical method heretofore undeveloped in natural history. Indeed, from Humboldt's perspective, nature might only be known through its constituent parts empirically, in a first-order way. This method thus required careful observation and a thorough commitment to the interplay of facts and theory—objective data-collection and thoughtful synthesis. Goethe was well aware of these philosophical issues and explicitly addressed them, but Humboldt exhibited a commitment to the gathering of natural history facts which was highly consonant with Thoreau's own style and directly influenced the development of the American's nature study.

We might construe several unifying themes at work concomitantly. Thoreau and his mentors, separated by more than a generation and living in three different countries, shared a common sensibility—the organic unity of thought and the harmonization of all knowledge—each linked by an aestheticism of Imagination. And putting Thoreau closer to Goethe and Humboldt in their respective scientific alignments than to Coleridge (primarily because of the highly speculative character of Coleridge's thought—he had a deeper sympathy for Schelling's *Naturphilosophie*), we see, nevertheless, that each was firmly committed to certain precepts about nature: 1) nature was unified, and thus material independence was countered by polar or some other principle of connectedness; 2) nature was composed of active beings, as opposed to passive materiality; and 3) forces and objects were inextricably entwined, so the same laws must apply to both the organic and inorganic domains. But there is a fourth element that served as the point of departure, namely the relation of mind and nature, the so-called correspondence between them. Do mind and nature have the same source (thereby exhibiting harmonies, symmetries, and parallelisms), or is there an irredeemable split between ourselves and the cosmos?

"Correspondence" comes in two Romantic modes (Cameron 1985, pp. 44–45). The Emersonian variety plays on the mirroring of man and nature, a sharing of vital rhythms and an epistemological "sympathy"; the other type, inherited from Coleridge, "suggests that a fertile tension, a rise in consciousness, results from the recognition of the 'polarity' of man and nature rather than their connection" (Slovic 1992, p. 21). Of course, "polarity" demands connection along some continuum; after all, dipoles cannot exist apart. But the point of emphasis is the difference or tension. Recent critical comment has emphasized, as evidenced by the later Journal, Thoreau's growing distance from Emersonian harmony and confluence, and it is fair to concur that Thoreau's original position regarding Correspondence, and his understanding of nature more generally, evolved from something close to Emerson's ideas to something quite different (Porte 1966, pp. 117 ff.; Cameron 1985, pp. 44 ff.; Slovic 1992, pp. 21 ff.). This is the critical issue which focuses Cameron's provocative argument concerning Thoreau's writing. She notes how the later Journal revolves around Thoreau's contemplations of the relation of the mind and the world it contemplates ("Apparently to write about nature is to write about how the mind sees nature, and sometimes about how the mind sees itself" [p. 44]), and how on that axis Emersonian Correspondence fails:

> [T]he Journal proposes and subverts the idea of correspondence. The whole of nature may be a metaphor for the human mind, but Thoreau's formulations emphasize *failed* attempts to make sense of the congruence. (Ibid., p. 45)

Without reiterating my differences with Cameron, at least on this fundamental matter we agree: Thoreau wrestled with defining the gap between the inquring mind and the world of its scrutiny. Our differences lie in my interpretation that Thoreau, except in the extraordinary mystical state, saw the self and its world as irredeemably separate. Support for that position has already been offered above and will be reiterated in different ways in the ensuing chapters. My argument now turns to the "currency" of thought—facts—as illustrating Thoreau's pervasive self-conscious awareness of himself as a "knower"—a self distinct from and yet in nature.

THE WORLDING OF NATURE

It is true, we are such poor navigators that our thoughts, for the
most part, stand off and on upon a harborless coast . . . or steer for
the public ports of entry, and go into the dry docks of science,
where they merely refit for this world, and no natural currents
concur to individualize them.

Walden, 1971, p. 292

Thoreau's "worlding" (Peck 1990)[15] may be fairly regarded as an attempt to capture nature in all of its multitudinous states from a myriad of perspectives to achieve some final synthetic vision. *Walden* was the most sustained and successful venture, but all of Thoreau's writings aspire to this coherent vision. His project is composed of two elements, critical observation and memory in reconstruction. Like social history, which is only partial, highly selective, and always oriented toward some thematic goal, natural history is similarly personalized and fractured by the hammer of creating an image of the world that conforms to an integrated image. In Thoreau's epistemological "topography" this inner faculty, which I have called a "personal image" or "vision," must marshal a first-order perception into an artistic expression. The integrity of that experience, its *wholeness*, if you will, is thus a product of the creative inner faculty, and in this respect we might see Thoreau as operating with a "split self." Except during rare mystical reveries, he seemed always conscious of himself observing nature. In this sense his self is divided: the observer of nature is being assessed by another consciousness—censoring the first and using its data to construct a second-order expression, the artistic product. Thus Thoreau's modes of knowing always relate his knowledge to some substratum of consciousness that, ill defined as it might be, must reside separate from the world, and yet be part of it. In short, as a Romantic, Thoreau is precariously perched on a divide separating a radical solipsism—a world of his own making—from the "world" beyond him.

The constant interplay of the self's introspection and the inspection of the other—society, persons, the natural world—leaves Thoreau with a tripartite structure that he attempted to integrate and make whole: the world (nature); the observation; and the observation/observer scrutinized by self-consciousness. Thoreau was very well aware of the integrative challenge this structure demanded, and he sought to find "the point of interest . . . somewhere *between*" himself and the natural world (November 5, 1857, *Journal*, [1906] 1962, 10:165). The particular orientation, and perhaps the core issue for the Romantics, was, given the reality of the world, how to give primacy to the knower without pushing him into the solipsistic abyss. Their stance was intrinsically unstable, and "the interaction—the 'dance'—of the creative self and the world" (Peck 1990, p. 123) must remain awkward, forever hobbled by the deep tension of the epistemological prominence given idealism and the centrality of the subjectivity inherent in the primacy of imagination and creative seeing. Thoreau himself was very much subject to that tension. Ultimately he strove to personalize the world, real in its own right but meaningful to him only on his terms.

We might best understand his difficulty in the context of Transcendentalism and his relation to that movement. Although often situated there, he seems to me an outlier of that group, and the differences separating them reach deeply into his unique epistemology. Before proceeding further, let me sketch Thoreau's project in the setting of the Transcendentalism with which he is typically identified.

Thoreau struggled to elaborate his own philosophy in relation to Emerson and other Transcendentalists. Indeed, when the secretary of the Association for the Advancement of Science questioned him about what branch of science interested him, Thoreau ironically offered a self-definition that played to the spectrum of his interests and which finally rested with his Concord friends:

> I felt that it would be to make myself the laughing stock of the scientific community–to describe or attempt to describe to them that branch of science which specially interests me–in as much as they do not believe in a science which deals with the higher law. So I was obliged to

speak to their condition and describe to them that poor part of me
which they alone can understand. The fact is I am a mystic–a transcendentalist–& a natural philosopher to boot. Now I think–of it–I should
have told them at once that I was a transcendentalist–that would have
been the shortest way of telling them that they would not understand
my explanations.

How absurd that though I probably stand as near to nature as any of
them, and am by constitution as good an observer as most–yet a true
account of my relation to nature should excite their ridicule only. If it
had been the secretary of an association of which Plato or Aristotle was
the President–I should not have hesitated to describe my studies at
once & particularly. (March 5, 1853, *Journal 5*, 1997, pp. 469–70)

This Journal passage is interesting in several respects relative to the issues
we are now considering. Obviously, Thoreau is rather uncomfortable with
his relation to the scientific community, for although he is involved in a
"naturalist" project, he does not comfortably assume any recognized scientific persona, an issue discussed in detail in the next chapter. Not that his
methods differed so radically from that of a taxonomist, or perhaps even an
ethologist, but the rationale for his studies was hardly scientific.[16] Apart
from one presentation late in his career, he made no attempt to publish scientific reports in professional journals and was satisfied instead to report
his observations in artistic venues: literary essays, books, and, most importantly, his Journal. As he himself admitted, his observations of nature,
instead of falling under the rubric of professional scientific discourse, led to
another forum altogether, that of the Transcendentalists. Professional scientists, he correctly realized, were only distant intellectual cousins. The
Transcendentalists were his brothers. So although Thoreau is, to a certain
extent, a "natural philosopher"—or what we would call a scientist—he lists
first, and then as a single designation, "transcendentalist." At this point, his
contemporaries, as well as modern commentators, diverge in assessing
Thoreau's success in placing himself either within (e.g., Paul 1958) or outside (e.g., Porte 1966) that family.[17] Sketching the contours of Thoreau's differences with Emerson—the major foil to Thoreau's own philsophical identity—will serve to help us better situate Thoreau's epistemology and its
metaphysical foundations.

There is little doubt that a profound parting of the ways finally, and irrev-
ocably, separated Thoreau and Emerson in 1851, a break that was already
well under way by the late 1840s (Harding 1965; Lebrieux 1984; Richardson 1986, 1996). To what extent this represented a psychological clash (personality incompatibilities, dependency needs, personal competition, jeal-
ousy) need not concern us here. Rather, it serves to highlight their intrinsic

differences, which only surfaced once Thoreau reached his philosophical maturity. The critical issue is to understand Thoreau's later epistemological project in reaction to his mentor and to the Transcendental movement more broadly. The problem in doing so begins, appropriately enough, with defining Transcendentalism—no easy task. After all, Transcendentalism represented a diverse array of beliefs and practices (religious and antireligious), arising from diverse cultural sources (German, English, American). The diversity of Transcendentalism itself is a fundamental difficulty with the subject and explains the continued fascination with attempting to adjudicate Thoreau's placement.[18] Here, I will simply enumerate some of the key issues which pertain directly to outlining Thoreau's epistemology relative to Emerson's in the hope that by juxtaposing them, Thoreau's own position will become clearer.

Although critics have divided on how closely one might place Thoreau in Emerson's shadow,[19] I regard their later animus as indicative of wide philosophical differences. If we attend strictly to the epistemological issues informing their respective philosophies, Emerson embraced a radical idealism, while Thoreau affirmed that, as a Transcendentalist, he was both an idealist and a materialist. This distinction reflects Emerson's general posture vis-à-vis nature, which he regarded only from a homiletical distance. As Sherman Paul noted, "The nature [Emerson] invoked was more programmatic and conceptual than actual: he did not need to go to Walden Pond to find it" (1958, pp. 176–77). Indeed, Emerson built his entire program at a certain distance from nature, so that he might remain an independent observer and so survey the world; Thoreau, in contrast, sought the particularities of nature in careful observation (at times in literal immersion in a river or a pond), bringing himself into the closest proximity to nature to glean from nature jewels of insight. As Olaf Hansen observed, "Where Emerson would claim that 'every natural fact is a symbol of some spiritual fact,' Thoreau would have insisted that every natural fact *is* a spiritual fact" (1990, p. 133). So while Emerson would write philosophically *about* nature, Thoreau *read* her (ibid., p. 135).

Idealism was Emerson's linchpin. "Having obliterated the world as matter . . . [he] could give it back as pure idea" (Porte 1966, p. 53), which was derived from the primacy he gave the soul as finer, higher, and truer than matter.[20] Indeed, idealism fulfilled Emerson's need for a theory to accommodate his essentially religious attitude, which he elaborated as a vision of moral law.[21] Emerson preached against the sensuous trap that matter portended, for in his view, nature must properly be regarded in its higher use—that is, to serve as a spiritual guide and inspiration for man. So Emerson "went to nature for confirmation and illustration of his a priori ethical system, not for mystical ecstasy inseparable from its ineffable meaning" (ibid., p. 62). In short, as exemplified in "Nature," "Emerson's idealism really signifies . . . a simple denial of the inherent worth of matter and sense experience" (ibid., p. 63). More, such a philosophy both allowed and justified the sovereignty of man over nature.

Thoreau thought utterly otherwise.[22] Nature was to be embraced first and foremost for its own sake, its sensuous beauty, and the pleasure derived from contemplating it. Rather than dominate and use nature, Thoreau was committed to celebrating the wild, seeing it as the primal source of civilization and his own vitality. Nature assumed a value *sui generis,* and he refused to contemplate nature as the Transcendentalists did, from their parlor armchairs: "We often hear the expression the natural life of man—we should rather say the unnatural life of man. It is rare indeed to find a man who has not long ago departed out of nature" (October 15, 1843, *Journal 1,* 1981, p. 475). More than anything else, Thoreau was committed to reconnecting this disjointed relationship. Against their comfortable dualism, he strove to find the bridge between spirit and matter, between the knowing self and nature. For him, sensuous experience initiated a cascade of emotive and philosophic responses that might end in some moral understanding, and along the way brought variegated perceptions and experiences, intellectual and mystical. Man's study of nature might direct, inspire, and otherwise instruct morality, but these were ultimately subordinate to nature's own standing, independent of the human use of it. Indeed, nature was *real* and might be known through perception, through engagement by sensory faculties. Thus an active interplay between the external and inner worlds created images of external reality that could be apprehended and understood. Mind then does not rest above, beyond, or superior to matter, but lives in active exchange with nature. Thus the world "is not a servant merely standing in for its Platonic master" (Porte 1966, p. 123) but is indeed primary and encompassing.

So, how would Thoreau appreciate *reality,* not just an intellectual distillation of it? As he wrote in *A Week,* "Are we to be put off and amused in this life, as it were with a mere allegory? Is not Nature, rightly read, that of which she is commonly taken to be the symbol merely?" (1980a, p. 382). Thoreau accordingly shed excess intellectual and moralizing baggage, which he deeply mistrusted.[23] Instead he immersed himself in a sensuous engagement with nature. Consider the following Journal passage, one of Thoreau's myriad reports that celebrate the sensuality of his experience:

> I am thrilled to think that I owe a perception to the commonly gross sense of taste–that I have been inspired through the palate–that these berries have fed my brain. After I had been eating these simple– wholesome–ambrosial fruits–on this high hill side–I found my senses whetted–I was young again. They fed my brain–my fancy & imagina- tion–and whether I stood or sat I was not the same creature. (July 11, 1852, *Journal* 5, 1997, pp. 215–16)

Thoreau could hardly have distanced himself further from Emerson's cir- cle: "We need pray for no higher heaven than the pure senses can furnish, a purely sensuous life" (*A Week*, 1980a, p. 382). This orientation in turn became the direction of Thoreau's own moral trajectory: "Our present senses are but the rudiments of what they are destined to become" (ibid.). And to what purpose? Simply because of the pure wonder of nature and the amazement evoked in her contemplation.

> In her midst I can be glad with an entire gladness. If this world was all man I could not stretch myself– I should lose all hope. He is constraint; she is freedom to me. He makes me wish for another world– She makes me content with this. None of the joys she supplies is subject to his rules and definitions. What he touches he taints– In thought he moral- izes– (January 3, 1853, *Journal* 5, 1997, p. 422)

So much for Emerson's moralizing and the constraints that intellectual stric- tures would put on Thoreau's immediate engagement of nature.

Given his celebration of nature's sensuousness, the intensity of his com- munion, the exuberance of his pleasure, and the detail in which he recorded his naturalist experiences, we might fairly conclude that if Thoreau truly was a Transcendentalist, he represented the opposite pole to Emerson's ide- alism. I emphasize their differences, but there is no neat divide, and Emer- son was to experience a continuum of feelings for Thoreau from outright disapproval[24] to admitting a susceptibility to Thoreau's own mystical incli- nations. There are many levels at which Thoreau and Emerson parted com- pany, and in an intellectual study we are bound to examine the more promi- nent philosophical issues. But just as I have read Thoreau's epistemology through what I regard as his own "personalized" prism, so too might we enlist another glimpse of Thoreau from the same general vantage point with Emerson's own testimony, one offered before their rupture. In a telling jour- nal entry, Emerson writes poetically and enchantingly of Thoreau as a latter- day Pan who, conversant with a dark and mysterious nature, appears as a guide to the deeper, perhaps mystical currents that might have similarly drawn Emerson, but which he resisted:

Then the good river-god has taken the form of my valiant Henry Thoreau here & introduced me to the riches of his shadowy starlit, moonlit stream, a lovely new world lying as close & yet as unknown to this vulgar trite one of streets & shops as death to life or poetry to prose. Through one field only we went by boat & then left all time, all science, all history behind us and entered into Nature with one stroke of a paddle. Take care, good friend! I said, as I looked west into the sunset overhead & underneath, & he with his face toward me rowed towards it,—take care; you know not what you do, dipping your wooden oar into this enchanted liquid, painted with all reds & purples & yellows which glows under & behind you. Presently this glory faded & the stars came & said "Here we are," & began to cast such private & ineffable beams as to stop all conversation. (June 6, 1841; Emerson 1969, p. 454)

But this sympathy did not characterize their later relationship; and Thoreau soon grew increasingly independent. A telling discussion recorded by Emerson's wife, Lidian, illustrates how far Thoreau—already in February 1843—had fallen outside Emerson's circle:

Mr Lane decided . . . that this same love of nature—of which Henry was the champion . . . was the most subtle and dangerous of sins; a refined idolatry, much more to be dreaded than gross wickedness, because the gross sinner would be alarmed by the depth of his degradation, . . . but the unhappy idolators of Nature were deceived by the refined quality of their sin, and would be the last to enter the kingdom. Henry frankly affirmed to both the wise men that they were wholly deficient in the faculty in question, and therefore could not judge of it. And Mr. Alcott as frankly answered that it was because they went beyond the mere material objects, and were filled with spiritual love and perception (as Mr. T was not), that they seemed to Mr. Thoreau not to appreciate outward nature. (Letter to Emerson; Thoreau, *Correspondence*, 1958, pp. 91–92)

And Thoreau was hardly shy in voicing his disdain for parlor-bound Transcendentalists, as he wrote in *A Week*.

Very few men can speak of Nature . . . with any truth. They overstep her modesty, somehow or other, and confer no favor. They do not speak a good word for her . . . The surliness with which the wood-chopper speaks of his woods, handling them as indifferently as his axe, is better than the mealy-mouthed enthusiasm of the lover of nature. Better that the primrose by the river's brim be a yellow primrose, and nothing more, than that it be something less. (1980a, pp. 108–9)

The Journal was more caustic: "Better that the primrose by the river's brim be a yellow primrose and nothing more, than the victim of his bouquet or his herbarium—to shine with the flickering dull light of his imagination, and not the golden gleam of a star" (March 13, 1841, *Journal* 1, 1981, p. 287). According to Thoreau, without immersing in the particular, in the immediate experience of the sensuous, one could hardly expect to reach the "ideal." Truth was to be found in the actual process of *seeing*, it would be discovered in the particular, for the particular's own sake. Thus to turn the primrose into a symbol of something higher was actually to reduce its value: this is a key divergence in Thoreau's and Emerson's respective philosophies.[25]

But there was a second dimension to Thoreau's criticism, one derived from what he must have regarded as a naive and narrow view of nature, which spoke even more persuasively to the distorted posture of Emersonian Transcendentalism. Like Emerson's "pastoral" vision of nature, Thoreau's vision allowed for intimate intercourse. After all, Thoreau's so-called immersion took place in the placid confines of a subdued, harnessed, rural setting, which allowed the free interplay of a cultivated man in his "wild garden." But Thoreau was jolted out of this complacent posture on an excursion to Maine's Mount Ktaadn in September 1846. As we saw in the preceding chapter, the Ktaadn experience forced Thoreau to recognize that nature was not always benevolent. In contrast to the pastoral setting, nature-in-the-raw has an independent integrity (absent from most of his nature writing) which disallowed Thoreau free and easy access or projection of humane value. The Transcendental project thus could be brought up short by not scrupulously picking one's object. So while Thoreau characteristically engaged in a close interplay between himself as observer and his object of scrutiny, the stunning experience on Mount Ktaadn forced him to recognize that nature might not always comply with our sympathetic demands and thus might deny service as a congenial "canvass to our imaginations" (*A Week*, 1980a, p. 292). This experience thus had profound metaphysical meaning for him, and epistemological significance as well.

The standing of facts, their grounding in the world, and their relation to the knower remained a quandary for Thoreau and stimulated much of his self-reflection regarding his own relation to nature. Indeed, we might regard Thoreau's facts as the counterpositions to Emerson's Ideas. No matter what "facts" Thoreau presents, he regarded them as material to be arrayed for another mission, namely to construct a portrait of reality, in the process enunciating a metaphysics of the self. As discussed most extensively in chapter 5, facts became the vehicle by which a knowing self might mediate the world, and thus they would served as the linchpin of Thoreau's deepest epistemological contemplations. This was an understanding that matured during his young adulthood. In an early Journal entry Thoreau wrote: "How indispensable to a correct study of nature is a perception of her true meaning– The fact will one day flower out into a truth" (December 16, 1837, *Journal* 1, 1981, p. 19), that is, a symbolic interpretation. But within six years a critical shift had occurred. As he wrote in his first important article, "Natural History of Massachusetts" (*The Dial*, July 1842 [1980c]), "Let us not underrate the value of a fact; it will one day flower in a truth" (1980c, p. 28). The fact, not some postponed "true meaning," is now Truth's flower: accurate observation and appreciation thereof. Emerson relied on finding Correspondence through idealist contemplation; Thoreau used careful observation "and left the spiritual laws to fend for themselves" (Porte 1966, p. 118). He would discard the "din of religion, literature, and philosophy" for "brave" science, by which he meant direct perception of nature and the appreciation of her beauty ("Natural History," 1980c, p. 4). By lifting his eyelids and opening his ears, Thoreau would engage nature directly not for any symbolic venture, but for her own sake. "The true man of science will know nature better by his finer organization; he will smell, taste, see, hear, feel, better than other men. His will be a deeper and finer experience" (ibid., p. 29).

So, a new identity issue arises. On the one hand, Thoreau recognizes that he is not a scientist (detailed in the next chapter); yet on the other hand, he rejects the Transcendentalists' moralizing of nature. He was never comfortable in any camp. Although identifying with the Transcendentalists, Thoreau was careful to eschew too close an affinity with Emerson's circle.[26] From an early age (well before the Walden experiment), he had little patience for the moralisms supposedly derived from studying nature, as he attests in his Journal of 1841:

> In reading a work on agriculture I skip the author's moral reflections, and the words "Providence" and "He" scattered along the page, to come at the profitable level of what he has to say. There is no science in men's religion–it does not teach me so much as the report of the committee on Swine. My author shows he has dealt in corn and turnips–and can worship God with the hoe and spade–but spare me his morality. (April 1, 1841, *Journal* 1, 1981, p. 295)

Thoreau went public in *A Week*:

> What he calls his religion is for the most part offensive to the nostrils[.] He should know better than expose himself, and keep his foul sores covered till they are quite healed. There is more religion in men's science than there is science in their religion. (1980a, p. 78)

And he was no less harsh on himself in this regard:

> What offends me most in my compositions is the moral element in them[.] The repentant say never a brave word–their resolves should be mumbled in silence. Strictly speaking morality is not healthy. Those undeserved joys, which come uncalled, and make us more pleased than grateful, are they that sing. (January 8, 1842, *Journal 1*, 1981, p. 361)

In other words, nature would address him directly, and abstract, referential musings are inauthentic as well as ultimately spiritually unhealthy as they distort or interfere with direct experience. To see nature is to move in a realm beyond ordinary human categories of good and evil.

> The best thought is not only without sombreness–but even without morality. The universe lies outspread in floods of white light to it. The moral aspect of nature is a disease caught of man–a jaundice imported into her– To the innocent there are no cherubims nor angels. Occasionally we rise above the necessity of virtue into an unchangeable morning light– . . . to live right on and breathe the circumambient air.
>
> There is no name for this life unless it be the very vitality of *vita*–Silent is the preacher about it–and silent must ever be. for he who knows it will not preach. (August 1, 1841, *Journal 1*, 1981, p. 315)

In short, Emerson's cosmic vision of moral law, and the Transcendental Correspondence which must support it, have been upstaged. Thoreau rejects moralizing about nature, since in his view, one should not, indeed cannot, speak of the deepest recesses of what we might perceive as nature's spirituality. This is not to say that Thoreau's relationship with nature is "amoral," only that to commune with nature has an "untranslated," indeed untranslatable, moral standing.

The relationship of Emerson and Thoreau is obviously complex (e.g., Paul 1958; Porte 1966; Richardson 1985), and I will not further delve into it here, except to note that a key separation, evinced by Thoreau's scientific interests and frankly greater "immersion" in nature, suggests that, far more than Emerson, Thoreau was interested in defining nature's structure, both spiritual and material, for its own sake as opposed to discerning how nature might subserve humanity (Buell 1995, p. 116). Emerson's judgment that "Nature . . . is made to serve" and that it "receives the dominion of man as meekly as the ass on which the Saviour rode" (Emerson 1983a, p. 28) can hardly be more anti-Thoreauvian in sentiment. Thoreau was, of course, to make his own translation of the basic Emersonian precepts concerning how he might understand nature's coherent system of signs and her Transcendental meanings, but this radically opposed orientation in regard to man's integration versus domination of nature may be the key to their eventual separation.[27]

Thoreau, of course, did contemplate nature and drew ethical inferences, but this kind of referencing was only one faculty of the complex exchange between observer and his object of study. It was not the goal of his project in the same way it was Emerson's. And more, Emerson would hardly have recognized Thoreau as advocating a formal ethical or religious agenda: "The Wisest man preaches no doctrines; he has no scheme; he sees no rafter, not even a cobweb, against the heavens. It is clear sky" (*A Week*, 1980a, p. 70). But indeed, Thoreau was erecting a moral agenda for himself, and his community:

> Men nowhere, east or west, live yet a *natural* life, round which the vine clings, and which the elm willingly shadows. Men would desecrate it by his touch, and so the beauty of the world remains veiled to him. He needs not only to be spiritualized, but *naturalized,* on the soil of earth. (*A Week*, 1980a, p. 379)

"Correspondence attempts to divert our attention beyond the visible reality; Thoreau was determined to stick with the thing-in-itself" (Porte 1966, p. 122). His engagement of nature—pantheistic and direct, sensuous and immediate—forthrightly rejected Emersonian Idealism and helped create a new way of relating to nature, one that has had a more lasting appeal.[28]

All these differences being cited, still, Thoreau's commitment to empiricism did not obviate his search for meaning. So, while Emersonian Idealism was radically transfigured by Thoreau's project, we must not lose sight that in his nature writing, Thoreau, like Emerson, was committed to seeking the same basic Romantic metaphysical truths: evidence for nature's unity and beauty; man's harmonious placement therein; clues as to the moral structure of the universe by which man might be ethically informed and guided. Their underlying vision of nature and man's relation to her were divergent, and their modes of knowing were separated by a great divide. Yet, while Thoreau practiced a more complex epistemology, one in which he sought natural facts, oftentimes in the guise of science, he still lived in Emerson's metaphysical neighborhood and therefore called himself a Transcendentalist. Thoreau's nature study, as empirical and "immersed" as it might be, was still characteristically Romantic—personalized and placed within a poetic vision: "We do not learn by inference and deduction and the application of mathematics to philosophy, but by direct intercourse and sympathy" ("Natural History," 1980c, p. 29). This personalized faculty, the poetic and spiritual modes of knowing, were thus integral to his project; and thus Thoreau's vision of himself, the very metaphysics of the self, underlies each and all of the epistemological matters we are addressing. This will serve as a key theme in the chapters to follow. But here we must note that Thoreau's own regard of nature is not so easily schematized and that we risk falsely characterizing his project by maintaining a singular point of view.

I draw these caveats not so much to blur the differences Thoreau exhibited with Emerson as to reemphasize Thoreau's Romantic character. I do so to keep in mind our own goal of discerning the structure of Thoreau's notion of his own personhood, the foundation by which we might better understand the distinctive quality of his project. Perhaps the philosophical differences that developed between Thoreau and other Transcendentalists over Correspondence is the key point upon which Thoreau would create his unique approach to the study of nature. But this is only one of the multiple issues that were at play in Thoreau's creation of his own worlding. So while it is interesting to cite Thoreau's rebuttal of Emersonian Transcendentalism, or to demonstrate his use of Humboldtian empiricism, or to show his employ of Coleridgean notions of individuation and polarity, or to trace his Goethian self-consciousness in the pursuit of the universal, Thoreau's endeavors cannot be readily placed in, or compete with, one schema or another. His was a complex calculus of thought and feeling, one that swung between established styles of discovery and exposition, and new ones that would be made uniquely his own. The question remains, after we dissect the intellectual forces being exercised in Thoreau's creative self-discovery— the one which is at the heart of my own inquiry—What was the relation of the observer to the object of study? And more specifically, How was (subject/object) "synthesis" achieved? What indeed did such a "synthesis" depend upon? Thoreau's distinction must be sought in understanding the responses (not answers!) he offered, and to do so we must place him struggling against the onrushing currents of positivism. To press further, let us unpack the amalgam of "science" and "sympathy" Thoreau attempted and determine how he dealt with the ascendancy of a radical separation of the knowing agent from nature, which not only objectified nature but isolated the self. To do so, we must first present a portrait of science during his era.

4   Thoreau at the Crossroads

Bought a telescope to-day for eight dollars. Best military spyglass with six slides, which shuts up to about the same size, fifteen dollars and very powerful.

> Thoreau, March 13, 1854,
> *Journal*, [1906] 1962, 6:166

Counted over forty robins with my glass in the meadow north of Sleepy Hollow, in the grass and on the snow.

> Thoreau, March 14, 1854,
> *Journal*, [1906] 1962, 6:167–68

Thoreau's movements into and out of science are delicately balanced. While we cannot simply dismiss him altogether from the ranks of mid-nineteenth-century scientists, neither can we place him within that community. Scholars have debated the scientific character of his work in great detail. Contemporary discussion is in large measure framed by, and often in reaction to, Nina Baym's assessment (1965) that Thoreau grew increasingly alienated both from science and from the scientific character of his own work the more he recognized that Transcendentalism, and by extension his own project, were out of line with the science of his period (Rossi 1993). So too earlier critics who, in placing Thoreau among the Transcendentalists—an admission he himself readily made (March 5, 1853, *Journal* 5, 1997, pp. 469–70; discussed in chapter 3)—thereby excluded him from "science." However, subsequent commentators (Howarth 1982; Angelo 1983; Hildebidle 1983; Richardson 1986; Sattelmeyer 1988; Rossi 1993; Walls 1995; McGregor 1997) have countered that this conclusion does not adequately address Thoreau's complex epistemological persona. On this latter view, Thoreau was well aware of the scientific advances of his day and employed scientific method in his own way. Indeed, some would endeavor to place him more firmly within the boundaries of science proper and have construed him as a hybrid figure in whom "scientist" figures prominently.

Some of Thoreau's nature study was indeed respectably scientific, characterized by scrupulous objective data-gathering guided, to varying degrees, by theory. His specimen collecting and classifying certainly qualified as "scientific," and as he matured, his projects became more ambitious and comprehensive. For example, his study of the dispersion of seeds he undertook as an attempt to show that the generation of plants was dependent on seeds alone, and that the variety of mechanisms available for propagation required scrupulous examination of plant patterns, weather conditions, topographical opportunities, and potential animal and insect carriers, to name just some of the factors he considered (Thoreau 1993). Indeed, it has been asserted that this project was different in character from his other efforts inasmuch as it was informed and directed by an underlying hypothesis (Richardson 1993). But as William Rossi notes (1993), Thoreau's allegiance to Transcendentalism, albeit in his own formulation, remained a steadfast commitment even after this so-called mature scientific project had focused much of his interest.[1]

At the very least, Thoreau regarded science throughout his life with strong ambivalence, and his various studies of nature were highly varied and only loosely structured. More to the point, Thoreau self-consciously pursued a course that he readily appreciated was different from the science of his time. Indeed, he expressly sought a different mode of knowing, one which recast an older scientific tradition into a new personalized form, the genre of nature writing. To get there, Thoreau had to find his place relative to the science of his era, maintaining a safe distance from its objectification of nature, yet at the same time employing "facts" to create an aestheticized vision of nature that confirmed his vision of her splendorous reality. In short, Thoreau, characteristically out of step with his peers, eyed with mistrust the rising tide of positivism which began to sweep the scientific community of the 1840s and 1850s, because it would obstruct his own vision of what a description of nature must and should achieve. What was he reacting to?

THE POSITIVIST CHALLENGE TO ROMANTIC SCIENCE

There is no such thing as pure *objective* observation. Your observation, to be interesting, *i.e.* to be significant, must be *subjective*. The sum of what the writer of whatever class has to report is simply some human experience, whether he be poet or philosopher or man of science.

> Thoreau, May 5, 1854,
> *Journal*, [1906] 1962, 6:236–37

Objectivity cannot be understood in isolation from the notions of subjectivity with which it is aligned. Lorraine Daston has made this coupling her seminal trope when tracing the historical development of the idea of "objectivity." She has persuasively argued that

[o]bjectivity is a fundamentally negative notion: it is defined by what it is not, by the subjectivity it opposes, as impress is defined by seal. And as shades of subjectivity differ, so do the shades of objectivity they stamp. (2000)

In her schema, originally coauthored with Peter Galison (Daston and Galison 1992), two forms of objectivity address different challenges of subjective experience. So-called "mechanical objectivity" counters the subjectivity of projection onto nature, which includes such elements as scientific judgment and aesthetic idealization. Mechanical objectivity relies on self-registering instruments and photographs to replace human observers as much as possible. "Communitarian objectivity" seeks to minimize idiosyncratic observation with standardized methods and instruments organized into large observational systems. Each of these forms of objectivity was formulated to address different epistemological concerns: the mechanical, to minimize individual human distortion of phenomena; the communitarian, to capture phenomena that individual observers might miss. The salient point for our discussion is that both forms of objectivity, despite their genesis in the early modern period, fully emerged as mature philosophical attitudes in the middle decades of the nineteenth century. Paying scant attention to this pre-nineteenth-century history and disregarding the revolutionary practical and theoretical results of this recast scientific philosophy, we will focus upon how Thoreau responded to the revised agenda of a scientific objectivity that "sought not to erase the self but rather cultivate self-consciousness" (Daston 2000).

The Romantics interested in science fell on a complex subjective continuum. Some were highly contemplative and idealist in orientation, like Coleridge and Emerson; others, like Goethe and Humboldt, were committed to the careful empirical investigation of nature. For our purposes here, the striking character of both of these Romantic genres of speculation is their assertion of the self-consciousness of the observer in his study of nature, and the active role they assign to imagination and aesthetic sensitivity toward the goal of discovering (or, perhaps, reaffirming) a cosmic unity. Whatever separates Thoreau, Goethe, Humboldt, Coleridge, and Emerson in the particulars of their scientific practice and philosophical outlooks, their shared notions of creative intuition pervade their respective epistemologies. By the 1840s, however, this active faculty of the investigator became increasingly eclipsed by an altogether different, "positivist" standard of observation.

"Positivism" carries several meanings and has been notoriously difficult to define. A philosophical position articulated by August Comte shortly before the deaths of Goethe (1832) and Coleridge (1834), it may be summarized as building on two precepts: 1) human thought and social life are continuous with the natural world and therefore susceptible to the same modes of investigation, and 2) knowledge may be regarded as falling into three grand stages where progression from a theological to a metaphysical stage culminates finally in a "positive" stage in which the world is explained in terms of scientific truth (Simon 1963, p. 4). This particular philosophy had limited success and applicability (ibid.), but if we regard Comte as only contributing another chapter to positivism's history, then a more broadly applicable concept emerges. Positivism sought a collection of rules and evaluative criteria by which to distinguish true knowledge from what Wittgenstein famously called "nonsense." Thus positivism is a normative attitude which would regulate how we use such terms as "knowledge," "science," "cognition," and "information" (Kolakowski 1968). As developed in the 1850s, positivism came to be understood as a normative philosophical belief which held that the methods of natural science offer the only viable way of thinking correctly about human affairs. Accordingly, empirical experience served as the basis of all knowledge. Facts, the products of sensory experience, were first ascertained and then classified. "Hypothesis" was defined as the expectation of observing facts of a certain kind under certain conditions; and a scientific "law" could be defined as the proposition that under conditions of a certain kind, facts of a certain kind were uniformly observable. Any "hypothesis" or "law" that could not be defined in terms like these would be written off as "pseudo-hypothesis" or "pseudo-law" (Collingwood 1940, p. 144)—the ultimate fate of, by these lights, theology and metaphysics ("pseudo-knowledge").[2]

While we may date the birth of modern social sciences to Comte's program, positivism has a complex history that may be traced from the Greeks to Francis Bacon and most directly to the seventeenth-century scientific revolution and the British empiricists, especially David Hume (Kolakowski 1968; Simon 1963, 1973). It contrasted sharply with the Romantic view of the world, by denying any cognitive value to value judgments. Experience, positivism maintained, contains no such qualities of men or events as "noble," "good," "evil," or "beautiful." In radical reaction against Romanticism's pursuit of aesthetic totalization, positivists sought instead to objectify nature, banishing human prejudice from scientific judgment. The total separation of observer from the object of observation—an epistemological ideal—reinforced the positivist disallowance of "value" as part of the process of observation. One might interpret, but such evaluative judgments had no scientific (i.e., objective) standing. Simply put, where the Romantics privileged human interpretation (exemplified by the artistic imagination), the positivists championed mechanical objectivity (e.g., thermometer, voltmeter, chemical analysis). This polarization, however, must be balanced with those elements of scientific investigation shared by both approaches. Specifically, we must distinguish the *aims* of science in contrast to its *methods*.

While positivism argued for a radical shift in investigative methods, its basic goals remained similar to those of its Romantic forebears. The deepest commitment of science has always been its search for "understanding" (the discernment of a rational pattern in natural events), its attempt to define "reality," and its pursuit of predictive power. These aims—and we might list others—have a distinctive scientific character because of the objective methods emerging in the nineteenth century. Despite how its methods contrast with Romantic subjectivity, positivism also pursued these metaphysical aims; indeed, its champions argued that their objectifying methods would lead to deeper understanding of reality than would a science compromised by subjectivity. Post-Romantic science did not necessarily repudiate aesthetic concerns, and indeed, key scientists and philosophers of science throughout the latter half of the nineteenth century explicitly attempted to integrate a Romantic sense of imagination and beauty as important factors in the appreciation of the scientific worldview. In other words, they saw no inconsistency in gleaning objective facts by a radical separation of subject and object, and then synthesizing and interpreting those data with the required human sensibility.[3] Therefore, while I am building on the common notions of opposition between Romanticism and positivism, an important caveat to this discussion is that implicit in the positivists' own program are two abiding concerns: 1) a search for a totalizing theory of nature and knowledge, and 2) a realization that the aesthetic had some role, albeit poorly understood or acknowledged, in that agenda. Thus the most obvious contrast between Romanticism and positivism lies in their respective notions of method, not in these fundamental goals, albeit the terms of characterization were strikingly different.

The radical separation of the observing/knowing subject and his object of scrutiny is the single most important characteristic of positivist epistemology. Because of this understanding, positivists claimed that science should rest on a foundation of neutral and dispassionate observation. The more careful the design of the experimental conditions, the more precise the characterization of phenomena, the more likely the diminution of subjective contaminants. Thus the strict positivist confined himself to phenomena and their ascertainable relationships through a vigorous mechanical objectivity. In the life sciences, for example, positivism exercised new standards in the study of physiology that applied the objective methodologies of chemistry and physics to organic processes. This approach allowed newly adopted laboratory techniques to establish physiology as a new discipline and gave birth to biochemistry, whose central tenets held that organic and inorganic chemistries shared the same fundamental principles, differing only insofar as the molecular constituents of living organisms were governed by complex constraints of metabolism. Demonstrating the oxidation of glucose, its synthesis in the liver, and the heat production of contracting muscle confirmed by mid-century the applicability of biochemical methods to the study of organic function and the unity of a science based on such methods of investigation (Fruton 1999, pp. 234 ff., 333 ff.). The powerful results obtained in physiology soon inspired new standards of study in natural history by documenting animal and plant life histories at a new level of detail and sophistication (Nyhart 1996).

Positivism's methodology was intimately linked to the assumption that all of nature was of one piece and that the study of life was potentially not different in kind from the study of chemical reactions, the movement of heavenly bodies, or the evolution of mountains. Thus, if all of nature was unified—constituted of the same elements and governed by the same fundamental laws—then the organic world was simply on a continuum with the inorganic. So, according to this set of beliefs, there was no essential difference between animate and inanimate physics and chemistry, and the organic world was therefore subject to the same kinds of study so successfully applied in physics. The new problem was both to reduce the organic to the inorganic, that is, to exhibit the continuity of substance and operation, and concomitantly to understand the distinct character of life processes. To accomplish this twofold agenda, positivism was soon coupled to another philosophy, reductionism. The reductionists did not argue that certain organic phenomena were not unique, only that all causes must have certain elements in common. They connected physics and biology by equating the ultimate basis of their respective explanations (Galaty 1974). Interestingly, the reductionists, like their Romantic opponents, were following Kant—not Kant of the *Third Critique*, who argued that the physical and organic worlds were fundamentally different in character, but the Kant they saw in the *Metaphysical Foundations of Natural Science* (1786) (ibid.).[4]

Reductionism, specifically physical reductionism, was a scientific program enunciated by German physiologists (led by Hermann Helmholtz) to eradicate vitalism from biology. The ostensible issue was the uniqueness of life and the basis of that distinctiveness, vitality. The notion that life possessed a special "life force" served as the focus of scientific debate, in both medicine and physiology, where it would play its key role, and also in the understanding of the history of organic life. Vitalism was at the nexus of debate because it belied the unity of nature offered by various sixteenth- and seventeenth-century mechanistic philosophies by imposing a duality to explain life. Vitalism assumed its modern garb as an escape from mechanistic speculation with George Stahl's *True Theory of Medicine* (1708), which argued for the complete separation of living beings from inorganic matter on the basis of an inbred "anima sensitiva" undetectable by physical means. Thus the early-eighteenth-century solution to Western mind-body dualism, namely that soul infused matter, revived the Greek concept of *pneuma*, which the ancient Stoics thought endowed all organic matter with life. It was also similar to the later Enlightenment solution which named activity and change (force and motion) rather than structure and permanence as nature's essential characteristics (Hankins 1985).

By 1740 the antimechanistic sentiment was at full tide, reaching its highest mark in 1802 when William Heberden declared, "[T]o living bodies belong many additional powers, the operations of which can never be accounted for by the laws of lifeless matter" (quoted by Schofield 1970, p. 191). Newton's atomism had been replaced by a nebulous dynamism: corpuscularity succumbed to vital force, vital energy, or simply "Life." However, in the process of imbuing the organic with a special and mysterious property, the holistic construct so crucial to Romantic science now became unnecessarily entangled with the confounding metaphysics of the vitalistic perspective. Indeed, Coleridge, by the beginning of the nineteenth century, urged chemists and biologists to consider the continuity between the animate and the inanimate in terms of shared forces, a complex and poorly articulated philosophy that implicitly invoked the unity of a vitalistic nature (Levere 1981).

These issues were largely resolved by three key developments: Helmholtz's demonstration (1847) that heat generated by contracting muscle could be accounted for by chemical metabolism (i.e., no special vitalistic force was necessary); Louis Pasteur's demonstration about a decade later that bacteria could not arise through spontaneous (i.e., vitalistic) generation; and finally Darwin's publication of *On the Origin of Species* (1859), which presented the case for a blind materialism to explain the evolution of species. The appeal of vitalism was not totally extinguished by mid-century, but certainly a new scientific ethos had taken over the life sciences by then. This battle over vitalism, and the character of the organic world more generally, may be regarded as an aspect of the quest for a single unity of nature. Thus in at least one sense, the Romantic notion of vitalistic nature was overturned, but on the other hand, the more important precept of nature's unity was reconfirmed, and adamantly so.[5] No wonder Thoreau could embrace Darwinism with such enthusiasm and regard the unity of nature as the paramount character of this new theory. Indeed, as Laura Walls has argued (1995), this overriding preoccupation with finding the integrated wholeness of nature profoundly guided Thoreau's nature studies, stretching from his careful "scientific" observations to his more contemplative reflections built on those studies. But it would be artificial to separate this concern from a third metaphysical component of the Romantic view of nature that undergirds the others, namely idealism.

Idealism takes several forms in this context: To look at nature as a source of beauty is an aesthetic idealism, which for Thoreau served as a "tonic" (*Walden*, 1971, p. 317) and spiritual delight. On this view, nature has its own divinity, and Thoreau would seek its expression in the beauty of animal and plant life, in the expanse of the landscape, and in the endless variety of the climate and the heavens. There was no end to the aesthetic rapture he found in his various sojourns, where he sought direct intercourse with nature and sympathy with it. This matter we consider in the next section. A second form of idealism is moral in character, the Romantic projection of human value onto nature initiated by Rousseau, who celebrated the primitive as the most "natural" and thus most virtuous man. Thoreau too made a central tenet the correspondence of spiritual order and unity as the natural paragon for human virtue. In many places this correspondence is explicitly articulated—for instance, "The universe constantly and obediently answers to our conceptions" (*Walden*, 1971, p. 97) or "What I have observed of the pond is no less true in ethics" (ibid., p. 291). We will return to this idea in later chapters. Here I wish to focus on a third kind of idealism, one most germane to this discussion, namely, the idealist epistemology of the Romantics.

Thoreau might well have taken heed of Goethe's response to Schiller's penetrating remark regarding the *Urpflanze* (the Primal Plant): "This is not an experience: it is an idea" (Goethe [1794] 1988). As such, it was poor science. Indeed, the center of positivism's assault on Romantic science was idealism. Goethe had understood the persistent conflict inherent in his own scientific efforts:

> In the idea, then, simultaneous elements are closely bound up with sequential ones, but our experience always shows them to be separate: we are seemingly plunged into madness by a natural process which must be conceived of in idea as both simultaneous and sequential. Our intellect cannot think of something as united when the senses present

it as separate, and thus the conflict between what is grasped as experience and what is formed as idea remains forever unresolved. (Goethe
[1818] 1988)

The archetype ("formed as idea") was not an empirical object. While the
universal, the essence, the idea is particularized by a given object and thus
perceived through the senses, the organizing idea defines and establishes
that object's cognitive standing. Despite his strong empirical tendencies,
Goethe clearly understood this idealist epistemology:

> my thinking is not separate from objects; . . . the elements of the object,
> the perceptions of the object, flow into my thinking and are fully per-
> meated by it; . . . my perception itself is a thinking, and my thinking a
> perception. (Goethe [1823] 1988, p. 39)

Thus Goethe accepted the intermingling of perceiving subject, the scientific
agent, and the object perceived, which could not stand alone. Only by allowing the subject's full integration into nature, which in turn depended on a
correspondence between man and nature, could such an epistemological perspective be supported. Mastery of the whole is precisely that: a whole must
include subject and object.[6] Goethe embraced that fusion.

But this orientation was soon replaced by a new objectivism, one that
spawned positivism's attempt to radically separate the observing subject
from the object of scrutiny. By the mid-nineteenth century, under the sway
of positivism, the ideal of objectivity had rendered the ideal scientist, too,
invisible, absorbed by his instrument or machine (Keller 1996, 1997). In the
most simplified version of this scientific romance, the scientist had become
a simple reporter of universalized data, erased as a subjective factor. The
ostensible goal of a completely detached observer, one independent of subjective foibles and prejudices, whose conclusions come from "somewhere
else," in principle offered a "view from nowhere" (Nagel 1986).[7] Complementary to this mechanical objectivity, communitarian objectivity set criteria for standardized observation: ultimately it subsumes the individual
observer in a larger scientific community. This communal scientific ideal
may also be traced back to the late seventeenth century when, focusing on
experimental procedures, Robert Boyle successfully promoted a shared
research program which generated a "multiplication of the witnessing experience" through public demonstrations and the adoption of a rhetoric that
emphasized the public character of observed phenomena (Shapin and Schaf-
fer 1985, p. 488). For objectivity to assume its current meaning of being
"aperspectival," extensive rhetorical and methodological refinements were
developed by the positivists, who finally merged the mechanical and com-

munitarian precepts so that a singular subjective observation was effectively co-witnessed and translated into a shared public objectivity through a machine's results. Biology lagged well behind the physical sciences in this regard, but as Thoreau sat at Walden Pond, positivist ideals were already well established for the life sciences, placing his natural history pursuits outside the professional practices of the day.

THE "SANCTITY OF FACTS"

Facts collected by a poet are set down at last as winged seeds of truth–samarae–tinged with his expectation. O may my words be verdurous & sempiternal as the hills. Facts fall from the poetic observer as ripe seeds.

> Thoreau, June 19, 1852,
> *Journal 5*, 1997, p. 112

To see Thoreau either as aspiring to some "objective" epistemology or as wishing to dissolve his self in nature is to put him at the extreme poles of mid-nineteenth-century nature study. This misconstrues him. To be sure, he was both a mystic and a careful observer of nature, practicing one mode and then the other, but there is a weighted center to his project that combines these elements, as well as others. I suggest rather that Thoreau practiced an array of approaches to studying nature, Romantic in inception, but moving toward some synthesis with the ascendant scientism of the age. Thoreau's notions of "facts" served a complex epistemological role as he fashioned them in order to construct his personalized view of nature. The significance, and meaning, of this personal vision directs my inquiry, for it is finally this juncture between self and world that underlies Thoreau's thought. In this respect, the questions he posed regarding the nature of facts, their construction and function, truly are fundamental to our understanding his study of nature.

Thoreau understood the epistemological challenges he faced from a rapidly changing scientific culture. Nevertheless his recorded insights into the issues positivism raised were hardly sophisticated; and, indeed, he embraced the Romantic position without apology or philosophical justification. For example, in a 1858 Journal entry, he laments the illusionary character of human relationships and concludes that only an ideal image of a friend is sustaining. Then he turns to the epistemological standing of nature, presumably, at least in a conventional sense, amenable to a more objective and stable relationship:

> I am not so ready to perceive the illusion that is in Nature. I certainly come nearer, to say the least, to an actual and joyful intercourse with

her. Every day I have more or less communion with her, *as I think*. At least, I do not feel as if I must withdraw out of nature [as with society]. I feel like a welcome guest. Yet, strictly speaking, the same must be true of nature and of man; our ideal is the only real. It is not the finite and temporal that satisfies or concerns us in either case. (November 3, 1858, *Journal*, [1906] 1962, 11:282; emphasis in original)

Two cardinal points should be emphasized in this passage. The first refers back to our discussion of Cameron's version of Thoreau's writing of nature, where the subject-object dichotomy is blurred. Here, late in his maturity, Thoreau explicitly accepts that he communes with nature *as he thinks it*, as he thinks *of* nature. In this sense he distances himself from Goethe's self-conscious mingling of the observer and the observed. This distancing is not to be confused with the *product* of that observation—the communion *with* nature. These are two distinct categories of experience: one is epistemological (the relation of subject and object), and the other is metaphysical (the spiritual or mystical union of man with divine nature). The second point rests on the key theme of the passage: "our ideal is the only real." "Ideal" may be understood as "rarefied" or "exemplary," but I think it safe to expand Thoreau's meaning to "idea." The concrete now of the finite is not the only object of his inquiry. While immediate experience is the vehicle of his project, this would not gratify him, for he is always contemplating, pondering, seeking a metaphysical reality literally "beyond" the physical. This effort was integral to his moral life, one enacted deliberately and self-consciously.

Here we face squarely the solipsistic element of Thoreau's entire project. He knows the world ultimately in relationship to himself. He constantly inquires *about* the world, which he understands not solely by some "objective" standard or shared public knowledge, but to varying degrees in his own terms. Thoreau, the knowing subject, perceives in many modes, but ultimately he affirms that it is only what he as a self-generating, self-referential knower knows that "satisfies" him. To reiterate: Thoreau's epistemology was in full service to his ethical metaphysics,[8] wherein he as subject, the knowing self, was guided by the moral project of seeking meaning. But here we come to another key question: What then is Thoreau's epistemological currency? What is the status of "facts"?

Here, we again return to Goethe, who also wrestled with understanding experience, with the discovery and construction of facts, and with their relation to more comprehensive structures of knowledge. The first lesson Thoreau might have learned from Goethe was that "facts" do not reside independent of a theory or hypothesis which must "support" them, a point well developed in twentieth-century philosophy of science (e.g., Hanson 1958;

Suppe 1977). Goethe's precept that "everything factual is already theory" (Goethe, *Maximen und Reflexionen*, no. 575) was offered as a warning about the epistemological complexity of supposedly objective knowledge:

> We can never be too careful in our efforts to avoid drawing hasty con-
> clusions from experiments or using them directly as proof to bear out
> some theory. For here at this pass, the transition from empirical evi-
> dence to judgment, cognition to application, all the inner enemies of
> man lie in wait: imagination, which sweeps him away on its wings
> before he knows his feet have left the ground; impatience; haste; self-
> satisfaction; rigidity; formalistic thought; prejudice; ease; frivolity; fick-
> leness—this whole throng and its retinue. Here they lie in ambush and
> surprise not only the active observer but also the contemplative one
> who appears safe from all passion. (Goethe [1792] 1988)

It is fascinating to see Goethe, the poet, rein in the Imagination, but he understood the potential danger of subjective contamination of scientific observation and, more to the point, the tenuous grounds of any objective "fact" that relied in any way on interpretation. Interpretation stretches from inference to direct observation, for any perception must ultimately be pro-cessed to fit into a larger picture of nature and must cohere with previous experience.

The synthetic project of building a worldview thus begins by placing "facts" within their supporting theory, and continues with integrating that scientific picture with the broader and less obvious intellectual and cultural forces in which science itself is situated. Thus "facts" as independent prod-ucts of sensory experience are *always* processed—interpreted, placed into some overarching hypothesis or theory; and, indeed, natural facts are *his-torical*, that is, they are recorded, stored, interpreted, and used in a fashion analogous to the way that historians use historical facts (Collingwood 1940, p. 145). In short, observations assume their meanings within a particular context, for facts are not just products of sensation or measurement, as the positivists averred, but rather they reside within a conceptual framework which "places" the fact into an intelligible picture of the world. To varying degrees, this constructivist interpretation was denied by the positivists. A world built from their principles would appear essentially the same to all viewers, for "facts" for them have independent standing and universal acces-sibility, so that irrespective of individual knowers, facts constitute shared knowledge. The Romantics placed important caveats on that approach to nature, on both epistemological and metaphysical grounds. From their per-spective, each inviolate observer held a privileged vantage, and the vision so obtained was jealously protected.

Goethe's chastised view of objectivity built from epistemological apprehensions, and while Thoreau generally shared Goethe's skepticism, the Transcendentalist rejected positivism more because of the metaphysical limitations imposed by that doctrine. Simply stated, Thoreau gathered facts in the employ of his personal agenda. But in the end, Goethe and Thoreau, regardless of how we mix their respective epistemological and metaphysical concerns, seem to intimate postmodern science, because they understood that knowledge in all of its guises—facts, perceptions, conclusions—is caught in irreconcilable tensions between varying "degrees" of objectivity which must be finally posed in contrast to the irreducible subjectivity of the knower. Neither argued philosophically about these matters, but each was sensitive to the perspectival ways in which facts were produced and used.[9]

But this was an old problem. The conflict between the objectified world of scientific facts and the private domain of personalized experience of those facts dates from the very origins of science, which aspired to discover facts "out there" divorced from a subjective projection of the mind upon nature. Descartes initiated and Locke completed the philosophical stance of a newly defined science which, in separating mind and body, split the "I" and the "world." In this view, humans are subject to an irreducible duality: the mind, *res cogitans*, surveys the world, *res extensa*. This division, irreparable and absolute, framed epistemology for the next four centuries, and in the context of a positivist-inclined science, to study natural phenomena demanded a dissociated self: to see "objectively," disallowed projection of the self, a contamination of attaining neutral knowledge. But this dualism bequeathed the dilemma of rendering whole what was broken in the division between self and world. The Cartesian reductive method imparts an irresolvable anxiety: after dissecting the world into parts, how are those elements to be reintegrated? Cartesianism itself offers no solution. Further, the epistemological standing of the observer is ambiguous: how indeed does the observer *know?* The rationalists and the empiricists thrashed out this question for almost two centuries preceding Thoreau's birth, and while Kant offered the grandest synthesis in his transcendental formulation, the question was never put to rest.

The positivist movement was a response to this problem. If facts could be universalizable, the "private" mind could be "opened" to public discourse. Objectivity at its most basic calling is the attempt to solve the imbroglio of unifying minds which are not only separated from the world but also dangerously isolated from each other. So the Cartesian mind/world split resurfaces in the public and private scientific experience of "fact," specifically: Who "knows" facts? How are facts used? What do they mean? in a community of distinct knowers. Although the discovery—or, more precisely, the construction—of a fact is intimately linked to the observer, the dynamics of the fact can hardly be limited to the private domain of the observer's experience. Others have a claim to a fact, which is often shared in the narrow proprietary sense, but always as the expected outcome of the scientific process. A scientific fact is fundamentally public, for it must be universalized by the scientific community at large. A hidden fact is useless to that community; discourse demands scrutiny. Scientific objectivity focuses upon the discovery or creation of facts and the public debates surrounding them. Scientific facts acquire the status of public entities as they become objectified, circulated, and finally identified increasingly less with the subjective, private report of the scientist. Critical to the development of modern science was precisely this process by which shared experience was universalized among scientific practitioners. Within this domain, "objectivity" is attained.

Yet there remains a second, private sphere of the fact, which arises from the scientist's identity as an autonomous epistemological agent. The integrity of the scientist as a private, knowing agent remains an implicit and critical characteristic of scientific activity. To know the world remains a fundamental individual aspiration in the age of the self (Tauber 1994, pp. 141 ff.), and while we emphasize the social aspects of science as a cultural activity, the scientist remains that Cartesian agent who experiences the world independently.

Scientific knowledge thus has strong commitments to Cartesian dualism, especially to its concept of a universalized corpus of fact and theory, which arises as the product of individual experience. We are left with a complex dialectic between the observer's "personal" relations to those facts as the product of his autonomous personhood and the need for entering that experience into the public sector. It is on this point that the epistemological, political, and moral ideals of Thoreau's own views on science converge. He was less a modern Prometheus, intent on conquering nature in all of its richness, than a self-conscious Janus, who sought to resolve the split caused by peering into the public and private domains, simultaneously.

I have used "fact" as a discursive vehicle, because at first glance, a fact seems to represent something "out *there*." From the positivist orientation, this independence of the known "fact" rests on its correspondence to a reality which any objective observer might know. This assumes *both* 1) a universal perspective, "a view from nowhere,"[10] *and* 2) a correspondence theory of reality. But the subjective components cannot be entirely eliminated, and as stubborn as the positivists might have been in attempting to stamp out subjective influences, they only succeeded in making them seem disreputable (Daston 2000). There is no escape from the constraints of an observer fixed by his individual perspective, contextualized in some observational setting, and committed to processing information through some interpretative (i.e., subjective) schema. Such an observer cannot adhere to a rigid identification of "facts" based on an idealized separation of the knower and the known. This seemingly postmodernist point was appreciated by Goethe, who recognized the complex tension between the detached observer, supposedly divorced from theory, and the creative scientist. From his point of view, the ideal or theoretical distillation of nature ultimately required personal and aesthetic faculties. Thoreau followed Goethe in seeking to encompass the widest scope of experience and to integrate it, *personally*.

This brings us squarely back to the subject/object divide imposed by positivism. If "scientist" increasingly came to be defined as one who adhered to a distanced, dispassionate regard of nature, then we see how out of step Thoreau found himself. He resisted the label of "scientist" or any variant of that designation, and for us to make him into a hybrid, a "poet-scientist," is to impose upon him our own divided sensibility of a two-culture world. Whereas Goethe and Thoreau regarded a unified nature with a unified mind and sensibility, our current fragmented world sees the poet and the scientist as necessarily viewing the same object in differently refracted experiences. But to the Romantic, experience is ultimately integrated by an arbitrating, aesthetically sensitive observer who is intimately connected to nature through all his faculties. Again and again we see Thoreau resisting an imperialistic vision of the world that would constrict his unique appreciation and understanding of nature. He did not so much reject science's contributions to knowing the world as its insidious power to stigmatize his own subjective processing of that world.[11]

PHILOSOPHICAL SUPPORT

Thoreau was at least vaguely aware of the outlines of this philosophical discussion, and during the 1840s and 1850s the Anglo-American intellectual community fully debated scientific method as well as the logical process of scientific discovery. Fundamental questions were posed most famously by three English critics: William Whewell (1794–1866), John Stuart Mill (1806–1873), and John Heschel (1792–1871). Whewell's philosophy of science is most relevant to Thoreau's own project inasmuch as each man sought to balance empiricism with Imagination. In *The Philosophy of the Induc-*

tive Sciences (1840), Whewell sought a middle ground between the strong English "sensationalist" school (having grown from the British empiricist tradition) and science based on the a priori of German idealists (Fisch 1991). Whewell appreciated that even the most commonplace perception must go beyond mere sensation and be ordered by the mind, and from this position he argued that science, and all true knowledge, was intellectually governed by what he termed "antitheticals"—composites of sensation/conception, things/ideas, fact/theory. These "mutually irreducible . . . [and] inseparable empirical and conceptual components" (Fisch 1998) left Kant's notion of the noumena intact, yet served a useful function in dissecting the process of scientific discovery. For Whewell, Baconian inductionism was naive, and in its place he saw the Imagination, very close to the Lake Poets' vision, as reading meaning, structure, regularity, and law into the facts, rather than gleaning such information from the empirical data alone. Facts were thus "colligated" by a superimposition of the mental concept over the empirical data (ibid.). Creative genius was required to bring the confusion of disparate inductive results into some sort of structural unity and significance. Moreover, science, according to Whewell, was closely aligned to natural theology, for scientific imagination in league with a cosmic Imagination would be able to reveal God's mind and purposes.

This was hardly inductionism in the traditional sense, and Whewell's proposals initiated vigorous debate over the nature of scientific discovery and verification (Yeo 1985; 1993; Smith 1994). As we will see, later postpositivist interpretations of science's mode of discovery and theory formation also have focused upon the intuitive, tacit, and aesthetic character of insight required for synthesis and the role of deductive reasoning at play with investigative induction—insights not so alien from Whewell's position. But in the mid-nineteenth century, Whewell's idealist philosophy strongly clashed with the growing positivist ethos concerning the objective status of scientific laws. Critics were dismayed at the prospects of a renewal of a speculative neo-*Naturphilosophie*. The argument was decided not in philosophical debate but in the laboratory. The practices and methodologies of the laboratory scientists were best described by other philosophies of science, both more strictly inductive in character and pragmatic in approach, and because of the congruence with actual practice these anti-Whewellian philosophies became more influential.[12] Thoreau might have been not only aware of these discussions but sympathetically drawn to Whewell's position (Rossi 1993). To be sure, Whewell's efforts to place a Romantic orientation within an increasingly objectified science resonate with Thoreau's own parallel attempts to personalize his experience of nature, but their respective projects at best were analogous, never identical. They were more like two trains heading for the same destination from different directions, at times traveling on parallel tracks and at other points diverging. Furthermore, each carried very different freight.

Thoreau, struggling with the same issues as Whewell, was driven into the active debate in other quarters of the intellectual establishment stimulated by the crisis of Romanticism's ebb and positivism's flow. The Romantic response to positivism assumed various forms, but all asserted the premier place of Imagination in the inquiry into nature. Thoreau pursued an agenda largely outside formal scientific and philosophical enterprises. His was the work of "poets," and philosophical debate, irrespective of the merits of its analytical sophistication and intellectual tradition, was not Thoreau's forum. Only by the most exercised inference might we place him more firmly within those formal discussions. Plainly stated, the issues pertinent to the analytical understanding of the nature of scientific knowledge did not concern him. Interested though he might have been in a general way, he formulated his own unique response to the contending issues quite apart from that discourse. So, while Thoreau was well acquainted with the controversy concerning the relationship of facts and theory, and although he read Sir David Brewster's attack on Baconian induction philosophy of science (*Life of Newton* [1831]) in 1856 (Thoreau, June 2, 1856, *Journal*, [1906] 1962, 8:362])—a critique aligned with Whewell's—it is not clear that Thoreau had intimate acquaintance with any of the arguments as *formally* presented. We might appreciate Thoreau and Whewell in alliance, even congruent from our perspective, but Thoreau himself is not readily placed in any philosophical orbit.

The segregation of discourses—scientific, philosophical, and literary—was just beginning in this period, so there still was a free exchange of ideas across disciplines during the 1840s and 1850s. (This same point will be amplified in my discussion of Thoreau's relationship to professional science below and in the next chapter.) The subject/object relationship, the nature of facts and their relationship to theory, and the metaphysical unity of the world were prominent issues "in the air," so to speak, and Thoreau's original and provocative contributions are self-evident (Peck 1990; Rossi 1993). But he never sustained a clear argument or exposition of a philosophical position, epistemological or otherwise, and offered, instead, scattered observations, aphorisms, asides of one kind or another. We have a sense of where he is going philosophically, and his message has philosophical import, but his discussion itself is not *philosophical. We* might analyze him philosophically, but that does not mean that he worked as a philosopher. And analogously, as we will see in the next chapter, while we might attempt to place

Thoreau's nature study in the context of science, that does not mean that he regarded his project as falling within a scientific agenda. He was too keenly aware of the restrictions of that worldview and too dedicated to his own, as he repeatedly asserted.

Committed to the aestheticization of experience, subordinating the objective study of nature to poetic enterprise, Thoreau regarded the relationship of the observer to the observed as a problem of poesis. The issue was not *subjectivity* in a prejudicial or solipsistic sense, but rather the transposition of experience from the objective parlance of science to a language of *meaning:*

> There is no such thing as pure *objective* observation. Your observation, to be interesting, *i.e.* to be significant, must be *subjective*. The sum of what the writer of whatever class has to report is simply some human experience, whether he be poet or philosopher or man of science. (May 5, 1854, *Journal*, [1906], 1962, 6:236–37)

And this was to be a celebration of life in its fullest deployment, a moral mandate:

> The man most of science is the man most alive, whose life is the greatest event. Senses that take cognizance of outward things merely are of no avail. It matters not how far you travel . . . but how much alive you are. (Ibid.)

Thoreau could not abide any categorization of himself as "scientist," which was, from his point of view, too restrictive. After all, he was pursuing a theory of life, not a theory of biology. As already noted, when invited to join the [American] Association for the Advancement of Science, Thoreau confided to his Journal a self-appraisal which put him in league with the Transcendentalists. Nine months later, when writing the Association's secretary, he declined membership by evoking his affinity with earlier naturalists, who belonged to a Romantic tradition that he undoubtedly felt was out of step with the current standards of scientific endeavor.[13] To this matter in particular, and the general standing of science in his day, we next turn.

THE ACADEMY

> According to Linnaeus's classification, I come under the head of the *Miscellaneous* Botanophilists.
>
> > Thoreau, February 17, 1852,
> > *Journal*, [1906] 1962, 4:309

Even by his contemporary standards, Thoreau cannot be counted among those who were becoming an increasingly professionalized group. Thoreau himself carefully eschewed formally affiliating with the scientific community, and to the extent that he had any interaction, it was in the role of amateur naturalist—in his day, to be sure, a serious commitment. In that capacity, he lectured, wrote various natural history essays, was enrolled by Louis Agassiz, the newly Harvard-appointed Swiss biologist, to collect specimens (beginning with turtles and fishes in the spring and summer of 1847), and was elected a corresponding member of the Boston Society of Natural History in December 1850. He joined that society largely for the same reason he had petitioned Harvard College in September 1849, namely, to have library privileges. (Thoreau declined to join the Association for the Advancement of Science at least partly because there was no such ostensible reason to justify his affiliation.) Founded in 1830, the Boston Society published both a *Proceedings* and a *Journal,* both of which were highly valued in European and American libraries.

For Thoreau, the most important appeal of these societies was not this venue for publication so much as the access to the libraries of Boston and Cambridge they provided. By 1850 these libraries were premier in scholarly resources (Bruce 1987, p. 39). Boston in particular, and Massachusetts in general, led the nation in total volumes; more significantly in this context, they excelled in the categories of collegiate and learned-society libraries. This statistic indicates the character of the Boston intellectual community. In the spring of 1846 the geologist Josiah Whitney called Boston "the only city in America where anything of any account is done for science" (cited by Bruce 1987, p. 32). A hyperbolic statement, perhaps, but based on an assessment of the actual distribution of major scientists and the institutions supporting them. Through the last quarter of the nineteenth century, a disproportionate number of those educated in the Boston constellation would emerge as the leaders of the larger scientific community. Despite being half the size of Philadelphia and a third of New York's population, by 1846, when Thoreau was living at Walden Pond, Boston had taken the lead in American science by possessing the deepest infrastructure to support scientific inquiry. As Robert Bruce has documented (1987, pp. 29 ff.), the factors that came into play for Boston to assume this role indicate deep historical and cultural roots, the most important being a strong educational tradition in Puritan New England and the support offered by Boston's social and commercial elite who, in underwriting institutions of learning, expressed an ideal of stewardship and *noblesse oblige.* Combined with a strong Yankee competitive work ethic and a cultural ideal that opportune circumstances might be translated into material gain, the key institutions supporting science—societies, libraries, colleges—were richly endowed.

Such resources promoted the professionalization of scientists. By 1846, two out of every three scientists confined themselves to a single major field, and specialization was even more practiced than this statistic indicates. The third of the scientists who apparently worked in several disciplines were actually more likely to perform minor interdisciplinary research. For instance, the number of crossover geologists might be increased by counting a chemist who analyzed geological specimens, or a physicist who measured terrestrial magnetism. On closer scrutiny, there was widespread application of specialized interests and skills (ibid., p. 94).

So in the mid-1840s, of the life scientists listed in the *Dictionary of American Biography*, 10 percent bore the old-fashioned label of "naturalist." While there was a rich tradition of natural history in America (e.g., the well-known travels of the Bartrams, the celebrated Lewis and Clark expedition, the popular paintings of Audubon), by this time the work of the naturalists was being eclipsed by a descriptive biology based on another scientific agenda. Zoology heavily influenced by an intellectual explosion in geology and paleontology expanded prodigiously; growing controversy over the nature of species would swell into the polemics over Darwinism in 1859; descriptive embryology was radically changing as a result of the acceptance of the cell theory in the 1840s and the preoccupation with species relationships; physiology was emerging as a new discipline, stimulated in large measure by attempts to make medical correlations. And botany was growing as a specialty area, led by Harvard's Asa Gray, whose *Manual of the Botany of the Northern United States* (1848) made an organized science out of American systematic botany. But Americans, despite their professionalization in the various life sciences, lagged behind Europe in experimental biology. Indeed, there was no significant research before 1880 in that arena, and despite ambitious American enterprise, the instrumentation and technology required to support sophisticated scientific research also remained largely European until the next century.

Much of the growth of American science in the nineteenth century depended upon the colleges and the societies, both of which lobbied the government and wealthy patrons for support. By promoting science and presenting its advances to the public at large, scientific societies served to increase the cultural presence of science generally. Strong amateur participation characterized these societies. Both the Boston Society of Natural History and the older American Academy of Arts and Sciences (founded 1780) housed a majority that was made up of "gentlemen who, to use an expression of . . . [the] founders [of the Academy of Natural Sciences in Philadelphia], are 'friendly to science' and its cultivation. Many of them pursue science only as a recreation during leisure hours, some are pleased to observe and know what others do, and others are content to encourage those who work" (from a report on the Academy of Natural Sciences in Philadelphia; cited by Bruce 1987, p. 36). During the 1840s, even a small village might form a "scientific society" to organize discussion groups and host lectures, for the insularity of professional exchange had yet to be created, and those inclined could still engage directly with the latest discoveries and theories.

Mid-nineteenth-century science was thus accessible to a broad population, both conceptually and socially. The larger scientific societies played an important role in science's "democratization" by distributing information and serving as important repositories of books, periodicals, specimens, and apparatus that might be employed even by the amateur. Amateurism was part of the general democratic ethos of American society of this post-Jacksonian period, and so we might well imagine that Thoreau could affiliate comfortably with the Boston Society of Natural History and still maintain a strong aloofness from the trend to professionalize. He lived in multiple worlds. Indeed, Emerson and Whitman, like Thoreau, not only respected scientists, they sought their company and welcomed interchange with them (Bruce 1987, p. 118). But the tides were, in fact, changing, and the respected amateur scientist was rapidly being eclipsed by the professional. In 1846, when Thoreau was studying Walden Pond and its surrounding forests, only 15 percent of the leading scientists (as determined by their listing in the *Dictionary of American Biography*) were amateurs, drawing no income from their science-related work; by the time of Thoreau's death sixteen years later, the percentage had shrunk to 9 percent (Bruce 1987, p. 135). In regard to natural history in particular, Agassiz was instrumental in relegating its field studies to second-rate status, reducing its field-based model to an amateur standing (as opposed to specialty training offered at Harvard), and essentially disfranchising the scientific role of its supporting institutions like the Boston Society of Natural History (Kohlstedt 1976; Walls 1995, p. 146). Already in the 1840s, research and study groups at Harvard were superseding the training, cooperative enterprises, and research activities of the Boston Society, so that by 1867, when the society opened its own Museum of Science, its goals had become almost entirely educational as opposed to research-oriented.

Agassiz's sentiments were formed in Europe, where natural history, especially in the German-speaking states, was already being professionalized (Nyhart 1996, pp. 426–29). With an emphasis on morphology and physiology, a new journal (founded in 1848), *Zeitschrift für wissenschaftliche Zoologie*, sought to establish a more scientific approach to what passed for natural history as Thoreau might have understood it. Excluding what they deemed applied topics and plain taxonomy, the editors wrote:

> We desire to give our journal the most scientific character possible. . . . To this purpose we exclude all announcements of new genera and species that do not relate to this task, unless they offer us a more thorough-going insight into plant and animal structure [*Bau*], into the life-history of animals and plants, or in the lawful organization of the organic realms. For the same reason we will exclude any kind of simple notes and natural history news. (Quoted by Nyhart 1996, p. 429)

With the publication of Darwin's *Origin of Species* in 1859, the boundaries of natural history were again redrawn, and the fate of life histories in the evolving discipline of biology followed a complex path. This move toward a scientific ethos which emphasized "structure" and "organization" and disregarded nonsystematic natural history "notes" and "news" reflected the influence of an increasingly stringent view of the organic realm. To a large extent this attitude drifted in from German reductionism, born in the 1840s (Galaty 1974), and in the drive toward a reductionist account of nature we witness the most dramatic contrast to Thoreau's own endeavor. Not only did reductionism reflect an orientation radically different from his holism, but the adherents of its approach were professional scientists, who were little concerned with the practice of what they perceived to be an outmoded style of studying nature.

Thus by the 1850s, despite the democratization of science, a perceptible widening schism had opened between the professionals and their supporting culture. Some scientists of the period admittedly deplored the political and social necessity of promoting and popularizing their profession. For instance, in 1854 James Dana complained that to satisfy the "vulgar appetites of the people," science had to be "diluted and mixed with a sufficient amount of the *spirit of the age*" (cited by Bruce 1987, p. 115). It is not clear what Dana meant specifically by "spirit of the age," but he might well have had in mind the lingering Romantic airs, which were not easily mixed with the emerging clouds of invention and burgeoning technology issuing forth from laboratories revitalized by a new scientific ethos.

TENSIONS

> When I heard the learn'd astronomer,
> When the proofs, the figures, were ranged in columns before me,
> When I was shown the charts and diagrams, to add, divide, and measure them,
> When I sitting heard the astronomer where he lectured with much applause in the lecture room,

How soon unaccountable I became tired and sick,
Till rising and gliding out I wander'd off by myself,
In the mystical moist night-air, and from time to time, look'd up in
    perfect silence at the stars.
                                    Walt Whitman, *By the Roadside* (1865)

Walt Whitman was not sanguine about the education he received in popular lectures, and more to the point, he intuitively resisted objectification of the cosmos. The world of letters had a complex relationship to science, but certainly it is no exaggeration that a dominant theme was the deep fear about science's unleashed power (e.g., as framed by Mary Shelley's *Frankenstein* [1818]). Mid-nineteenth-century literati offered a tenacious resistance to the allure of scientific knowledge and its attendant technological promise. As a young Henry Adams predicted in 1862, shortly before Thoreau's death,

> Man has mounted science, and is now run away with it. I firmly believe that before many centuries more, science will be the master of man. The engines he will have invented will be beyond his strength to control. Some day science may have the existence of mankind in its power, and the human race commit suicide by blowing up the world. Not only shall we be able to cruize in space, but I see no reason why some future generation shouldn't walk off like a beetle with the world on its back. (Letter to Charles Francis Adams, London, April 11, 1862, Adams 1920, 1:135)

Famously, Romantic criticism called into question the legitimacy of science both as a mode of cognition and as a social institution (Marx 1979). The theme that seems to connect both elements of the Romantic critique is Schiller's warnings against "disenchantment." Disenchantment here comprises the belief that there are no mysterious forces at play, that "one can, in principle, master all things by calculation" (Weber [1922] 1946).[14] At one level this clearly optimistic outlook elevates science as the bearer of all (only *seemingly* esoteric) knowledge. On the other hand, the process of scientific analysis evidently denied any possibility of a metaphysical/religious/ "enchanted" response to nature. This Romantic indictment charged science with wrenching man out of his privileged niche, where he once resided unique in nature, a privileged creature in communication with God. It laid modern metaphysical disjointedness at the feet of an imperialistic scientific worldview which not only defined nature and humankind in antispiritual language but called into question the legitimacy and value of other modes of knowing the world. Science subordinated human intuition, imagination, and feeling to intellectual abstraction. Thus the Romantics' revolt against the positivists. Against the reductionists, critics accused science of breaking unified nature asunder, incapable of reassembling the fragments. The consequences, they railed, were dire for both man and society: an inevitable metaphysical vacuum yawned where once religion stood. Any of these accusations and concerns express a profound remorse for a lost innocence.

Science, however, had never claimed to address the problem of meaning; to do science is, practically and pragmatically, to believe in its methods and its results. Consequently, to ask science to answer moral questions is to make a fundamental category error. The scientific language does not allow this sort of question to be asked *within the confines of its own grammar.* Science does not "partake of the contemplation of sages and philosophers about meaning in the universe" (Weber [1922] 1946). Thoreau did not want to disfranchise science from metaphysical meaning. He would have disagreed with Max Weber, who despaired that these "ultimately possible attitudes towards life are irreconcilable, and hence their struggle can never be brought to a final conclusion" (ibid.). Rather, Thoreau sought to place scientific insight within a broader humanistic universe. Ultimately, he would interpret morally the world that science presented, creating a portrait of nature from atomistic facts, ordered and signified by the aesthetic and spiritual vision which informed his own worldview. In these pursuits he was in good company.

A stark division between Victorian science's worldview and the literary reaction to it is too neat and prescriptive, and certainly did not apply universally either to the scientists or to the literati. In fact, the broadest intellectual concerns of some leading scientists during the Victorian period attest to the humane character of their scientific endeavors and the falsity of dividing the intellectual world into simple pro-science and anti-science groups. Nineteenth-century science was too multifarious an enterprise to be delineated so clearly, and more to the point, the deepest metaphysical aspirations of its practitioners arose from concerns shared with their poetic brethren. Tess Cosslett (1982, pp. 11–30) has outlined the values of Victorian science in this humanistic context along the following lines:

1.   Truth: The search for truth should reject the easy consolations of religion, for nature never lies and she provides a standard of veracity. This scientific fidelity to the truth of nature alone was seen by Thomas Huxley as the basis of morality, for

> the foundation of morality is to have done, once and for all, with lying; to give up pretending to believe that for which there is no evidence, and repeating unintelligible propositions about things beyond the possibilities of knowledge. (Huxley 1886, p. 146)

On this view, those holding science as the standard of veracity seize the moral high ground from those embracing the fantastic revelations of religious tradition, and instead help establish ethics on a foundation of reason.

2.   Law: Science discerns laws of natural causation and thereby can perceive a deeper order in the universe than that expressed by poetic or religious imagination. For instance, John Tyndall (a celebrated physicist and popular commentator on science [1820–93]) saw science as the effort to place man harmoniously within the natural cosmos. Scientific culture is

> based upon the natural relations subsisting between Man and the universe of which he forms a part. . . . The world was built in order: and to us are trusted the will and power to discern its harmonies, and to make them lessons of our lives. (Tyndall 1854, p. 302)

Huxley similarly believed that moral order might derive from natural order, for the same faith in, and search for, laws of cause and effect learned from nature might be applied to the understanding and the regulating of human conduct. This extrapolation was also sought by the Transcendentalists, albeit with different methods (see chapter 3).

3.   Kinship with nature: Natural causation not only implies regularity but also confers an inherent unity with nature (as discussed in chapter 3; Postlethwaite 1984; Dale 1989). So, while Darwinian evolution or Lyellian geology was metaphysically destabilizing in one sense, to be intelligible these theories still had to be coherent. Thus the interconvertibility of light and heat, the evolution of species, the rise and fall of mountains sounded the keynotes of unity and continuity. As a popularizer wrote in 1888, "all things are made of the same stuff differently mixed, bound by one force, stirred by one energy in divers forms" (Clodd 1888, p. 231). The barriers between inorganic and organic were thus broken down by the universal operation of scientific law and a universal materialism. Tyndall and Huxley insisted that this view did not degrade the "organic" but rather dignified the "inorganic," a position also championed by Coleridge and Thoreau, as well as many others.

> So instead of the material analogy being extended upwards, the analogy of life could equally well be extended downwards, and the whole of Nature, including man, be seen as one living organism, rather than one dead machine. Instead of feeling an alien in a hostile universe, man can just as well have a new feeling of kinship with the rest of Nature. (Cosslett 1982, p. 22)

On this view, "mechanism" has become "organism" and "matter" has been transmuted into "process." These formulations humanize nature into categories analogous to human agency and action.

4. Organic interrelation: While the organic view of nature rests on the integrated unity of nature as its primary characteristic, in addition it holds the critical corollaries that each organic part is integral to the whole and each element has an essential effect on that whole. This view had deep aesthetic and moral implications, especially telling when human history and natural history were seen as one. Humanity from this vantage can be viewed as one perpetual, self-renewing, transgenerational organism. Regarded as of one piece, each constituent is responsible for, and to, the whole. So, as discussed in chapter 1 in regard to the moral value of the present, each act, no matter how seemingly inconsequential or trivial, assumes a cosmic significance both in its own right and by its effects on subsequent human history.

5. Scientific imagination: While they rejected Romanticism's subjectivity, some Victorian scientists (e.g., Tyndall) recognized that scientific creativity still rested upon Imagination, and they used the notion in the same way Coleridge did. Because of its affinity with idealism and an older Naturphilosophie, this notion was highly controversial, and while embraced by certain philosophers of science (e.g., William Whewell and David Brewster), it must be regarded as a retained characteristic of Romanticism that did not readily find a compatible environment in a scientific culture increasingly dominated by a materialist positivism. In the perspective of this residually Romantic view, Imagination referred to the unifying, all-encompassing vision which, by grounding theory, offered the connecting apparatus for disjointed objective observations. For instance, in order to perceive nature as a unified organism, the scientist must look at nature as integrated in the first place. A theory of such an organic construction then follows, and then facts and data can be placed within that formal model. Thus Imagination in the employ of the scientist underlies both the gathering of data and the construction of theory. Moving between particular fact and general theory, the visible and the invisible, the real and the ideal, scientific imagination was not "unbridled" (since it always referred back to the particulars of nature), but its ability to serve as a metaphysical "glue" depended on its reference to the Real.

Yeo (1985) maintains that a transmutation of this form of Romantic idealism took place later in the nineteenth century, when the orienting role of hypothesis was increasingly recognized, so that intuitive generalization became constitutive of scientific reasoning. This said, deep and abiding tensions between the poet's and the scientist's approach and resulting world-views remained. The mystery and transcendental quality conferred by scientific insight fundamentally lies outside formal science praxis. Science has no voice to articulate its vision in terms that are subjective. So when the scientist faces the ultimate mysteries, he must step across the line dividing science from religion and poetry and acknowledge what Herbert Spencer called "The Unknowable." John Tyndall eloquently attested:

> In one sense [science] knows, or is destined to know, everything. In another sense it knows nothing. Science understands much of this intermediate phase of things that we call nature, of which it is the product; but science knows nothing of the origin or destiny of nature. Who or what made the sun and gave his rays their alleged power? Who or what made and bestowed upon the ultimate particles of matter their wonderous power of varied interaction? Science does not know: the mystery, though pushed back, remains unaltered. (1865, 2:52)

Humane scientists like Darwin, Huxley, and Tyndall, in promoting the power of scientific explanation, acknowledged the limits of the scientific dominion. With an appreciation that could only be developed from an education steeped in humanistic values, they understood that science's values of objectivity were, indeed, *values*. Science is ultimately based on a belief in the values of objectivity, rationality, and order as construed within certain limits and prescriptions. These are chosen for particular purposes and undergo historical development: in this sense, scientific principles are themselves historically and culturally conditioned. Thoreau could join this liberal company and stretch himself, as they did, between two intellectual universes, which at the time did not appear as disparate as they do today: the world of humane letters and the world of science. To us, now, it may seem self-evident that the two discourses are governed by different rules of thought, that their respective rationalities possess a different character, and that their objects of study demand different methods of exploration. But in the mid-nineteenth century a synthesis was still possible in the mind of the individual whose eclectic interests allowed diverse pursuits. The tensions and potential contradictions that resulted were regarded as problems, not dilemmas.

Thoreau, in some sense, was a synthesizer, but we situate him among the scientists of his era, even the most poetically inclined, only with difficulty. While he respected the power of scientific knowledge to "capture" a fact and hold it up to scrutiny, Thoreau had a conflicted view of that public fact, and ultimately he gave primacy to the "private" fact and the intimate truth it revealed to him. Concomitant with his personal quest, he found his own facts in his own characteristic fashion, and to do so, he self-consciously placed himself outside the scientific community even as he visited it. However, Thoreau could not escape his scientific culture: science only heightened his self-consciousness—epistemologically, metaphysically, and existentially. And as scientific objectivity increasingly asserted itself against the centrifugal forces of subjectivity, Thoreau attempted to maintain his own true orbit, balancing the centripetal pull of objectification against the collapsing attraction of solipsism. He lived a delicate equilibrium.

MEANINGFUL SCIENCE?

The eye which can appreciate the naked and absolute beauty of a scientific truth is far more rare than that which is attracted by a moral one. Few detect the morality in the former, or the science in the latter.

Thoreau, *A Week*, 1980a, p. 361

I suspect that the child plucks its first flower with an insight into its beauty & significance which the subsequent botanist never retains.

Thoreau, February 5, 1852,
Journal 4, 1992, p. 329

The scientist never sees anything for the first time.

Bachelard 1969, p. 156

Thoreau lived in a transitional period in our culture, when the inspiration offered by a Goethian view was still sympathetically appreciated and the self-conscious positivist approach to nature was in active ascendancy. Thoreau keenly felt the tug of each, and we see the swings of attitude toward formal science as an expression of his own ambivalence. Only when we restrict our vision of Thoreau to him as a "naturalist" or a "scientist" in the narrow sense do we oblige ourselves to scrutinize his observations by the standards of those disciplines. To be sure, he suffers our critique quite well, but that is beside the point. For Thoreau, the observation of nature served another purpose beyond a value in and of itself. The naturalist was in the employ of the artist who in turn served the moralist. When Thoreau concludes *Walden* by observing, "We know not where we are" (1971, p. 332), he is not acknowledging defeat but alluding to a means for fulfillment. It is precisely in being aware of our confusion and looking for our place that we might begin the redemptive task: "Not till we are lost, in other words, not till we have lost the world do we begin to find ourselves, and realize where we are and the infinite extent of our relations" (ibid., p. 171). In the process, the situating of man in nature remains ongoing.

Thoreau is distinguished from the positivists by his assertion of the inextricability of human value from our assessment and study of nature. During a period when ideas on nature were undergoing radical objectification, he maintained the primacy of the subject to behold nature with a personalized vision, which brought a set of values and self-judgments that could not be escaped. His views have found posthumous support in the rise of a popular attitude toward nature that we now refer to as the environmental movement, and more generally in later philosophical reassessments of positivism. The modern environmental movement expresses a popular disenchantment with a sterile survey of nature and seeks instead to view the world in humane terms—aesthetic or moral—where the human mediator's centrality in interpretation is always given. This general perspective has also received a renewed legitimacy in mid-twentieth-century post-positivist critiques of science, which are useful to situate Thoreau's own views.

Positivism continued to garner strength into the twentieth century, and its program achieved its major influence from the 1920s into the 1950s under the guise of logical positivism (also called logical empiricism). This movement, often identified as the Vienna Circle, extended well beyond science into the social sciences and largely shaped analytic philosophy, whose principle concerns dealt with how sentences might be verified and thus determined as truthful or not (Ayer 1959; Kolakowski 1968; Giere and Richardson 1996). Putting aside the issues concerning the analytic basis of truth statements in ordinary language, logical empiricism, extrapolating from its key tenet that scientific method alone provides knowledge, regarded a statement as cognitively meaningful only if it was "scientific," that is, empirically veridical. In this context, propositions are meaningful only if they can be assessed by an appeal to some foundational form of sensory experience. Thus proponents of this Vienna Circle position espoused science as the gold standard of knowledge, because sense data—especially in the form of mechanical objectivity—were treated as worthy of foundational status; and, conversely, given such criteria for a basis for truth claims, these positivists judged religious, metaphysical, and ethical statements "meaningless."

This strong empirical orientation has been justly challenged on many philosophical, historical, and sociological grounds. Most celebrated of those assailants was Thomas Kuhn, who, in *The Structure of Scientific Revolutions* (1962; 2d ed., 1970), argued that scientific evolution did not exclusively follow such precepts and that other social and aesthetic factors were important determinants of scientific truth.[15] Indeed, according to Kuhn, scientific evolution occurred in two modes: "normal" science was the ordinary confirmation of encompassing theory; "revolutionary" science radically altered the entire structure of scientific investigation, redefining a worldview. Once a new construction was in place, this so-called "paradigm" again determined normal praxis. Famously, paradigms were the conglomerate of cultural, political, economic, aesthetic and sociological ingredients that constituted the highly complex activity we refer to as science. The pursuit of truth, of course, remained science's cardinal aspiration. But truth, rationality, and objectivity evinced by the historical record were more contingently constructed than the positivist ideal acknowledged. Coupled to historically based critiques, philosophers, led by Paul Feyerabend (1975, 1981a, 1981b), argued that there was no prescribed, orthodox scientific method and that science was better characterized as a plurality of philosophies and practices. Finally, sociologists firmly placed science among other social institutions and showed how scientific practice was influenced by a vast intellectual and cultural infrastructure (Hollis and Lukes 1982; Jasanoff et al. 1995). In short, argued the critics, science was hardly normative, and because of an intricate matrix of philosophical, historical, and cultural contingencies, it could not possess a singular universal and prescribed method of discovery or verification. Some further argued that as a result of these critiques, even science's cognitive content was open to new skepticism.[16]

The 1960s and 1970s witnessed a blossoming of alternatives to the rational models of scientific progress that increasingly put the positivist proponents on the defensive. Instead a constructivist argument became dominant which, in its broadest interpretation, disallowed the insularity to the practicing scientist sought by the logical-empirical perspective.[17] Accordingly, in seeking objectivity, the researcher works under the auspices of pragmatic, realist demands as well as within an intricate web of social and linguistic constraints. Debate ensued about to what degree such "extraneous" factors determined the cognitive content of scientific descriptions. Contemporary philosophical, historical, and sociological perspectives largely converged in concluding that objectivity cannot be arrived at by transcendental, timeless norms of scientific practice (Megill 1994). Yet these critical perspectives diverge in the degree to which they see social forces effecting scientific content. And here we find the locus of contention. Those embracing a radical constructivist orientation hold that objectivity is achieved primarily as a matter of rhetorical practice and communal praxis.[18] Because the individual cannot achieve objectivity as a private mental condition, monitoring objectivity then becomes a matter of broad social policy, and a communal notion of objectivity takes on a new dimension.

If Kuhn spawned the major thrust of "social" critiques of positivist science, others drove the discussion back into the cognizing scientist, a perspective most relevant to our discussion of Thoreau's personalized epistemology. The clearest articulation countermanding positivist injunctions for logical empiricism at this level of discourse was offered by Michael Polanyi, who wrote *Personal Knowledge* in 1958 just as the positivist crest was about to crash. I think it informative in exploring Thoreau's views to understand how his concerns were later reframed and legitimated by Polyani's critique proposed a century later.

Personal Knowledge begins with the bald assertion, "I start by rejecting the ideal of scientific detachment" (Polanyi 1962, p. vii), and proceeds by analyzing the word "knowing" to show that its connotations refer to many levels of understanding. Impersonal, "objective" knowledge is only one kind aspired to, but even this category, according to Polanyi, is a conceit, and a limiting one at that. His complex argument attacks the positivists' position essentially from within the strictures of their own logic (incidentally, very different from the strategy employed by Kuhn), and I will only highlight certain aspects. Much of the argument concerns the logical futility of establishing any fixed framework which could critically test the positivist program. In other words, the positivists offer no perspective from which their own axioms might be examined critically. Specifically, we cannot escape our own perspective, the personal assessment that is intrinsic to any knowing. Simply put, Polanyi regarded the positivist view of science's logic as too narrow. He saw "rationality" as a broader category than the criterion of objectivity construed in a narrow sense. He notes,

> the act of knowing includes an appraisal; and this personal coefficient, which shapes all factual knowledge, bridges in doing so the disjunction between subjectivity and objectivity. It implies the claim that man can transcend his own subjectivity by striving passionately to fulfill his personal obligations to universal standards. (Ibid., p. 17)

Polanyi explicitly discounts *subjectivism* and substitutes *personal.* In this fashion he still aspired to objectivity's ostensible goals. This is not an either/or choice, for Polanyi would simply broaden our cognitive category of "objectivity" to include those mental faculties which play in the realm of discovery and cannot be, in any formal fashion, finalized in logical format. He also explicitly recognizes the "legitimacy of pretheoretical experience— which is not the same as random subjectivity!" (Hansen 1990, p. 14). He was to call this broadened realm of knowing the "tacit dimension" (Polanyi 1966), and in that domain the full panoply of knowing—aesthetic sensibility, probabilistic judgment, intuition, metaphoric extension, and the like—comes into play. In short, Polanyi argued that we see the world through different cognitive lenses, each of which has a part to play in scientific discovery.

In still offering an objective vision of the world mediated by the active person in his or her various knowing modalities, Polanyi resurrects the deeper metaphysical goals of science. Sounding a rich Thoreauvian theme, he employs objectivity as a humane tool:

> Objectivity . . . does not require that we see ourselves as a mere grain of sand in a million Saharas. It inspires us, on the contrary, with the hope of overcoming the appalling disabilities of our bodily existence, even to the point of conceiving a rational idea of the universe which can authoritatively speak for itself. It is not a counsel of self-effacement, but the very reverse—a call to the Pygmalion in the mind of man. (Polanyi 1962, p. 5)

For Polanyi, science is a passion, which despite its apparent austerity and aloofness must reflect a deeply personal way of viewing the world.

> [P]ersonal knowledge in science is not made but discovered, and as such it claims to establish contact with reality beyond the clues on which it relies. It commits us, passionately and far beyond our comprehension, to a vision of reality. Of this responsibility we cannot divest ourselves by setting up objective criteria of verifiability—or falsifiability, or test-ability, or what you will. For we live in it as in the garment of our own skin. Like love, to which it is akin, this commitment is a "shirt of flame," blazing with passion and, also like love, consumed by devotion to a universal demand. Such is the true sense of objectivity in science . . . the discovery of rationality in nature, a name which was meant to say that the kind of order which the discoverer claims to see in nature goes far beyond his understanding. (Ibid., p. 64)

Wary of becoming ensnared in the confines of restricted theory or disciplines of thought and, more importantly perhaps, limited to only a narrow wedge of experience and modes of knowing, the scientist by the latter third of the twentieth century again becomes the arbiter of what warrants inclusion (the problem of different layers of reality) and endeavors to widen his or her scope of investigation and worldview to become as inclusive as possible. I would not suggest that Polyani is reviving "subjectivism," but he is espousing sub-jectivity's recognized role in scientific discovery and theory formation. Rather than deny the selective process of observation and the interpretative character of scientific investigation, Polyani embraces them. Thus "personal knowledge" becomes a catchall for the necessary creative elements which cannot be accounted for in the positivist rendition of science.

As presented earlier, objectivity is intrinsically coupled to notions of sub-jectivity: one cannot speak of one without at least implicit reference to the other. Our regard of the subjective has been recast. We no longer are inspired by Goethian *Sturm und Drang* nor guided by Coleridgean Imagination, but we do appreciate the unfathomable depths of creativity and celebrate its application to science. Further, we understand that scientific discovery follows no prescribed "rules": scientific methods evolve and have no final structure; verification is never complete, and theory is always "underdetermined"; "facts" are invariably embedded in complex structures which may range from formal laws to informal models to nebulous hypotheses, and thereby facts have no clear status or meaning. To render order with such pliable cognitive structures, we must interpret, and interpretation requires judgment in all of its various guises, ranging from a positivist ideal to the vaguest of intuitions. Having no final calculus of scientific reasoning, we might fairly regard the Romantics' scientific project, and their epistemology more generally, with greater sympathy. We are less prone to dismiss their struggle of placing the subject-object distinction in a humane framework now that we recognize that indeed there is no escape from our own perspective. In philosophy, this so-called "perspectivism" is most often traced to Nietzsche, but in studying Goethe or Thoreau, we witness the unresolved tension between achieving various degrees of objectivity and maintaining—indeed, insisting on—the integrity of the observer. Theirs was a sensitive appraisal of how individual assignment of significance and meaning conferred value on their observation.

While the cognitive confluence between subject and object was formalized and developed in twentieth-century philosophy as an epistemological problem in science, Goethe's "solution" (followed by Thoreau), namely, that the aesthetic experience may serve to integrate self and the world, was essentially ignored (Tauber 1993, 1996a). Yet we must acknowledge that scientific knowledge is variegated and complex, incorporating what I have called "raw observation" as well as "contextualized observation," of which "the beautiful" is a crucial component. It is insufficient merely to call upon such notions as "key insight," "beautiful experiments," and "elegant theory," as glosses for the "extrascientific" aspects of the experiences of a few scientists of titanic creativity. The very practice of everyday science, beyond its drudgery and frustration, must embody recognition and realization of a personalized ideal which governs the undertaking as much as impersonal standards of objectivity. While this position may be supported by a variety of strategies, it is most effectively advanced in the recognition that science, being essentially a creative project, must acknowledge that component of the personal which we call the aesthetic.[19] Thoreau, led by Goethe and other Romanticists, keenly understood our predicament, embracing the notion that the poet's eye might serve science in seeking nature's true design. As

Thoreau confided to his Journal, "the laws of nature are science but in an enlightened moment they are morality and modes of divine life. In a medium intellectual state they are aesthetics" (September 28, 1843, *Journal* 1, 1981, p. 468). The aesthetic in this sense serves as a crucial faculty reintegrating experience. In short, the aesthetic dimension may be the bridge that unifies the objective, qua scientific, with the subjective, qua personal. As Goethe wrote, "Nowhere would anyone grant that science and poetry can be united. They forgot that science arose from poetry, and did not see that when times change the two can meet again on a higher level as friends" (Goethe [1817] 1988). From this perspective, the scientist, just as the poet, draws upon the same aesthetic resources as a primary component of his experience (Tauber 1996a).[20]

While science often appears most driven by its quest for technical mastery, its aspirations for explanation draw upon a deep aesthetic reservoir, one steeped in the metaphysical thirst for meaning.[21] The dissection of the world has yielded a kind of knowledge which beckons to be coordinated in our full human experience. The scientific object may reside seemingly separate—"out there"—the focus of an inquiry of what it is, in itself (ignoring the philosophical difficulties of that expectation), but the challenge is to integrate that object into our full experience, rational *and* emotional. The search for this common ground is the elusive synthesis of our very selves in a world ever more objectified from us—a beguiling reminder of the lingering fault of our very identity. To the extent that we appreciate that our two-culture world reflects a disjunction of that integration, we gain insight into a metaphysical chasm that may still be mended. Thoreau has offered hope that such a project might still be successful. Instead of regarding science and poetry as disparate, he chose to integrate them within his own expansive experience, knitting their apparent divergence into a creative composite, a new vision of nature.

How then do the crucial and variable elements of creative intuition, deduction, observation, replicable method, and assembly of disparate information create "objective" reality? This has been the question informing most discussion in the philosophy of science during the twentieth century, and we might judge that Thoreau's project had philosophical merit on many levels as evident from the course of our own debates. At a minimum he might well have argued that science, too, is governed by values, which of course are both chosen and developed, hardly existing as steadfast and unchanging. Indeed, as Hilary Putnam (1982) has urged, we must get past the rigid fact/value dichotomy, for science itself is subject to assuming value judgments regarding its own practice and can hardly be said to proceed by any formal, final method. When theory and fact conflict, sometimes one is given up, sometimes the other, and the choice as often as not is made "aesthetically," by adopting what appears to be the simplest, the most parsimonious, or elegant, or coherent—qualities which themselves are *values*. These are what Putnam calls *action-guiding* terms, the vocabulary of justification, also historically conditioned and subject to the same debates concerning the conception of rationality. The attempt to restrict coherence and simplicity to predictive theories is self-refuting, for the very logic required even to argue such a case depends on intellectual interests unrelated to prediction as such. Putnam concludes that if coherence and simplicity are values, albeit the objective values governing science, then the classic argument against the objectivity of ethical values is undercut, for *all* values suffer of the same "subjective softness." The point is to dispel the intellectual hubris of the scientific attitude and allow "that all values, including the cognitive ones, derive their authority from our idea of human flourishing and our idea of reason" (ibid.). This is a matter to which we must return, but let us first complete situating Thoreau's own immediate concerns.

The final ingredient—one we have considered from several vantages already—is to regard nature as of one piece, where each part—ourselves included—must be understood in relation to the whole. This is what Polanyi referred to as nature's "rationality," and as Thoreau affirmed in *Walden*,

> If we knew all the laws of Nature, we should need only one fact, or the description of one actual phenomenon, to infer all the particular results at that point. Now we know only a few laws, and our result is vitiated, not, of course, by any confusion or irregularity in Nature, but by our ignorance of essential elements in the calculation. Our notions of law and harmony are commonly confined to those instances which we detect; but the harmony which results from a far greater number of seemingly conflicting, but really concurring, laws, which we have not detected, is still more wonderful. The particular laws are as our points of view, as, to the traveller, a mountain outline varies with each step, and it has an infinite number of profiles, though absolutely but one form. Even when cleft or bored through it is not comprehended in its entireness. (1971, pp. 290–91)

This vision also requires a poetic faculty whereby one might see the integration of diverse nature into a single whole. The communal flash might occur observing a hawk flying (ibid., pp. 316–17), contemplating the weeds in a field (ibid., p. 166), or while fishing:

> It was very queer, especially in dark nights, when your thoughts had wandered to vast and cosmogonal themes in other spheres, to feel this

faint jerk, which came to interrupt your dreams and link you to Nature again. It seemed as if I might next cast my line upward into the air, as well as downward into this element which was scarcely more dense. Thus I caught two fishes as it were with one hook. (Ibid., p. 175)

In this sense, science—as observation of nature—also becomes personalized, that is, personally meaningful at a level of comprehension beyond that experienced by those confined to a narrow positivist definition of what might be scientific. For our culture, dominated by a scientific worldview that too often is regarded as competing against humane values, the path leading to personalized knowledge begins at the door of Thoreau's cabin at Walden Pond.

5 Thoreau's Personalized Facts

> The problem of restoring integration and cooperation between
> man's beliefs about the world in which he lives and his beliefs
> about the values and purposes that should direct his conduct is
> the deepest problem of modern life. It is the problem of any
> philosophy that is not isolated from that life.
>
> John Dewey [1929] 1984, p. 204

I have already intimated that Thoreau regarded epistemology as fundamentally a moral problem of situating objective knowledge within a humane
context. The value one placed on kinds of knowledge and their respective
placement in a hierarchy of significance were key issues that undergird all
of the Romantics' reaction to science. *Meaning*, they insisted, must be
sought outside of an objective knowledge of nature, that activity which we
call science or natural history. Science in its origins embraced an epistemology whose ideal—the separation of the subject (the scientist) from his
or her object of study—was itself potentially alienating. Science thereby
stratified along a continuum between "objective" and "subjective" poles of
experience. In the 1840s and 1850s, this fragmentation of knowledge was
only in its infancy; a century later, the transformation of culture and forms
of understanding it wrought were well evident. C. P. Snow named the
widening schism between the worlds of the humanities and of science/
technology in *The Two Cultures* (1959). There he argued that the two different intellectual modalities echoed a broad cultural conflict, wherein the
analytical, mechanical, and abstract qualities of science displaced the elements of the primary encounter characterized in terms of the personal, emotional, or aesthetic. When the poet communes with nature, the artist does
so almost always in rejection of the scientific stance.

Contemporary culture has been riven by the schism between the Two
Cultures, and their partition remains deeply problematic. But in his day,
Thoreau could still believe in some grand synthesis, wherein science might
"enchant" through the aesthetic dimension of the observer's experience.
From his vantage, the scientific view might be extended to encompass
beyond nature more elusive dimensions—the emotional, the subjective. Not

all scientists would regard these as properly or even possibly within the province of science, but for Thoreau the scrutiny of nature entailed multiple levels of knowledge, and consideration of the aesthetic facet of science provided him a way to attend to these nebulous dimensions of human experience. The issue for him was not how the scientist attempts to be objective but rather how knowledge of the world becomes personally meaningful. The import of that synthesis concerns the very nature of objectified knowledge itself, which is transformed into personal knowledge, wherein "events are not counted but weighed, and past events not explained but interpreted" (Heisenberg 1979, p. 68). Thoreau is a paradigmatic example of this perspective at work.

Although Thoreau matured beyond a youthful disdain of science, he nevertheless subordinated that form of knowledge relative to a more personalized experience.[1] On the one hand, he sought to "capture" nature through meticulous observation of natural processes; and on the other hand, he sought in nature a "personalized" reality so that he might situate himself in the order and beauty of the natural world. This, of course, is a traditional Romantic project, and Thoreau assumed a typically Romantic persona in viewing nature as a sacred source of human moral direction. But in so doing, he put himself at odds both with the idealist moralizing philosophy of Emersonian Transcendentalism and with ascendant professionalized positivistic science which divorced nature from the knowing subject. Thoreau instead sought to reenchant nature while employing certain scientific methods to do so—a synthetic approach that pursued the unification of objective and subjective experience. He thus appears as a powerful practitioner of the aestheticization of science which, he demonstrated, need not be at odds with careful, albeit unorthodox, methods of scientific inquiry. More than a literary naturalist (the way we tend to see him now), Thoreau was able to straddle the literary/scientific divide in an attempt to place science within its broadest humanistic tradition. This orientation undergirds the discussion of this chapter.

Thoreau was suspicious of science's efforts to objectify to the extent that such fragmentation of experience would interfere with his experience of nature, specifically, the personal significance that observation might yield.[2] Science does not attend to humane significance. The poetic power of imagination, however, transforms the inert fact into personal meaning, an emotional category. Thoreau stated the issue quite plainly:

> I think that the man of science makes this mistake, and the mass of mankind along with him: that you should coolly give your chief attention to the phenomenon which excites you as something independent on you, and not as it is related to you. *The important fact is its effect on*

me. He thinks that I have no business to see anything else but just
what he defines the rainbow to be, but I do not care whether my vision
of truth is a waking thought or dream remembered, whether it is seen
in the light or in the dark. It is the subject of the vision, the truth alone,
that concerns me. The philosopher for whom rainbows, etc., can be
explained away never saw them. With regard to such objects, I find that
it is not they themselves (with which the men of science deal) that concern me; the point of interest is somewhere *between* me and them (*i.e.*
the objects). (November 5, 1857, *Journal*, [1906] 1962, 10:164–65; first
emphasis added)

How are we to understand Thoreau's efforts to remove this uneasy relation between science and poetry?[3] I might agree with Loren Eiseley that
Thoreau "never resolved his philosophical difficulties" (1978, pp. 229–30),
if we understand by that pronouncement that no one philosophical argument or doctrine might account for his epistemology in a formal sense. But
Thoreau illustrates a way by which splintered experience—objective and
subjective—might be knit together by recognizing the full legitimacy of
each. He arrived at this position primarily by acknowledging the limitations
of rationality and the proper placement of scientific knowledge. To "see"
fully, other faculties of knowing must be enlisted:

We shall see but little way if we require to understand what we see–
How few things can a man measure with the tape of his understand-
ing–how many greater things might he be seeing in the meanwhile.
(February 14, 1851, *Journal* 3, 1990, p. 192)

In his view, man's supposed autonomous aloofness as scientific observer
actually mirrors his own personal fragmentation. This might be mended by
engaging the full panoply of various forms of knowing. Instead of relegating experience to one domain or another, Thoreau "simply" allowed the free
integration of various kinds of understanding and admitted that there
are different forms of knowledge that may, indeed must, be self-consciously
regarded. His concern with becoming too "scientific" seemed to rest primarily on the fear of fragmenting experience, of losing the whole:

I fear that the character of my knowledge is from year to year becoming more distinct & scientific– That in exchange for views as wide as
heaven's cope I am being narrowed down to the field of the microscope– I see details not wholes nor the shadow of the whole. I count
some parts, & say 'I know'. (August 19, 1851, *Journal* 3, 1990, p. 380)

Thoreau's daunting challenge—how to unify the aesthetic, scientific, and
moral universes—remains our own. Let us examine how he proceeded.

THOREAU'S SCIENCE

It is hard for the least philosophic intellect to conceive of a value in science which is not potentially a human value also. . . . Yet the researcher knows that the end must never overshadow the means. The goal may be the subjective wish, but the research must be conducted as if it were an end in itself, otherwise we get no science but the results of wish psychology. This was Thoreau's weakness as a scientist. Fearing that he would lose his sense of the living reality behind the appearance, he never gave his whole mind to the discipline of observation.

Canby [1939] 1958, pp. 329–30

In the context of American science's exponential growth during the nineteenth century, its rapid and effective application to technology with its attendant mechanization of a pastoral world (Marx 1965), and its implicit assault on subjectivity, Thoreau's consistently focused and clear conviction about his own mission is indeed remarkable in light of his own ambivalence toward scientific inquiry. On the one hand, he held fast to his own naturalist tradition; on the other, he remained intellectually engaged with and receptive to new scientific discoveries. In short, despite competing interests, Thoreau was able to follow his own path in studying nature, guided by the same fierce independence that marked both his experimentation in personal economy and his political advocacy.

An important example of Thoreau's relationship to science is offered by the case of the bream.[4] At Walden Pond in late November 1858, Thoreau discovered frozen fish previously unencountered, which were "shaped like bream, but had the transverse bars of perch" (November 25, 1858, *Journal*, [1906] 1962, 11:345). He made meticulous notes of their appearance, took careful measurements (ibid., pp. 346–47, 348–49, 363–64, 368), drew a profile of his discovery, and exclaimed in obvious excitement, "Are they not a new species?" (ibid., p. 347). Thoreau presented the fish at the Boston Society of Natural History, and several members concurred that he had indeed made a discovery. The Boston newspapers reported the findings and the expert disagreements, and upon further study announced that the putative new species had been previously identified (notes to November 27, 1858, entry, ibid., pp. 348–49). Irrespective of the final adjudication, his Journal records Thoreau's extraordinary exhilaration as a result of this scientific adventure. Dominant is the metaphysical import of his *relation* to the fish. I quote a large portion of his reflection, because perhaps more clearly than any other evidence, it reveals Thoreau's enthusiastic appreciation of the organism's part in the cosmic whole, as opposed to the meager meaning permitted by the isolated scientific fact:

[I]n my account of this bream I cannot go a hair's breadth beyond the mere statement that it exists,—the miracle of its existence, my contemporary and neighbor, yet so different from me! I can only poise my thought there by its side and try to think like a bream for a moment. I can only think of precious jewels, of music, poetry, beauty, and the mystery of life. I only see the bream in its orbit, as I see a star, but I care not to measure its distance or weight. The bream, appreciated, floats in the pond as the centre of the system, another image of God. Its life no man can explain more than he can his own. I want you to perceive the mystery of the bream. I have a contemporary in Walden. It has fins where I have legs and arms. I have a friend among fishes, at least a new acquaintance. Its character will interest me, I trust, not its clothes and anatomy. I do not want it to eat. Acquaintance with it is to make my life more rich and eventful. It is as if a poet or an anchorite had moved into the town, whom I can see from time to time and think of yet oftener. Perhaps there are a thousand of these striped bream which no one had thought of in that pond,—not their mere impressions in stone, but in the full tide of the bream life. (November 30, 1858, *Journal*, [1906] 1962, 11:358–59)

Thoreau goes on to decry scientific knowledge as prideful and mortiferous:

Though science may sometimes compare herself to a child picking up pebbles on the seashore, that is a rare mood with her; ordinarily her practical belief is that it is only a few pebbles which are *not* known, weighed and measured. A new species of fish signifies hardly more than a new name. See what is contributed in the scientific reports. One counts the fin-rays, another measures the intestines, a third daguerreotypes a scale, etc., etc.; otherwise there's nothing to be said. As if all but this were done, and these were very rich and generous contributions to science. Her votaries may be seen wandering along the shore of the ocean of truth, with their backs to the ocean, ready to seize on the shells which are cast up. You would say that the scientific bodies were terribly put to it for objects and subjects. A dead specimen of an animal, if it is only well preserved in alcohol, is just as good for science as a living one preserved in its native element. (Ibid., pp. 359–60)

Thoreau is most critical of a science that cannot, because of its very method, examine the specimen in its living context, a part of the greater whole. This is the early ecologic sensitivity that such critics as Buell (1995) have emphasized. But I suspect that Thoreau is at least equally, probably more, concerned by the necessary distortion demanded by the reductive methodology of science. Only by inference could a scientific assessment be related to the world of the living—for Thoreau, the only true frame of relevance. The dead specimen is as worthy and useful to Thoreau's scientist-peer as the living animal, and the process of accruing tiny bits of information is deadening to both object and subject, who each suffer death throes in the alcohol of preservation.

Thoreau, rather, explores the metaphysical wonder of the natural world as the source of scientific inquiry. He sees science itself as achieving its motive power from this sense of awe:

> What is the amount of my discovery to me? It is not that I have got one in a bottle, that it has got a name in a book, but that I have a little fishy friend in the pond. How was it when the youth first discovered fishes? Was it the number of their fin-rays or their arrangement, or the place of the fish in some system that made the boy dream of them? Is it these things that interest mankind in the fish, the inhabitant of the water? No, but a faint recognition of a living contemporary, a provoking mystery. One boy thinks of fishes and goes a-fishing from the same motive that his brother searches the poets for rare lines. It is the poetry of the fishes which is their chief use; their flesh is their lowest use. The beauty of the fish, that is what it is best worth the while to measure. Its place in our systems is of comparatively little importance. Generally the boy loses some of his perception and his interest in the fish; he degenerates into a fisherman or an ichthyologist. (Ibid., p. 360)

Particularly interesting in this entry is Thoreau's juxtaposition of his metaphysical musings with the scientific knowledge that triggered his excitement. The contrast is stark and absolute: the fish as a living creature is a microcosm of an entire cosmos; the scientific appreciation of that organism is essentially devoid of human meaning and significance. The image of the scientist standing at the ocean's edge—with his back to the water and picking up mere scraps of the sea's bounty—stands in contradistinction to Newton's peering at the horizon in realization of how little he knew or understood. The majesty of nature's beauty and its beguiling mystery are lost to the ichthyologist, while Thoreau exuberantly regards the bream as "another image of God."

We might well regard Thoreau's excitement as an expression of what may be called his pastoral sensibility. That Romantic view of harmony and beauty was, of course, balanced by the awesome and terrifying power of nature that he experienced on Mount Ktaadn (1846) or at Margaret Fuller's shipwreck death (1850).[5] Within that complex continuum, Thoreau would gather facts, sometimes with the view toward aesthetic construction, at other times toward a more formal description of nature, one tinged less with emotion and directed toward a particular scientific description—that is, the soundings of Walden Pond, the dating of the appearance of flora, the meteorological descriptions. As attested by his Journal entries, the listing of "facts" in his later years became more of a preoccupation (Foerster 1923, pp. 92–93), which reflects a changed character in his scientific work (Walls 1995). But Thoreau's personalized musings on nature would never be eclipsed, and his basic assessment of science and its relationship to other modes of knowing did not significantly change during his adulthood.

What unsettled Thoreau's relationship to science was fundamentally his need to find value. His last systematic investigations well illustrate this point. Concurrent with his "discovery" of the bream, Thoreau worked on two comprehensive studies which have been regarded as the most systematic, if not the most scientific, of his nature observations: the dispersion of seeds to uncover the mechanisms of forest succession and a thorough compendium of wild fruits in the Concord environs. Both projects represented compilations from observations begun in the early 1850s and, while incomplete, offer a unique amalgam of science and Romantic interpretation.

Wild Fruits (2000) is basically a complex catalogue, whose descriptions of various botanical details of the fruit and their supporting plants is supplemented with discussions of nomenclature and listing of phenological data, geographical range, local growth characteristics, and history of use and discovery. Interspersed with these more orthodox descriptions are heavy doses of Thoreauvian commentary about personal encounters with the vegetation, most often aesthetic descriptions and reflections on the respect these plants command for their contribution both to natural order and to human well-being. The catalogue is obviously incomplete and erratic: some plants are extensively discussed (e.g., the black huckleberry receives twenty-three pages [pp. 37–59]), whereas others, like the black ash, are cited with one line (p. 175). While the text has bountiful scientific data, it is clear from Thoreau's introductory remarks that *Wild Fruits* was intended to sensitize the reader to the natural world, specifically the ready opportunity to become intimate with an aspect of the wild:

> The value of these wild fruits is not in the mere possession or eating of them, but in the sight and enjoyment of them. . . . Of course, it is the spirit in which you do a thing which makes it interesting, whether it is sweeping a room or pulling turnips. Peaches are unquestionably a very beautiful and palatable fruit, but the gathering of them for the market is not so interesting to the imagination of men as the gathering of huckleberries for your own use. . . .

It is a grand fact that you cannot make the fairer fruits or parts of fruits matter of commerce; that is, you cannot buy the highest use and enjoyment of them. You cannot buy that pleasure which it yields to him who truly plucks it. You cannot buy a good appetite, even. In short, you may buy a servant or slave, but you cannot buy a friend. (Pp. 4–5)

Wild Fruits then would serve both as a contribution to the ambitious Kalendar project and as a user-friendly field guide. The text ends with a plea for the establishment of natural parks or primitive forests for "instruction and recreation" (p. 238).[6] And then in the closing paragraph, Thoreau draws a direct correspondence between human health and receptivity to nature, so that the wild fruit becomes the elixir of civilization's discontent:

Live in each season as it passes; breathe the air, drink the drink, taste the fruit, and resign yourself to the influence of each. Let those be your only diet-drink and botanical medicines. . . . Open all your pores and bathe in all the tides of Nature, in all her streams and oceans, at all seasons. Miasma and infection are from within, not without. . . . For all Nature is doing her best each moment to make us well. She exists for no other end. Do not resist her. With the least inclination to be well, we should not be sick. Men have discovered, or think that they have discovered, the salutariness of a few wild things only, and not of all Nature. Why, Nature is but another name for health. (Pp. 238–39)

A similar fusion of personal sensibility and scientific discourse marks Thoreau's other major project of his last years. Although he pursued studies of plant propagation in the late 1850s, Thoreau actually first noted seeming anomalies concerning the growth of trees and the possible role of animals and wind in dispersing seeds in 1850. Concentrating on the growth of oaks on land cleared of pine trees, Thoreau, by 1856, was meticulously noting forest succession. Stimulated by reading *On the Origin of Species* in early 1860, he modeled his research on the full character of a scientific study. His work on seeds is fairly accounted as scientific not only because of its careful observations but also because of the structure of his inquiry that tested a hypothesis framed by Darwin's theory. The bulk of the manuscript has only recently been published (1993), but a portion of this larger work, "The Succession of Forest Trees" (1980f), was delivered in 1860 at the annual Concord Middlesex County Cattle Show and published soon after in the New York *Weekly Tribune*.

"The Succession of Forest Trees" is Thoreau's only published scientific account and was part of a larger project (*The Dispersion of Seeds* [1993]), a treatise concerning the propagation of plants written very much as Darwin would write *The Fertilization of Orchids* (1862), *Climbing Plants* (1875), or

Insectivorous Plants (1875). Thoreau, of course, had long been committed to documenting the distribution of wildlife around Concord, but in this book he explicitly extended his observations to promote the Darwinian argument against spontaneous generation of plants and animals and to show how plants were propagated by seeds and sought their appropriate ecological niche. The power of Thoreau's observations, careful measurement, and meticulous note-keeping afforded him the tools to now turn his naturalist descriptions from a catalogue project to one brought into service to promote a biological theory. Indeed, he self-consciously observed, "my theory was confirmed by observation" (Thoreau 1993, p. 29).

On the Origin of Species presented nature's evolution as a materialistic, blind process governed by a force Darwin saw as analogous to a Newtonian cause, natural selection (Depew and Weber 1995). While this theory presented a challenge to theology, Thoreau's enthusiastic reception suggests that he understood it to be conducive to his own view of nature.[7] In many respects Thoreau had anticipated the Darwinian paradigm (Harding 1965; Richardson 1985) in the sense that he regarded *all* of nature as integrated and of a whole, so descent by differentiation from a common ancestor was readily accepted. Darwin's theory offered Thoreau a grand foundation upon which he might finally have rested not only his scientific endeavors but also the metaphysical queries which dominated his concerns.[8] Thoreau was attracted to those elements which addressed the organic world as a vastly intricate unit, one that beautifully intertwined each element in the most complex, yet harmonious, order. Adaptation to ecological opportunity explored the constructive expansiveness of life. Presented in terms of adaptation, this vision of the natural world posed a naturalistic response to the metaphysical quandary that framed Thoreau's own pursuits, namely, how to situate himself within nature. By deliberate choice and self-willed direction, man might not only find his place but work to create it.

Thus even in Thoreau's most scientific endeavors, he continued to celebrate the integration and order of nature, which in turn reflected both aesthetic splendor and transcendental higher laws. Man must be included in that divine structure. In this sense he was most taken by nature as community, and at times he had expressed an almost pantheist euphoria ("Am I not partly leaves and vegetable mould myself?" [*Walden*, 1971, p. 138]). This is not to say that Thoreau did not recognize his own savagery ("We have a wild savage in us" ["Walking," 1980b, p. 125]), but "the Wild" Thoreau celebrated was the natural, the appreciation of man *in* nature, indeed, integral to nature. Thoreau sought both to *know* nature (a cognitive enterprise) and to be one with it (a mystical aspiration). This was, in fact, a single enterprise, for these two faculties—epistemological and meta-physical—were joined by the desire both to understand and to be existentially part of nature's flux—life in its ceaseless movement.

Critics usually designate the seed study the most "scientific" of Thoreau's research, and it represents the best effort he made to synthesize science with his own more idiosyncratic naturalist style. In coining the term "succession," Thoreau was the first to emphasize the importance of seed dispersal in plant succession. This contribution is of scientific significance, not withstanding that twentieth-century ecologists might regard his focus as too narrow (studying only a few tree species as opposed to the full botanic context) and his description oversimplified (Caswell 1974; history of the idea and significance for modern ecologists reviewed by Foster 1999, pp. 134 ff., 186–91, 244–46). But whatever its shortcomings, this work was Thoreau's most systematic and conventional effort.

The paper's presentation is respectably scientific, its ethos not. Even in this most "respectable" scientific essay, Thoreau begins with an ironic identification: "Every man is entitled to come to Cattle-Show, even a transcendentalist; and for my part I am more interested in the men than in the cattle" (1980f, p. 72). He might just as easily have said, "than in the trees," for even though he gives an eloquent account of how animals disperse seeds and the natural succession of hardwoods and pines, he ends the introductory portion of the essay with a most Thoreauvian invitation, "Let me lead you back into your wood-lots again" (ibid., p. 74). Even in this ostensibly scientific report, what Walter Harding has called "Thoreau's major contribution to scientific knowledge" (1965, p. 439), he could not resist the opportunity to sensitize his audience to the wonders of nature and the pleasure of an intimate knowledge of its workings. Thoreau in his full maturity has finally forged an alliance between scientific and moral discourses: science, like all knowledge, must be in the employ of human—that is, humane—sensibility. There were economic benefits to Thoreau's observation (the rational cultivation of the woodlands), but the principal issue is the metaphorical meaning offered by his studies: "I have great faith in a seed,—a, to me, equally mysterious origin for it. Convince me that you have a seed there, and I am prepared to expect wonders" (Thoreau 1980f, p. 91). Just as with the bream, paramount for Thoreau is life's mystery and the meaning of that mystery for knowledge.

Ultimately, Thoreau explored nature for the spiritual treasures it held. Science was simply another way to dig for bounty, as he ends this essay with the admonition of the seer:

> Perfect alchemists I keep who can transmute substances without end,
> and thus the corner of my garden is an inexhaustible treasure-chest.

> Here you can dig, not gold, but the value which gold merely
> represents. . . . Yet farmers' sons will stare by the hour to see a juggler
> draw ribbons from his throat, though he tells them it is all deception.
> Surely, men love darkness rather than light. (Ibid., p. 92)

Thoreau might dress his message in different guises—categorical scientific description, poetic revelry, self-contemplation, aesthetic portrait—but the essential lesson was the same: nature and man are of a single piece, and one must seek their essential nexus.[9] His quest led him to formulate a new genre of nature writing. Indeed, natural history as a scientific discipline was passing him by.

Walter Harding and others have attempted to salvage Thoreau's scientific standing by invoking him as a founding father of ecology:

> Nearly a century ahead of his time, he was fundamentally an ecologist.
> He would have had fewer complaints about the narrowness of the scientific view if he could have read some of our twentieth-century ecological studies. And, reciprocally, twentieth-century scientists have
> begun to realize the values of his broader approach. (1959, p. 138)

This is not a unique view (Buell 1995, pp. 362–64), and recent biographies have emphasized Thoreau's late natural-history investigations (e.g., Howarth 1982; Richardson 1993; Rossi 1993; McGregor 1997) and his scientific sophistication and interactions with other scientists (Richardson 1986).[10] Indeed, Walls (1995) would like to assign Thoreau a role as a scientist, albeit with a unique identity.[11] I am not sanguine about any such attempt. We need not legitimate Thoreau's efforts by calling them "scientific." Clearly, Thoreau was breaking a new path. "Natural history, as Thoreau found it in Gilbert White's letters and in Darwin's journal, was an open form, what Emerson called an 'unclosed genre' " (Paul 1992, p. 24), and Thoreau made that genre his own. While Thoreau followed a literary tradition of naturalist history (Hicks 1926, pp. 81–99), he stamped this literary form with his unique vision, establishing a literary genre that grew in influence and became the foundation of twentieth-century environmentalism (Buell 1995, n. 19, pp. 429–30).[12] Indeed, Thoreau's first biographer, his friend William Ellery Channing, entitled his work *Thoreau: The Poet-Naturalist* (1873) in an attempt to place him in a singular category, and literary critics have refined the point. Thoreau's place in the American pantheon is not as a scientist.

He is better placed with the naturalists if we accept that "The true naturalist . . . is interested in explaining the marvelous; Thoreau's concern is to make the ordinary marvelous" (Hildebidle 1983, p. 25). Unlike even those naturalists doing life-history studies (which might be construed as also including Thoreau's own endeavor), Thoreau sought parables, self-made myths, mystical insights, which strove not so much for clarity as for an evocative obscurity (ibid., p. 47). Thoreau's oeuvre is not necessarily consonant with that of other practitioners of the naturalist's art, but he shares with them the broad commitment to encompass greater wholes to allow the observer to extract personal meaning from his scrutiny. And here is where the great divide with science occurs:

> The danger of solipsism is clear; the reading of nature as a reflection of the self can easily be a mis-reading. But to the natural historian— Romantic or pre-Romantic—there is really no choice but to risk the danger. The only alternative would be as pointless as observing stuffed birds in order to understand the migration of the sparrow. . . . Rather than abandon this principle, the naturalist usually abandons the name of scientist, and along with it the respect which is more and more commonly accorded that name. (Hildebidle 1983, pp. 58–59)

But Thoreau cannot rest easily in the world of naturalists, either. His practice of natural history has been attacked on the basis of its own professional standards, so that those who would place him within the naturalist tradition do so at the risk of exposing him to charges of being second-rate. For instance, John Burroughs, demonstrating the numerous ornithological mistakes in Thoreau's Journal, comments:

> What he saw in this field everybody may see who looks; it is patent. He had not the detective eye of the great naturalist; he did not catch the clews and hints dropped here and there, the quick, flashing movements, the shy but significant gestures by which new facts are disclosed, mainly because he was not looking for them. . . . He was more intent on the natural history of his own thought than on that of the bird. To the last, his ornithology was not quite sure, not quite trustworthy. (Burroughs 1904, pp. 38–39; quoted by Hildebidle 1983, p. 53)

This opinion is hardly unique,[13] but to argue the "professionalism" of Thoreau's naturalist observations is only to move him from the stocks of science critics to those of the naturalists. With due respect to those who would credit or discredit Thoreau's scientific sensibility or his naturalist skills, I do not believe his importance rests on his observational abilities. We forgive his lapses—perhaps we are oblivious to them—because, his flaws notwithstanding, we understand that he was writing for purposes other than scientific accuracy alone. While he respected the objective frame of mind, individual vision was paramount.

Thoreau, beholden to Kant, found Reality in the *interplay* of mind and world. On this view, the world is known only insofar as our mental faculties allow, so that perception depends on the particular character of the mind. Objectivity universalizes many minds into a single, universalized vision, so that individual perceptions are made uniform. The Romantic attempted to hold objectivity at bay, arguing instead that there is no single, objective Reality we all share. That is not to say that if confronted with an object or a panorama, we might not all agree on its basic characteristics and share a common, general description. But at the next level of cognition, the bestowing of significance on that object, each of us has a deeper or more superficial "understanding," placing that object in a constellation of knowledge and experience that must differ from individual to individual. *Meaning* in this sense is singular. Unique vision—the opportunity of discovering and creating a world of individual standing—was Thoreau's key insight and moral claim. His was no fantasy, for he probed in order to see what others had missed or ignored. To see is to see dialectically, where the mind actively selects and orders the world according to prior values of signification. This is the moral attitude at work—the *valuing* of experience. As important as objectifying nature might have been, it would be subordinated to Thoreau's greater purpose. Thus naturalist observations were in service to intimate experience. Observing nature—qua scientist, qua naturalist—was only a tool in that personal project.

For Thoreau, objectification captured only a part of nature, serving certain ends but ultimately requiring a second arm upon which to lean to present some semblance of reality. He records this early lesson in his Journal:

> I learned to-day that my ornithology had done me no service– The birds I heard, which fortunately did not come within the scope of my science–sung as freshly as if it had been the first morning of creation, and had for background to their song an untrodden wilderness–stretching through many a Carolina and Mexico of the soul. (March 4, 1840, *Journal* 1, 1981, p. 115)

Not only would Thoreau be unable to capture the birds' song; science (he seems to stress here) in some insidious manner would have interfered with his appreciation. To hear melody required a listening soul, as fresh as the wilderness from which the music emanated. As he wrote in *A Week*, "A true account of the actual is the rarest poetry" (1980a, p. 325), which means, plainly, to know nature requires both observation (science) and sympathy (poesis). This sentiment appears again and again in Thoreau's musings on the relationship of "knowing" to "Knowing" aesthetically, morally, spiritually. The visual nature of Thoreau's work, the "aesthetic of nature" which he sought (Peck 1990, pp. 49 ff.), dominated his epistemology. He did, after all, write that "the humblest weed is indescribably beautiful" (January 11, 1854, *Journal*, [1906] 1962, 6:63); and as he fervently attempted to live deliberately—which entails this aesthetic and spiritual embrace of nature—Thoreau was ever vigilant in order to be true to his project. His just standing as a seer of our contemporary ecological self-consciousness was achieved by this aesthetic sensitivity to nature and, more profoundly through this recognition, by his understanding that human relationship to the earth and all therein was essentially an ethical relationship. Seeking the real—aesthetically and spiritually—was Thoreau's life's work, and as his Journal attests, he proceeded tirelessly. I will argue that, ultimately, Thoreau's nature writing was motivated by his acceptance of an overarching mission to integrate the scientific, aesthetic, and spiritual components of his appreciation of nature. So let us now turn to the aesthetic dimension of this enterprise and to how such poesis expressed Thoreau's deepest concerns.

THE CONUNDRUM OF BEAUTY

The rain bow . . . What form of beauty could be imagined more
striking & conspicuous . . . Plainly thus the maker of the Universe
sets the seal of his covenant with men . . . Designed to impress
man[.] All men beholding it begin to understand the significance of
the Greek epithet applied to the world–name for the world–
Kosmos [?Kalos] or beauty. It was designed to impress man. We
live as it were within the calyx of a flower.

> Thoreau, August 6, 1852,
> *Journal* 5, 1997, pp. 284–85

Thoreau's natural history was a history of a world of his own making, one guided by a powerful aesthetic. To grasp this dimension of Thoreau's project, consider again the sand bank he describes in the "Spring" chapter of *Walden*. There Thoreau not only uses evocative descriptions, free and poetic, but self-consciously regards the scene as the work of a divine artist, the sand and clay the medium of His handiwork. Turning to the spring 1848 Journal entry from which this passage derives, we perhaps more clearly see the aesthetic dimension in the raw:

> These little streams & ripples of lava like clay over flow & interlace one
> another like some mythological vegetation–like the forms which I seem
> to have seen initiated in bronze– What affects me is the presence of the
> law–between the inert mass and the luxuriant vegetation what interval

is there? Here is an artist at work–as it were not at work but–a-playing designing – – (*Journal 2*, 1984, p. 383)

In these few lines we see Thoreau associating freely: clay is the medium of the sculptor; the interlacing is the weaving of a tapestry; the mythological vegetation is evocative of fantasy; forms are like bronze statues, again evoking sculpture. Then he raises a theme that is repeated throughout the rest of the entry (and later included in the published passage of *Walden*—e.g., "There is nothing inorganic" [1971, p. 308])—namely, the seamless continuity of a shared life that encompasses the organic and the inorganic. The greatest of artists molded a seemingly inanimate sand bank into movement replete with color ("bluish clay now clay mixed with reddish sand–now pure iron sand–and sand and clay of every degree of fineness and every shade of color" [*Journal 2*, 1984, p. 383]) to present to the discerning eye a veritable life form.[14] This is a rush of insight. Thoreau sees the connectedness of all nature and places himself within that verdure wherein he shares the complete interrelatedness of nature: "I perceive that there is the same power that made me my brain my lungs my bowels my fingers & toes working in other clay this very day– I am in the studio of an artist" (ibid., p. 384).

The splendor of nature always dominates. As he ends the sand bank passage in *Walden,* Thoreau perceives the earth as a great living entity, "with whose great central life all animal and vegetable life is merely parasitic" (1971, p. 309). We see only the most superficial expressions of a throbbing earth whose inhabitants are but "plastic in the hands of the potter" (ibid.). The artistic trope is more than metaphor for Thoreau. He wants to capture the essence of his own understanding through aesthetic sympathy with nature, which he sees as "living poetry" (ibid.). But a certain knowledge haunts his reverie. Whereas the Artist effectively works the "soil," Thoreau can present no such vehicle—music or image—to his reader. He is constrained by lexicon and grammar when portraying his perception, and we sense his own artistic frustration. As he confided to his Journal in the year of *Walden's* publication, and published in somewhat different form in its "Conclusion" (p. 324):

> I fear only lest my expressions may not be extravagant enough,—may not wander far enough beyond the narrow limits of our ordinary insight and faith, so as to be adequate to the truth of which I have been convinced. I desire to speak somewhere without bounds, in order that I may attain to an expression in some degree adequate to truth of which I have been convinced. From a man in a waking moment, to men in their waking moments. Wandering toward the more distant boundaries of a wider pasture. Nothing is so truly bounded and obedient to law as

music, yet nothing so surely breaks all petty and narrow bonds. Whenever I hear any music I fear that I may have spoken tamely and within bounds. And I am convinced that I cannot exaggerate enough even to lay the foundation of a true expression. As for books and the adequateness of their statements to the truth, they are as the tower of Babel to the sky. (Thoreau, February 5, 1854, *Journal*, [1906] 1962, 6:100)[15]

Nevertheless, Thoreau regarded himself as an artist committed to perfection—an ideal that he could never attain. He comes as close to a confession as we possess in *Walden*'s Kouroo artist fable.[16]

I close these short comments on Thoreau's aesthetic venture by drawing a circle back to Goethe and commenting on Thoreau's relation to him—his indebtedness and, perhaps more saliently, their differences. In this latter case, we clearly discern how Thoreau thought of himself as a poet. First, as already noted, Thoreau endorsed the universality of the Primal Plant image Goethe discovered as the basis of botanical variation. But Thoreau would take that insight a step further. In the sand bank passage, the leaf not only fulfills the botanic role Goethe assigned it, but also assumes a universal significance, serving as the template of rivers, feathers, wings, ice, because all of nature—inanimate and animate—follows a selfsame law. In the erupting sand, one finds

> an anticipation of the vegetable leaf. No wonder that the earth expresses itself outwardly in leaves, it so labors with the idea inwardly. *The atoms have already learned this law,* and are pregnant by it. The overhanging leaf sees here its prototype. (*Walden*, 1971, p. 306; emphasis added)

In a sense, Thoreau would go one step further than Goethe. The Young Turk can make this move because of a complex reading he gives Goethe. The clues are offered in testimonials made before *Walden* was published. In *A Week*, Thoreau devotes several pages to Goethe, appreciating his descriptions,[17] and he goes on to laud Goethe as a writer, indeed as the possessor of characteristics we might well imagine that Thoreau himself wished to have. Perhaps Thoreau modeled himself in part on Goethe's own example of power and thoroughness in the descriptions found in his notebooks of the *Italian Journey (1786–1788)*.

But then a fascinating critique emerges, one that sets the stakes much higher, for Thoreau proceeds to assess Goethe as an artist. A distancing now emerges: "Goethe's whole education and life were those of the artist. *He lacks the unconsciousness of the poet*" (*A Week*, 1980a, p. 327; emphasis added). Thoreau explains that Goethe was hampered by living in the city, surrounded by artists and cultural refinement, where neither nature nor a more primal life might have been experienced. "He was defrauded of much which the savage boy enjoys" (ibid.)—obviously a liability given Thoreau's own orientation toward the value of the wild, the celebration of the common man, his pride in American democratic ideals (too often unfulfilled in his opinion), and the general disparagement of effete Europe relative to the rigor and promise of the West. But beyond Goethe's "cultural deprivation," which one might well imagine Thoreau thought devastating for a poet, the American takes a potentially lancing cut at the German's character: "The Man of Genius may at the same time be, indeed is commonly, an Artist, but the two are not to be confounded" (ibid., p. 328). The former is original, inspired, producing "a perfect work in obedience to laws yet unexplored," while the Artist follows in his wake, applying "rules which others have detected" (ibid.). And so who is who?

Thoreau offered a critical clue in a lecture on poetry ("Homer. Ossian. Chaucer."), which he delivered to the Concord Lyceum in 1843. In his lecture, Thoreau takes pains to describe true poetry ("distinguished . . . by the atmosphere which surrounds it") and poets: "There are two classes of men called poets. The one cultivates life, the other art," and correspondingly there are two kinds of writing, "one that of genius or the inspired, the other of intellect and taste." The former

> is above criticism, always correct. . . . It vibrates and pulsates with life forever. It is sacred, and to be read with reverence, as the works of nature are studied. . . . We do not take his words on our lips, but his sense into our hearts. It is the stream of inspiration. . . . The other is self-possessed and wise. It is reverent of genius, and greedy of inspiration. . . . The train of thought moves with subdued and measured step, like a caravan. But the pen is only an instrument in its hand, and not instinct with life. . . . The works of Goethe furnish remarkable instances of the latter. (Thoreau 1975b, pp. 171–72)

Thoreau, the man of nature, thus contrasts himself with the refined European court functionary. Goethe is conversant with "life" but hardly in intimate step with the rhythm of nature, is unable to participate in the exuberance of inspiration, and therefore must, by implication, follow the true poet, the man of true genius, the individual immersed in nature who might traverse the barrier of experience to truly communicate the awesome splendor and unity of nature. Although Thoreau attests that "there has been no man of pure Genius" (*A Week*, 1980a, p. 328), there are indeed a select few who are so gifted—"only one in a hundred millions [is awake enough for] a poetic or divine life" (*Walden*, 1971, p. 90). The true poet's standards are, indeed, Thoreau's thinly disguised descriptions of his own work. Regardless of the poems actually composed—and Thoreau certainly wrote a lot of poetry—the true work of the poet, of the genius, was to place himself within the pulse of life, to commune with nature intimately, and then to "brag [of his findings] as lustily as chanticleer in the morning, standing on his roost, if only to wake my neighbors up" (*Walden*, 1971, p. 84; epigraph on title page of first edition). Thoreau's writings—the works of a true poet in his view—testify to this mandate.

Thoreau thus distinguished himself primarily by his acute sense of nature. But interestingly, he failed to acknowledge the deeper source of his indebtedness to Goethe. Goethe's influence on Emerson (Van Cromphout 1990) and Thoreau, indeed on nineteenth-century thought generally, can hardly be overestimated: "Goethe was simply the paramount intellectual influence upon the age. . . . [I]n a very real sense, his achievement defined modernity" (ibid., p. 9). Van Cromphout uses "modernity" to refer to an awareness of self, a sense of disrupted tradition, and a rejection of authority. Most saliently, nineteenth-century modernity was in a state of "perpetual crisis and an unceasing exercise in self-definition" (ibid., p. 14).[18] The "definition" of the self resulted in a self-conscious ego peering at itself in bewilderment. Any form of knowledge—whether history, science, poetry— arose from a consciousness divided against itself in endless reappraisal, but deliberate "self-definition," the effort of defining applied to "the self," was endlessly recursive (Taylor 1989). Emerson was well aware that *Faust* was the exemplar text of such self-awareness (ibid., p. 18), and Thoreau too faced this fundamental divide in every aspect of his intellectual and spiritual pursuits. Indeed, this is the critical key for understanding Thoreau's projects, each of which was in service to mending the self's division.

THOREAU'S COORDINATES OF THE KNOWING SELF

I think that the existence of man in nature is the divinest and most startling of facts– It is a fact which few have realized.

> Thoreau, May 21, 1851,
> *Journal 3*, 1990, p. 229

Thoreau's nature writing, stemming from his "scientific" observations of natural phenomena, must be seen as of one piece with his poetry, for there is no division either in his sensibilities or even in his method. Closing the circle with the Journal entry with which the previous chapter opened (June 21, 1852), we can now more fully appreciate the three perspectives which have framed our consideration of Thoreau's nature writing: imperative of attention, aesthetic imagination, and self-consciousness. As mentioned in the Introduction, this entry is from the period in which Thoreau was involved in various pursuits: surveying, lecturing on various subjects (including chapters from *Walden* and what became "Walking," first presented in April 1851 [1980b, pp. 93–136]), collecting and classifying botanical specimens, and turning to his Journal more and more as a focus of his literary interests and the repository of an increasingly rich trove of observation and self-reflection. By June 1852 Thoreau had fully embraced his Romanticism (or completed his Romantic turn [Adams and Ross 1988, chap. 9) and was devoting increasing attention to nature in the ways detailed above. This typical report—given here in its entirety—describes an ordinary summer evening hike, commencing about two miles southwest of Concord and proceeding southerly for another couple of miles (from map of Concord area, *Journal* 5, 1997, pp. 536–37):

> 7 Pm. To Cliffs via Hubbard Bathing Place. Cherry birds–I have not seen though I think I have heard them before–their *fine* sering-o note–like a vibrating spring in the air. They are a handsome bird with their crest–& chestnut breasts. They are ready for cherries, when they shall be ripe. The adders tongue arethusa smells exactly like a snake. How singular that in nature too beauty & offensiveness should be thus combined. In flowers as well as in men we demand a beauty pure & fragrant–which perfumes the air. The flower which is showy–but has no or an offensive odor–expresses the character of too many mortals.
>
> The swamp pink bushes have many whitish spongey excrescences– Elder is blossoming. flowers opening now where black berries will be by & by. Panicled andromeda–or Privet andromeda. Nature has looked uncommonly bare & dry to me for a day or two. With our senses applied to the surrounding world we are reading our own physical & corresponding moral revolutions. Nature was so shallow all at once I did not know what had attracted me all my life. I was therefore encouraged when going through a field this evening, I was unexpectedly struck with the beauty of an apple tree– The perception of beauty is a moral test. When in bathing I rush hastily into the river the clamshells cut my feet.
>
> It is dusky now– Men are fishing on the Corner bridge– I hear the veery & the huckleberry bird–& the catbird. It is a cool evening past 8²⁰ [8:20] o'clock. I see the tephrosia out through the dusk–a handsome flower[.] What rich crops this dry hill side has yielded. First I saw the v. pedata here–& then the Lupines & the Snap-Dragon covered it–& now the Lupines are done & their pods are left–the tephrosia has taken their place. This small dry hill is thus a natural garden– I omit other flowers which grow here & name only those which to some extent cover it or possess it. No eighth of an acre in a cultivated garden could

be better clothed or with a more pleasing variety from month to month–& while one flower is in bloom you little suspect that which is to succeed & perchance eclipse it. It is a warmly placed dry hill side beneath a wall–very thinly clad with grass. Such spots there are in nature–natural flower gardens.– Of this succession I hardly know which to admire the most. It would be pleasant to write the history of one hill side for one year. First and last you have the colors of the rainbow & more–& the various fragrances which it has not. Blackberries–roses–& dogs bane are now in bloom here– I hear neither toads nor bull frogs at present–they want a warmer night. I hear the sound of distant thunder though no cloud is obvious. muttering like the roar of artillery. That is a phenomena of this season– As you walk at evening you see the light of the flashes in the horizon & hear the muttering of distant thunder wher some village is being refreshed with the rain denied Concord. We say that showers avoid us–that they go down the river–i.e. go off down the Merrimack–or keep to the south. Thunder and lightening are remarkable accompaniments to our life–

    The dwarf orchis O. herbiola Big (P. flava Gray) at the bathing place in Hubbards meadow, not remarkable. The purple orchis is a good flower to bring home– it will keep fresh many day & its buds open at last in a pitcher of water. Obtuse galium. I observe a rose (called by some moss rose) with a bristly reddish stem, another with a smooth red stem & but few prickles–another with many prickles & bristles.

    Found the single flowered broom rape in Love lane under the oak. (June 21, 1852, *Journal* 5, 1997, pp. 120–22)

This entry begins and ends with self-awareness. Thoreau clearly situates himself in time and place. He notes the route, the data, and the exact time of his observations. In fact, in the manuscript he changes the original "8 o'clock" to "8^{20}" to be exact (ibid., Textual Notes, p. 601). But a second level of self-consciousness is at play, and this resides in self-reflection. There are three obvious examples to cite and at least one other, more obscure. The first is the plain comparison of flowers with human character. Thoreau assigns human value to a flower (adder's-tongue arethusa)—beauty (the visual appearance of the flower) and offensiveness (its smell)—and notes how one would not expect their combination. Why? Because he has indulged in a subjective projection, in which humans associate fairness and fragrance. And then he goes on with a disingenuous comment about flowers that are "showy" (this particular orchid has a striking rose-purple color and distinctive bearded appearance of its lip) but have no odor: they express the "character of too many mortals." Presumably Thoreau does not include himself in this class of men, but the importance of the remark is that he *sees* the human dimension—himself and others—in nature, in particular as per-

sonified by an orchid. If there is any doubt, consider the paragraph following, where he self-consciously acknowledges his own recent lapse in interest in nature and recognizes his state as one reflecting physical well-being
and, more importantly, the state of moral alertness. Again, in attending
nature, Thoreau *reads* his own character. The self-conscious placement of
himself in nature is his route to self-awareness.

Next, note the juxtaposition of his insight regarding the nexus of beauty
and morality ("I was unexpectedly struck with the beauty of an apple tree–
The perception of beauty is a moral test") with an obscure, almost free association: "When in bathing I rush hastily into the river the clam-shells cut
my feet." Here, Thoreau reminds himself that conventional reality, the
world of the everyday, harshly imposes itself to interrupt his poetic reverie.
He realizes, even as he jots down what is indisputably a critical insight—
the very fulcrum of his entire project that allows the self to "lift" the world
to capture experience in a moral, indeed spiritual, frame—that he cannot
reside too long to rejoice in a tree's beauty. Awakened, he pursues his work
of observing and reporting, in this case the flora of a hillside. And then again,
he cannot withhold his personalized judgment. As with a well-cultivated
garden, he "admires" the hill and contemplates that "it would be pleasant
to write the history of one hill side for one year." Pleasant! Hardly a scientific project that would place his eye to the magnifying glass in the drudgery of careful scientific observation. That indeed may be enjoyable, but work
in a conventional sense is not what Thoreau had in mind. No, Thoreau
would admire and enjoy the vegetation's rich colors and fragrances. Again,
the poetic reverie appears in the midst of the minutiae he recalls—the particular flowers, sounds, temperature—and he relates nature to himself as an
aesthetic experience. Finally in this regard, note the last line of the entry:
"Found the single flowered broom rape in Love lane under the oak." It is
unclear which plant he has identified (there are 180 species), but the entire
family is a herbaceous root parasite that lacks chlorophyll and thus receives
nourishment from the roots of other plants. What is the relation of this
plant to Love lane? Is this a simple observation or a veiled comment about
love as a parasitic relationship? If the latter, what then is Thoreau saying
about his own solitude? We cannot say, but our interest is pricked.

Briefly, let us consider other themes, namely the attention to detail and
the aesthetic dimensions. Note that his description is hardly scientific in any
usual fashion. He makes no attempt to compile a complete catalogue of wild
life; indeed, he admits that he lists only those hillside plants "which to some
extent cover it or possess it." In other words, he surveys the scene as a whole
and its details are of little consequence. He, in fact, offers an impression, the

image that most readily falls under his attention. Neither the number of a given species (plant or animal) nor their distribution nor their variation is given. Only in passing does Thoreau remark on the appearance of blooming or otherwise notable plants, the striking cherry birds' song (likened to a vibrating string), or thunder in the distance. In almost every case, when he presents a detail, he uses it as a dab of paint to compose a prose portrait of the hike. In capturing the highlights, Thoreau has effectively offered a coherent picture of what it was like on that June evening just outside Concord, the town of consonance. Indeed, the aesthetic "wholeness" and integrity of the scenes he conjures represent both the harmonized vision of nature itself and Thoreau's ability to perceive and appreciate that harmony.

Thus Thoreau effectively employs detail to present an image—the cultivated, integrated, and successive order of the hillside. This coordinated splendor of variation reflects the grand "design" of the Artist who bestowed this beauty for us to enjoy and contemplate. Thoreau's attention to particulars is in service of two other faculties, the aesthetic and the spiritual, each reflections of a self-conscious awareness so that this man might know his place and his time. But a conceit looms over this passage—indeed, a pretense. The "nowness" of this journal entry, the supposed immediacy of experience, unmediated and direct, is actually a reworking of a memory, an attempt to capture an inner life or its seemingly accessible sensations. But ultimately the description is locked into a conventional "space" by the confines of writing which must, by its very nature, translate private experience into a public tongue, a language foreign to the soul. As he writes, presumably to and for himself, we see Thoreau creating a poetic world under the guise of *re-creating* the scene that he witnessed. This scene is idealized, and represents a vivid example of the world romanticized and in the process "created."[19]

Thoreau is offering a code here, clues of overlapping fragments of experience, whose piecemeal impressions and contemplative reflections conjure a literary portrait of that evening. The extent to which Thoreau is successful in leading us back through his experience depends on our following with him what he called the "scent," which he regarded as "more primitive . . . and trustworthy" than the eye, or his critical faculty (May 9, 1852, ibid., p. 45). I would suggest that "scent" is a form of intuition that guides the outward eye to nature's images. And in the frame in which I see Thoreau, this deepest sense of guidance is "moral," that is, seeking value. The meeting ground of these two faculties—the guiding ethos and the perceiving eye—is "contemplation," those few moments of reverie which quell Thoreau's deep disquiet. Whatever understanding we might share of

Thoreau's experience depends on sharing this vision of his innermost moral perception. We do so by picking up the "scent" of the experience—the clues he leaves for us—the very same he used himself.

So at one level, through his aesthetic faculty, Thoreau is able to see nature, specifically "the beauty of an apple tree," and recognize again how nature holds spiritual value for him as his gaze integrates him into nature's order. But from another perspective, the scene is composed of the hillside and its flora, on the one hand; and on the other, there is Thoreau, who stands attentive, yet fundamentally separate, outside, observing. He must be aware that he is in some fashion constructing the scene, that it is he, as sensitive observer, who confers meaning and significance, a function of his poesis. So we witness the inherent tension of the detached self, observing the world, and at the same time—through sympathetic Imagination—a poetic, spiritualized self which communes with or perhaps is incorporated into that microcosm. And then there is a second divide: the metaphysics of self-awareness, a keen and ceaseless vigilance of the self's place within its world. This bespeaks a profound irony: even as Thoreau would bury himself into the bosom of Mother Nature, he does so acutely aware of his selfness, of his discreteness, of his irreducible individuality, and it is his self-consciousness that makes him "other," a resident alien. This essentially irreconcilable Janus-quality of the self is the tension inherent in Romanticism. The self always and simultaneously peers at the world while scrutinizing its own inquiry in an endlessly recursive spiral of self-contemplation. Thoreau is trapped: attempting to integrate himself into nature, he cannot release himself from the self-consciousness of his own effort. This posture will both support and destabilize his efforts to establish his moral agency.

6 Thoreau's Moral Universe

Our whole life is startlingly moral.
    Walden, 1971, p. 218

What is Thoreau's enduring moral appeal? That question generates responses that revolve around many issues: the first, and the most accessible, pertains to his formative effect on modern environmentalism. In many respects he set that agenda. His genre of nature writing became an exploration of the unstable relationship between the wild and the pastoral; of the predicament of defining or constructing nature; of the metaphysical placement of the self in the universe. Thoreau relentlessly pursued these issues with an honesty and poignancy unique and powerfully evocative. To get to know Thoreau is to achieve an enriching dialogue, and to know him well is to engage a worthy confidant to explore these matters. But more than as a premier American naturalist, an admirer and chronicler of natural history, Thoreau was philosophically self-conscious in these pursuits. This introspective cognizance reflects a deeper source of inquiry as he engaged in perplexing and oftentimes agonizing meditations on his personhood and the meaning of his life in the context of nature.

This leads to the darker side of Thoreau's moral vision, one that dates to the birth of the social universe. How does one balance the interests of the individual with that of the community in which he lives? From Antigone to our present day, this question has been at the heart of ethics, and Thoreau's response is noteworthy for the adamant and uncompromising primacy he gives the individual. The moral vision which so guided his life was derived from an inner sense of his own personhood, the preservation of his own autonomy, the sanctity of his self-determined choice. In the end, Thoreau's moral philosophy is dangerously solipsistic; narcissistic to the extreme, Thoreau's morality was built from the precept that the protection of his autonomy was the crucial and abiding parameter of moral action. In striving for that independence, Thoreau erected a universe around himself.

Belying the mystical aspirations, Thoreau's self-conscious appraisal of the world and himself left him self-contained and thus often isolated from the larger communal universe in which ethics are ultimately enacted.

Thoreau effectively exercised his perspectivism to bring his nature writing to a new standard of literary achievement. And in his history writing, we discussed how he engaged and reconstructed the "radically irrecoverable pastness" (Krell 1990, p. 7) into his own vision that prefigures much of our own historiography. I have stressed the personal imprimatur with which Thoreau stamps each project, for in each instance the moment of creation can only be reenactment, and ipso facto "the whole performance of writing becomes such a reenactment" (Hansen 1990, p. 135). In both genres, Thoreau's imagination celebrates his vantage on the world and time, and he fashioned narratives of vitality and verve that in the process affirmed—and defined—his own selfhood. Indeed, we might note a strong resonance between the writing of a history of culture and autobiography, for both are, in fact must be, cohered by what Husserl called "the hidden unity of intentional inwardness which alone constitutes the unity of history" ([1935] 1970, p. 73). But there was, of course, a high cost for this independence and individuality. Thoreau suffered the throes of isolation and was keenly aware, in this second aspect, of a solitude based on the divide of knowledge—moral and otherwise—separating him from his fellow citizens. The poignancy of writing to himself about his existential solitude speaks volumes:

> The stars go up and down before my only eye– Seasons come round to me alone. I cannot lean so hard on any arm as on a sunbeam– So solid men are not to my sincerity as is the shimmer of the fields. (March 17, 1841, *Journal 1*, 1981, p. 289)

This is not simply a theme of a disaffected youth but one that continued to haunt him. As he confided to his Journal during the Walden period, he, at the very least, felt sequestered from any true sharing of experience:

> No man lives in the world which I inhabit–or ever came rambling into it– Nor did I ever journey in any other man's– Our differences have frequently such foundation as if venus should roll quite near to the orbit of the earth one day–and two inhabitants of the respective planets should take the opportunity to lecture one another[.] (December 2, 1846, *Journal 2*, 1984, p. 355)

Thoreau did not always feel so despondent (see, e.g., May 21, 1851, *Journal* 3, 1990, p. 229), and his entire literary output as a public activity belies this assertion; but at the same time he was all too aware of the difficulty, and at times the futility, of communicating his experience and, more to the point, of having others take him seriously in the full force of his argument. He struggled alone.[1]

Thoreau responded to his isolation by both further retreating into a world of his own making, a place in nature (or what he described as having "a room all to myself; it is Nature . . . a prairie for outlaws" [January 3, 1853, *Journal* 5, 1997, p. 422]), and also by reaching out to the world of men by writing a grand, albeit idiosyncratic, autobiography. The ever-dominant "I" of *Walden*, the vigilant observer and commentator of the essays, *A Week, Cape Cod,* and *The Maine Woods,* the introspective Journal, all attest to a vast attempt to reach to another—the listening ego of Thoreau's split-screen consciousness. Indeed, in the "Solitude" chapter of *Walden*, Thoreau forthrightly uncovers the deepest stratum of his isolation, which is neither emotional (i.e., psychological) nor social, but rather metaphysical, the solitude of the core self, which he refers to as his "doubleness" (already discussed in the previous chapter): "I only know myself as a human entity; and am sensible of a certain doubleness by which I can stand as remote from myself as from another" (*Walden*, 1971, p. 135; written in somewhat different form in the *Journal*, August 8, 1852, [1906] 1962, 4:291). One might hear this statement as an early voice of existentialism if Thoreau had lingered peering at himself as some sort of post–World War II French literary character, pondering his alienation and ennui. But after acknowledging this existential solitude, Thoreau marched on with purpose and self-assertion, capturing his dual identity as it voiced its musings and doings of a man in constant dialogue with himself.

Thoreau recognized how the self might be imprisoned by its selfness, and in the Romantic tradition of actualizing in the context of the other, he relentlessly pursued a transfiguration, which would exchange his autonomous self for one whose boundaries have been blurred in the communion with nature. But there is an unresolved tension between an expansive, expressive view of the person, and the self-actualization of an autonomous entity. So on the one hand there is a circumscribed character to the self, where a moral mandate defines the telos of one's development; and on the other hand, the entity cannot be defined in any circumscribed fashion. In short, there are competing claims for the self—one of independence and one of responsibility; one based on autonomy, the other on relation. Thus the Romantics' preoccupation with the psychological independence of the individual also inherited the Enlightenment tradition of relegating responsibility and freedom to a self-governing ethical agent. Obviously, adherence to a divinely inspired moral code characterizing this latter case long predates the Romantic reaction that asserted the primacy of the "expressive self," the pronouncement of self-will, and the ethical essentiality of the autonomous moral agent. In many ways, the declaration of the self, the free spirit, the actualizing individual characterizing the age of Byron, Keats, and Shelley, made strong claims on an earlier vision of the autonomous self, but now the contours of that agent were elusive and obscure. And it is here that we must search for Thoreau's moral agent and its vision.

VIRTUE

How to observe is how to behave.
> Thoreau, March 23, 1853,
> *Journal*, [1906] 1962, 5:45

[E]ach of us literally *chooses*, by his ways of attending to things, what sort of universe he shall appear himself to inhabit.
> William James [1890] 1983, p. 401

Much of my discussion has been based on a persistent yet unarticulated view of Thoreau's moral philosophy. Here I wish to outline its configuration explicitly. The foundation is the exercise of self-determination, the Romantic mandate to build the self from within in the face of the challenge of "the other." He was thus beholden to Fichte's notion of "self-positing," which by these lights is fundamentally moral:

> Ethics thus considers the object of consciousness not as something given or even constructed by necessary laws of consciousness, but rather as something to be produced by a freely acting subject, consciously striving to establish and to accomplish its own goals. The specific task of Fichte's ethics is therefore to deduce from the general obligation to determine oneself freely the particular obligations of every finite rational being.
>
> Viewed from the perspective of practical philosophy, the world really is nothing more than what Fichte once described as "the material of our duty made sensible," which is precisely the viewpoint adopted by the morally engaged, practically striving subject. (Breazeale 1998, p. 650)

So in this fashion, Thoreau's moral project might be seen in the same way Nietzsche was to construct his own forty years later:[2] Self-responsibility as moral action is grounded in itself; moreover, that self is always striving toward some ideal of itself. Self-consciousness then becomes moral as actions are scrutinized as meaningful and ethically significant. Self-awareness is not only a virtue: it is the origin of morality. But there is a more social or public aspect to Thoreau's ethics, one that in many ways is traditionally ethical and conforms to a moral system that is less abstract and better articulated as a course of action. I will explicate that program by describing its major tenets in terms of virtue ethics and then return to assessing the success of such a construction.

What was virtue for Thoreau? This is a complex issue, for he offered no succinct pronouncement that might guide us. In fact, one might easily argue that Thoreau's entire life's work might be regarded as a project in virtue ethics. Virtue ethics revolve around the idea of the "good life." There are, to be sure, many ways in which a happy and good life has been defined. Consider, for instance, Homeric *arete* (excellence), Socratic self-knowledge, Aristotelian friendship and *phronesis* (wisely applied knowledge, practical wisdom), Christian faith, hope, and love. Plato advised turning our attention to the idea of pure Goodness, which might guide our own lives through disciplined attention to purification of the intellect and passions. Augustine believed that only divine grace might bestow the power to act virtuously, but he advised that prayer and a contemplative religious life would help achieve such grace. Kant argued that virtuous people act precisely from, and because of, respect for moral law which is universalizable. Knights of the Round Table and Victorian gentlemen had their respective codes for a life of virtue, and our own era seems to have evolved to the position that in a pluralistic society virtue comes in various forms and standards, of which tolerance of diversity is itself a cardinal virtue. Indeed, each era and culture has adopted a set of virtues which might even characterize that society. What standards are then applied remains a perplexing quandary for moral theorists. There seemingly are no core virtues or even a unity to the concept. There is simply too much variation in the history of social orders and accompanying philosophical theories to suggest a coherent "doctrine" of virtue.

Nevertheless, Alisdair MacIntyre (1985) does offers us a conceptual scaffolding by which we might understand the nature of virtue, and from this point we can turn to Thoreau's own venture. MacIntyre's approach is to glean from the history of ethics the major conceptions of virtue and then search for an underlying conceptual structure that may hold them all (1985, chap. 14). To be sure, virtue has served as a quality which 1) enables an individual to discharge his or her social role (Homer); 2) makes possible the achievement of a specifically human telos, whether natural or supernatural (Aristotle, Christianity); and 3) enables one to attain earthly and heavenly success. To bring these characteristics together, MacIntyre argues that virtue must rest on character and that character in turn must rest on a common sense of the meaning and purpose of life which is firmly lodged in the philosophical and religious tradition of a particular society. He builds a neo-

Aristotelian definition, by adopting Aristotle's understanding that virtue is related to the skills involved in living a good life, which in turn depends on grasping what a good life looks like by reference to natural and historical ends. According to MacIntyre, the exercise of virtue always exhibits a "practice," by which he means a socially established cooperative human activity. "Bricklaying is not a practice; architecture is. Planting turnips is not a practice; farming is" (ibid., p. 187). There are, to be sure, both internal and external "good" to such practices, but even the internal practice has expression in the community and presumably benefits all. Thus the distinction of "internal" and "external" pertains to the placement of action. Practice pertains to the final standards of excellence and obedience to rules as well as the achievement of ends (ibid., p. 190). Such standards may be modified in history, but judgments as to adherence and achievement are based on objective (communally defined) criteria, not on subjective or emotive analyses. In other words, virtue is ultimately a social act and demands

> a certain kind of relationship between those who participate in it. Now the virtues are those goods by reference to which, whether we like it or not, we define our relationship to those people with whom we share the kind of purposes and standards which inform practices. (Ibid., p. 191)

All this depends on seeing a human life as a continuous narrative rather than as a series of isolated acts and events, which of course raises a profoundly disturbing question for the moderns to answer:

> The question is: is it rationally justifiable to conceive of each human life as a unity, so that we may try to specify each such life as having its good and so that we may understand the virtues as having their function in enabling an individual to make of his or her life one kind of unity rather than another? (Ibid., p. 203)

In other words, is virtue in some fundamental sense a lens by which we peer at a life, or is it the internal compass by which an individual orients his or her own behavior? In either case, it is the narrative of selfhood that is being told. In this regard, narrative itself formulates ethical problems and solutions. Novels, poems, plays, and personal accounts offer vivid moral lessons not by elaborating a systematic ethics but by tapping into collective experience and the wellsprings of the "social imaginary." It is here that we encounter moral choice—solution and impasse—in the full range of human behavior. As MacIntyre observes, "I can only answer the question 'What am I to do?' if I can answer the prior question 'Of what story or stories do I find myself a part?' " (MacIntyre 1985, p. 216). Narrative thus not only becomes a legitimate source for philosophical comment but presents us with the very possibility of developing moral inquiry.[3] The centrality of narrative will serve us in placing Thoreau within his own moral philosophy, for in many respects, by regarding Thoreau as "writing a life" we might appreciate his ethics at work.

The question remains, What did Thoreau regard as virtuous? A study of his political writings—from "Resistance to Civil Government" (1973b) to his late defenses of John Brown—offer us a political philosophy both particular to his time and more generally relevant to our own. (We will consider this aspect in the next section.) In addition, or alternatively, we might glean from Thoreau's correspondence and the rich trove of biographical anecdotes a moral portrait of the man. And perhaps most richly, we could simply cite *Walden* and list the opinions, stipulations, criticisms, and exonerations offered in each chapter, and come up with a virtual moral index ranging from abolitionism to the Zen of direct and intuitive insight. There is an explicit moral code elaborated there in detail, so that one might attain a utopian economy, a utopian life based on its principles (see, e.g., Cafro 1997). But do any of these strategies present a core formulation by which we might understand Thoreau's singular concept of virtue?

"Virtue" hardly appears as an explicit issue in Thoreau's Journal after April 1842. There are numerous references in his early entries, but the problem of virtue as an abstract, philosophical issue largely disappears from his musings, only to erupt occasionally again (e.g., a "prayer" discussed in the next chapter: July 16, 1851, *Journal* 3, 1990, pp. 311–12). Although one might perceive that Thoreau is alluding to "virtue" throughout his oeuvre, after the first volume of the Journal—noteworthy for nineteen separate entries on "virtue"—there are scant direct references. And even in these early writings, "virtue" is given no sustained comment and is cited only in aphorisms, punctuating inferences to an underlying ethos.[4] Virtue was clearly on his mind, but these ethical nuggets can only be understood in the context of a fuller accounting of what virtue might be for Thoreau.

Most obviously, to live a virtuous life was to live deliberately, or, as we might put it, self-consciously. Whether as a day laborer, naturalist, or writer, Thoreau carefully chose his path of action, one he determined as meaningful. When he wrote in *Walden*'s "Higher Laws," "Our whole life is startlingly moral" (1971, p. 218), he was obviously advising us of what he perceived as a fundamental fact.[5] We see this most evidently in those activities which were guided by his sense of a proper relation to the natural, where he attempted some communion with nature in an immediate awareness. Under these auspices, Thoreau approached nature as a member of its congregation: "The constant query Nature puts is Are you virtuous? Then you can behold me" (June 5, 1852, *Journal* 5, 1997, p. 79). Only if pure and worthy would he be allowed to behold nature and drink of her splendor: "Beauty–fragrance–music–sweetness–& joy of all kinds are for the virtuous" (ibid.). There is a quality of the lover enjoying the pleasures of his partner in this passage, but in addition to the intensity of his spiritual delight, Thoreau reckons he enjoys admission to that altar because of his purified state, the trial of cleansing and the exercise of virtue that has brought him to that place. These religious and rapturous overtones are not to be neutralized as some kind of metaphoric or poetic account. Thoreau indeed was committed to nature, and because of his devotion he was elected to a special standing, which warranted his sermonizing tone. As Thoreau's orienting pole star and spiritual object in all matter and form, nature truly was regarded devoutly and with extraordinary intensity. If we understand him in conventional terms, we might miss the utter absorption he experienced, and exhibited, in his nature worship.

In examining Thoreau's vision of time, history, memory, and natural observations we are struck not only with the personal aspect of his recording but with his self-conscious intention of fulfilling a self-defined quest directed toward a moral vision of himself in self-conscious awareness of his relation to nature. This is the vision of the ethical life as one that champions the wild as the first principle of nature herself, but more saliently, as the basis of our own link to the world. In seeking the core of our own being, Thoreau asserts that the wild is the essential element and that by domesticating it through civilization we lose contact with the deepest source of our spirituality. Justly, "Walking" is regarded as a national anthem to a new moral standing of nature. The essay begins with a cry to arms:

> I wish to speak a word for Nature, for absolute freedom and wildness, as contrasted with a freedom and culture merely civil,—to regard man as an inhabitant, or a part and parcel of Nature, rather than a member of society. I wish to make an extreme statement. (Thoreau 1980b, p. 93)

The slogan "in Wildness is the preservation of the World" (ibid., p. 112) truly captures Thoreau's moral stand.

But as I have endeavored to show, as central as this relationship is to Thoreau, it is an epiphenomenon of something deeper—the discovery of the self and its perfection. In this Romantic context we see Thoreau's relationship to nature as the *expression* of that effort. He might have sought self-definition in another context, but he *chose* nature, and thereby nature became the moral vehicle by which he explored his own identity and developed his personhood. The Journal, more than other project, became the narrative which, again following MacIntyre, allowed him the "practice" that virtue ethics demands as constitutive of its structure: the narrative record gave coherence and continuity to a life that was literally being written. Walt Whitman published *Song of Myself;* Thoreau kept, in private, "a book of myself." It served as the repository of a life we might share.

The telos of a good life in Thoreau's view is best described by Thoreau himself:

> Virtue is incalculable, as it is inestimable. Well man's destiny is but Virtue–or manhood–it is wholly moral–to be learned only by the life of the soul. God cannot calculate it–he has no moral philosophy–no ethics[.] The reason before it can be applied to such a subject will have to fetter and restrict it–how can he step by step perform that long journey–who has not conceived whither he is bound– How can he expect to perform an arduous journey without interruption who has no passport to the end? (April 3, 1842, *Journal* 1, 1981, p. 401)

One might read this passage as a prayer, where "the life of the soul" is its own life, beyond morality—that is man's rational construct, which will only fetter it—and is given directly to man by God's grace. There is indeed some "passport to the end," and we are obligated to pursue our destiny, which, because it is chosen, could only be virtuous.

Thus, according to Thoreau, our destiny is prescribed as following the character of our personhood. In this sense our lives are composed both from the contingencies of circumstance *and* from the creative responses arising from our moral personalities. To the extent that each of us is able, we pursue, and discover, our own self-made fortune. Thoreau does not develop the philosophical foundations of this thought, but he draws from implicit assertions of free will the imperative of the rational, and the core organizing force of moral agency. Like Nietzsche after him, morality becomes the ethics of self-responsibility, and Thoreau, the Romantic individual, answers only to himself.[6]

In the "Conclusion" to *Walden,* Thoreau writes perhaps the clearest credo for a life governed by the virtue ethics of what Coleridge had called individuation (see chapter 3). It might be termed, in the American context, the creed of individuality. All of the elements for virtue ethics—practice, telos, and achievement—are contained here, encapsulating the life of simplicity, communality with nature, and the paramount place of self-actualization:

> I learned this, at least, by my experiment; that if one advances confidently in the direction of his dreams, and endeavors to live the life which he has imagined, he will meet with a success unexpected in common

hours. He will put some things behind, will pass an invisible boundary; new, universal, and more liberal laws will begin to establish themselves around and within him; or the old laws be expanded, and interpreted in his favor in a more liberal sense, and he will live with the license of a higher order of beings. In proportion as he simplifies his life, the laws of the universe will appear less complex, and solitude will not be solitude, nor poverty poverty, nor weakness weakness. If you have built castles in the air, your work need not be lost; that is where they should be. Now put the foundations under them. (*Walden*, 1971, pp. 323–24)

The key to this passage, and indeed to *Walden,* is that one's life may be constructed from within—as a germ that must be cultivated to flourish. In this respect, the self is fundamentally organic and self-determined.

The Imagination—as close to a vital center as we might find in Thoreau's moral cosmos—is more than our faculty by which to understand nature, or create art, for it serves as the means by which the self might grow according to its own telos. The stultification of a repressive culture is the gravest threat to this thriving, and besides the direction nature offers us, more basically, it is the freedom from civilization's inhibition that affords us the opportunity to flourish. This is Thoreau's well-known and celebrated credo. But I venture to argue that his moral attitude extended beyond ethical action as normally understood. When he declared that "our *whole* life is startlingly moral" (*Walden,* 1971, p. 218; emphasis added), I take him literally. Beyond social consciousness and individual action, Thoreau's moral universe extended to investing the natural world with his own vision. Plainly stated, Thoreau's world-making is value-laden, which simply means that he *chose* how to see, and in so doing, he discovered a world that was uniquely his own. No doubt there is a "real" world to encounter, but how that engagement occurs is a moral, namely *human,* choice—one dictated by a host of factors which play together to direct attention, perception, and final signification. As already detailed in previous chapters, by focusing on certain elements of a panorama or the behavior of a particular animal, Thoreau allowed his inner eye—the poetic and spiritual "organ"—to direct his optical vision and attune his ear. Thus there is a cognitive component to Thoreau's moral vision, one fully integrated with ethical conduct in a more ordinary sense. To *see* creatively was itself, for Thoreau, a value.

And now we come to Thoreau's dilemma: How might he translate his private experience into the public domain? His own tortured path fell precisely at this divide. In one sense, he protected his inner life and regarded his virtue as a private affair:

> Men should hear of your virtue only as they hear the creaking of the earths' axle and the music of the spheres. It will fall into the course of nature and be effectually concealed by publicness. (February 10, 1841, *Journal* 1, 1981, p. 263)

On the other hand, he was not shy to lecture his fellow Concordians on politics and the moral life more generally. Indeed, following MacIntyre, Thoreau's virtue ethics required the discharge of a social role and the attainment of some private telos. Both elements are important to Thoreau—the public and the personal—indeed, they are not easily separated. Thoreau was well aware that he, in the endeavor to create a life he regarded as honest, was doing so in a public forum. After all, for all of his talk about solitude, Thoreau lectured actively. But more to the point, he was frustrated by the lack of the literary success that would have enabled him to assemble a large, attentive audience. He aspired to being recognized as a seer, one whom the ordinary would hear and follow. His was the work of the prophet, and Thoreau unabashedly regarded himself as engaged in heroic work.[7] But heroes are not always successful; indeed, the tragic hero is defined by his failure. So in terms of his moral venture we must now assess Thoreau's achievement, first as a writer of nature and than as a political moralist.

THE LIMITS OF WRITING

The sound of the *dreaming* frogs prevails over the others.
                                   Thoreau, June 13, 1851,
                                   Journal 3, 1990, p. 263

Thoreau's claim of showing us a life of virtue rests most apparently upon his position as godfather of the environmental movement, the leading figure in the pantheon of naturalists. He has achieved that status not because he was a self-conscious and careful observer. To be sure, he was, but the character of that enterprise was to seek the metaphysical origins of his morality. This aspect of his moral project ultimately "succeeds" despite the "failure" of his epistemology, by which I mean that Thoreau could not capture nature in his writings as he *experienced* it. At best, he might "present a scene in which the gap between man and nature will seem *virtually* closed" (McIntosh 1974, p. 156; emphasis added)—but not quite. As beautiful and evocative as any of his descriptions might be, there was a gulf separating his primary encounter with the self-consciousness of reflection and composition. And even more fundamentally, no matter how deeply he sought correspondence with nature, he realized that "[h]is [the poet's] thought is one world, her's [Nature] another. He is another nature–Nature's brother"

(March 3, 1839, *Journal* 1, 1981, p. 69).[8] But it was in the *doing*, in the exercise, in the pursuit of the vision he experienced, that we witness most clearly Thoreau practicing what he considered to be a virtuous life.

Thoreau's entire project depends on the personalization of experience: "the truth respecting *his* things shall naturally exhale from a man like the odor of the muskrat from the coat of a trapper" (November 1, 1851, *Journal* 4, 1992, p. 158; emphasis in original). Note the emphasized possessive adjective, *his*. Truth is not assessed or attained through some positivist standard, but rather falls squarely within the personal domain. This is not to say that Thoreau creates "truth" in the idealistic sense: for him, the world indeed exists independent, real, and knowable. But a dialectic plays here between the subject and his object of inquiry. Ultimately, the observing eye must gather "facts," but these are ordered into an interpretative description of nature, whether under the guise of science or poetry.

Thoreau was not always sanguine about his ability to transmit his vision, and some of his "facts" are not ordinary perceptions readily transmitted to the public domain. Many times Thoreau recognizes the ultimate privacy of his experience. Consider, for example, the following early Journal entry:

> Perhaps I may say that I have never had a deeper and more memorable experience of life–its great serenity, than when listening to the trill of a tree-sparrow among the huckleberry bushes after a shower. It is a communication to which a man must attend in solitude and silence, and may never be able to tell his brother. (September 28, 1843, *Journal* 1, 1981, p. 469)

This is a particularly poignant passage. It stands alone, and we are witness to Thoreau's solitude—indeed, isolation. This takes on deeper significance as we recall Emerson's famous judgment in his eulogy of Thoreau:

> I cannot help counting it a fault in him that he had no ambition. Wanting this, instead of engineering for all America, he was the captain of a huckleberry party. Pounding beans is good to the end of pounding empires one of these days, but if, at the end of years, it is still only beans!— (Quoted in Rossi 1992, pp. 331–32)

Many commentators have been struck by Emerson's lack of insight into Thoreau's enterprise, and the choice of the huckleberry setting is particularly revealing given Emerson's own lost dreams of youthful exuberance.[9] Further, the slap at the hoeing of beans is particularly callous considering the ethical import of the entire Walden experiment. Emerson, who himself had followed the same deserted path into the woods in his youth had apparently come to deny or ignore one of Thoreau's key messages:

at the same time that we exclude mankind from gathering berries in our field, we exclude them from gathering health and happiness and inspiration and a hundred other far finer and nobler fruits than berries. (Thoreau, *Journal*, [1906] 1962, 14:56)

If Emerson misunderstood Thoreau, only finally to reject him, no wonder Thoreau so profoundly felt his solitude. And this was not solely a function of the limits of language or the adequacy of facts to convey his experience. The other intractable limitation was the inability of others to hear, to comprehend, to appreciate the world as Thoreau did:

> I heard the dream of the toad. It rang through and filled all the air, though I had not heard it once. And I turned my companion's attention to it, but he did not appear to perceive it as a new sound in the air. Loud and prevailing as it is, most men do not notice it at all. It is to them, perchance, a sort of simmering or seething of all nature. That afternoon the dream of the toads rang through the elms by Little River and affected the thoughts of men, though they were not conscious that they heard it. (October 26, 1853, *Journal*, [1906] 1962, 5:453)

Dreaming frogs appear frequently in the spring Journal entries of 1851 (May 21, 25; June 13, 14) and 1852 (April 30, May 3, 5, 7, 8) during Thoreau's Romantic turn. He only alludes to their significance for him, and we may surmise that in hearing the frogs' inner voice, he detects the faint pulse of nature itself, the measure of its nearness. But beyond the intimacy of nature, Thoreau is keenly aware of its supernatural standing, and he uses the frogs to declare that reality:

> The frog had eyed the heavens from his marsh, until his mind was filled with visions, & he saw more than belongs to this fenny earth– He mistrusted that he was become a dreamer & visionary–leaping across the swamp to his fellow what was his joy & consolation to find that he too had seen the same sights in the heavens–he too had dreamed the same dreams.
> From nature we turn astonished to this *near* but supernatural fact[.] (May 21, 1851, *Journal* 3, 1990, p. 229)

This passage immediately follows an almost rapturous observation of Thoreau's deepest hope to communicate with his fellow citizen:

> There is a representative of the divinity on earth–of all things fair & noble are to be expected. We have the material of heaven here. I think that the standing miracle to man is man–behind the paling–yonder come rain or shine–hope or doubt–there dwells a man. an actual being who can sympathize with our sublimest thoughts. . . .

> I think that the existence of man in nature is the divinest and most
> startling of all facts– It is a fact which few have realized. (Ibid.)

Thoreau is like the frogs, consoled by the ability of another sentient being
to appreciate that which he perceives as a "supernatural fact." Unfortunately,
two years later Thoreau admits that his companion could not hear the
dreaming frogs, and we thus witness the unresolved tension between
Thoreau's striving to communicate his vision and the inability of his fel-
lows to understand him. He is left essentially alone: "I hear the dreaming
of the frogs– So it seems to me & so significantly passes my life away. It is
like the dreaming of frogs in a summer evening" (May 25, 1851, *Journal* 3,
1990, p. 237).

At the same time, Thoreau was compelled to write. As he confided to his
Journal well in his maturity:

> I see that my neighbors look with compassion on me, that they think it
> is mean and unfortunate destiny which makes me to walk in these
> fields and woods so much and sail on this river alone. But so long as I
> find here the only real elysium, I cannot hesitate in my choice. My
> work is writing, and I do not hesitate, though I know that no subject is
> too trivial for me, tried by ordinary standards; for, ye fools, the theme is
> nothing, the life is everything. (October 18, 1856, *Journal*, [1906], 1962,
> 9:121)

The "life" of writing indeed is Thoreau's life; he is in effect writing his autobiography, but it is a most circumscribed aspect of his full experience. More,
in the process of writing ostensibly about nature, the self emerges:

> We touch our subject but by a point which has no breadth, but the
> pyramid of our experience . . . rests on us by a broader or narrower
> base. That is, man is all in all, Nature nothing, but as she draws him out
> and reflects him. (Ibid.)

Much has been written regarding Thoreau's imperative of writing (e.g.,
Cavell 1981; Cameron 1985; Garber 1991), which builds basically on
Thoreau's own aspiration: "As you see so at length will you *say*" (November 1, 1851, *Journal* 4, 1992, p. 158), and I hardly would dispute Thoreau's
principal identity as writer. He self-consciously and ambitiously pursued
his art and adopted the ethos of the literary circle.[10] After all, Thoreau's primary vocation was writing, and he pursued his craft with passion, distinguishing "recording" from "creation."

> Writing may be either the record of a deed or a deed.
>   It is nobler when it is a deed. . . . Its productions are then works of
> art. And stand like monuments of history– To the poet as artist his

words must be as the relation of his remotest and finest memory. And older and simpler antiquity– Contemporary with the moon and grasshoppers. (After January 1, 1844, *Journal* 1, 1981, p. 495)

The moon and the grasshoppers refer to the supernatural, and while Thoreau claims that the *memory* of that experience might inspire his writing, he does not assert that he accomplishes more than the creation of a work of art that might well stand in history. That is, of course, worthy in itself, but that is not the issue with which we are now concerned, namely, What is the relation of the writer—the conscious intellect, the knowing ego—to his immediate experience?

Thoreau was keenly aware of the "levels" of experience by which objectivity divided the world. While partaking in the keen observation of nature, albeit ultimately for poetic or spiritual purpose, he recognized, like the phenomenologists after him, that experience was distilled and in the process "refined"—categorized, objectified—and thus filtered through various conceptual channels and changed accordingly. The implications of that self-conscious appraisal had far-reaching effects, most directly in the experience of nature. Nature was always "processed" by the mind and accordingly was experienced as a product of "the Wild" (as a Kantian noumenon) and a cognitive faculty.[11] This represents a personalization of the radical other: "Through our conceptual domestication of nature, we extinguish wild otherness even in the imagination" (Evernden 1992, p. 116).

How can one respond to the dilemma implicit in these constructions of nature? One may simply acknowledge the duality of the subject-object dichotomy, leaving man to "know" the world as best he might, a consequence of our epistemological posture. On this view, we accept different degrees of dualism and different degrees of knowing, so that there may be things we might vaguely appreciate but not *know*, such as the wild. With this concept of the wild, there must persist a domain that remains "unknown," that is, unapproached by human understanding. Thus Thoreau's battle cry, "in Wildness is the preservation of the world" ("Walking," 1980b, p. 112), becomes a slogan celebrating this inexhaustible reservoir for human experience. So while we may study nature scientifically, employ it for technology, model it for art, and ponder it as a spiritual resource, each modality adheres to the basic epistemological subject-object divide. Thus nature (the Wild) is never truly tamed or known.

Yet Thoreau "sensed" the Wild, both in mystical revelry and as some kind of personal savagery. These were elusive experiences, and oftentimes we get the sense that he was incapable of offering us the descriptive means to witness his vision. "Frogs' dreams" is a fecund metaphor, an allusion to an appreciation of nature and reality; but at another level we might take the image as the only language available—an evocative but hardly explicit description. "Frogs' dreams"—whatever they might be—was as forthcoming as the experience would allow. Simply, there are supernatural facts, and these are not to be understood—or communicated—by conventional, that is, public, means. In this realm, science and its search for positivist facts is irrelevant. Thoreau believed that "we do not learn by inference and deduction . . . but by direct intercourse" (October 11, 1840, *Journal 1*, 1981, p. 187), and by "direct" he meant unmediated. If no mediation is required to appreciate and *know* nature, then no language is required either. "Direct" implies no distance between subject and object; so when the knower is immersed in nature, intellectualization—reflection, contemplation—is suspended. But that experience when communicated as knowledge then requires a radical reformulation, for cognitive categories must be applied. Where language was unnecessary in the primary encounter because it was "thoughtless," that is, mystical, it becomes something else in public transmittal. "The whole point is, of course, that the senses are always 'too late,' once we become aware of them they already have meaning. They have become attached; they are, to use Thoreau's own phrase, 'made' for something" (Hansen 1990, p. 134).

So much of Thoreau's writing seems to move toward an ephemeral point—an imprecise triangulation between nature, himself, and his reader—because frequently the experience he is recording is preconscious and must employ in these cases, as the best approximation, prose poetry. Thoreau would valiantly push the limits of language, but he was caught on the horns of an intractable dilemma: on the one hand, he sought the "miracle" of man to hear and respond to him; on the other hand, no matter how carefully he wrote, Thoreau could barely achieve a fair transmission of his experience and vision into words. His was a lonely vigil. No wonder he felt as if he resided with the frogs in their dreams—and they in his.

Thoreau's frustration may be the reason why he intrigues us so powerfully. To refer to Thoreau's naturalist writings as in some sense a disappointment may be jolting. He is, after all, justly celebrated as a seer of the environmentalists' imagination, a consummate practitioner of his art. As an observer of nature, his careful descriptions, meticulous note-taking, comprehensive recordkeeping, and eloquent accounts of encounters with landscapes and natural life of all sorts are exemplary naturalist writings. If indeed he is a naturalist extraordinaire, on what basis did he "fail"?

His was no ordinary failure. But if one sees Thoreau as striving for metaphysical integration as his ultimate ambition, his writing repeatedly forced him to face his own self-consciousness. He was all too well aware that he was *writing.* In offering his experience, specifically his integration with, and knowledge of, nature, he produces a representation, which must, by its very character, be a "translation." In this sense, his medium of communication consumes what he would communicate. Thoreau cannot do what Sharon Cameron takes him to be doing; that is, he cannot "write" nature, dissolve the subject-object relationship, efface his own identity, and in the literary product offer us his own consciousness (1985, pp. 46–48, 88–89; previously discussed in chapter 3). By Cameron's lights, the natural world and Thoreau's writing are somehow of one piece, seamlessly connected. I maintain (as discussed in chapter 3) that this putative fusion rests on a category error. One must not confuse the description with its object. For example, if I describe a bottle in every detail, even if I photograph the bottle from a dozen different angles, my description can never *be* the bottle. As Magritte wrote at the bottom of his painting of a pipe, "Ceci n'est pas une pipe." The representation is by its nature derivative and interpretative; Thoreau could only depict the world, just as a painter might. This is a classic semiotic snarl, but the signified/signifier difference is fundamental. We may gaze upon the object of inquiry, but to confuse that gaze with the object itself is to make the most basic of category errors. Cameron makes such a conflation in her interpretation of Thoreau's Journal writing. But did Thoreau?

Thoreau was ever mindful of *not* "writing nature." The reconstruction of experience accomplished in and by his writing is an artistic rendering *of* that experience. But Cameron has pointedly brought into focus the intriguing question that deserves fuller attention, for it falls squarely in the midst of the epistemological standing of Thoreau's writing: namely, What is the relation between the object of inquiry—the natural world—and this method of study and reporting (whether as formal scientific description or as descriptive narrative, namely natural history, or its philosophical or psychological extensions of those observations)? I do not contest that in mystical union the subject-object divide may be dissolved. I acknowledge that Thoreau suspended the self-other dichotomy in mystical states, and that he quite forthrightly attempted to report those experiences. But his testimony is a mere allusion. And when he engaged in studying nature, seeking careful measurement and observation in many different venues, he divested himself of his mystical cloud and strode forth to engage the world in minute detail, well aware of the self-other separation. He certainly knew what it meant to apply systematic thinking to a problem, whether to record the first appearance of flowers or to determine the best mixture of clay and graphite to make a better pencil (Petroski 1989). In other words, Thoreau knew what it meant to engage in the science of his day, and he readily drew upon the most recent scientific contributions of geology, taxonomy, ornithology, entomology, botany, ichthyology, albeit in an older naturalist tradition. But then Thoreau also practiced an "intermediate" literary venture, situated somewhere between self-absorbed mystical reverie and objectivity-oriented positivist science. This was the art of his nature writing, the distillation and translation of a self-conscious encounter with nature, one posed specifically as an intimate exchange, one imbued with significance and beauty.

Cameron's description best suits not what Thoreau *accomplished* but rather what he *attempted*. This venture sustained him, because of its *moral* intent: attending many needs, most importantly Thoreau's writing satisfied an ethical calling. As readers, we readily perceive that he is prescriptive: Integrate experience! Personalize knowledge! See self-consciously with a poetic eye! Boldly stated in many places, his exhortations have no ambiguity and no subtlety. But he also enacts another morality play. In this less direct guise, Thoreau remains coyly evocative, offering us only vague indications where we too might pursue a path similar to his own, but one which we must discover individually. This is Thoreau's deeper lesson: the recognition that there are no formulae or prescriptions, but only a nebulous approximation of the vision a great mystic might hope to report. He indicated the direction he followed: each, he tells us, must find his own path. Thoreau's writing can only suggest the contours of his own insights. His rhetoric is full of dreams, frogs, mists. It is a world of mirages, symbols, fables, myths, and fantasies. It is the world of poetry.

At about the same time as Thoreau lived at Walden Pond, Kierkegaard was writing of the leap beyond rationality to the dominion of the divine. There was no philosophical hope of adjudicating belief, and Kierkegaard clearly voiced a religious existentialism that would have reverberated sweetly in Thoreau's Massachusetts woods. Thoreau would indeed have agreed with Kierkegaard's cardinal point about the immiscible nature of logical discourses and metaphysical experiences. At the nexus of the self-conscious rational mind, each of them would have forgone the attempt to reconcile that faculty's knowledge of the world with the frogs' dreams emanating from supernatural or moral universes. Each approached the issue from his unique perspective—as religionist and naturalist—but each testified to the same lesson. As Thoreau wrote,

> The destiny of the soul can never be studied by the reason–for its modes are not extatic– In the wisest calculation or demonstration I but play a game with myself– I am not to be taken captive by myself.
>
> I cannot conceive myself–God must convince– I can calculate a problem in arithmetic–but not any morality. (Thoreau, April 3, 1842, *Journal* 1, 1981, p. 401)

Thoreau recognized that indeed there was a spiritual domain that might be exhibited to him, but his analytical tools were not to be applied in its understanding. His "wisest calculation" is only reduced to "a game," and morality resides beyond reason. That is not to say that the ethical life was beyond man, only that its call is not derived logically, nor understood in a conventionally rational sense.

Aside from the differences in orientation, this is Kierkegaard's theme in *Fear and Trembling*, a work published in October 1843, written precisely when Thoreau penned this Journal entry. The Dane was dealing with "understanding" of the divine encounter, the "beyond rationality" of faith, and the inability of language to convey that experience, for, being outside comprehension and the intellect (in any logical sense), speech can grasp no hold to express the meeting of God and man. Kierkegaard's discussion revolves around Abraham taking Isaac for sacrifice to God, and toward the end of the essay, he discusses the role of language in the context of Abraham's inability to explain what he is about:

> Abraham is silent—but he *cannot* speak, therein lies the distress and anguish. . . . He can say what he will, but there is one thing he cannot say and since he cannot say it, i.e. say it in a way that another understands it, he does not speak. . . . [H]e doesn't say anything, and this is his way of saying what he has to say. (Kierkegaard [1843] 1985, pp. 137 and 142)

This is the same conclusion Wittgenstein drew in his famous adage at the end of the *Tractatus*, "Whereof one cannot speak, thereof one must be silent" ([1922] 1981, p. 189). Kierkegaard and Wittgenstein meant that language—using the presumption of logic—could make no sense of the metaphysical. From this point of view, when we speak of such matters, it is either "nonsense" (Wittgenstein) or "universal" (Kierkegaard); nonsense is nonsense and the universal is the universal, that is, prosaic. In both cases speech is, at best, distorting, and, more fairly, simply false to the experience. Thus both Kierkegaard and Wittgenstein, despite their vastly different orientations, arrived at the same point—"[F]aith [the metaphysical generally] begins precisely where thinking leaves off" (Kierkegaard [1843] 1985, p. 82)—and language stops at that point.[12] When Kierkegaard explores the domain of faith, he offers us a few hints about this unintelligibility:

> Here we see the need for a new category for understanding Abraham. . . . Abraham cannot be mediated, which can also be put by saying he cannot speak. The moment I speak I express the universal, and when I do not no one can understand me. . . . Perhaps what the

believer intends just cannot be done, after all it is unthinkable. (Ibid.,
pp. 88–89)

Language is, after all, the expression of our thinking; without thought there
is nothing to *say*. Thoreau might well have concurred: he wrote of dreaming frogs that their sound "is such a sound as you can make with a quill on
water–a bubbling sound" (Thoreau, May 5, 1852, *Journal 5*, 1997, p. 29).
Hardly language anyone else might understand. And even more explicitly,

> There is no name for this life unless it be the very vitality of *vita*–
> Silent is the preacher about it–and silent must ever be. for he who
> knows it will not preach. (August 1, 1841, *Journal 1*, 1981, p. 315)

So Thoreau swings between the requirement that he write, knowing that
he can capture only a small portion of his experience, and the admission
that the profoundest insight cannot be discussed at all.

Yet much of Thoreau's accomplishment as a writer hinges on his ability
to describe nature and his relation to it, and it would be perverse simply to
dismiss his literary efforts as a doomed effort to speak the unspeakable. A
tension then needs to be further explored to make the point I wish to stress
here. Indeed, other philosophers, most notably Stanley Cavell, have vexed
themselves over this issue. Cavell makes the salient point that language,
despite the problem of transmitting private experience does, must, carry
meaning. "Writing is a labor of the hands" (Cavell 1981, p. 27), and it is in
the *doing*, in the effort, that meaning is forged, both for the writer writing
and for the reader reading. Each must do his own work. Somewhere then,
between the inert deadness of words and understanding, we must translate.[13] And here we find language's meaning: "*What* gives it life?—In use
it is *alive*. Is life breathed into it there?—Or is the *use* its life?" (Wittgenstein 1953, p. 128e). Wittgenstein's thesis is that the miracle of language is
in its use—that, indeed, language is fundamentally functional in its own
doing. So too would Thoreau regard his writing as the act of giving life to
words that could only point to experience, and hopefully beckoning his
reader to his or her own work in the reading of those words. The reader is
intimately linked to Thoreau's project, for "reading is not merely the other
side of writing, its eventual fate; it is another metaphor of writing itself"
(Cavell 1981, p. 28).

Obviously, some writing is more amenable to communication than other
kinds. For instance, when Thoreau describes the economy of his experiment,
it is clear what he is about; when he draws a word picture describing a landscape, he evokes an image and its accompanying emotion with broad, if
indistinct, strokes of his pencil; when he refers to feelings of the sublime,

we float in foggy vapors and language begins to fail us. Both Kierkegaard and Thoreau do indeed write of the spiritual, the experience that knows no words. They wrote, in fact, a lot, and thus their *action* belied their own doubts. This, of course, follows the tradition of great mystics—whom we know of!—who sought words to convey their experience and yet knew that their efforts diminished, even distorted, what they had experienced. There are, to be sure, different ways of dealing with transcendence: silence; distinguishing between ways in which the transcendent is beyond discourse and ways in which it may not be; and, finally, refusal to resolve the dilemma, that is, acceptance of a genuine aporia (Sells 1994). This last response leads to a particular kind of discourse, where any saying demands a correcting proposition, an unsaying, so to speak; and in the "space" between the names, we might approximate meaning. This is the technique employed by Plotinus, Ibn Arabi, Meister Eckhart, among many others, but it is not Thoreau's method, which, for lack of a more comprehensive description, I will call "poetic." In verse, but more often in prose poetry, Thoreau, very much in the tradition of his circle, used nature as the spiritual muse to whom he responded by writing of his experience. He spoke for the most part with confidence, admitting on occasion the "dullness" of his ability. So, while he appreciated the limits of thought, rationality, and poesis, Thoreau remained a writer, and in this context, a courageous one.

But there is another level of insecurity with the writing project. Although Thoreau endeavored to capture nature in his writing as a translation of his unmediated experience, beyond what he directly perceived through his senses and intellect, there were intimations that a supernatural world beckoned, more ideal and real than nature as he might see or understand it—Plato's cave in a different guise. This then represents a second level of inaccessibility: that is, beyond what he experienced but could not express, there were clues of a spiritual dimension he did not even apprehend. While we might sense this hidden sublime reality, it is not accessible to our imperfect intelligences and thus remains unarticulated even by our most profound poetic or aporiatic language. Ideal nature is not only simply out of reach of rational consciousness, it is unknowable in any sense and thus beyond Thoreau's pencil, in any mode.

> I believe that there is an ideal or real nature, infinitely more perfect than the actual as there is an ideal life of man. Else where are the glorious summers which in vision sometimes visit my brain[.]
> When nature ceases to be supernatural to a man—what will he do then? Of what worth is human life—if its actions are no longer to have this sublime and unexplored scenery. Who will build a cottage and

dwell in it with enthusiasm if not in the elysian fields? (Thoreau,
November 2, 1843, *Journal 1*, 1981, p. 481)

In fact, Thoreau did, by moving into his Walden cabin less than two years
later.

Thoreau was modest in his expectations of Rational Understanding, but
he was stalwart in pursuing nature's moral order, for he indeed had seen a
spiritual vision that sustained and guided him. For all the homage Thoreau
paid the critical faculty, when he faces the metaphysical, reason is subordinated to the insight offered by divine revelation:

> On one side of man is the actual and on the other the ideal– The former
> is the province of the reason[.] it is even a divine light when directed
> upon it–but it cannot reach forward into the ideal without blindness.
> The moon was made to rule by night, but the sun to rule by day. Rea-
> son will be but a pale cloud like the moon when one ray of divine light
> comes to illumine the soul. (April 3, 1842, *Journal 1*, 1981, p. 401)

From this perspective, the nature of language, for all its breadth and miracle
of communication of experience, simply cannot eclipse its inherent limits.
Our overreliance on language is simply the product of an older metaphysics.
So discussions regarding the self's relation to nature can offer no bona fide
knowledge. Instead, we speak in generalities, poetics, and metaphors, which
may easily be misunderstood or disputed, depending on the perspective
adopted or the evidence that one chooses to bring to discourse. Although
such discussions may be important, we must recognize their true character:
perhaps holding relevance and revealing erudition within religious, literary, psychoanalytic, political, ideological, or historical contexts, such com-
munications may never be confused as meaningful in Wittgenstein's sense.[14]
Yet, Thoreau no doubt persisted in his own attempts to capture his experience in words. At the same time, he knew, and told us, that the deepest experience and the clearest sightings of reality were private. As he wrote in
Walden, "perhaps the facts most astounding and most real are never communicated by man to man" (1971, p. 216). Note that Thoreau was not stat-
ing that we could not perceive such reality as nature offered us, but that
each of us must engage that spiritual realm independently and directly. The
poet might guide us there, but ultimately we are responsible for our
encounter, individualized and personal.

Thoreau was indeed a writer, one who could not abide the impasse later
philosophy might have offered him. Despite his frustrations, he would *write*,
and in so doing, would deny Wittgenstein's solipsism. Even in the splendid
seclusion of his cabin at Walden Pond, Thoreau always had his eye directed

to his reader, endeavoring to bridge his own social and psychological separation through literary efforts. They hardly shared the same reservations, for, after all, Thoreau proposed "to brag as lustily as chanticleer . . . if only to wake my neighbors up" (*Walden*, 1971, p. 84). In some essential fashion, Thoreau *had* to write. Why? At Walden Pond, we witness Thoreau's writing, the *doing* of a "literary man," and in that literary heritage we appreciate the full import of his endeavor as a moral one. Thoreau was a self-fashioned Romantic hero in the sense that he would not succumb to the anxiety of the self separating from its world in some final and irretrievable way, and to a large extent, writing was the means to his salvation. So, by inscribing his selfhood, in writing his life, Thoreau exercised his most basic understanding of moral agency by fulfilling the imperative of deliberate, self-determined action and by forging the various elements of his life into a coherent whole, indeed, a new alloy.

A HERO AMONG US?

Is not the poet bound to write his own biography? Is there any other work for him but a good journal? We do not wish to know how his imaginary hero, but how he, the actual hero, lived from day to day.

> Thoreau, October 21, 1857,
> *Journal*, [1906] 1962, 10:115

To note Thoreau's self-consciousness is only to place him among Romantics generally; what distinguishes Thoreau from other Transcendentalists of his neighborhood was how he engaged nature actively and, unlike Emerson, went forth *into* the wild, leaving the armchair for active engagement as a self-appointed hero in the American quest of the West. Thoreau's moral example falls into two categories: the first is this environmental ethic which he espoused so eloquently; the second is, in a sense, even more universal, namely, the basis of moral action as residing in a radically self-determined agent. In the end, we must ponder how these two moral elements relate to each other and what are their ethical consequences. Thoreau certainly saw them as of one piece, crucial to a grandiose, heroic self-image.

It is perhaps a bit odd to think of his quiet, uneventful life as heroic, but Thoreau certainly considered himself engaged in some epic contest. From his early Journal, we glean a cardinal principle of Thoreau's life: "any age is a heroic age to the heroic individual" (Richardson 1986, p. 26). Thoreau's identification with the Greeks and Romans suggested to him how he might envision "a new heaven and a new earth for Greece" (Thoreau, February

16, 1838, *Journal 1*, 1881, p. 29). After all, "The past is only so heroic as we see it–it is the canvass on which our idea of heroism is painted–the dim prospectus of our future field. We are dreaming of what we are to do" (July 3, 1840, ibid., p. 148). So the quiet town of Concord was as fitting a battle-field as the plains of Troy.[15] Thoreau played out this drama in the "Bean Field" chapter of *Walden,* a venture important not just to illustrate economic austerity but, because he "was determined to know beans" (p. 161), to serve as a parable of a heroic battle:

> A long war, not with cranes, but with weeds, those Trojans who had sun and rain and dews on their side. Daily the beans saw me come to their rescue armed with a hoe, and thin the ranks of their enemies, filling up trenches with weedy dead. Many a lusty crest-waving Hector, that towered a whole foot above his crowding comrades, fell before my weapon and rolled in the dust. (Pp. 161–62)

This is a humorous passage, sustained by a dose of ironic self-mockery, but nevertheless the moral lesson stands in relief. Thoreau cultivated himself: "my labor . . . yielded an instant and immeasurable crop" (ibid., p. 159). While he tabulates his expenses and yields, and calculates a profit, his profit can hardly be measured in dollars and cents:

> The true harvest of my daily life is somewhat as intangible and indescribable as the tints of morning or evening. It is a little star-dust caught, a segment of the rainbow which I have clutched. (Ibid., pp. 216–17)

Just as in the battle of the ants in "Brute Neighbors" (*Walden,* 1971, pp. 228–31), we are indeed in struggle, and the point is to choose our battle and engage fully. Are we to live some false materialism or commercialism to no end, or cultivate our own fields, vanquish the inner enemy of our own weaknesses, and become the best that we might be? How to enlist ourselves to better purpose is the basic theme of *Walden,* and Thoreau regarded that matter *very* seriously. Indeed, the metaphysical import of his business—to glimpse "a life unlived," to "trust the remotest," to "look under the lids of Time"—was "all that I have imagined of heroism" (January 30, 1841, *Journal 1,* 1981, p. 242).

We are repeatedly summoned to enlist and march in Thoreau's army, albeit in pace with our own drummer (*Walden,* 1971, p. 326). This military image portends a cosmic struggle, one witnessed by heavenly forces.[16] And so Thoreau ended *Walden,* imploring us to follow our dreams, by which he meant pursue a heroic contest. His own meanderings over the cultivated hills and through the manicured forests of Concord's suburbs was heroic in his mind: "For every walk is a sort of crusade, preached by some Peter the Hermit in us, to go forth and reconquer this Holy Land from the hands of the infidels. It is true, we are but faint-hearted crusaders" (Thoreau, "Walking," 1980b, p. 94). Therefore Thoreau admonishes us to "go West" and, in seeing the sunset, to imagine the gardens of the Hesperides, as did Columbus when discovering the New World.

The West, of course, is "but another name for the Wild" (Thoreau, "Walking," 1980b, p. 112). The West, the Wild, is the mythic source of civilization, for "the founders of every state which has risen to eminence have drawn their nourishment and vigor from a similar wild source" (ibid.). To experience "the Wild" renews and invigorates us in our epic struggle to free ourselves from the clutches of civilization. A bit overstated? Not at all, if one perceives this battle as one of life and death: "Life consists with wildness. The most alive is the wildest. Not yet subdued to man, its presence refreshes him" (ibid., p. 114); there is no substitute—no philosophy, no poetry ("the best poetry is tame" [ibid., p. 120])—although, not surprisingly as the discourse of the heroes, mythology comes nearest to adequately expressing this yearning for the wild, for life. For Thoreau, the struggle is a morality drama, for "all good things are wild and free" (ibid., p. 122). So not only must we protect nature, we must find our own goodness within our own wildness. To the extent that Thoreau regarded himself as fulfilling that search, he was a hero. Whether we recognize him as misguided or as prophetic, the integrity of his pursuit should not be denied.

Heroic leaders almost always earn this role by their own personal triumph in struggle. Like Jacob at Jabbok, Thoreau wrestled with himself;[17] again like Jacob, he took a new name, exchanging "David Henry" for "Henry David" shortly after he graduated from college (Harding 1965, p. 54). Scholars have since debated the psychological significance of this shift,[18] and I would suggest that he changed his name, at least in part, because he regarded his personal quest as heroic, one requiring a self-appointed name to signify his own self-willed forging of a new identity. In assuming a "new" name, he also put on a mantle to lead his fellow Concordians upon the beckoning road to the West. *Walden* may be read as "scripture" (Cavell 1981, p. 14), and Thoreau himself may be seen, following a line beginning with Emerson's eulogy and continuing through Joseph Wood Krutch (1948) to Edward Abbey and the Sierra Club, as "prophet,"[19] or perhaps "hero-prophet"—a mix of both types.

Thoreau's strong emphasis on individuality, on isolation, and on experience bind together the way he saw the world and how he led his life. To break out of his self-imposed confinement—real and potential—and speak to his fellow men and women was truly a heroic effort for Thoreau, and given the quandary of the personal, we can appreciate why. When we regard Thoreau as "hero," we most clearly appreciate how he regarded the moral dimensions of his struggle and what was at stake. The hero stands out from the crowd, steadfast, in clear sight for all to see and follow. There is no doubt about the self in this mode, presented with confidence and with the ability to inspire. No less a project did Thoreau set for himself, and he spoke with the authority of the Right.[20] Certainty is reasserted, and it is accomplished by the only authority we have—ourselves (as he famously proclaimed in "Resistance to Civil Government," 1973b). While necessary, is this standard sufficient? Thoreau had ample opportunity to test his moral code, and he left us a rich record by which he could be judged.

Thoreau lived in turbulent political times, and counting himself a Transcendentalist, he was hardly noteworthy for being nonconformist. After all, the likes of Bronson Alcott, Orestes Brownson, Emerson, Theodore Parker, and Elizabeth Peabody took critical stances against church and state at times more radical than Thoreau's. But opinion has been sharply divided about the nature of Thoreau's political philosophy (Taylor 1996), ranging from Emerson's lament that Thoreau was content with leading a huckleberry party to Bob Taylor's recent assessment "that contrary to Emerson's evaluation . . . there has been no writer with more ambition for America than Henry Thoreau, nor one more deeply concerned with the future moral character of our political community" (1996, p. 13). To draw such a sympathetic portrait, Taylor reads *A Week* and *Walden* as political accounts, where the problem facing the nation "is not primarily moral error [so much as] moral fear and indifference" (ibid., p. 33). On this reading, Thoreau rejects simple moralism ("conscience really does not, and ought not to monopolize the whole of our lives, any more than the heart or head" [*A Week*, 1980a, p. 74]) and attempts to bring history and memory into moral action. Thus memory becomes a moral exercise (e.g., "When the Indians die, we do not even remember, or care to remember, where they are buried" [Taylor 1996, p. 21]). In constructing the past, we must make our own reckoning of our social inheritance. This understanding of history served as the theme of chapter 2. We might also regard Thoreau's natural history through a political prism, where the deeply humanistic link with nature, the respect for nature in all of its manifestations, has broad social and political ramifications.

More accessible to political analysis are Thoreau's reform writings, which may be divided between more general statements that outline his political philosophy (e.g., the "Economy" chapter of *Walden*, 1971, and "Life without Principle," in *Reform Papers*, 1973a) and those more specifically addressing the moral challenge of slavery (e.g., "Herald of Freedom," in *Reform Papers*, 1973a; "Slavery in Massachusetts," 1973c; and "A Plea for Captain John Brown," in *Reform Papers*, 1973a). While undoubtedly important in illustrating Thoreau's public ethics, I have paid scant attention to these reform papers or his activism more generally. Indeed, I regard these concerns as derivative of a deeper personal philosophy and thus of secondary interest for this study. But these papers do illustrate, very clearly, the egocentric focus of Thoreau's moral philosophy, which, like his nature writing and historiography, are dominated by his own individual concerns. It is, perhaps, ironic that in a fundamental sense Thoreau was at odds with democratic ideals, for while celebrating America, he almost exclusively placed the individual above or beyond the community. Therefore, instead of a detailed discussion of Thoreau's specific political views, I think it more appropriate to summarily situate his political philosophy within the context of his personal concerns and see how even in the political domain, Thoreau could not escape his preoccupation with himself.

Because of the tensions between his social maladroitness and his need to lead his fellow citizens in a radical moral reform, Thoreau moved along a private-to-public continuum in the political writings. Various commentators have noted that Thoreau eschewed reform organizations as vigorously as churches, but despite this aversion, he did become actively involved with the abolition movement. Beyond his early lectures, Thoreau exhibited little overt activism, restricting himself to limited participation in the underground railroad and going to jail for a night (July 1846) as a result of refusing to pay the poll tax—an act of civil disobedience over the issue of the slave status of Texas and the resulting Mexican War. But Thoreau's political posture also embraced a more overt activism, for while he regarded personal reform, rugged moral self-reliance, and the assertion of individual virtue as constituting the bedrock of social responsibility (e.g., "The Service" and "Reform and the Reformers," in *Reform Papers*, 1973a), he also asserted that the individual ultimately acts in a political context to effect his moral agency—either actively (e.g., "Wendell Phillips," in *Reform Papers*, 1973a) or passively (e.g., "Resistance to Civil Government," 1973b).[21]

We can see Thoreau's political philosophy unified if we understand that his underlying moral philosophy underwent no significant modulation but that his participatory politics did. Thus we can trace a progression of his activism from the mid-1840s to that reached with the fugitive slave issue revolving around Anthony Burns ("Slavery in Massachusetts," 1973c). From passive noncompliance and self-removal, Thoreau, by the time John Brown attacked Harper's Ferry in 1859, was fully, even passionately, invested in personal action against the state. In a sense, his support for Brown reflects a complete outward turning of moral sentiment from personal outrage to public denunciation. It is as if Thoreau were no longer satisfied to reside in solitude or to resist government passively, so that by 1850, when the Fugitive Slave Law was enacted, his moral umbrage at the state's participation in the return of escaped slaves propelled the public participation that he had hitherto avoided. And by the end of the decade Thoreau came to regard John Brown as a true American hero, one he eulogized without restraint ("The Last Days of John Brown" and "Martyrdom of John Brown," in *Reform Papers*, 1973a). Coupled with his admiration was, apparently, the realization that passive resistance was an inadequate response to state aggression. As Len Gougeon notes, "self-culture cannot be practiced in a society where freedom is either denied or actively threatened" (1995, p. 205). The philosophical position remained steadfast; the political expression had become radicalized.

Thoreau's political philosophy rested on one key principle, as famously declared in "Resistance to Civil Government":

> The authority of government, even as such as I am willing to submit to . . . is still an impure one: to be strictly just it must have the sanction and consent of the governed. It can have no pure right over my person or property but what I concede to it. . . . There will never be a really free and enlightened State, until the State comes to recognize the individual as a higher and independent power, from which all its own power and authority are derived, and treats him accordingly. (1973b, p. 89)

In short, for Thoreau, government, majority rule, and courts of law would never compromise sacrosanct individuality. The quiet militancy of nonviolent, passive resistance reflects a deep and uncompromising resoluteness, and Thoreau's later more overt activism hardly reflected a shift in his basic philosophy, for the essential lesson of "Resistance to Civil Government"— that government must protect the freedom of its citizens—was to be reiterated in later activist writings. Let us consider "Slavery in Massachusetts" (1973c) as illustrative of the themes I wish to emphasize.

This lecture was delivered in 1854 to an abolitionist audience shortly following the abortive attempt to free Anthony Burns, a fugitive slave, from being returned to Virginia (von Frank 1998, pp. 276–85).[22] The federal Fugitive Slave Law had superseded the state's Personal Liberty Laws, which were enacted to protect runaway slaves in the 1840s. Thoreau then, ironically in respect to the clash over states' rights resulting in the Civil War, argued heatedly against the loss of state sovereignty: "The whole military force of the State [Massachusetts] is at the service of a Mr. Suttle, a slaveholder from

Virginia, to enable him to catch a man whom he calls his property; but not a soldier is offered to save a citizen of Massachusetts from being kidnapped!" (Thoreau 1973c, p. 94). And consonant with "Resistance to Civil Government," Thoreau proclaims a moral law higher than the Constitution, and, more pointedly, the right of the moral individual, in the face of an immoral majority, to assert and enact his own sense of probity (ibid., p. 104). Again, the themes of self-responsibility are clearly declared:

> The fate of the country does not depend on how you vote at the polls— the worst man is as strong as the best at that game; it does not depend on what kind of paper you drop into the ballot-box once a year, but on what kind of man you drop from your chamber into the street every morning. . . .
>
> Let each inhabitant of the State dissolve his union with her, as long as she delays to do her duty. . . . Only they are guiltless, who commit the crime of contempt of such a Court. (Ibid., pp. 104–5)

There is a dark streak of elitism in Thoreau's confidence in knowing the Right, in his disdain of the democratic process, and in his lofty self-righteousness.

The key indictment against Thoreau's moral authority is how he casts Burns's rights in his own: Thoreau regards the return of Anthony Burns to enslavement as a critical infringement on his own freedom: "the State has fatally interfered with my lawful business" by interrupting "me and every man on his onward and upward path" (ibid., p. 107). And so the underlying rationale for protest rests on Thoreau's outrage that his own freedom had been compromised—not that of Burns! Here we come squarely to the moral implications of Thoreau's narcissism. I can offer no better critique than that offered by Orestes Brownson about Emerson's Divinity School Address (1838), but which could just as easily have been written about Thoreau:

> "The highest good they recognise is an individual good, the realization of order in their own individual souls." Can a person who adopts this moral rule really be called moral? "Does not morality always propose to us an end separate from our own, above our own, and to which our own good is subordinate?" It is indeed necessary to achieve harmony within the individual soul, but that is only a preliminary step. "Above the good of the individual, and paramount to it, is the good of the universe, the realization of good of creation, absolute good." The man who forgets himself is "infinitely superior to the man who merely uses others as the means of promoting his own intellectual and spiritual growth." (Cited and edited by Barbara Packer 1995, p. 437)

So, on the basis of Thoreau's own sense of personal infringement, action was now justified, and he lauded those who acted to free Burns.[23]

Thoreau, in this most public exhortation, cannot remain in the public sector, and instead returns to the private sphere as the ultimate source of action. How then would Thoreau proceed in his everyday life? Or, as he asks, How can one "be serene in a country where both the rulers and the ruled are without principle?" (Thoreau 1973c, p. 108). He quickly answers: in nature—as mediated by a sensitive soul. Thoreau turns, as he did in *Walden*, to the higher laws and the eternal truths he perceived in the natural world, and thus in the pursuit of his art he affirmed a moral order, as exemplified by natural beauty. Almost rhapsodically, Thoreau closed his tormented remarks by citing the simplest pleasure of observing flowers, in which he found solace for, if not specific answers to, the pressing political questions and moral laxity of his feverish time:

> But it chanced the other day that I scented a white water-lily, and a season I had waited for had arrived. It is the emblem of purity. It bursts up so pure and fair to the eye, and so sweet to the scent, as if to show us what purity and sweetness reside in, and can be extracted from, the slime and muck of earth. . . . What confirmation of our hopes is in the fragrance of this flower! I shall not so soon despair of the world for it, notwithstanding slavery, and the cowardice and want of principle of Northern men. It suggests what kind of laws have prevailed longest and widest, and still prevail, and that the time may come when man's deeds will smell as sweet. . . . If nature can compound this fragrance still annually, I shall believe her still young and full of vigor, her integrity and genius unimpaired, and that there is virtue even in man, too, who is fitted to perceive and love it. It reminds me that Nature has been partner to no Missouri Compromise. I scent no compromise in the fragrance of the water-lily. (Ibid.)

This passage is noteworthy in three respects: The first is that Thoreau's moral direction is self-determined, self-perceived, and ultimately self-centered as he uses his intercourse with nature as the foundation for his political action. It is evident, then, that he uses no corrective external standard—political or moral principles—and relies entirely on his own sensibility, which to our ears appears precious and even drunk with rapturous delight. Second, given the egocentric character of this essay, Thoreau still is able to move beyond himself and offers his ultimately optimistic prediction about the political process for social justice. Indeed, the reformer, in the very act of arguing his case, must, at some basic level, believe that he might effect change for the better. In Thoreau's case, given that natural laws are the oldest and ultimately the dominant ones, man must—if he only *sees* what nature provides, that is, if properly attuned to her lessons—achieve the same kind of social harmony that Thoreau witnesses in the lily. In other words, the transcendental principles sought for the individual may also be applied to man in the collective. This, in short, is his basic political philosophy. Finally, social reform rests on the moral reform of the self, because political action is not determined by a particular crisis but reverberates to the very foundations of the moral agent himself. There can be no retreat from the world's challenges, and Thoreau does not offer some naive gloss in this passage but rather enunciates the key insight first expressed in "Paradise to Be Regained" (in *Reform Papers*, 1973a), namely, that man must "reform himself" before effecting social reform. As Sherman Paul noted, the central task was "self-reform, which was Thoreau's way of reforming the outward life" (1958, p. 153), and reform here is expressed as the appreciation of nature and the attestation of values consonant with that purpose. Accordingly, before attempting to reform the world, Thoreau's turn to nature was the primary "political" act, albeit personal and private. In the process of truly seeing the beauty and order of nature, Thoreau believed he was provided with the values which would guide his worldly endeavors.

By this reading, the perfectibility of the collective and the reform of the individual each stem from the same crucial source: self-examination. Thus, whether regarded from the perspective of the political arena of social choice or from that of a particular person's ethics, Thoreau's reform writings derive from his central celebration of individuality, one he achieved through his unique manner of communing with nature. As the intensity of debate surrounding slavery increased, Thoreau's own rhetoric also heightened in intensity, but the basic political themes were already clearly articulated in the moral philosophy of *Walden*'s first draft—the assertion of the individual's sanctity, the willed pursuit of self-improvement, the denial of false social values at the expense of the attainment of meaningful personal ones, and the centrality of man's relation to nature and the discovery thereby of his own divine character. Thus, we may understand the basic structure of "Resistance to Civil Government" (written during this same period) as an *applied* civics lesson from the Walden experience. When Thoreau asserts that "the only obligation which I have a right to assume, is to do at any time what I think right" (1973b, p. 65), he does so fully confident that he has been inspired by the "higher laws" of nature and that he indeed perceives them correctly because "through the exercise of an active conscience a person maintains a transcendent spiritual life" (Gougeon 1995, p. 202). Thoreau's movement from passive resistance to a more rigorous activism is of secondary concern to the underlying moral precept: each individual is responsible for his or her own actions, and the sense of right is not to be found in the world of social intercourse (i.e., conventional morality or majority rule) but in the private domain of conscience and self-realized personhood. The structure of moral agency was thus based on individuality—the choice of fulfilling one's own agenda—and the willing of that personal identity along a continuum of perfection.

Thoreau's self-image of hero, prophet, and political conscience rested on an assured sense of personal identity. But our age is wary of heroes, self-proclaimed or otherwise. And the banner of the self—under which a hero, if there is one, must appear—has been tattered. We are unsettled by the suspicion that the self is but an interpretative scheme, an almost discarded remnant of an eclipsed sociohistorical period. Our very identities seem all too plastic and contingent. And guidelines vanish as mysteriously as they appear. Philosophically, the very notion of selfhood was a problem bequeathed to Thoreau by his own era. What we glean, putting aside the vexing psychological issues, in studying the quest for his personhood is the assertion of the self's reality, and a powerful affirmation at that. From our vantage, this posturing may seem a "conceit" (Cavell 1981, p. 19), but such a judgment says as much about ourselves as about Thoreau. We are deaf to prophets, and we mistrust leaders. In Thoreau's self-creative effort of making himself into a political voice, we see the moral boundaries of his personhood in highlight. On this note, which addresses the particularly vexing modern conundrum of the self, we most clearly hear Thoreau's trumpet. Is his song a rhapsodic melody or the cacophony of postmodern atonality? In the concluding chapter, we consider Thoreau's basis of moral agency, the putative "triumph of the self."

7 The Self-Positing I

If I am not I, who will be?
   Thoreau, *A Week,*
   1980a, p. 156

The fate of having a self—of being human—is one in which the self is always to be found; fated to be sought, or not; recognized, or not.

Stanley Cavell 1981, p. 53

One might stretch Thoreau between two poles—the Real and the Good. He sought "reality" in all of its diverse guises—in nature, in man, in his own psyche. At the same time, he sought the moral—in social action and politics, in local society, in his dealings with his intimate constellation of friends and family, and, most importantly, in his self-deliberations about his own personhood—to define himself in his work and behavior. These two modes—the ontologic and the moral—are intimately linked, so that *knowledge* is formed from each and thus inseparable. In short, to know the world is to know it morally, in the sense of assigning it value.[1] Thoreau bound his world together through an endless dialectical process. His vision of nature—what he valued and thus *saw*—was framed by a particular attitude. In turn, the world informed and guided his own moral development as he matured and cultivated his ethical consciousness in response to what he experienced. *Seeing* consequently becomes a moral act. The prize was Reality. This theme recurs again and again in Thoreau's admonishments. Consider, for example, the passage in *Walden*'s "Where I Lived, and What I Lived For":

> Let us spend one day as deliberately as Nature, and not be thrown off the track by every nutshell and mosquito's wing that falls on the rails. Let us rise early and fast, or break fast, gently without perturbation; let company come and let company go, let the bells ring and the children cry,—determined to make a day of it. Why should we knock under and go with the stream? . . . If you stand right fronting and face to face to a fact, you will see the sun glimmer on both its surfaces, as if it were cimeter [scimitar], and feel its sweet edge dividing you through the heart and marrow, and so you will happily conclude your mortal career. Be it life or death, we crave only reality. (*Walden*, 1971, pp. 97–98)

Thoreau struggled both with processing experience, that is, making it conscious, and with transmitting that experience into words. As we saw in the preceding chapter, he was at times frustrated by the inability of words to convey experience: "When I hear a bird singing I cannot think of any words that will imitate it– What word can stand in place of a bird's note! . . . It has so little relation to words" (May 7, 1852, *Journal* 5, 1997, pp. 37–38). Thoreau regarded facts as representations of reality, a lexicon for nature. He would strive for a clear language by which to transmit his own experience, and facts had a crucial standing in that enterprise. But, as we can now appreciate, though Thoreau would invest them as agents of simplification—elements of composite wholes—facts are themselves complex. At one level they are the metier of Thoreau's life, and he would engage them "directly" (as he exclaims shortly after moving into his Walden cabin: "I wish to meet the facts of life . . . face to face" [July 6, 1845, *Journal* 2, 1984, p. 156]). He savored the morsels of truth which facts bespoke: "It is a rare qualification to be able to state a fact simply & adequately. To digest some experience cleanly. To say yes and no with authority– To make a square edge . . . Say it & have done with it" (November 1, 1851, *Journal* 4, 1992, pp. 157–58). Yet Thoreau was well aware that facts were not "simple," that they were in themselves a means of interpretation, and he recognized that "facts" depended on context. The contextualization of knowledge supported and defined the fact. That is, facts exist within certain milieux of understanding: "Statements are made but partially– Things are said with reference to certain conventions or existing institutions– not absolutely" (ibid., p. 158).

Indeed, Thoreau understood that facts must be processed by the knower to attain their full significance and meaning:

> See not with the eye of science–which is barren–nor of youthful poetry which is impotent. But taste the world. & digest it. It would seem as if things got said but rarely & by chance– As you *see* so at length will you *say*. (November 1, 1851, *Journal* 4, 1992, p. 158)[2]

The intimation underlying this passage, and many others, concerns the role of the self in signifying the world, a theme reiterated in different contexts throughout this study. Thoreau self-consciously admitted that science and poesis are only vehicles of knowing or expressing, and may be regarded as products of a deeper agency. One's approach to, and vision of, nature arise from the processes of selecting, organizing, and finally signifying observations to create a picture of the world. Correspondingly, the individual's values, sensitivities, and experiences place such facts into a context that ultimately determines their meaning. Thus seeing, at least for Thoreau, was a deliberate and oftentimes self-conscious effort, and, ultimately, an ethical imperative. For him, moral agency assumed new dimensions, expanding from the domain of ethics to include epistemology as well.

A PRAYER

Let me forever go in search of myself.

> Thoreau, July 16, 1851,
> *Journal* 3, 1990, p. 312

In the summer of 1851 Thoreau offered what can only be described as a prayer. It becomes an ode to the self and a proclamation of virtue ethics. Through it we see Thoreau's own vision of selfhood and the construction of moral agency:

> What more glorious condition of being can we imagine than from impure to be becoming pure. It is almost desirable to be impure that we may be the subjects of this improvement. That I am innocent to myself. That I love & reverence my life! That I am better fitted for a lofty society today than I was yesterday to make my life a sacrament– What is nature without this lofty tumbling[.] May I treat myself with more & more respect & tenderness– May I not forget that I am impure & vicious[.] May I not cease to love purity. May I go to my slumbers as expecting to arise to a new & more perfect day.
>
> May I so live and refine my life as fitting myself for a society even higher than I actually enjoy. May I treat myself tenderly as I would treat the most innocent child whom I love–may I treat children & my friends as my newly discovered self– Let me forever go in search of myself– Never for a moment think that I have found myself. Be as a stranger to myself never a familiar–seeking acquaintance still. May I be to myself as one is to me whom I love–a dear & cherished object– What temple what fane what sacred place can there be but the innermost part of my being? The possibility of my own improvement, that is to be cherished. As I regard myself so I am. O my dear friends I have not forgotten you[.] I will know you tomorrow. I associate you with my ideal self. I had ceased to have faith in myself. I thought I was grown up & become what I was intended to be. But it is earliest spring with me. In relation to virtue & innocence the oldest man is in the beginning earliest spring & vernal season of life. It is the love of virtue makes us young ever– That is the fountain of youth– The very aspiration after the perfect. I love & worship myself with a love which absorbs my love for the world. The lecturer suggested to me that I might become a better than I am–was it not a good lecture then? May I dream not that I shunned vice– May I dream that I loved & practiced virtue. (Thoreau, July 16, 1851, *Journal* 3, 1990, pp. 311–12)

This hymn sounds the classic prayer motif of purification. Life has become a process of self-improvement.[3] In places it is almost childlike in its innocence, as if Thoreau is remembering, "every day a little bit better." And then the voice in the middle of the passage changes to serious introspection regarding the nature of his selfhood. This ode to himself frankly proclaims that his "love and worship" of himself absorbs "my love for the world." Clearly, Thoreau is radically egocentric, his narcissism dominating all other concerns, and it is difficult to argue with Bob Taylor's appraisal of Thoreau as "self-congratulatory" and "at his most morally perfectionist and egoistic" (1996, p. 9). In assessing the basis of Thoreau's political comment about the fugitive slave in the preceding chapter, it became evident that Thoreau's moral philosophy developed from a selfish perspective. Indeed, his communal civility emanated from a fiercely protective stand for his own autonomy. This was the price of his self-conscious preoccupation. Never complacent that he has found himself, Thoreau seems embarked on an endless search for his own identity, seemingly to the exclusion of serious attempts to integrate himself in the larger community. Rather than seek his place in the world (the thesis Garber [1991] sees as dominating Thoreau), he would search for his true person within. In this prayer, the image of spring, of renewal and growth, dominates the portrait of a dynamic self, one that aspires to attain an ideal state. He will follow the course of virtue, and indeed it is "virtue," a "fountain of youth" that bestows eternal youth and vitality. In short, he would make his life a sacrament, and he would do so by living what he conceived as a virtuous life—to be sure, self-absorbed and isolating. But this was the posture he assumed in constructing his personhood, and he saw that enterprise as morally worthy.

What, then, did it mean to "construct" the self?

PHILOSOPHICAL INTERLUDE

Peculiarities of the present Age . . . It is said to be the age of the first person singular.

> Emerson, Journal entry,
> January 30, 1827 (Emerson 1963, p. 70)

"In the wake of Descartes's meditations, modern philosophy becomes a *philosophy of the subject*" (Taylor 1989, p. xxii). For the Romantics, this became a crisis which has yet to be resolved. From the mid-seventeenth century through the Kantian project, the self, although difficult to define, still remains to offer a perspective on the world and thus order it, becoming the locus of certainty and truth (Nagel 1986; Taylor 1989). For Kant, transcendental apperception is the structured unity—the pure ego or self—of consciousness, which precedes (transcends) the content of perception and makes possible its experienced order and meaning. Kant posited that transcendental apperception was the necessary condition for experience and for synthesizing experience into a unity. In this sense, the self is an entity. And therein lies the rub for the Romantics. An entity has boundaries, limits. It would not suffice for the expressive, Romantic elusive self.

The self, for the Romantics, was neither rigidly restricted by social convention nor confined to a particular rationality. The expressive self reveled in the world's splendor and thereby enriched its own experience. One found fulfillment not in preserving identity but in expanding it. (It is no accident that Coleridge took mind-altering opiates and, like Icarus, sought to reach the sun.) The self, no longer set, established, or structured, was imagined as an organic *process* of experience. In loosening the self-contained (and self-sufficient) nature of personhood, the Romantic self became largely defined in relation to its object. That object could be the outside world or some inner self-consciousness. Relation became the key precept, for when one is in dialogue, or communion, or rapture, the experiencing self is absorbing and responding. In the process of experience, which now becomes the watchword of Romanticism, the very idea of a set identity, one fixed and unchanging (and thus incapable of evolution), becomes anathema. The cardinal rule is self-reflection, and in an endlessly recursive process, the self experiences itself, more particularly its world, the other, and its own experience. *Relation* replaces entity.

How did this transfiguration of the self occur? Without digressing too deeply into the history of philosophy, it is fair to say that philosophers at the dawn of Romanticism—and by extension, or perhaps in concert, the poets—were attempting to break the confining impasse in which the self had been placed by John Locke's construction of a detached, observing "eye" that would perceive the world, know it directly, and retain its objective autonomy. In many ways, "autonomy" was the key issue, serving both as the basis of an epistemological system and as the fundamental element of a moral and political philosophy. This idea of autonomy was recognized at the crest of Newton's epochal discoveries in the philosophy of Locke, who effectively translated the objectifying scientific ideal into the political and moral domains. Locke's philosophy hinged upon arguing for the ability of the individual to detach from the world, and from himself, and observe each objectively.

This view had profound ethical ramifications, for objective disengagement becomes a moral requirement in knowing not only the world but also the self. Autonomy is thereby a value, limited only to the extent that an individual's freedom infringes upon the freedom of others. Entwined in Locke's epistemological definition we find his legal foundation, for the individual so defined becomes the unit of government, divided between its freedom and the rights of the majority. "Self" becomes a forensic term to which the law is applicable, and "possessive individualism" (MacPherson 1962) is thus celebrated and moreover assured as established by the epistemological system from which an independent ethical unity consistently arose. Liberalism was based on the self as an independent knowing entity, one that might act rationally and freely. Thoreau was a *Romantic* heir of this seventeenth-century liberalism and became a celebrated interpreter of that tradition. When he proclaimed the essential independence of man in *Walden*'s opening chapter, "Economy"—"What a man thinks of himself, that it is which determines, or rather indicates, his fate" (1971, p. 7)—and proclaimed his anthem in the "Conclusion"—"If a man does not keep pace with his companions, perhaps it is because he hears a different drummer" (ibid., p. 326)—we see the figurative bookends of his entire enterprise: the essence of man is the proprietorship of his person.

Romanticism's expanded view of nature and man's place in it resulted in a crisis for this view of the autonomous self. Nature's laws are not moral ones, and thus a distinction between natural law (the mechanical laws of cause and effect) and moral law (governing humans) became apparent. On this view, human free will, the basis of self-determination, thus functions with one form of rationality, while the natural world, governed by deterministic laws, functions with another. Rejecting the idea of the self as an isolated entity then requires a single Reason, one that might both discern the mechanical universe and at the same time operate within the human soul. Here, too, Kant set the terms of this later discussion when he distinguished between "theoretical reason" and "practical reason" as the key categories for understanding human intelligence and moral agency. Kant had attempted to establish a metaphysics of nature (consisting of the *a priori* principles of our knowledge of what *is*) and a metaphysics of morals (comprising the *a priori* principles of what *ought to be*). While he sought to ground both realms in a unified Reason, Kant recognized that reason assumes a different character in the natural and moral realms. Simply stated, the respective "objects" of thought—nature, governed by one set of natural laws, and human behavior, following a different set of laws—reflected the distinct ontologies of what *is* and what *ought to be*.[4]

In proposing this structure, Kant bequeathed to German and English idealism the problem of seeking the unity of reason, for Kant's distinctions presented a necessary tension: Can the view of the world that follows from the principles of theoretical reason (a world of natural events occurring in accord with natural causes) be reconciled with the kind of world required by the laws of man's practical reason? Whether Kant set these forms of reason in opposition or was successful in synthesizing them is a question,[5] but indisputably, he sought their unification. As he wrote at the end of the second *Critique*,

> Two things fill the mind with ever new and increasing wonder and awe ... the starry heavens above me and the moral law within me. I do not merely conjecture them and seek them as though obscured in darkness or in the transcendent region beyond my horizon: I see them before me, and I associate them directly with the consciousness of my own existence. (Kant [1788] 1993, p. 169)

Generally, three possible solutions were sought (Neuhouser 1990, pp. 12 ff.): theoretical and practical reason 1) were compatible with each other, 2) were derivative of a unitary and complete system of philosophy (and requiring some first principle), or 3) comprised a structural identity constituting in essence a single activity. Hardly restricted to the esoteric debates among philosophers, this presentation of unified knowledge had profound cultural ramifications, refracting in different ways the deeper philosophical issue raised by Kant's attempt to establish the distinctive metaphysics of nature and morality and to conceptualize the forms of rationality that operated in each.[6]

The philosophers attempted to resolve this issue in the terms of Critical Philosophy, but artists, poets, and novelists of the period also responded to a form of the same basic problem: How might a common Reason unify science, religion, and aesthetics? Admittedly, this issue was of a different order and was posed in a different context than as originally presented by Kant, but a shared motivation drives the question of how to formulate a unitary Reason to account for both theoretical and practical knowledge, since each of these human activities seemed to be governed by different faculties of understanding. The fundamental issue was the unity of knowledge.

The question whether a single rationality could bind both science and art was close to the quandary that Thoreau himself faced. In seeking to unify the world as seen spiritually, aesthetically, and scientifically, he likewise sought some basis for a common mode of knowing, what the philosophers were calling Reason. Beginning with the Transcendentalist legacy, he pondered that question in the form of deciphering the character of human reason that bridges the gulf between the autonomous self and the seemingly separate natural world (e.g., How might one place human action and understanding in concert with nature's perfect harmony?).

But Thoreau moved beyond the strictures of seeking a common Reason, to an answer so ingenious and fecund that I suspect it is still not fully appreciated: instead of seeking a unifying Reason, instead of attempting to bridge a divide between ourselves and nature, he admonished that we should recognize that we *are* nature, or, as he put it, that we should acknowledge our own wildness. In asserting that nature, the wild, is within us, our mission is to discover and become intimate with that primitive essence which connects us with the cosmos. The wild, because of its very character, cannot be "known," that is, tamed or rationalized, made a species of consciousness. All those modes of knowing that we must pursue are sorry residues of a primary knowing. In the wild, Reason does not rule; it can, at best, only mediate. So in some sense, Thoreau "solved" the Kantian imbroglio by asserting that no essential divide separated man and nature, only one's self-consciousness. We are at base wild and thus integral to nature. The "problem" of human agency arises only when we become self-conscious knowers, who must contemplate and objectify our experience so that the recognition of our primary experience may be reported—to others and, more fundamentally, to ourselves. So while it is true that Thoreau's philosophical mileu was idealism, he reached beyond Reason to a realm of unprocessed experience that required translation, which in itself was only a derivative problem of self-consciousness. In that formulation, Thoreau fundamentally reframed the defining question of his age.

Thus Thoreau would not postulate unified Reason, thought, or consciousness to unite his experience, but would take a phenomenological approach in experiencing the wild. By "phenomenological" I mean that Thoreau thought that the experience of the wild was primary and unmediated, in contrast to its later translation into consciousness, which is mediated by various "reasons" in the effort to capture that primary experience. Ever mindful of his own experiencing, Thoreau processed the wild through various intellectualized formats, drawing on his intuition of the originally immediate experience. In his Journal we see him struggle with the expression of these different faculties of knowing, which were in essence his attempts to harness the wild into his self-conscious pursuit of nature. This translating process was multilayered and most conspicuously required different kinds of reporting to effect a full synthesis.[7]

But derived from the spiritual epiphany of his own sense of wildness, *unknown* and preconscious, Thoreau's attempts, at some level, must "fail." He lived an intense paradox: to be was not to be. He understood that in his merger with nature (to truly "be"), his self was "dissolved" (he no longer existed as a knower, his self-consciousness suspended). This natural state was the source of vitality, creativity—the truest self—and in this preferred condition, he was freed from the shackles of civilization and exuberant in that liberty. Yet the gulf between that original epiphany and his writing of it remained as a constant reminder that Thoreau was *not* (ordinarily) wild, and to the extent that he remained civilized, reasoned, literary, and self-conscious, he denied his full vibrancy. This is the conundrum of self-consciousness and those actions based on a reflective faculty. The "self" only appears in its own self-awareness, and the products—self-reflection, memory, and writing—are the voices of the knowing ego trying to recapture its primary experience. But in that capture, both the object (nature) and the knower's own subjectivity (feelings and perceptions) become something else from the original "dissolved" state experience. While the "spiritual birth" Thoreau described to Harrison Blake[8] remained his inspiration, he would not be satisfied with his mystical epiphanies. In his commitment to writing, Thoreau translated that experience by the typical Romantic modes of self-consciousness. Thus to recognize and appreciate nature and to integrate it in order to effect some kind of metaphysical unity were problems presented to Thoreau as a result of his self-consciousness, namely, in his confronting the mystery of his independent ego.

THE PROBLEM OF THE SELF

Around 1800 the self stood in unprecedentedly high esteem.
                               Cunningham and Jardine 1990, p. 1

Thoreau may easily be placed in the Romantic tradition of unfolding the expansive, self-determined self. When Goethe left Weimar to journey to Italy and Coleridge hiked with his friend Wordsworth through the hills of England, their poetic quests were more than aesthetic excursions, as were Thoreau's own sojourns. They sought to redefine themselves in the broadest context of their natural setting, driven by the conviction that their own true selves were best situated there. This projection of the individual psyche into the cosmos with a preoccupied concern for nature is a basic Romantic sentiment. It represents a dethroning of Rationality's dominance to be replaced with a more comprehensive participation in the world. To achieve such an integration of self and world, the boundaries of the self were first loosened and then set free altogether. And the entire enterprise required a self-willed self, whose action in the world determined that world and the moral orientation to it. The Romantics' expressive psyches were expansive, even plastic to the contours of their experience of nature and the self-reflexive process of their awakening to its glory. Deliberately and self-consciously, they sought to refashion their identities by exploring nature, human and nonhuman, in order to establish new contours to their souls. They sought rapturous insight and aesthetic pleasure. A narrow construal of Rationality would not restrict their journeys, nor would conventional notions of socially prescribed achievement. The Romantic wanderers with whom Thoreau aligned himself reached beyond themselves as defined by an Enlightenment ideal to novel personae ruled by the primacy of subjectivity and emotional fulfillment.

Recall Thoreau's "prayer": "Let me forever go in search of myself– Never for a moment think that I have found myself. Be as a stranger to myself never a familiar–seeking acquaintance still" (*Journal* 3, 1990, p. 312). The "self" is an internal other, and Thoreau in a sense is divided between one who observes this inner self—indeed, he writes an ode to it—and a core self that is somehow oblivious to this examining eye. So there is this innermost identity, the "source" of his personhood, and a conscious observing self who is taking note of this familiar, yet different, self. In the famous discourse on solitude in *Walden,* after rhapsodically discussing how he was never truly alone in nature, how "[e]very little pine needle expanded and swelled with sympathy and befriended me" (1971, p. 132), Thoreau entertains the themes concerning self-consciousness discussed above:

> With thinking we may be beside ourselves in a sane sense. By a conscious effort of the mind we can stand aloof from actions and their consequences; and all things, good and bad, go by us like a torrent. We are not wholly involved in Nature. . . . I only know myself as a human entity; the scene so to speak of thoughts and affections; and am sensible of a certain doubleness by which I can stand as remote from myself as from another. However intense my experience, I am conscious of the presence and criticism of a part of me, which, as it were, is not a part of me, but spectator, sharing no experience, but taking note of it; and that is no more I than it is you. When the play, it may be the tragedy, of life is over, the spectator goes his way. It was a kind of fiction, a work of the imagination only, so far as he was concerned. (1971, pp. 134–35)[9]

Thoreau is aware that he is splitting his consciousness, but he asserts that he is "sane."[10] This is interesting, inasmuch as he must take cognizance that such an introspective exercise is not "normal." We do not characteristically look at ourselves as some kind of interior object, yet he does so, and in that act he realizes that his selfhood is subject to the same kind of scrutiny as is his examination of the rest of the world, both nature and society. This self-reflection also prompts from him an important admission: "We are not wholly involved in Nature," which, by admitting his separation from nature, in a sense undermines his mystical aspirations, restraining his rapturous involvement with a touch of epistemological realism. It is an honest moment, not only portraying a self-aware insight about his own "doing" but also providing him with a perspective about his own place in time. Despite Thoreau's efforts to capture time, he well recognizes the ephemeral quality of his own passing.

One of Thoreau's clearest statements about the self is contained in a lengthy Journal entry of 1852, which has three parts: The first third is an evocative landscape description, poetically recording a play of fog and sunlight; the last third predominantly catalogues flora and the weather. But the middle third is a commentary on personal identity. Thoreau begins by noting the ability of thought to carry him from one era to another, and thus he feels contiguous with "Sadi" who "entertained once identically the same thought that I do–and thereafter I can find no essential difference between Sadi and myself" (August 8, 1852, *Journal* 5, 1997, p. 289). No longer a Persian seer, lost in time, "by the identity of his thought" with Thoreau's, Sadi

> still survives. It makes no odds what atoms serve us. Sadi possessed no greater privacy or individuality than is thrown open to me. He had no more interior & essential & sacred self than can come naked into my thought this moment. Truth and a true man is something essentially public not private. If Sadi were to come back to claim a *personal* identity with the historical Sadi he would find that there were too many of us–he could not get a skin that would contain us all. The symbol of a personal identity preserved in this sense is a mummy from the Catacombs–a whole skin it may [be] but no life within it. (Ibid.)

At one level Thoreau is commenting on the integrated character of the life of the mind, how he might attain intimacy with the ancients through common thought. But at another level he is writing on the nature of personal identity, where the essential character of the individual holds some kind of universal confluency, open to others of like mind. He then goes on to deconstruct his own identity with a pronouncement: there is no sanctity of the self—we are in some sense composed of a "conscious" self, which is aware of a deeper self that in a fundamental sense is not ourselves as we might "know," consciously. This schizoid splitting of personhood is destabilizing to say the least. But then there is another recasting of the identity of the individual ego and some universal Mind, where various minds, in communication through shared thought, merged, thus obliterating the integrity of individual identity. Personal identity is only some kind of a mummy, a shell of who we *really* are.

Thoreau thus seeks his truest self beyond his conscious self, exploring the depth of his personal identity to delve for that core, generative self.

Physical solitude is then insignificant, for in this vast mental syncytium, Thoreau was never truly alone (although in a conventional way he might admit, "I love to be alone" [*Walden*, 1971, p. 135]). Physical isolation was trivial, the life of the mind bringing him into intimate contact with himself, other minds, and the world. From this perspective,

> no exertion of the legs can bring two minds much nearer to one another. What do we want most to dwell near to? Not to many men surely, . . . but to the perennial source of our life. . . . [which] will vary with different natures, but this is the place where a wise man will dig his cellar. (Ibid., p. 133)

The trope of loneliness simply articulates Thoreau's deep existential awareness that his moral character demands attention not to the protection of personal identity but rather to its development and expansion. He would not rest "alone" in society, distracted by the demands of those whose values were inimical to this quest. Thus he writes confidently, "I am no more lonely than the loon in the pond that laughs so loud, or than Walden Pond itself" (ibid., p. 137). The loon and the pond have no self-consciousness and thus have no consciousness of being separate, or, in this parlance, "alone." Thoreau, by identifying with nature, achieves a communion with God, who visits him in various guises—as the old settler "who is reported to have dug Walden Pond" and an elderly dame whose "memory runs back farther than mythology" (ibid.).

Nevertheless, there is an unresolved tension. In the insistence on maintaining his personalized view of the world, Thoreau dangerously skirted the black hole of solipsism—one's consciousness (mind, self) cannot know anything other than its own content. The balance between confinement and maintaining a self-aware identity which was always tested against some version of objective reality—natural and social—represented a pervasive epistemological challenge arising from the very metaphysics of self-conscious awareness of oneself as alien in the world (Jonas 1958, 1963; Evernden 1985, 1993). And to whatever extent he might have engaged the world and written of it, the solipsism issue simply would not go away, but always hung over Thoreau and threatened to envelop him in the exclusive universe of his own making. In short, the danger of asserting the self as constitutive of its world is the peril of constructing a world known only to that self. Thoreau was no solipsist. He recognized that "it is vain to think either that the mind can *be* a place, or that the mind alone can *find* a proper place for itself or for us. It must look outside of itself into the world" (Berry 1983, p. 179; quoted by Buell 1995, p. 279). At the same time, however, he was relatively isolated as the result of the perspectivism that arose from his radically personalized view of the world.

Thoreau became acutely aware of his selfness, and, indeed, it became a problem for him. His dilemmas were symptomatic of the age, and there are many testaments—poetic and philosophic—of others' attempts to deal with them. To better situate Thoreau's conundrum and his own achievement, we must better understand the notions of selfhood which undergirded his own formulations, which in fact "allowed" him to proceed. Thoreau employed, knowingly or not, a philosophical scaffolding that bestowed primacy on the self—in particular, on a self-conscious ego.

The theory of subjectivity proposed by Johann Gottlieb Fichte (1762–1814) best articulated the Romantic understanding of the self that Thoreau himself utilized. Thoreau need not have been intimately familiar with Fichte's philosophy itself to have benefited from its formal articulation. The ethos was in the air, and others composed similar rhapsodies in different keys and with assorted harmonies. Thoreau had many sources to learn the particulars of Fichte's program, if he so desired.[11] That is not the issue. Fichte's orientation of the self in action was widely accepted in its most general outline, and, more to the point, Thoreau's response to this Romantic challenge closely followed Fichte's philosophical prescription, or other ones that approximated it. Today few know Fichte's *Wissenschaftslehre*, while *Walden* is part of the canon, but they belong on the same library shelf.

Fichte's thought is notoriously difficult to summarize, and his philosophy of the self evolved most radically after 1800 (presented in various versions of his *Wissenschaftslehre*). But if we focus on his formulations during the 1790s, a relatively coherent picture emerges, one very useful for posing the issues Thoreau implicitly, and at times explicitly, dealt with. Fichte was one of those post-Kantians who sought to mend the fault lines separating theoretical and practical reason. As Thoreau did later, Fichte gave primacy to the knowing self in whose unity all forms of knowing must be derived. In other words, Fichte sought to establish the nature of a self that comes prior to any faculty of knowing, and this fundamental activity of the mind Fichte called "self-positing." Thus the nature of consciousness, most specifically self-consciousness, is at the heart of Fichte's philosophical project, and specifically the effort to find the unity and coherence of the knowing subject. Whereas Kant posited the coherence of the ego in a transcendental quality, the unity of apperception, Fichte investigated the "unconditionedness" (*Umbedingtheit*) of the "I" as residing in a radically self-referential metaphysic:

> Life does not begin with disinterested contemplation of nature or of
> objects. Life begins with action. . . . External nature impinges upon us,
> and stops us, but it is clay for our creation; if we create we have free-
> dom again. Then [Fichte] makes an important proposition: Things are
> as they are, not because they are so independent of me, but because I
> make them so; things depend upon the way in which I treat them, what
> I need them for. . . . "I do not accept what nature offers because I
> must": that is what animals do. I do not simply register what occurs
> like some kind of machine—that is what Locke and Descartes said
> humans do, but that is false. "I do not accept what nature offers because
> I must, I believe it because I will". . . . [E]xperience is something I
> determine because I act. . . . I make my world as I make a poem. (Berlin
> 1999, pp. 88–89)

Fichte's Romantic anthem attests to the yearning expression of a free self,
which was commonly celebrated, one that sought its own self-perfection.[14]
The implications for moral philosophy cannot be overestimated.

The other cardinal feature of Fichte's philosophy posits that the self could
not exist alone and could only be constituted in tension with, or even in
opposition to, an "other." In fact, there are two levels of otherness: the self
itself in its own self-positing, and the empirical world that must be brought
within the self's knowing—incorporated and integrated only as the self
might comprehend it. In this process of knowing, the self would be articulated in tension with the "outside" world. Fichte's basic construction of alterity became widely utilized. For instance, otherness for Coleridge was the
divine other; more radically, for Hegel the other became an ontology.[15]
Hegelian dialecticism regarded all action as governed by confrontation and
synthesis. Applying the ipseity-alterity axis to the self, the sovereign subject would relate only to that which it constructs or confronts. In that meeting the realization of the self is determined in a complex duality, the encountered world comprising one element of the synthesis and the person's own
self-consciousness the other. Their meeting—their synthesis—modulates
the self, which thereby evolves. Like Fichte's construction, the self becomes
a relation, fundamentally an activity which never rests. The general lesson
was universally applied: the self depends intimately on its relation to the
other, whether God, nature, culture, history, or other selves. Otherness
becomes constitutive of the self—quite a different vision of the self from
that of Kant, where the person retained individuality by some postulated
transcendental quality.

Alterity revolves around whether, and how, in response to an encounter,
the self articulates itself or is altered as a consequence of that engagement.
How might the engaged self alter its object and their shared world? How

> The I *posits itself*, and it *exists* by virtue of this mere self-positing. . . .
> *What* was I before I came to self-consciousness? The natural answer to
> this question is: *I* did not exist at all, for I was not an I. The I exists only
> insofar as it is conscious of itself. (Fichte, *Wissenschaftslehre* [1794],
> quoted by Neuhouser 1990, pp. 45–46)

According to Fichte, this self-intuition is the grounding, indeed the self-
grounding, of the self, and from it all forms of human knowing are derived.[12]
From this initial formulation, he further developed his philosophy upon the
notion of the self's practical freedom, what he described as a "feeling of
[one's] freedom and absolute self-sufficiency" (Fichte, *Wissenschaftslehre*
[1797], quoted by Neuhouser 1990, p. 54). If the self existed as self-positing,
then the self's self-determination of itself and its world rested on regarding
the "absolute self-activity of the I as independent of everything outside of
oneself" (ibid.). The goal was genuine autonomy. But Fichte drew a crucial
distinction between the "intellectual intuition" of the self and the self as a
knowing faculty, and thereby made autonomy a "problem":

> If, in intellectual intuition, the I *is because* it is and *is what* it is, then
> it is, to that extent, *self-positing*, absolutely independent and autono-
> mous. The I in empirical consciousness, however, the I as intellect, *is*
> only in relation to something intelligible, and is, to that extent, depen-
> dent. But the I which is thereby opposed to itself is supposed to be not
> two, but one—which is impossible, since "dependence" contradicts
> "independence." Since, however, the I cannot relinquish its absolute
> independence, a striving is engendered: the I strives to make what is
> intelligible dependent upon itself, in order thereby to bring that I which
> entertains representations of what is intelligible into unity with the
> self-positing I. (Fichte [1792] 1988, p. 75; emphasis in original)

Three key features highlight this passage: first, the primary self-sufficiency
of the I;[13] second, the aspiration for autonomy; and third, the dialectic of the
other in the self's self-constitution. This construction of the world's dependence on the knowing I was a "solution" to Kant's challenge of defining a
unifying Reason, but Fichte's radical primacy of the self also begat solipsism.
Before delving into that quandary, let us consider what Fichte did offer.

In Fichte's philosophical system the self is no longer an entity but rather
is regarded as an activity, one which is self-constituting in a way that an
object cannot be. The guiding characteristics of this sensibility (epistemologically) assert the self in a pragmatic mode and (metaphysically) free it
with self-determination. In offering the architectonics of a free, self-willed
self, Fichte provided the Romantics with a philosophical foundation by
which the Romantic quest might proceed:

might the self live in its world and in a universe of other selves? The self alone is either isolated, hence alienated, or else it actively engages the world and thereby becomes actualized. This was the basis of Marx's economic theory of self-alienating work and Kierkegaard's religious philosophy of dialogue with the divine, where the self's authenticity resided in its responsiveness to that call. *Relation,* whether to work (Marx) or to God (Kierkegaard), was based on taking the dialectical structure of Hegel's (and Fichte's) philosophy in new directions.[16]

The relational construct as applied to the specific issue of personhood converges on how the potential for self-aggrandizement must be realized *in* the world, and the self must ultimately actualize itself in the encounter with the other. The "other"—as self-consciousness—includes the self itself, and herein lies the essential mystery of the Romantic understanding of selfhood. On the one hand, we are self-consciously aware of our selfhood as arising from our thinking about being a self; but there is a critical caveat to that observation: the self thereby dissolves. We become locked into a relentless recursive reflection where "the self" no longer abides as a circumscribed, self-contained entity. In *The Principles of Psychology* (written from a very different orientation but still indebted to this Romantic sensibility [Goodman 1990]), William James clearly articulated the elusiveness of mind, specifically the core of the self-consciousness: "[I]t [consciousness] is not one of the *things experienced* at the moment; this knowing is not immediately *known*. It is only known in subsequent reflection" (James [1890] 1983, p. 290). Accordingly, like Fichte before him, James held that consciousness can only be regarded as a process, where, in the attempt to objectify experience—that is, to share it and make it public—consciousness is transformed into something else altogether. Our reflection on our thought, perception, and feelings is irretrievably distinct from the source of that process, which we would like to refer to as our inner or core self. The act of recognition is a function of our self-awareness; and as consciousness or actions are reviewed, a continual generation of new experience must in turn be contemplated. The act of introspection is thus perpetually incomplete in the attempt to capture the primary experience. Because the review process is fundamentally oriented as a retrospective act of analysis, it can never be the act itself. The reflection itself is a thought, but then the recursive spiral begins and there is no end, as Kierkegaard so elegantly observed forty years earlier.[17]

The psychological elusiveness of "selfhood" elicits a beguiling puzzlement. The self has become immersed in its world, and when one attempts to arrest that experiencing subject by reflecting on its experience, subjectivity is lost and an alien objectivity is substituted that is essentially and fundamentally incapable of capturing what is intuitively referred to as inner identity, the experiencing self. The self is truly unaware of itself as it acts, but as soon as the identity of personhood is sought, it slips away into its own recesses. From this point of view, there is no ready definition of the self outside of specific contexts, independent of particular languages and social or physical settings. For instance, selves as citizens have certain rights and obligations as defined by law; soldiers as selves are defined by their military roles and duties; patients are defined by their respective pathologies and reports of illness. So when we speak of the self, we are actually only referring to a commonly accepted construction, one formed out of the contingency of a particular time and place. The self has become a convenient vehicle for speaking about various social roles. When extended to our personhood, the concept becomes a conundrum.[18] This was precisely the issue Thoreau set himself to address.

From the orientation adopted here, we might say that Thoreau found the "other" in several contexts, of which nature is the most prominent. As a naturalist, he saw nature not as a reflection of himself but as radically other: "Man is but the place where I stand & the prospect (thence) hence is infinite. It is not a chamber of mirrors which reflect me–when I reflect myself–I find that there is other than me" (April 2, 1852, *Journal* 4, 1992, p. 420), or as he might have said, the other establishes the finitude of the self. He embraced his self-consciousness to turn his peering at the world into an aesthetic and spiritual order, and accepted his metaphysical separation from nature with a self-willed mandate to explore that relationship. In so doing, he articulated and, in the context of this philosophical formulation, created his personhood. To know Thoreau's work is to perceive that he was in constant dialogue with nature, not only absorbing her beauty and facts of being but, more personally, ascertaining himself in relation to the natural. Various critics assess that process by different criteria and see this project in different lights. I will not attempt any further adjudication here, for my purpose is not to further show how nature as other served as constituent to Thoreau's self-definition of his personhood—it clearly was to a large extent the measure and counterpoise of his own identity—but rather to see this examination as a means of exploring an even deeper other, namely the otherness of himself, one he discovered as the wild.

So, as with Fichte, Thoreau would give primacy to his agency—the knowing self and the self in self-determined action. But unlike the idealist philosophers—from Fichte to Emerson—Thoreau would articulate himself in dialogue over his place in nature through active empiricist pursuit. In a way heretofore unappreciated, Thoreau celebrated sensual experience and made that experience the wellspring of his own selfhood. And by exposing that source, Thoreau finally found his union with the other.

IN SEARCH OF THE SELF

I went in search of myself.

> Heraclitus

While Thoreau deserves scrutiny in his own right, his relevance grows if we effectively place him more securely among those who gave serious responses to our own metaphysical predicament. I am not referring here to the environmental crisis, albeit that issue is certainly germane, but rather to a deeper malaise. We live with a deep uncertainty about certainty. We are insecure about criteria of objectivity, rationality, and truth. What indeed is real and how do we know it? Is there a "self," and if so, what is it? The foundations of knowledge are weakened by the uncertain metaphysics of the knowing agent. These fundamental grounding questions are posed in many different guises under the rubric of postmodernism and seem to dominate discussions in diverse human sciences, art, literature, politics, philosophy, and religion. Thoreau, of course, was no "postmodernist." But his way of posing the question of epistemological and moral agency resonates with many current such discussions, though his "answer" of course differs radically from postmodern ones.

In many respects, postmodernism may be regarded as a continuation of the Romantic reaction to the Enlightenment, and it is on that continuum that we might place Thoreau's own project. We have yet to complete the deconstruction of the self that began in the early nineteenth century. The Romantics had no intention of eliminating the idea of selfhood, but in their initiating its expansion, the concept of identity began to lose its boundaries. Eventually the very question of an entity that we might designate "the self" became highly problematic, so the very authenticity of such an entity was challenged. Post–World War II literary and artistic expression extended this orientation so that we now speak of the self's "indeterminacy," the emblematic slogan for the difficulties in identifying the agency of cognition or moral action (Tauber 1994).[19] When the subject is "decentered," no longer a stable entity—a reference, an origin, or a source—it becomes only the contingent result or product of multiple historical, social, and psychological forces. On this view, the unity of the self is at best a deceptive construction, a remnant of an older and discarded metaphysics. Instead, such an object might only be described in its "doing."[20] And here we come to a fascinating resonance with Thoreau, who similarly would define himself in his doing—in his work and literary product.

Thus in the assertion of agency, in the life work in which he fully engaged, Thoreau defied the forces that conspired to confuse his perspective. Outside any social role or an identification with any movement or group, Thoreau insisted on his own self-made integrity. Presenting it as the work of a hero, he proclaimed his own personhood. By regarding Thoreau from the vantage point of the assault on personal identity, I have endeavored to show that prior to his various roles as naturalist, historian, environmentalist, or polemicist, Thoreau asserted the knowing self. He assumed this mantle of self-positing as a task. In his rebellion against the ascendant positivism of his age, in his insistence on personalizing experience, he gave primacy to his individuality grounded in his particular abilities to see and do. Yet, ironically, in the positivist's world, the self is assumed as given. In Thoreau's universe, where the world is known only as refracted through a personal lens, the knowing self becomes a problem, for it has no universal structure, or even a basis for shared experience with other knowers. The self is fundamentally alone, and only through prodigious effort could Thoreau portray the moral universe he appreciated. He did so despite his isolation and angst.

Thoreau's is a critical counterposition to the postmodern dissolution of agency. We peer at him across our historical divide and ponder to what extent his triumph might be our own. The problematic status of the self, irrespective of the force of contemporary critiques, cannot be regarded as an issue unique to Thoreau's era, or our own. Indeed, we may discern the roots of Thoreau's conundrum in earlier thinkers—in Augustine, Descartes, Rousseau—and project the problem in its later forms in late-nineteenth-century psychology, postanalytic philosophy, and post-1945 art and literature.[21] From this perspective, postmodern critiques of the self's unity, even of its very basis, is a current expression of a deep tradition in our culture, where individualism is

> energized by an inner dynamic of loss, conflict, doubt, absence and lack which feeds into our culture's obsession with control, its sense that the identity of everything, from self to nation, is under centrifugal and potentially disintegrative pressures which have to be rigorously controlled. This is a kind of control that is always exceeding and breaking down the very order it restlessly seeks and is forever re-establishing its own rationale even as it undermines it. (Dollimore 1997, p. 254)

The elusive self has had a complex history, and Thoreau comes late to the stage, as we do. In attempting to assess his venture from our own vantage only a few generations removed from him, we see, more clearly than he could, the trajectory of the crisis he grappled with. In some sense, his innocence of our future enables us to see in him a response still fresh in its hope, sustained by the vigor of a conviction we seem to have lost.

Given his current popularity, it is apparent that Thoreau's mode of inquiry, largely discredited as science and discarded as corrupted Transcendentalism in his own time, remains a potent idealistic and aesthetic philosophy. Why? There are no short answers, and certainly no limits to our speculations, but the perspective adopted here is that Thoreau's lasting appeal resides in his articulation of his own character, what I am calling his "doing." The self-determined agency of his action is guided by a powerful inner sense of himself which brought coherence to his diverse activities and offered a singular direction to his life's work, whether expressed in the acts of writing or in manual labor, political activism, or mystical intercourse. His environmentalism is only one aspect of his project. The power of Thoreau's message consists, at least in part, in the persistent attraction of the Romantic sensibility in our own postmodern era, where the questions he posed remain ours, because the construction of the Romantic self in search of itself still prevails.

Thoreau continues to ride the crest of the Romantic wave that represents the "great break in European consciousness" (Berlin 1999, p. 8), a shifting "away from the notion that there are universal truths, universal canons of art, that all human activities were meant to terminate in getting things right, and the criteria of getting things right were public, were demonstrable" (ibid., p. 14). Romantics adopted a new "universal"—one dominated by the private, by the emotional, by the independent self, bequeathing the relativism that currently dominates. In this post-Enlightenment period, the universe is plastic; there is no abiding structure of things or thought or morality; objectivity has different meanings in different domains; no abiding "method" is universally applicable. The world and the modes by which it may be understood and governed become more pliable, require more tolerance, allow for plurality, and must be understood as amenable to acts of will and free choice. The Romantic world then might well encompass divergent and even contradictory characteristics—harmony and turbulence, unity and multiplicity, integration and fragmentation, joy and melancholia, order and chaos—for these in fact cannot be integrated beyond their own individual metaphysical standing. The radical shift in consciousness is more encompassing than some simplified holistic view of nature or human consciousness, for in its own contradictory fashion, Romanticism must incorporate its own disparate characteristics, which are bound together only in the ulti-

mate revolt against an Enlightenment stricture of some universal, fundamental order. In such a Romantic world, how do we find our bearings?

Thoreau offered us a map of this terrain. He followed in the tradition of
Rousseau's *Confessions* (and the *Reveries*) and Wordsworth's *The Prelude*,
autobiographies that deliberately analyzed personal development and in this
fashion attempted to form an understanding of personal identity.[22] Each
story is unique, and there is little to gain in any attempt to further compare
or contrast him with these other Romantic autobiographers. Instead, let us
briefly consider how autobiography articulates themes introduced at the
beginning of this study, namely, how memory reveals the character of the
self. Thoreau primarily used memory in the particular context of writing
history, but even the naturalist writings are recollections, reconstructions
of his experience, and thus must build from memory, fashioned around the
core issue of his own experience. From this perspective, the nature writing
and the cultural history are all of one piece. They are public discourses as
distillations of Thoreau's most intimate thoughts of himself in the domains
of nature and the past. Each required exercise of creative memory—imaginative, aesthetically driven, and thus deeply personal. For Thoreau, to
plumb these depths constitutes an important project in his discovering, and
enunciation, of the self. Indeed, autobiography as the expression of such
introspection is a critical component of the notion of a developing self, one
that not only changes but remains elusive in its evolution.

Thoreau was perhaps most cognizant of this issue as he pondered the
moral dimension of his poesis. *A Week* offers a remarkable testament to his
own vision of the poet-historian:

> The true poem is not that which the public read. There is always a
> poem not printed on paper, coincident with the production of this,
> stereotyped in the poet's life. It is *what he has become through his
> work*. Not how is the idea expressed in stone, or on canvass or paper, is
> the question, but how far it has obtained form and expression in the life
> of the artist. His true work will not stand in any prince's gallery.
> (1980a, p. 343; emphasis in original)

This is Thoreau's definition of a life of virtue. His morning work and his
dreams—waking or sleeping—are unified by a vision of moral action which
can be achieved only in doing—in intense experience, deliberate conduct,
and artistic achievement. But the completed essay was not Thoreau's final
destination; rather, the *experienced* life, which included the writing, was the
object of his efforts. He was "writing" his life, creating in word and deed,
so that in the end the presented public record was configured by the imperative to portray a vision of the self—one seen in the doing but only per-

ceived as the tip of an iceberg of experience. Thus Thoreau's literary project, whether he presented it as cultural history, natural history, or poetry, distilled a deeper consciousness.

In the end, the search for the self is a project complete unto itself. But we may well ask, To what end? Modern critics of autobiography have explored the tension between the person who says "I" and the "I" that is not a person but a function of language. In other words, the "I" does not properly refer to an entity inasmuch as it has a split agenda as authorial voice and object of that voice (Gilmore 1994, p. 6). This is simply a reformulation of the self-consciousness problem, and there are many ways to demonstrate it: Autobiography identifies centrifugal forces, which move away from the center—the "I" in one form—and centripetal forces, which move toward the center—the "I" in the other modality (Bergland 1994, p. 160). In this sense, "to find a self in autobiography inevitably fails because of the impossibility of language to represent a whole" (ibid., p. 161). Another way of looking at this issue is the intriguing observation made by Roland Barthes of photographic images of himself:

> In front of the lens, I am at the same time: the one I think I am, the one I want others to think I am, the one the photographer thinks I am, and the one he makes use of to exhibit his art. In other words, a strange action: I do not stop imitating myself, and because of this, each time I am (or let myself be) photographed, I invariably suffer from a sensation of inauthenticity, sometimes of imposture. . . . [T]he Photograph represents the very subtle moment when, to tell the truth, I am neither subject nor object but a subject who feels he is becoming an object. (Barthes 1981, pp. 11–14)

Barthes is describing "a dispersed self," one that

> seems never to coincide with its image. Barthes's treatment of posing is really about the impossibility of not posing. It questions the very concept of authenticity and turns it into a kind of simulacrum in which the subject cannot stop "imitating" himself. . . . But worse than the specter of inauthenticity is the specter of objectification, the fear that the always-inauthentic image does in fact constitute the objectified self. The problem Barthes's remarks on posing [reveal] is that the so-called profound or essential self can never be represented as such. Indeed the very nature of this essential self becomes paradoxical: its subjectivity is linked to a notion of authenticity, yet any image of that self is a sign of its objectification, and hence, its inauthenticity. The authentic self, in Barthes's terms, is finally an impossibility, for it would be a self freed from the process of becoming an object. (Jay 1994, pp. 194–95)

Responses to the existential anxiety provoked by this insight have led either to defense of the essential self or to an admission of the inevitability of its inaccessibility. Thoreau, unlike most twentieth-century existentialists, chose the former option. In a sense, his autobiographical narrative, like the photograph, freezes an image of time and person, a pose, if you will, that assumes a certain identity and then to some extent *becomes* that identity. Thoreau would constantly expand and refashion that self-portrait and thus attempt to close the circle. The self is constantly being made and remade, so that "in the end," written memory—the literary product—in large measure becomes the subject itself. The qualifications—"to some extent" and "in large measure"—are important, because the writing project remains incomplete and never can totally capture that "split-screen" character of identity. But the point is not whether or to what extent Thoreau "succeeds" but rather his moral imperative of attempting to do so. In the *doing*, the self is asserted.

Thoreau could not abide the uncertainty of our own age, and looking forward into the western sunset, he could proclaim, "As a true patriot, I should be ashamed to think that Adam in paradise was more favorably situated on the whole than the backwoodsman in this country" ("Walking," 1980b, p. 111). The American hero was about to add his "fables to those of the East" (ibid., p. 121), for this time, in this place, demanded a response to an epic opportunity:

> If the heavens of America appear infinitely higher, and the stars brighter, I trust that these facts are symbolical of the height to which the philosophy and poetry and religion of her inhabitants may one day soar. . . . For I believe that climate does thus react on man,—as there is something in the mountain air that feeds the spirit and inspires. Will not man grow to greater perfection intellectually as well as physically under these influences? . . . I trust that we shall be more imaginative, that our thoughts will be clearer, fresher, and more ethereal as our sky,—our understanding more comprehensive and broader, like our plains,—our intellect generally on a grander scale, like our thunder and lightning, our rivers and mountains and forests,—and our hearts shall even correspond in breadth and depth and grandeur to our inland seas. . . . Else to what end does the world go on, and why was America discovered? (Ibid., pp. 110–11)

This spiritual hymn to patriotism invokes divine purpose, and in that tradition, man, the divine's agent, has been made in His image. To be sure, this was not jingoistic patriotism, the blind ambition of imperialism, but a sense of the land's spirit. Without "*self*-respect . . . [p]atriotism is a maggot in their heads" (*Walden*, 1971, p. 321; emphasis in original).

The optimism such a view celebrates belongs only to a great individual-ist, who can assert the primacy of his own selfhood and its accompanying mandate. There is, in fact, a mission, and he knows its character and its demands. If presented with the postmodern challenge, Thoreau would have answered that the self indeed exists as groping for self-expression and knowl-edge in a world potentially alienating and distant. But rather than decon-struct the self and leave ourselves in limbo, untethered and floating in a sea of contingency, he would maintain that our deepest and most abiding core of "personhood" must be the assertion of that individuality as a moral man-date. Such is the stuff in which heroes are cast. The project he thus assigned himself, and us, is to capture our essence as character. His "solution"—to the extent that he had one—was to live in elusive nature, appreciate and inter-nalize her, and in the process of the acute self-consciousness of his scrutiny, actualize himself.

But Thoreau's recognition that he was a separate mind—in nature, yet segregated in his own self-consciousness—created an inner tension, never fully resolved. He was stretched between the autonomy of his own person and the world in which he lived. This balancing of the "autonomous-self" with the "self-in-the-world" is a dialectic in continual play. One way of gauging the tilt of Thoreau's balance is simply to look directly at a text. For instance, Buell (building on Clapper's [1967] key insight) makes the inter-esting observation that as *Walden* unfolds, the speaker as the self-creator of his environment, as evinced by the frequent appearance of "Thoreau's favorite pronoun, 'I,' " gradually yields, as the text proceeds, to the cluster of "Walden," "pond(s)," and the various nominal and adjectival forms of "wild" in which the self lives (Buell 1995, p. 122). This inverse relationship of the "autonomous-self" and the "self-in-the-world" reflects the thematic intent of the narrative and reflects, in perhaps a crude measure, the com-plex structure of the book. As Thoreau reaches out to nature, and to his audi-ence, we see him pushing aside the narcissistic mirror, and the inordinate "I" becomes contextualized. This represents the to and fro of Thoreau's struggle of defining his very personhood.

To the extent that he remains stuck in his self-awareness, the separated self is always peering at nature rather than being truly connected to it. This is, then, despite his extraordinary success as a writer, ultimately the "fail-ure" inherent in the "autonomous-self," which in its various epistemolog-ical projects can never fulfill the experience of that other "self-in-the-world." But the "problem" of self-consciousness might well be turned on its head. As Hans Jonas wrote in answer to the nihilistic challenges of our own era, it is precisely our consciousness that provides the guarantee of our personhood. In this view, then, the very inability to merge with nature assures us of our very humanity, our transcendence as moral creatures, and the metaphysical basis of our selfhood (Jonas 1958; 1963, pp. 320 ff.). At some level, Thoreau must have appreciated that, indeed, his separateness conferred his selfhood, and perhaps in an ironic turn, we appreciate that in Thoreau's consummate immersion in nature he came to realize the irony of Emerson's credo, offered from the contemplative podium: "And, in fine, the ancient precept, 'Know thyself,' and the modern precept, 'Study nature,' become at last one maxim" (Emerson 1983b, p. 56).

This brings us to a central debate about Thoreau, namely the "egocentric" versus "ecocentric" construction of his thought. Buell correctly notes that this division hardly allows a neat separation; placing Thoreau into one camp or the other is to oversimplify a complex shifting of contexts. Nevertheless, he would read Thoreau's nature writing with far more emphasis on its ecological and environmental ethical perspectives, portraying him in close proximity to the current green ethos. Thoreau is thus postured as moving toward a biocentrist awareness (1995, p. 394) but hardly as its full author: "the environmental imagination cannot live by Thoreau alone. But with him as a point of reference, we can move in all the necessary directions" (p. 395), that is, "helping to make the space of nature ethically resonant" (p. 394). Thus *Walden*, from Buell's perspective, should not be read solely as an autobiographical narrative (p. 394), but for its key moral lesson: "The path to biocentrism must lead through humanitarianism" (p. 386). This is what Buell refers to as "*Walden's* plot of relinquishment: the protagonist in the act of becoming weaned from the project of a solely individual fulfillment as primary subject of interest" (p. 389).

It is erroneous to read Thoreau as asserting *either* the disappearance *or* the self-assertion of the persona (Buell 1995, p. 178); as Peter Fritzell observes, there is rather a constant interplay, even a dialecticism at work:

> To present an environmentalist's point of view in a personal voice. To immerse the person, the personal voice, in an environment. To deny the self and affirm the environment. To deny the environment and celebrate the self. To view the self as a product of its environment and the environment as a product of the self. To view the self as a metaphor for the environment and the environment as a metaphor of or for the self. Such is the habit of the self-conscious ecologist, the man at Walden. (Fritzell 1990, p. 189)

Thoreau shared the great Romantic quandary of finding his place—the vantage point from which the world might be known—and in so doing, he would define himself. But Buell basically sees the ethos of nature writing, and Thoreau's own efforts, from the environmental point of view, which would efface the self:

> The effect of environmental consciousness on the perceiving self, as I see it, is not primarily to fulfil it, to negate it, or even to complicate it, although all of these may seem to happen. Rather the effect is most fundamentally to raise the question of the validity of the self as the primary focalizing device for both writer and reader: to make one wonder, for instance, whether the self is as interesting an object of study as we supposed, whether the world would become more interesting if we could see it from the perspective of a wolf, a sparrow, a river, a stone. This approach to subjectivity makes apparent that the "I" has no greater claim to being the main subject than the chickens, the chopped com, the mice, the snake, and the phoebes—who are somehow also interwoven with me. (Buell 1995, p. 179)

That is certainly true at one level: each component of nature (including ourselves) is just that, an element—a part of the whole. But that is not the issue as I see it. Rather, the question underlying this debate is that a story is being told, a narrative elaborated, with all the force that narrative bestows—a human perspective, imbued with meaning and signification.

Such questioning of the status of the self reflects a postmodern ethos, the insecurity of doubt about the "I"'s very standing. Thoreau, I expect, if given only a single choice, would cast his lot with the other side. Indeed, he might well have said, How can one know the world from a river's perspective? Aside from the absurdity of assigning consciousness to chopped corn or a stone, what could such a perspective be other than *our* perspective of the river's or tree's respective point of view? In the end, such a sighting is simply another one of our multitudinous vantages of the world in which we seek *meaning* and in the process project our own intentionality or rationality *onto* that world (Tauber 1998a). The question then becomes, How do we fool ourselves into thinking that we might shed our "I-ness"? Or more to the point, Why do we need to?[23] To seek a more intimate and caring relationship with nature need not necessitate deconstructing ourselves in the process. The very integrity of our own agency would be threatened. Why not simply promote a sympathy, recognizing that it is an "I" that must sympathize? Fritzell comes closer to the mark in claiming a play of perspectives as we build a multidimensional universe about ourselves. This Thoreau did with acute self-consciousness and consummate skill.

The controversy about Thoreau's placement as an "ecocentrist" versus an "egocentrist" is conclusively resolved in favor of the latter designation if one appreciates his diverse projects of one piece. His nature study was in service of defining the coordinates of knowing, a project which in turn was dedicated to establishing the agency of the knower. This venture informed all of his various projects—his literary career as a nature writer and historian, his crusades for religious and economic integrity, as well as his diverse scientific, political, and aesthetic pursuits. The various challenges Thoreau posed for himself—epistemological, ontological, ethical, and, not the least, psychological—may all be subsumed in this quest for his own self.

From this reading, the critical issue is not whether Thoreau was an ecocentrist or not, but rather what are the implications of his egocentrism. On the one hand, Thoreau's celebration of autonomy countermands the seemingly inescapable anomie of our own mass culture and offers an appealing answer to the quandary of conformity; yet, on the other hand, the ethics of his isolating individualism leaves us uneasy about the moral implications of such a stance in a world ever searching for an ethics to govern an increasingly complex, interdependent society. Thoreau, in the end, offers us only an incomplete portrait of moral identity, because he was so rigidly focused on the individual. This indictment may seem ironic considering how relentlessly he pursued an integrated, holistic vision of himself in the world. However, bereft of a sustaining social ethics, Thoreau was all too often left in splendid isolation with nature, whose responses to him, he testifies, were found at Walden Pond, whose surface—sometimes glassy, sometimes ruffled—always reflected his own image.

Epilogue: Mending the World

We can comprehend only a world that we ourselves have made.
Nietzsche [1904] 1967, p. 272

Thoreau, I have argued, moved from an idealist Transcendental tradition of mind contemplating nature to one embracing an empiricist-based self-consciousness of mind-in-nature. From this latter perspective, he offers extraordinary insights into the dilemmas and paradoxes of selfhood. His efforts to bridge nature and culture, to savor the wild and to translate that primary encounter with acute sensitivity, remain his abiding legacy. Not content to describe or create a mythic way of seeing nature, he enacted it. For us to "read" that myth demands that we appreciate that his "seeing" possessed a unique moral character. Indeed, Thoreau created a particular kind of vision of, and for, himself. This creation became an ethical venture, the imperative of seeing the natural world and his place in it, ever conscious of himself observing himself observing nature. In constructing Thoreau's metaphysics of the self, I have detailed how his epistemology was governed by this composite vision of the world and himself.

The centrality of his personal perspective was both the strength of his character and at the same time its weakness. In order to pursue his private goals, Thoreau often forfeited social intercourse, and even in his political activities he remained steadfastly centered on his own person. Ironically, Thoreau, like Nietzsche after him, attempted to serve as a physician to his culture, but in his famous isolation he remained a solitary figure, glorious in the celebration of his individuality and artistic accomplishment, yet sadly removed from the social world of other human beings. In short, Thoreau's vision, for all its power to articulate himself and celebrate the natural environment he inhabited, remained communally myopic and thereby restricted to a world of his own making. Others were simply not particularly germane for him.

The most poignant testimony to this aspect of Thoreau's character occurs around the enigmatic break with Emerson. Whatever the reasons for the schism, Thoreau's Journal reveals the deep disappointment in his own carriage.[1] He can adopt an ironic, humorous tone[2] or, more honestly, a laconic bent. Thoreau cut a sorry figure. At the same time he was complaining about Emerson, Emerson confided to his own journal in the fall of 1851:

> H.T. will not stick
> he is not practically renovator. He is a boy, & will be an old boy. Pounding beans is good to the end of pounding Empires, but not, if at the end of years, it is only beans.
>   I fancy it an inexcusable fault in him that he is insignificant here in the town. He speaks at Lyceum or other meeting but somebody else speaks & his speech falls dead & is forgotten. He rails at the town doings & ought to correct & inspire them[.] (1975, p. 404).

And this was not solely the assessment of an antagonist but seems to have been a general opinion, one Thoreau himself recognized as widely held.[3] Thoreau did not cultivate social graces, nor did he attempt to be "one of the boys."[4] And Thoreau reciprocated the quiet hostility of his neighbors:

> Since I perambulated the bounds of the town I find that I have in some degree confined myself– –my vision and my walks–on whatever side I look off I am reminded of the mean & narrow-minded men whom I have met lately there– What can be uglier than a country occupied by grovelling coarse & low-lived men–no scenery will redeem it–what can be more beautiful than any scenery inhabited by heroes!
>   . . . It is a charmed circle which I have drawn around my abode–having walked not with God but with the Devil. I am too well aware when I have crossed this line. (Thoreau, September 27, 1851, *Journal* 4, 1992, pp. 100–101)

The following Journal entry is striking as we witness Thoreau building a fortress about himself, an elaborate rationalization of a man misplaced. Writing a week after his birthday, he contemplates his existential standing at what becomes a major crossroads:

> Here I am 34 years old, and yet my life is almost wholly unexpanded. How much is in the germ! There is such an interval between my ideal and the actual in many instances that I may say I am unborn. There is the instinct for society–but no society. Life is not long enough for one success. Within another 34 years that miracle can hardly take place. . . . The society which I was made for is not here, shall I then substitute for the anticipation of that this poor reality. I would have the unmixed expectation of that than this reality.

If life is waiting–so be it. I will not be shipwrecked on a vain reality.
(July 19, 1851, *Journal* 3, 1990, p. 313)

Thoreau found his truer being in other realms—in nature, in the spirit, in himself.[5] His splendid solitude and the perspectivism he cultivated focused his intense vision. This would suffice.

For Thoreau, the world truly was there only to the extent that he *saw* it. To appreciate nature is one way to experience it; to experience it more acutely is to be aware of the *responsibility* of the observer to see to the degree that he has the capacity. In this sense, the character of the individual determines what is "out there."

> Objects are concealed from our view not so much because they are out of the course of our visual ray as because there is no intention of the mind and eye toward them. We do not realize how far and widely, or how near and narrowly, we are to look. The greater part of the phenomena of nature are for this reason concealed to us all our lives.
> (November 4, 1858, *Journal*, [1906] 1962, 11:285; also published in "Autumnal Tints," 1980d, p. 173)

Each has his own perspective; each sees somewhat differently; each sees something different. Thus what objects "one person will see . . . are just as different from those which another will see as the persons are different" (ibid.). Nature's reality is not at stake, but the individual's ability to know the world depends solely on his ability to observe and comprehend it. "Who can say what *is?* He can only say *how* he *sees*" (Thoreau, December 2, 1846, *Journal* 2, 1984, p. 355).

Thoreau's preoccupation with his own perspective drew on two sources: his personality, the self-centered, asocial inclinations of an eccentric bachelor; and from his deep intellectual interest in perception. When Thoreau observed during the Walden period, "As for the reality no man sees it–but some see more and some less" (Thoreau, December 2, 1846, *Journal* 2, 1984, p. 355), he not only was making a passing note of the Kantian noumena/phenomena distinction but also was writing the preamble to a significant portion of his later agenda. By the mid-nineteenth century, new insights into the psychology and physiology of vision raised novel questions about how fragmented sensory and psychological experience might cohere, and how objectivity might be attained. These issues became defining questions of personal identity, considering how closely "our sense of seeing connects with our sense of ourselves as unities" (Pick 1997, p. 199). Joining company with Müller, Constable, Turner, and Ruskin, Thoreau appreciated the mysteries of perception and made them central to his scientific and artistic inquiries. For him, scientific questions drifted into epistemological ones and, ultimately, metaphysical deliberations of how the transparency of the subject-as-observer was "clouded." And thus we might appreciate that Thoreau's concerns were in step with a broad contemporary reassessment about cognition, which entailed a new self-consciousness about the world's presentation—the beguiling puzzle of how the mind, in its interactions with nature ("reality"), creates a world of its own design and character.[6]

It is difficult, if not unfair, to name a single philosophical issue that captures Thoreau's epistemological project most adequately, but a general configuration of problems in the mainstream of philosophical discourse does compose his context. If we regard him in a broader tradition, Thoreau becomes both a proto-pragmatist and a proto-phenomenologist. Both philosophies later substituted for the positivist perspective, the ultimate expression of the distanced observer, a knower incontrovertibly *in* the world and *part* of it. Phenomenologists, beginning with Brentano, were preoccupied with the ways in which we "constitute" the world by personally signifying objects. Interaction in the world thereby confers knowledge of it, and thus "the world *as we know it* is always a world which is 'to hand,' and a world with which we deal" (Toulmin 1984, p. xii). American pragmatists from Pierce to James to Dewey arrived at a similar orientation, arguing that philosophy must turn to examining life in action, humans in their fully lived experience. Only in this "pragmatic" context would knowledge assume its appropriate role, in what Dewey would call its "naturalized" or "instrumental" function (Dewey 1984, p. 238). And from this perspective, Dewey concluded in his Gifford Lectures of 1929:

> Mind is no longer a spectator beholding the world from without and finding its highest satisfaction in the joy of self-sufficing contemplation. The mind is within the world as a part of the latter's own ongoing process. It is marked off as mind by the fact that wherever it is found, changes take place in a directed way, so that a movement in a definite one-way sense . . . takes place. (Dewey 1984, p. 232)

So, on these views, mind moves from a beholder of the world (Descartes and Locke) to an active participant in it, one distinguished in this orientation by intention. Imagination and Will have thus undergone metamorphosis, but these basic Romantic notions remain in the "infrastructure" of these later phenomenological and pragmatic philosophies.[7]

While the pragmatists were centering their interests on human action, the phenomenologists invoked the "gaze" as the pivotal focus of the subject's relation to the world, in the sense that consciousness and meaning depended quite literally on how things are seen (Husserl [1935] 1970; Koháck 1978). For phenomenologists, "the objects that surround us function less 'as they are' than 'as they mean,' and objects only mean for someone. . . . To see implies seeing meaningfully" (Morrissey 1988, p. xx). This was simply a more neutral, perhaps more flexible, position, which afforded escape from the subjectivism that so tainted Romantic epistemology. But in the end, the nineteenth-century Romantics and the twentieth-century phenomenologists come close to the same conclusion: the inextricability of subject and object that Goethe pronounced and modern phenomenology reaffirmed, clashed with the ideal of the scientist as independent from the world—an austere observer, a collector of data uncontaminated by a projected personal vision. In short, the aspiration of positivist objectivity— devoid of value judgment, leaving the facts to stand alone—is, from this phenomenological perspective, an odd conceit.[8]

The phenomenologists addressed the same question that Thoreau the Romantic had struggled with: How could subject and object be seamlessly connected? How could one mend the world? As science increasingly idealized a distanced observer, objectivity subordinated knowledge based on personal experience. But Thoreau, by moving across epistemological boundaries, resisted science's hegemony and firmly grasped for other modes of experience cut off by these new positivist standards. Coupled to this epistemological isolation of the subject, a metaphysics unifying man and nature had been lost. By the mid-nineteenth century, the older "vitalistic" monism had been replaced by a "materialistic" monism, and in that shift the Romantics and their heirs lost a unified reality, where humans—as distinctly "other"—are at one with nature and the cosmos (Jonas 1982).

At the heart, then, of Thoreau's quest for the elusive synthesis of "personal" and "objective" is the search for their common metaphysical foundation (Whitehead 1925). Husserl posed this problem dramatically in our own century in *The Crisis of European Sciences*. For him, scientism had recast Kantian rationalities (theoretical and practical) into a deep metaphysical schism in a two-step process. First, it fragmented knowledge: scientific reason was assigned to study, if not govern, nature, while a different kind of reason was applied to matters of value and ethics. This division was unstable and ultimately fractured experience. Second, the scientific ethos went on to dominate these other forms of knowledge and experience, subordinating them to its own standards and ways of knowing:

> Merely fact-minded sciences make merely fact-minded people. . . . Scientific, objective truth is exclusively a matter of establishing what the world, the physical as well as the spiritual world, is in fact. But can the

world and human existence in it, truthfully have a meaning if the sciences recognize as true only what is objectively established in this fashion . . . ? (Husserl [1935] 1970, pp. 6–7)

Husserl saw in this division the collapse of any attempt to define a unifying metaphysics (ibid., p. 13). Modern man would now be torn between a
naive faith in reason and a skepticism that admits only knowledge based on
positivist criteria. The "crisis" was the deeply divisive nature of objective
knowledge pitted against personal experience, aesthetic value, and spiritual
intuition. In place of this fragmentation, Husserl sought a unifying "Reason,"[9] recognizing the need to synthesize all experience.[10]

Albeit in a different format, this had been Thoreau's mission, one inherited from Goethe, who clearly articulated the problem in the early period
of the Romantic era. But by the end of the nineteenth century, the schism
was widening. Nietzsche proclaimed a fundamental impasse, an irredeemable gulf between the possibility of objective knowledge and personal
meaning (Tauber 1996a). Nietzsche's position, although the obverse of the
positivists' celebration of the scientific attitude, also rejected a composite or
holistic ideal that might attempt to incorporate personal passion and objective science.[11] In separating personal experience from what he viewed as a
despotic rationality, Nietzsche advocated the rejection of an ascetic science
and sided with the primacy of personal, self-creative experience. In this
sense, he articulated the two-culture impasse but placed the disjunction
within the individual (Tauber 1992, 1994). Thoreau, still embedded in a
Romantic optimism, sided with Goethe.

As I have endeavored to show, the scientific and the personal may be complementary to each other and, indeed, may serve to strengthen their respective forms of knowledge. The issue is one of balance, not of combat. In this
regard, the pluralistic universe of William James, where multiple forms of
knowing are not only tolerated but legitimated and encouraged, not only is
better tempered but moves toward the unification of reason Husserl advocated.[12] And one way of creating that synthesis, again a theme explored here,
is that objectified knowledge must be made meaningful. This was the program enunciated by Michael Polanyi, and, I have argued, this was also
Thoreau's own project. After all, there is no return to Romantic ideals in
the form of an imposition of the subjective into scientific methodology; yet
to displace the personal from scientific experience is to deny a large measure of the human dimension of the venture. With the truncation of the
knowing subject, the scope of the entire scientific enterprise is reduced and
impoverished as a personally meaningful activity. The issue then becomes
how to achieve integration of scientific knowledge and personal meaning.

This enterprise may well be regarded as a peculiarly contemporary project, one that addresses the current need to find integration in our fragmented postmodern condition. This is not to advocate a choice between rationality and emotion, an either/or predicament, but rather to admit self-consciously the need to acknowledge personal experience in a world increasingly objectified. To see science as possessing an aesthetic dimension is a means of making such knowledge "personally meaningful." What might otherwise escape as sterilized "objectivity" is thereby reintegrated within a fractured psyche and, universally, within culture at large. It is here that Thoreau's own example must account for much of his contemporary appeal.

And this question of coherence brings us back to the "fact." For Thoreau, facts truly exist as poetic elements, refashioned by the imagination and aesthetic appreciation into the most intimate experience. Consider the following Journal entry from February 18, 1852:

> I have a common place book for facts and another for poetry–but I find it difficult always to preserve the vague distinction which I had in my mind–for the most interesting & beautiful facts are so much the more poetry and that is their success. They are *translated* from earth to heaven– I see that if my facts were sufficiently vital & significant– perhaps transmuted more into the substance of the human mind–I should need but one book of poetry to contain them all. (February 18, 1852, *Journal 4*, 1992, p. 356)

Here we hear echoes of Goethe's own view that poetry and science stem from a common root, human imagination. Thoreau certainly gives primacy to the poet (e.g., ibid.), but the point is not that science is subordinated but that all experience can be integrated into a meaningful whole. For Thoreau, a fragmented world is a failure of Imagination, for the world—all within it—was of one piece. Thus he sought cohesion at several levels of experience: he might fall into a rapturous mystical union with divine nature as he watched Walden Pond at sunset; he would carefully follow the flight of a hawk or regard a landscape to contemplate nature's order and beauty; he scrupulously studied the distribution of acorns and sand-pine seedlings to pursue facts about plant propagation. Each of these activities was unified in his experience, and Thoreau's "work" was to assure that they remained cohesively together. Indeed, his self-consciousness was the key modality of his attempts to repair the rift separating the self and its world.

The centrality of creating and preserving his individuality not only drove Thoreau's quest to know, and thereby find meaning, but also fulfilled his original self-proclaimed charge to forge his personhood in experience. More than any particular political or social agenda, Thoreau's way of viewing the world and himself within it established his example for posterity. He did not succumb to the anxiety of the self separating from its world in some final and irretrievable way. In the passage quoted above, we see him (happily) anticipating the writing of "one book of poetry to contain them [facts] all," and indeed that was his overriding mission. In recognizing the legitimacy of his project, we might well ask, And what ordered that book? What was its theme? How, indeed, was it to be written? Finally, *who* will write the next volume? Thoreau's response: Each of us in his or her own way.

Notes

ACKNOWLEDGMENTS

1. Emmanuel Levinas (1906–95) was a French phenomenologist whose moral philosophy has established him as a major Continental figure. In a radical critique of autonomy-based ethics (and perhaps more broadly in reaction to Martin Heidegger), Levinas argued that philosophy must address the individual's unavoidable responsibility for others. But his ethics takes on a much more global quality than simply a narrow construal of civic duty or moral attitude. It is a comprehensive ethic which would ground epistemology and metaphysics in this ethical encounter. Levinas's philosophy then may be fairly regarded as an ethical metaphysics, within which the self not only is defined in relation to the other but regards persons only in relation to our relationships with others. Levinas's major works have been translated, the most important being *Totality and Infinity* ([1961] 1969) and *Otherwise Than Being, or Beyond Essence* ([1974] 1991). Excellent general reviews of his work include those of Edith Wyschogrod (1974) and Arthur Peperzak (1993); shorter comments in Cohen (1986) and in Bernasconi and Critchley (1991). This idea of an ethical metaphysics—how a moral philosophy offers a grounding to metaphysics and epistemology—permeates my own study of Thoreau. I regard the orienting force of Thoreau's moral character as shaping his distinctive vision of the Other—whether nature, history, or culture—so that his entire sense of identity and his relation to the world are joined parts of a deeply moral enterprise. Thus the most fundamental work of "knowing" is, for Thoreau, value-laden, an orientation profoundly instructive to our own time and perhaps key to his enduring popularity.

INTRODUCTION

1. For example, in 1841 Thoreau read Coleridge's *Aids to Reflection* (1829), which carefully explained the difference between Understanding and Reason,

"perhaps the key epistemological concept of the Romantic age" (Sattelmeyer 1988, p. 30). Thoreau's philosophical education began at Harvard but flourished in the first years of his friendship with Emerson (Richardson 1986; Sattelmeyer 1988).

2. *Walden* was to reflect this overtly Romantic shift, and while some regard *A Week* as also a Transcendental treatise (Buell 1973, p. 207), it is far less well articulated and clear, for Thoreau has achieved in *Walden* a sense of self-realization absent from the earlier work. Lynden Shanley, who was the first to make an extensive study of *Walden*'s creative evolution (completed by Clapper's comprehensive genetic text [1967]), maintained that its essential nature did not change from the first to the last (eighth) version of 1854 (Shanley 1957, p. 6), a critical opinion vigorously contested by many more recent studies (e.g., Adams and Ross 1988; Sattelmeyer 1990). *Walden*'s structure or theme need not be detailed here otherwise than to note certain key features of its architecture: As Charles Anderson (1968) argues, "The Ponds" is a central focus of the finished work, for it expresses Thoreau's mystical union with Walden Pond, which had evolved into a symbol of the ultimate reality, the limitless bounds of man's mind, and the potential of nature. With this vision Thoreau narrates, in the three chapters that follow, his attempted ascent to purity and perfection very much in keeping with the Journal entry just cited (Adams and Ross 1988, p. 183). A second climax occurs in the penultimate chapter, "Spring," where Thoreau witnesses an epiphany of natural renewal that he translates into personal rejuvenescence. Thus from this reading, the first half of the book attempts to illustrate a new moral and psychological perspective on the material world, with an emphasis on personal economy and a critique of competing social values. The critique is informed by the use of heightened imagination guided by an appreciation of the divine character of nature. In the second half of the text, Thoreau then espouses his own role as mythmaker, the prophet heralding the organicism of the world, and the mystical transcendence available to the cognizant individual. And in the "Conclusion," Thoreau calls us to live courageously—a life guided by the imagination is to live the life one has dreamed. As Adams and Ross document (1988, pp. 166 ff.), the substantive material added to the second half of the book in version IV (written during 1852) places this structure in the text.

3. Perhaps surprisingly, this is the first use of "transcendental" in Thoreau's Journal, and he uses it in three contexts in this same entry. The others refer to the intuition concerning time—"We review the past with the commonsense–but we anticipate the future with transcendental senses" (June 7, 1851, *Journal* 3, 1990, p. 245)—and the second refers to himself, "I am too transcendental to serve you in your way" (ibid.), referring to a practical social mission.

4. Harold Bloom schematizes them as an early-phase Prometheus struggling against nature, society, and all orthodoxies, to be followed by a later-stage Real Man, the Imagination, who in crisis steps back and internalizes the quest, now recentered in the self. In this latter mode, the Romantic hero is no longer "a seeker after nature but after his own mature powers," turning away, not from

society to nature, "but from nature to what was more integral than nature, within himself" (1971, p. 26). The widened consciousness seeks not a union with nature or the divine, but rather with the "self-less self" (ibid.).

5. This is a widespread view. Hicks was of the opinion that "his [Thoreau's] object was never scientific knowledge, nor, for that matter was nature his true subject" (1925, p. 72). This perspective was reiterated by Walter Harding (1959, p. 136) and Roderick Nash: "The crucial environment was within. Wilderness was ultimately significant to Thoreau for its beneficial effect on thought. Much of Thoreau's writing was only superficially about the natural world. Following Emerson's dictum that "the whole of nature is a metaphor of the human mind," he turned to it repeatedly as a figurative tool (1967, p. 89). Thoreau's putative "ecocentric" vision has been contested, reflecting the complex cultural trajectory of modern environmentalism (Buell 1995, pp. 364–69). Buell, more thoroughly and carefully than any other critic, has attempted to recast the *ego*centrist Thoreau—the Thoreau of Marx (1964) and Nash (1967)—into an *eco*centrist portrait (1995) (further discussed in chapter 7). This may well be a meaningful reading for those concerned with the environmental movement who wish to use Thoreau, as Buell writes, as a "point of reference." Taylor vehemently criticizes this position:

> Buell's analysis is, of course, remarkably patronizing toward Thoreau as a thinker. The unargued assumption is that our (Buell's) ideas are correct, and that the task is to legitimate these ideas by tracing them back to Thoreau, even though the fit is certainly less than perfect. In the process, Thoreau is made to look like little more than an immature, imperfect vision of ourselves. . . . Instead of discovering in Thoreau a powerful thinker, Buell instead finds only an "environmental saint," a symbol we can exploit in promoting our own views and fighting our own battles. Here Thoreau has been completely drained of his critical and philosophical power. (1996, pp. 141–42)

I have attempted to interpret Thoreau's maturation strictly within his own cultural moment—the mid-nineteenth century—as fulfilling a personal agenda, of which nature was an important element, a vehicle, as it were, to another consciousness. While Thoreau may be enlisted in our ideological wars of environmentalism, this question seems to me to be framed by a post-Thoreauvian audience, whose own program is enriched by his odyssey. To be sure, Thoreau's nature writing is a fecund resource for current sensibility, but such an interpretation is to a large degree a projection of our own concerns framed by our own time. Thus an ecocentric environmentalism does not fall within my purview, and, for that matter, I doubt it was a primary concern of Thoreau's either.

6. We may safely conclude that some "vision" inspired Thoreau deeply, sustaining much of his aesthetic and spirtual project. As he confided to his friend Harrison Blake, "I have had but one *spiritual* birth (excuse the word,) and now whether it rains or snows, whether I laugh or cry, fall farther below or approach nearer to my standard, whether Pierce or Scott is elected, . . . the same surprising & everlastingly new light dawns to me" (letter to Blake, February 27, 1853,

Correspondence, 1958, pp. 296–97). But as will be clear from this discussion, Thoreau lived easily in the world of fact and in the transcendental climes. To put him into one camp or the other is to restrict him inappropriately from the diverse arenas of his identity, a duality generally disregarded for at least half a century (Matthiessen 1941, pp. 92–93).

7. So in the end, unmediated, direct, mystical experience remains in its own domain, not to be conflated with the refined literary product, or even the intermediate Journal musings and recollections. Despite their intimacy, Thoreau would not confuse writing with the experience writing sought to capture, and this tension extended to all areas of his writing. After all, this is the fundamental conundrum of literary theory: "its skepticism about how texts can purport to represent environments in the first place when, after all, a text is obviously one thing and the world another" (Buell 1995, p. 82). This tension reflects the deeper impasse that has become a central theme in contemporary nature writing. As Edward Abbey writes in *Desert Solitaire,* "I dream of a hard and brutal mysticism in which the naked self merges with a non-human world and yet somehow survives still intact, individual, and separate" (1968, p. 6). Buell draws out the inner conflict: "This is a dream that cannot be fulfilled, partly because the dreamer does not unequivocally want it to be fulfilled" (1995, p. 72).

8. Olaf Hansen, in reference to this Journal entry, explicitly poses the issue in terms of selfhood:

> The clear view of the unattainable lends identity to our existence in this world *because* we cannot integrate the cosmos. So then, whatever shape each individual's existence will have, its identity is derivative of a purity of vision which can only be defined in terms of its unworldliness. Hence the worldly, practical consequences of our quest for identity. (1990, p. 4)

1. THE ETERNAL NOW

1. This dictum is reiterated, perhaps more clearly, in his next letter to Blake:

> When, in the progress of life, a man swerves, though only by an angle infinitely small, from his proper and allotted path . . . then the drama of his life turns to tragedy, and makes haste to its fifth act. When once we thus fall behind ourselves, there is no accounting for the obstacles which rise up in our path, and no one is so wise as to advise, and no one so powerful as to aid us while we abide on that ground. Such are cursed with *duties,* and the *neglect of their duties.* For such the decalogue was made, and other far more voluminous and terrible codes. (Letter to Blake, May 2, 1848, *Correspondence,* 1958, p. 221)

2. What is time? Who can explain this easily and briefly? Who can comprehend this even in thought so as to articulate the answer in words? . . . Provided that no one asks me, I know. If I want to explain it to an inquirer, I do not know. But I confidently affirm myself to know that if nothing passes away, there is no past time, and if nothing arrives, there is no future time, and if nothing existed there would be no present time. Take the two tenses, past and future. How can these "be" when the past is not now present and the future is not yet present? Yet if the present were always present, it would not pass into the past: it would not be time but eternity. If then, in order to be time at all, the

present is so made that it passes into the past, how can we say that this present also "is"? The cause of its being is that it will cease to be. So indeed we cannot truly say that time exists except in the sense that it tends toward non-existence. (Augustine, *Confessions* 11.14.17)

Augustine's discussion echoes philosophical debates among Platonists, Aristotelians, and Stoics, and he follows a skeptical course, inasmuch as he concludes that the human mind cannot formulate an "answer."

3. James quotes E. R. Clay (*The Alternative* [London: Macmillan, 1882], p. 167) approvingly:

"... Time, then, considered relatively to human apprehension, consists of four parts, viz., the obvious past, the specious present, the real present, and the future. Omitting the specious present, it consists of three ... nonentities—the past, which does not exist, the future, which does not exist, and their conterminous, the present; the faculty from which it proceeds lies to us in the fiction of the specious present." (James [1890] 1983, p. 574)

James goes on to make his own comment:

In short, the practically cognized present is no knife-edge, but a saddle-back, with a certain breadth of its own on which we sit perched, and from which we look in two directions into time. ... The experience is from the outset a synthetic datum, not a simple one; and to sensible perception its elements are inseparable, although attention looking back may easily decompose the experience, and distinguish its beginning from its end. (Ibid., pp. 574–75)

4. Peck reads Thoreau as ravaged by the trials of time (the death of John Thoreau) and as psychologically endeavoring to immerse himself "in the flow of time in order to overcome time ... and confront and experience the destructive force of history in order to recover from it his own and his region's lost past" (Peck 1990, p. 35). Thoreau's preoccupation with history and memory in *A Week* is thus explained by Peck as an elaborate psychological catharsis initiated by a grief response, whereby "remembrance becomes redemptive" (ibid., p. 14). My emphasizing the centrality of Thoreau's preoccupation with time reflects my indebtedness to this work in many respects.

5. Note that this is quite a different reading from the many interpretations of the circle or sphere in Thoreau's oeuvre, where, in placing man in the center of the circle, Thoreau follows 1) a Romantic egocentric epistemology (Tuerk 1975, p. 51), 2) an Emersonian construction (elaborated in "Circles," 1983d) which regards God as a circle whose center is universal and whose circumference is nowhere (Tuerk 1975, pp. 14 and 58), or 3) a cyclic view of time, an "eternal return, and in no matter what part of a cycle man may be, something in him remains constant" (ibid., p. 40). In these respects, the symbolism of Walden Pond itself may be variously interpreted according to these modes of circularity.

6. I am not concerned here with Augustine's vision of time's linear progression, i.e., time's eschatological progress, but with how Augustine, like Aristotle (Chadwick 1991, p. 230), as well as certain neo-Platonists, perceived time as a function of the soul. Aristotle spells out his views of time in the *Physics*, and in book 4 he refers to time's relation to the soul (if there cannot be someone to

count, there cannot be anything that can be counted either; it is impossible for there to be time unless there is soul [223a]); the cyclic nature of time as related to the homogenous primary movement in a circle or sphere (223b); and time's character in the now (220a): "Time depends on the now both for its continuity and for its differentiation into parts, as movement does on the moved body, and the line on the point. And . . . if it is by virtue of its nows that time is numbered, we must not suppose that nows are parts of time, any more than points are parts of a line. There is no least time as there is no least line" (Ross [1923] 1995, p. 91).

For the neo-Platonist Plotinus, time "is in every soul . . . and in the same form in every one of them, and all are one" (*Ennead* 3.7). Augustine shares the Platonic view that the true "I" was the incorporeal soul, but differs from Plotinus, who "begins with the universal soul and moves to individual souls which are somehow one with it, while Augustine . . . begins with individual human souls and moves to a universal mind or soul that embraces all of time" (Teske 1996, p. 54). But for each, time is primarily a distention of the soul by which form is given to the world; and because of the soul's dual individual and universal nature, time is experienced not only as subjective and private but also as objective and public (ibid., pp. 48 ff.).

7. It is interesting to compare this passage with a similar one found in the "Sunday" chapter of *A Week*.

> The shallowest still water is unfathomable. Wherever the trees and skies are reflected there is more than Atlantic depth, and no danger of running aground. We noticed that it required a separate intention of the eye, a more free and abstracted vision, to see the reflected trees and the sky, than to see the river bottom merely; and so are there manifold visions in the direction of every object, and even the most opaque reflect the heavens from their surface. Some men have their eyes naturally intended to the one, and some to the other object. (Thoreau 1980a, p. 48)

8. Much of this discussion follows Porte's (1966) presentation, but while he uses Thoreau's mysticism to contrast Thoreau with Emerson, I am concerned rather with how the mystical aspiration forms a component of Thoreau's metaphysics of the self, serving, in a sense, as a counterpoint to his scientific epistemology. Further, I disagree with Porte's conclusion that "unlike the other Transcendentalists, his [Thoreau's] concern was ecstasy—and ecstatic illumination— rather than ethics" (p. 164); instead I see Thoreau's mysticism as part of the greater moral enterprise which informed all of his activities.

9. Besides Thoreau's frequent allusions to Eastern mystics (e.g., the "Monday" chapter of *A Week*), Porte makes note of the inspiration Thoreau apparently drew from the great mystic philosopher Plotinus. "The union that Plotinus advocated was one involving a man's total being: the coincidence of ecstatic feeling with perfect vision. This was Thoreau's goal as a naturalist" (Porte 1966, p. 166). That union ties together Thoreau's naturalist project with his metaphysical inspiration. In his Journal (June 14, 1840, *Journal* 1, 1981, p. 127), he quotes from Plotinus's *Ennead* 6: "a kind of tactual union, and a certain presence better than knowledge, and the joining of our own centre, as it were, with the centre of the universe" ("Annotations," ibid., p. 519). Porte writes, "Being

'on the mount' was a way of describing that 'contact' with the One of Plotinus which led to the 'greater presence of knowledge.' Like Plotinus, what Thoreau brought back from his experience of union with the center of all things was teasingly ineffable" (1966, p. 166).

10. Thoreau described these experiences in various ways: the "vision" or "insight" of inspiration (e.g., December 29, 1841, *Journal* 1, 1981, pp. 348–49); the accidental and transient quality of the experience (e.g., November 21, 1850, *Journal* 3, 1990, p. 148); the intractability of capturing the experience in consciousness and then translation into writing (e.g., December 11, 1855, *Journal*, [1906] 1962, 8:45); and in public testament: "The most glorious fact in my experience is not anything that I have done or may hope to do, but a transient thought, or vision, or dream, which I have had. I would give all the wealth of the world, and all the deeds of the heroes, for one true vision" (*A Week*, 1980a, p. 140).

11. See n. 6 to Introduction.

12. As Robert Milder comments: "Fallen into history (or adulthood), we are obliged to press onward *through* history in a pilgrimage toward the timelessness beyond it. In heightened moments, however, we miraculously pierce the veil of time to glimpse the 'perennial,' and if we are disciplined, or worthy, or fortunate enough, we can hope to string such moments together to make a beatific life" (1995, p. 31). See Giorgio Agamben's strikingly rich and original essay on the sources of history, memory, and language in infancy (1993). A theme I develop in chapter 5 concerns the self-reflective arc that commences with the primal recognition that we discern the world by splitting "pure experience"—that pre-semantic world of infancy and early childhood—into two domains: the knowing self and the world known, thereby constituting ourselves as the subject of language.

13. Stanley Rosen's essay "The Lived Present" (1999) offers a close parallel to this construction of time and its ethical structure from an entirely different perspective (that of a critique of Plato, Kant, and Heidegger). Rosen begins by rejecting conceptual analyses of time, whether in the language of mathematical physics or of ontology, and he also discards attempts to explain the present as some kind of synthesis of past and future. Instead, he builds on the provocative metaphor of time as played out as a "secretion" of living and uses the image of a spider's web to serve as the "structure" of temporality.

> Living is distinct from the spiderweb, which is not life but the structure of time. . . . [Thus] if human activity produces time rather than filling or occupying it like a place or a structure of places that already exists, then it makes no sense to ask for the temporal location of this activity. More precisely, it makes no sense to locate it in the present, as for example by saying that I (= anyone) am now, that is, presently, and so in the present, producing time, including the present. But neither does it make sense to locate this activity in the past or the future. In short, if I produce time, then the activity of production must be atemporal. (Pp. 24–25)

The present as a characteristic of human existence then becomes *presence.* In this formulation, Rosen is attempting to capture the immediate and embedded character of human experience *in* the world, but even more radically, the primacy of human existence as rank-ordering—the production of a world constituted and ultimately determined by human value. This so-called "erotic ascent" (Plato) interprets human activity as atemporal: the experience of the present is neither the moment, nor the synthesis of past and future, but the primary act of "opening" or making our world (in a sense, Heideggerian self-authentication).

> This "opening" is not temporal in itself; it is neither the present, the past, nor the future. Instead, we should think of it as the founding of presence as the atemporal condition that makes possible the articulation of past, present, and future. (P. 32)

Presence then is "the non-temporal foundation of the temporal present" (p. 33) and thus cannot be an object of perception but is praxis itself (p. 32). So the "present" is self-consciously constructed, while "presence" is human praxis or experience—immediate and unreflexive, "the pulsation of eros, that is the rank-ordering and world-constituting force of the human soul" (p. 33). These are themes highly resonant with my own reading of Thoreau.

14. This Romantic ideal was clearly enunciated in again a different mode by Emerson ("Self-Reliance" [1983c]), and perhaps most celebrated by Nietzsche. George Stack (1992) has made a compelling case that Nietzsche was heavily indebted to Emerson, not only in a general orientation regarding their respective philosophies of the self, but more particularly in the enunciation of man's relation to fate and the moral imperative of asserting responsibility for our destiny. One readily appreciates the general affinity of Emerson and Nietzsche in Emerson's insistence on the "intensification of subjectivity" and thus "forming his ideal of the man who has faith in himself, who values above all the integrity of the self, who is willing to stand alone, who strives to think, act, and live truth" (Stack 1992, p. 11). But beyond these general notions, which might have arisen independently, Stack documents how Nietzsche carefully studied Emerson (e.g., pp. 42 ff.), providing marginalia that clearly express his admiration ("the author richest in ideas of this century" [ibid., p. 45]), and shows how certain key Emersonian ideas were explicitly developed. Of concern here is the idea of the eternal recurrence. Each begin with the cyclicity of the moral development of the individual; and more broadly, for both Emerson and Nietzsche, the "circle" is the ideal representation of reality (ibid., pp. 198–99). From this point they each affirm that "the powers of the self are as real as the power of fate" (ibid., p. 200), and in regard to the eternal recurrence, "if we ourselves are fate, then we are part of the processes of fate, and in a sense, we 'condition it for all eternity' " (ibid., p. 205). Stack credits Emerson with the basic principles, albeit undeveloped, with which Nietzsche erected his own vision of the eternal return. In regard to the genesis of Nietzsche's idea of the eternal return, Stack concludes:

> Nietzsche would have had to have read Emerson with meticulous care and sympathetic understanding to have joined together four separately discussed conceptions in one of nature; the affirmation of life, of the entire circular process; and the notion of a lived experience of immortality. Given the symmetry between Nietzsche's idea of eternal recurrence and his emphasis upon the experience of eternity and Emerson's disjointed remarks on these topics, there is no doubt that he had assimilated and, consciously or unconsciously, synthesized these theoretical conjectures. (Ibid., p. 209)

Nietzsche of course was more of a philosopher than Emerson, and his thinking is sharper, deeper, more subtle, and more far-ranging than his. But it cannot be denied . . . that Nietzsche could not have constructed this part of his philosophical edifice without Emersonian foundations. (Ibid., p. 211)

A concurring opinion is offered by George Kateb (1995, p. 149), who offers an interesting comparison of Emerson and Nietzsche around the theme of individuality and self-reliance. Kateb essentially agrees with Stack's appraisal: "I believe Emerson's influence on Nietzsche's formulations is direct and profound" (ibid., p. 149). Thus an intriguing triangulation between Emerson, Thoreau, and Nietzsche is suggested.

15. In the context considered here, Nietzsche's own use of the cycle of time, which he called the eternal recurrence, is of most interest. Not to stretch their similarities, it is not too far-fetched to suggest that despite the great differences in their respective philosophical projects, the ethical structure of Thoreau's cycle of time and Nietzsche's own view of time share strong resemblances. Nietzsche's conception of the eternal return is coupled to two basic premises: 1) the circularity of the eternal process of becoming, and 2) a morality that had neither revealed status nor universal standing nor philosophical foundation—to wit, no ethical imperative other than the force of our will and the imperative of exercising choice. If God is dead, then our morality must be based on our self-willed sovereignty (e.g., *On the Genealogy of Morals*). The will, alone on its own axis, unselfconsciously knows no past or future, only the present. Responsibility then resides solely in the self, which lives in a radical present; the past and future are only constructions of the now. Time is framed not in the past or future, but it accompanies us, moving steadily forward within the present. The present vision of the self thus defines the past, and if the present is accepted, then all that has led to that juncture has been enjoined. Most important, the past as forming the future is acknowledged. Thus to accept the present in Nietzsche's terms is to have willed—or willed to choose to accept—all that led to this moment. The eternal recurrence, as an *ethical* mandate, becomes the ultimate assertion of individual free will and choice.

The present is, in a sense, pulled out of time—inasmuch as it has become the only mode of temporality. Further, being placed in eternity, the notion of time's passing has been radically altered. As life is eternally cycled, Nietzsche's recurrence does not refer to a life precisely *like* this one, but to this *selfsame* life. (This interpretation is informed by Arthur Nehamas [1985]; my own views are extended in Tauber 1994.) He would thus imbue every moment with the quality of eternity and lead us to a supreme self-awareness of our ultimate and inescapable responsibility for our acts. The last element of his ethic, then, is to accept the irrevocability of every choice, thereby allowing us to assume the mandate of responsibility for our life, a life to be lived again and again, eternally. In short, if life is to be eternally recurrent, then we must accept living in the present in its full and self-sufficient complement. If we deduct the extravagant poetic quality of the eternal recurrence, we might appreciate that the ethical structure of Nietzsche's formulation is essentially the same advocated by Thoreau, namely the assertion that each moment is not only immutable but precious, making us forever accountable to ourselves. By living each moment as if it is to recur again and again into eternity, Nietzsche sought to inspire an acute awareness of our "presentness." Indeed, in facing eternity, we must face ourselves. In this respect, there are strong similarities with Emerson and Thoreau, because the eternal recurrence is a metaphor for personal responsibility, which arises from an Emersonian-Thoreauvian sensibility, one shared by many other Romantics. While I am not attempting to pose Thoreau (or Emerson for that matter) as a proto-Nietzschean, Nietzsche does, nevertheless, serve as a useful foil for understanding Thoreau's metaphysics of time.

16. Considering the centrality of the present for Thoreau, it is intriguing how Jonas reads the progression of Nietzsche's thought to Heidegger's own philosophy of time:

> [The] "present" remains practically empty—at least as insofar as modes of "genuine" or "authentic" existence are concerned. . . . Actually a great deal is said about the existential "present," but not as an independent dimension in its own right. For the existentially "genuine" present is the present of the "situation," which is wholly defined in terms of the self's *relation* to its "future" and "past." It flashes up, as it were, in the light of decision, when the projected "future" reacts upon the given "past" (*Geworfenheit*) and in this meeting constitutes what Heidegger calls the "moment"(*Augenblick*): the moment, not duration, is the temporal mode of *this* "present"—a creature of the other two horizons of time, a function of their ceaseless dynamics, and no independent dimension to dwell in. . . . No present remains for genuine existence to repose in. (Jonas 1963, p. 336)

If we accept Jonas's interpretation of Heidegger, and in turn accept Heidegger's interpretation of Nietzsche's deeper metaphysics, the "present" assumes a very different meaning from Thoreau's understanding of it.

2. THREE APPLE TREES

1. Harding, in reviewing Thoreau's earliest works, concurs with Moser (1951) that "all of Thoreau's basic ideas are in the college essays, the seeds are all present, awaiting maturation" (quoted by Harding 1959, p. 43), a reading that is important in how we regard Thoreau's relationship to Emerson and the development of Thoreau's ideas, especially in light of the so-called Romantic conversion of 1851–52 (Adams and Ross 1988, pp. 143–90). (All these matters are considered in later chapters.) While I recognize that Thoreau certainly developed his ideas over two decades, I am far less concerned with tracing that development than in outlining the basic structure of his thought that I perceive as essentially established by the early 1840s.

> 2. If we could pierce the obscurity of those remote years, we should find it light enough; only *there* is not our day. . . . There has always been the same amount of light in the world. . . . Always the laws of light are the same, but the modes and degrees of seeing vary. . . . There was but the sun and the eye from the first. The ages have not added a new ray to the one, nor altered a fibre of the other. (*A Week*, 1980a, p. 157)

3. *A Week* was written in memory of a camping trip Thoreau took with his brother John in 1839. John's tragic death of tetanus in January 1842 was a profound loss for Henry, and Peck has interpreted *A Week* both as a memorial work to John and as a psychological conflict fought between an attempt to kill time ("by containing it, by taking the entire temporal order . . . within himself" and thereby "kill the vehicle of temporality in which the world and the self have their being and their relation; in this sense he has committed suicide" or at the very least become "trapped deeply within a solipsism of his own making" [Peck 1990, pp. 5–6]) and an effort to resituate the self in the world, or, in Peck's parlance, "to keep time without killing it" (ibid., p. 8). Thoreau's preoccupation with history and memory in *A Week* is thus explained by Peck as an elaborate psychological catharsis initiated by a grief response whose existential manifestation is an elaborate treatise on the nature of time and our attempt to understand temporality, whereby "remembrance becomes redemptive" (ibid., p. 14), a theme further developed by Burbick (1987; see note 7).

4. Duston was the first American woman to be honored with a commemorative statue, erected at the site of the escape, in Boscawen, New Hampshire, in 1874. A second monument, dedicated in 1879, may be seen in Haverhill, Massachusetts, the site of the Indian abduction. The story has routinely appeared in various histories of New Hampshire and Massachusetts (e.g., Chase 1861; McClintock 1889; Lyford 1903; Pillsbury 1927; Squires 1956; for further citations see Arner 1973, note 25), and might fairly be spoken of as "being now 'frozen' in the New England imagination" (Arner 1973, p. 22). Perhaps the most thorough recent review was made by a legislative historian, Leon Anderson (1973).

Duston remains a highly enigmatic figure for nineteenth- and twentieth-century commentators. In 1836, Hawthorne wrote for the *American Magazine*, "Would that bloody old hag been drowned in crossing Contocook river, or that she had sunk over head and ears in a swamp, and been there buried, until summoned forth to confront her victims at the Day of Judgement" (quoted by Ulrich 1982, p. 172). She figures as a historical foil for a contemporary murder mystery by Susan Conant (1997), who implies that Duston might have exhibited certain sociopathic or psychopathic tendencies dominant in her family by citing a relationship discovered by Laurel Thatcher Ulrich (1982): "Cotton Mather preached a sermon about Hannah Duston, who was in church when he proclaimed her a savior of New England. Four years earlier, Mather had preached a sermon of condemnation about a woman named Elizabeth Emerson. The unmarried mother of one child, Elizabeth Emerson had given surreptitious birth to twins and promptly killed them. In 1693, she was convicted of murdering her newborn babies. Hannah Duston's maiden name was Emerson. Hannah Duston and Elizabeth Emerson were sisters" (Conant 1997, pp. 114–15). To what extent the Emerson sisters were prone to violence and whether the psychodynamics of their family might have promoted such behavior it is impossible to decide. In any case, Ulrich's account of colonial women clearly documents their not so infrequent violent behavior (chapters 9 and 10) and notes that Hannah

Duston's exploits followed a long tradition of women defenders of the New England Zion—if not against aggressive Indians, certainly in the more traditional role of maintaining Puritan mores and protecting the family, writ large.

5. Mather's ecclesiastical history of New England devotes chapter 25, entitled "A Notable Exploit—Dux Femina Facti" (A Woman the Leader of the Deed), to Duston, who apparently told him,

> in Obedience to instructions which the French have given them, they [the Indians] would have *Prayers* in their family no less than thrice every day . . . nor would they ordinarily let their children *Eat* or *Sleep*, without first saying their *Prayers*.
>
> Indeed, these *Idolaters* were, like the rest of their whiter brethren, *Persecutors*, and would not endure that these poor women should retire to their *English Prayers*, if they could hinder them.
>
> Nevertheless, the poor women had nothing but fervent prayers to make their lives comfortable or tolerable; and by being daily sent upon Business, they had Opportunities, together and asunder, to do like another *Hannah*, in *pouring out their souls before the Lord*. Nor did their praying friends among ourselves forbear to *pour out* supplications for them.
>
> Now, they could not observe it without some Wonder, that their *Indian* master sometimes when he saw them dejected, would say unto them *What need you trouble yourself? If your God would have you delivered, you shall be so.*
>
> And it seems our God would have it so to be.
>
> . . . One of these women took up a resolution to imitate the action of *Jael* upon *Siseria*; and being where she had not her own *Life* secured by any *Law* unto her, she thought she was not forbidden by any law to take away the *Life* of the *Murderers* by whom her children had been Butchered. (Mather 1702, book 7, pp. 90–91; English spellings modernized)

This deist bent was subscribed to by Duston herself. A remarkable testimony is given in her 1727 membership application to the Haverhill Center Congregational Church: "I am thankful for my captivity, twas the Comfortablest time that ever I had; In my affliction God made his Word Comfortable to me. I remembered 43d ps. ult ["Hope in God; for I shall again praise him, my help and my God"]—and those words came to my mind—ps 118.17 ["I shall not die, but I shall live, and recount the deeds of the Lord"]" (Anderson 1973). Hannah Duston, 39 years old at the time of her celebrated exploits, gave birth to her last (thirteenth) child in October 1698 and lived to age 80.

6. In America these wars between England and France are generally known as King William's War (1689–97); Queen Anne's War (1702–13); King George's War (1744–48); and the French and Indian War (1754–63).

7. History is always value-laden, and certainly the historians to whom Thoreau was reacting wrote within a long line of committed religious ideology (see Buell 1986, part 3, "Reinventing Puritanism: The New England Historical Imagination" for an excellent survey). So the issue is not that of a lost objectivism as some positivist ideal, but rather that Thoreau was self-consciously writing history in opposition to the dominant tradition and ethos of his time. This point of view is consonant with that of Joan Burbick (1987), who similarly argues that Thoreau wrote an "alternative" history, one she characterizes as "uncivil" (i.e., natural) in contrast to the false civilized history of tamed Amer-

ica. This "redemptive" history became one of Thoreau's attempts to show the true relationship of man and nature, where the Puritan ethic of greed and dominance, the short-term economies of profit, might be replaced with another nature-related, communal, nonproprietary mode of existence (also developed by Berry 1987). The opening chapter of *Walden* is, of course, the clearest statement of this perspective, but Burbick gleans the essential ethical lesson by a systematic examination of Thoreau's early and late writings, not all of which are obviously "historical" in the usual sense. More importantly, Burbick regards Thoreau's historiography as firmly integrated within what we would normally characterize as his nature writing—or his translation of perception: In "his grand experiment of observation, Thoreau faces the dilemma of . . . extracting from sequences of perceived natural events a law or demonstrable pattern of redemptive growth," which would suit "his need to formulate a sustained vision of history" (pp. 123–24). Thus, while building on Hildebidle's (1983) insight of how Thoreau's natural history *methodologically* informed and guided his historiography, Burbick goes further in the direction I am proceeding in by insisting on emphasizing the *moral* character of Thoreau's historical project—how history was invoked to support his natural history and vice versa, both of which in turn were in service to his moral philosophy. It is all of one piece. In the following chapters I will more fully develop how Thoreau's moral attitude framed his natural history and more deeply the metaphysics of his selfhood.

8. This part of the story is particularly suspicious according to my Boscawen, New Hampshire, neighbors, who live along the river at the site of Hannah's escape. The Merrimack River at the end of March is in full rush from the melting snows of the mountains, and it is highly unlikely that Duston would have made the effort, even if it were possible, to execute an upriver navigation. Given that an Indian child and woman had escaped, Duston would well have made haste to place as much distance as possible between her and alerted Indians. Given the falls at Concord, another significant obstacle to her downriver run, Duston's delay might well have been a fatal mistake. Thoreau must have appreciated these factors, and therefore his keeping Mirick's embellishment over Mather's account can only be explained by Thoreau's larger literary intentions unencumbered by historical accuracy in a narrower sense. Thoreau remained intrigued with Duston and visited the original homestead after *A Week* was published (May 12, 1850, *Journal* 3, 1990, p. 64).

9. Although this general orientation dates to the Romantics, it was Nietzsche who perhaps best celebrated the need to mend the subjective-objective divide as the very basis of a meaningful epistemology. There are many vantages from which we might pick up his argument, but perhaps as a historian his early critique of his fellow philologists is most relevant to our own discussion. In *On the Advantage and Disadvantage of History for Life* ([1874] 1980), he argued that the historian must already possess something of the past within himself or he will fail to see what is being offered to him:

> And might not an illusion lurk even in the highest interpretation of the word "objectivity"? By this word one understands a condition in the historian in which his view of

an event with all of its motives and consequences is so pure that it has no effect at all on his subjectivity; one has in mind that aesthetic phenomenon, that detachment from all personal interest with which the painter sees his inner picture in a stormy landscape amid lightening and thunder on a rough sea, one has in mind the total absorption in things: yet it is a superstition to believe that the picture which things produce in a man in such a state of mind reproduces the empirical essence of those things. Or is one to think that things in such moments, as it were, retrace, counterfeit, reproduce themselves photographically on a pure passivity through their own activity? (Pp. 34–35)

Subjectivity in this view is then partially constitutive of objectivity, a view already articulated by Thoreau.

10. Of course engineers routinely design for likelihood of such a single incident per century—and rarely make allowance for it beyond that limit—but that is beside the point of historicity that Thoreau is making.

11. Ginzburg further explains: "The object is the study of individual cases, situations, and documents, precisely *because they are individual*, and for this reason get results that have an unsuppressible speculative margin. . . . Even if the historian is sometimes obliged to refer back, explicitly or implicitly, to a sequence of comparable phenomena, the cognitive strategy, as well as the codes by which he expresses himself, remain intrinsically individualizing" (Ginzburg 1989, p. 106).

12. "Scientist" was coined by William Whewell in 1833, and irrespective of his own philosophical intent in using the term, at first the designation had a somewhat derogatory connotation. Instead of being "philosophical" (in the sense of eighteenth-century natural philosophy being the global study of nature in both epistemological and metaphysical contexts), the "scientist" was generally understood to have interests in developing technology, which, of course, had commercial overtones that might sully investigation for its own sake.

13. "In 1802 Gottfried Reinhold Treviranus announced the birth of a new scientific discipline. He called it '*Biologie*,' the science whose aim was to determine the conditions and laws under which the different forms of life exist, and their causes. The significance of his declaration was not in denying that biological phenomena had been investigated previously . . . rather Treviranus sought to affirm a set of methods which characterized biology as a discipline in its own right" (Lenoir 1990, p. 119).

14. Thoreau's keen interest in Indian history highlights his concern that a balanced rendition of the colonial period include the native perspective. After all, "the Indian is absolutely forgotten but by some persevering poets. . . . For Indian deeds there must be an Indian memory–the white man will remember his own only– We have forgotten their hostility as well as friendship" (*Journal* 2, 1984, pp. 38–39). This is but one example of many in which Thoreau's critical acumen regarded what passed as scientific history with a jaundiced eye.

15. Emerson was heavily influenced by Thomas Carlyle and refers to him in many places. See especially Emerson's comments on Carlyle's *On History*, in *Critical and Miscellaneous Essays*, 4 vols. (Boston, 1838–39), 2:247. For Emerson's relation to Carlyle, see Richardson 1995. Thoreau also studied Carlyle carefully (see, e.g., Thoreau 1975a, pp. 219–67).

16. This passage from the first version of *Walden* (Shanley 1957) is, as expected, a hybrid between the Journal and the final *Walden:*

> 24 years ago I was brought from the city to this very pond—through this very field—so much further into the world I had but recently entered. It is one of the most ancient scenes stamped on the tablets of my memory. That woodland vision for a long time occupied my dreams. The country then was the world—the city only a gate to it. And now tonight my flute has waked the echoes over this very water. One generation of pines has fallen and I have cooked my supper with their stumps—and a new growth of oaks and pines is rising all around the pond to greet other infants' eyes. Almost the same Johnswort springs from the same perennial root in this pasture. Even I have at length helped to clothe that fabulous landscape of my dreams, and the result of my presence and influence is seen in these bean leaves and cornblades, and potato vines.
> I planted about 2 acres and a half of upland . . . (Pp. 177–78)

17. Robert Kuhn McGregor (1997) makes the salient and important point that Thoreau's interest in nature was quite limited—as attested by his writings—prior to the spring of 1846, almost midway in his sojourn at Walden Pond. If one surveys Thoreau's lectures and published writings from 1837 to 1849 (McGregor 1997, pp. 207–10), there is a paucity of natural history. " 'The Natural History of Massachusetts' was the only essay Thoreau published in the first ten years of his writing career in which he directly addressed the subject of nature" (ibid., p. 54), and this was hardly characteristic of his later nature writing. Other essays, "A Walk to Wachusett" and "A Winter Walk," are more travel essays, laden with symbolic inner examination. Nature is only " 'emblematic,' intended only to point the way to greater spiritual achievement" (ibid., p. 55). The exuberance of Thoreau's later nature writing, characteristic of a Romantic enchantment and psychological expansion, have been interpreted by some commentators (e.g., Adams and Ross 1988) as a dramatic and sudden Romantic turn (occurring in the 1850–51 period), well after the break with Emerson. McGregor, pointing out that the sensitivity to nature reflected an earlier transformation, cites suggestive entries in the May 1846 Journal entries, which show that the Walden experiment was more than originally designed: beyond establishing a haven to find solitude to write and conduct an experiment in home economics, the grand themes that were to preoccupy Thoreau's efforts in natural history were, in a sense, thrust upon him by simply living in one of the few remaining wild acres of Concord, a wood lot left relatively immune to the voracious appetite of the lumber and fuel-consuming industry. The mature sensibility soon followed, when Thoreau, on a trip to Maine's Mount Ktaadn in September 1846, encountered the awesome grandeur and terrifying aspect of nature, a cognitive/emotional experience that jolted him into realizing that Emerson's idealism was an inappropriate means of mediating man and nature. McGregor makes the mountaintop experience a critical turning point in Thoreau's (conscious) understanding of nature. I would argue, based on Thoreau's early Journal entries, that while he certainly had an epiphany on Mount Ktaadn, this only added a dimension to a deeply committed Romantic sensibility, vividly placing nature's awesome power in balance with a more pas-

toral vision. The essential aesthetic and spiritual quest remained unchanged. In other words, the structure of Thoreau's study of nature reflected a moral attitude already discernible in his earliest musings.

18. Peck notes that "while the river distinguishes the role of the observer, it also distances him from the object of his vision and in other ways also restricts and defines his possibilities" (1990, p. 23), a point well appreciated by Thoreau himself: "To . . . see the earth from the water side, to stand outside of it on another element, and so get a pry on it in thought at least, that is no small advantage" (March 25, 1860, *Journal,* [1906] 1962, 13:226–27).

19. Cited by Hovey (1966, pp. 62, 151) as *Original Manuscript of Concord and Merrimack River* in the Berg Collection at the New York Public Library, p. 6.

20. "As yesterday and the historical ages are the past, as the work of to-day is present, so some flitting perspectives, and demi-experiences of the life that is in nature, are, in time veritably future, or rather outside to time, perennial, young, divine, in the wind and rain which never die" (*A Week,* 1980a, p. 8). Thoreau is, of course, referring to the ever-present present. Don Gifford notes that this general tenor is central to the Romantic project:

> Thoreau's longings for sustained visionary consciousness, suggest attempts to reify memory in time so that the process of memory, fully contemplated in time-past, can be reversed, anticipated as a future experience to be reentered and fully realized in an ideal time-present. That is what I call Romantic time. (1990, p. 80)

But this "time-present" is, of course, never fully captured or replayed, and by 1857 Thoreau was resigned to accepting the poetics of his memory—incomplete and thus, in some sense, inadequate, but at the same time the more salient and "truer" report. (March 27, 1857, *Journal,* [1906] 1962, 9:306; quoted in chapter 1).

> 21. That man does not believe that each day contains an earlier, more sacred, and aural hour than he has yet profaned, has despaired of life, and is pursuing a descending and darkening way. After a partial cessation of his sensuous life, the soul of man, or its organs rather, are reinvigorated each day, and his genius tries again what nobel life it can make. All memorable events, I should say, transpire in the morning time and in a morning atmosphere. The Vedas say, "All intelligences awake with the morning." Poetry and art, and the fairest and most memorable of the actions of men, date from such an hour. All poets and heroes, like Memnon, are the children of Aurora, and emit their music at sunrise. (*Walden,* 1971, p. 89)

22. In our own post-positivist era, objectivity is regarded as arising from consensus, and communal standards are recognized as always changing; criteria of proof have a long history of metamorphosis; assumptions about rationality change similarly; even Truth can no longer be designated as stable. Thus objectivity, whether in the sciences, social sciences, or humanities is built from a value system, and these values are themselves constantly under scrutiny and modulated as our needs and sophistication evolve (Megill 1994). Postmodern historians have been particularly conscious of these unstable foundations (e.g., Friedlander 1992; Fay, Pomper, and Vann 1998), and their perspective enables us to see more clearly the anti-positivism of Thoreau's own project.

3. ANOTHER APPLE TREE

1. Thoreau continued,

I realized what the Orientals mean by contemplation and forsaking of works. For the most part, I minded not how the hours went. . . . [I]t was morning, and lo, now it is evening, and nothing admirable is accomplished. My days were not days of the week . . . nor were they minced into hours and fretted by the ticking of a clock; for I lived like the Puri Indians, of whom it is said that "for yesterday, to-day, and to-morrow they have only one word, and they express the variety of meaning by pointing backward for yesterday, forward for to-morrow, and overhead for the passing day" [Ida Pfeiffer, *A Lady's Voyage Round the World* (1852); cited by Rossi 1992, p. 76 n. 1]. This was sheer idleness to my fellow-townsmen, no doubt; but if the birds and flowers had tried me by their standard, I should not have been found wanting. A man must find his occasions in himself, it is true. The natural day is very calm, and will hardly reprove his indolence. (*Walden*, 1971, p. 112)

2. Thoreau's interest in oriental literature began while he was residing with Emerson in 1841, and by the time he published *A Week*, he could confidently write, "The reading which I love the best is the scriptures of several nations, though it happens that I am better acquainted with those of the Hindoos, the Chinese, and the Persians, than of the Hebrews" (1980a, p. 71). See Harding (1959, pp. 98–100) and Richardson (1986, pp. 106–9) for review of the significance of the oriental influence on Thoreau.

3. See n. 1 to Acknowledgments.

4. When the frost comes out in the spring, and even in a thawing day in the winter, the sand begins to flow down the slopes like lava, sometimes bursting out through the snow and overflowing it where no sand was to be seen before. Innumerable little streams overlap and interlace one with another, exhibiting a sort of hybrid product, which obeys half way the laws of currents, and half way that of vegetation. As it flows it takes the forms of sappy leaves or vines, making heaps of pulpy sprays a foot or more in depth, and resembling, as you look down on them, the laciniated lobed and imbricated thalluses of some lichens; or you are reminded of coral, of leopards' paws or birds' feet, of brains or lungs or bowels, and excrements of all kinds. (*Walden*, 1971, p. 305)

5. Thoreau's enterprise seems one of exchange—an identity for an occupation, the externalization of the self for the internalization of the seasons.

Insisting that the self could substitute its attributes for those of the elements, Thoreau spells it out: "You who complain that I am cold–find Nature cold– . . . That I am cold means that I am of another nature" (December 21, 1851 [*Journal* 4, 1992, p. 214]). The self, not dispensed with, is converted to "another nature" in the words of one passage, or to a "second person" in the words of another, and can see its own reflections as if from outside them. In the separation of the self into two discrete persons (one who watches the self who in turn watches nature) the second person is foreign. "Who is this?" Thoreau asks. The second person is alien not simply because it is a projection wholly defined by impressions of nature, but because these impressions are then conceived as if they were inseparable from the elements they were recording. (Cameron 1985, p. 86)

6. In Thoreau's *Journal* nature and the mind are *not* like each other, or if they are, it is because man has been naturalized, because nature has been as if driven into the mind. Descriptions of nature at once displace our idea of what thoughts are, and, as these pic-

tures exist instead of thoughts, in that replacement, seem inseparable from them, very much as subjects and examples have been made inseparable. (Cameron 1985, p. 150)

I think Thoreau would have differed, inasmuch as he was forthcoming concerning the limitations of his success in fusing with nature. For instance, in the great description of the loon in the "Brute Neighbors" chapter of *Walden*, Thoreau acknowledges his inability to be anything but an encumbered observer: As the loon dived, Thoreau could not predict his reappearance, and its cry mocked him in its "demonic laughter" (1971, p. 236). The object remains aloof and independent, and the bird's consciousness inaccessible to Thoreau; so try as he might, their respective intelligences remain disparate and noncommunicative: "While he was thinking one thing in his brain, I was endeavoring to divine his thought in mine" (ibid., p. 235). There may have been moments of the most intimate joining, but more often than not, his epistemological self-consciousness was paramount, or, said in another fashion, his pantheistic impulse was stymied.

7. Neil Evernden's study is a rich amalgam of Foucauldian analysis, the philosophical insights of Hans Jonas, historical commentary, and environmental activism. Evernden is writing from the perspective that "the environmental crisis is as much a social phenomenon as a physical one" (1992, p. 7), and thus "what matters is not what ecology is, but how it functions, how it is perceived and used" (ibid., p. 15). The object of inquiry, then—"nature" as it might "exist" in its asocial state—is constructed by social forces and epistemological understandings to yield a human category: "nature." Evernden stresses that in this sense, nature cannot be simply described as an object but "is also an assertion of a relationship" (ibid., p. 21). He then draws upon Roland Barthes's (*Mythologies*, [1957] 1972) fecund observation that while it generally appears that history or culture rests on nature, the reverse is in fact the true state of affairs: nature as a social creation turns history into nature (i.e., history becomes a subcategory of nature). Nature is thus contingent, pliable, and subjective—fully vulnerable to human judgment; natural law is, then, hardly "natural," and, of course, there is no normative content to nature; nature becomes, from this perspective, our appropriation, what we have self-consciously assigned to the "other." Indeed, self-consciousness becomes the basis of establishing the otherness of nature as we see her in what Evernden calls "a category, a conceptual container" (1992, p. 89). Empathy suggests that the subject and object are akin (ibid., p. 41), and thus the Romantic notion of nature as a source of human inspiration and a directive to the moral venture represents a "loosening" of the subject-object dichotomy. Evernden would like us to do away with the nature-culture dualism altogether:

> The absorption of ourselves into Nature is simply the absorption of ourselves into ourselves, or rather, into our own conception of how it "ought" to be. The paradox we encounter, of this perpetual oscillation between the domains of nature and culture, arises from a fundamental error. The dualism cannot actually be resolved, *because it never existed*. The dualism we fret over exists only because of our own decision, not only to constrict the nature-tube into two domains, but to create the container in the first place. One might even say that there is no "nature," and there never has been. (Ibid., p. 99)

This proposal is doubtful, and as I read Thoreau, he too would discount it for all the reasons discussed in this chapter.

8. Buell make the cogent point that "humanity *qua* geographer is *Homo faber*, the environment's constructor, and the sense of place is necessarily always a social product and not simply what is 'there' " (Buell 1995, p. 77).

9. For instance, in *Walden*, in describing the sounds of screech owls, we are struck with the evocative description of a bird's song, but it is accompanied by a heavily laden emotional veneer to show us how we should read the anglicized melody. The birds cried

> like mourning women their ancient u-lu-lu. Their dismal scream is truly Ben Jonsonian. Wise midnight hags! It is no honest and blunt tu-whit tu-who of the poets, but, without jesting, a most solemn graveyard ditty, the mutual consolations of suicide lovers remembering the pangs and delights of supernal love in the infernal groves. Yet I love to hear their wailing, their doleful responses, trilled along the wood-side, reminding me sometimes of music and singing birds; as if it were the dark and tearful side of music, the regrets and sighs that would fain be sung. They are the spirits, the low spirits and melancholy forebodings, of fallen souls that once in human shape night-walked the earth and did the deeds of darkness, now expiating their sins with their wailing hymns or threnodies in the scenery of their transgressions. They give me a new sense of the variety and capacity of that nature which is our common dwelling. *Oh-o-o-o-o that I never had been bor-r-r-r-n!* sighs one on this side of the pond, and circles with the restlessness of despair to some new perch on the gray oaks. Then—*that I never had been bor-r-r-r-n!* echoes another on the farther side with tremulous sincerity, and—*bor-r-r-r-n!* comes faintly from far in the Lincoln woods. (*Walden*, 1971, pp. 124–25)

10. For instance, "Color . . . acts on man's inner nature . . . [and] hence we will not be surprised to find that its effect has a direct connection with the moral realm. . . . A tiny imperceptible shift changes the beautiful impression of fire and gold into a muddy one. The color of honor and joy becomes the color of shame, loathing and disquiet. This may explain the yellow hat of the bankrupt and the yellow circles on the Jew's mantle" (Goethe [1810] 1988, pp. 278, 280). Thus, despite Goethe's aspirations toward objectivity, he was sometimes guilty of what seems to us to be extraordinarily brazen subjectivism. But this is a complex matter, for Goethe was no subjectivist in the usual sense. After all, he espoused a rigorously detached view of observed phenomena. The scientist is supposed to "observe and survey [the objects] with a uniformly calm eye and to take the criterion for his perception and the date for his judgement not from within himself, but from the sphere of things he observes" ([1792] 1988), but the theoretical (archetypal) construction of his major scientific works on plant morphology and light are testaments to the dangers of his own theoretical formulations. In addition, his observations themselves frequently suffered from bias, relating phenomena as pleasant or unpleasant, useful or useless, etc. For him, the quest for objectification only went so far, leaving the phenomena to become integrated and "meaningful" by some active, perhaps creative process. See Amrine et al. 1987; Bortoft 1996; Seamon and Zajonc 1998.

11. This divorce of subject and object was belied by quantum mechanics, which showed how measurement in the atomic world imposed an effect, so that

the assessment of the momentum of a particle altered the ability to determine its position. Thus there is an irreducible measurement effect that cannot be canceled, placing the observer intractably within his system of study. Strict "objectivity" is thereby lost. (See Tauber 1997, pp. 91–124.)

> 12. It struck me that these ghost leaves and the green ones whose forms they assume, were the creatures of the same law. It could not be in obedience to two several laws, that the vegetable juices swelled gradually into the perfect leaf on the one hand, and the crystalline particles trooped to their standard in the same admirable order on the other. (Thoreau, November 28, 1837, *Journal 1*, 1981, pp. 15–16)

> 13. I define life as *the principle of individuation,* or the power which unites a given *all* into a *whole* that is presupposed by its parts. The link that combines the two, and acts throughout both, will, of course, be defined by the *tendency to individuation.* Thus, from its utmost latency . . . there is an ascending series of intermediate classes, and of analogous gradations in each class. To a reflecting mind . . . [classes] are homogeneous, and . . . are but degrees and different dignities of one and the same tendency. (Coleridge [1848] 1970, pp. 42–43)

14. Thus Coleridge is a particularly interesting case of Kantian, Hegelian, and Schellingian philosophies of life intermingling, and thus serves as an important example of *Naturphilosophie* at work. For analysis of *Theory of Life,* see Levere 1981, pp. 42–45, 161–66, 215–19.

15. The "worlding" theme serves as a major scaffolding for Daniel Peck's *Thoreau's Morning Work* (1990), which he explains as follows:

> This phrase ["worlding" of the world] comes from an essay by Richard Pevear, who uses it in a discussion of the poetry of George Oppen. Pevear places Oppen's work in contrast to the "solipism of so much contemporary writing" and understands it as an antidote to the "worldlessness" of the postwar period. It was, of course, a nineteenth-century version of worldlessness—the condition of "quiet desperation"—that sent Thoreau to the Pond to recover *his* world, and *Walden* may be considered the "poem" he wrote toward his recovery. He was, as many have observed, prescient in understanding how the technology and coercive social structures emerging in his time could alienate people from nature and turn them into machines. One of his reasons for going to Walden, like many another utopian of his day, was to recover the very ground of being, to "world" the world in this quite literal sense. (Pp. 125–26)

16. This view, despite recent attempts to overturn it (e.g., Walls 1995; see next chapter) has been long recognized. For instance, consider Hicks's assessment: "There was every reason why, with his keen, sensuous perception, his zealous and incessant observation of the facts of nature, and his intensive study of a single, small district, Thoreau might have become one of the foremost field naturalists of modern science. He chose to be something else" (1925, p. 87).

17. I will adopt Porte's basic reading. Suffice it to note here only that Paul regards Thoreau as "fortunate to find in an emerging Transcendentalism a program for his life" (1958, p. 1); accordingly, his challenge was "to apply transcendental ideas, to bring them to the test of living" (ibid., p. 16), and thus most of Emerson's treatise [*Nature*] was embodied in *Walden* (ibid., p. 301). Thus Thoreau, from this perspective, attempted to prove Emerson's philosophy

(p. 274), although the naturalist method, writ large, was ill suited for the disciple's greater task (ibid., pp. 275 ff.). This of course was Emerson's own view, as he wrote in 1841: "I told H. T. that his freedom is in the form, but he does not disclose new matter. I am very familiar with all his thoughts,—they are my own quite originally drest" (1970, p. 96), and then reiterated after Thoreau's death: "In reading him [Thoreau], I find the same thought, the same spirit that is in me, but he takes a step beyond, & illustrates by excellent images that which I should have conveyed in a sleepy generality" (June 24, 1863, 1982, p. 353). Matthiessen (1941, p. 80) quotes the first journal entry and then more fairly balances the ledger with the following general assessment: "his [Emerson's] failure to concentrate squarely on the fact that here, among all his followers, was the rare artist for whom he had been looking" (ibid., p. 81). An interesting commentary on Emerson's dismissal is offered by his own son, Edward Waldo Emerson, who, in 1917, wrote an appreciative correction on the occasion of the centennial anniversary of Thoreau's birth:

> His close association, under the same roof, for months, with the maturer Emerson [Ralph Waldo] may, not unnaturally, have tinged his early writings, and some superficial trick of manner or of speech been unconsciously acquired, as often happens. But this is all that can be granted. Entire independence, strong individuality were Thoreau's distinguishing traits, and his foible was not subserviency, but combativeness in conversation, as his friends knew almost too well. Conscious imitation is not to be thought of as a possibility of this strong spirit. (1999, p. 12)

Notwithstanding a possible family tension, the younger Emerson was particularly irked by James Russell Lowell's view of Thoreau (e.g., 1899, p. 25).

My own favorite defense of Thoreau was that offered by his early biographer, Henry Salt:

> I would hazard the suggestion (though well aware that it must at present seem fantastic) that Thoreau's genius will eventually be even more highly valued than Emerson's. No sane critic could for a moment doubt the mighty influence which Emerson's great and beneficent intellect wielded among his contemporaries, or dream of comparing Thoreau with him as a nineteenth-century power. But the class of mind which has the most lasting hold on men's interest and homage is not always, and not often, the same as that which rules contemporary thought. . . . Of all the Concord group, the most inspired, stimulating, and vital personality is Thoreau's; and when time has softened down the friction caused by superficial blemishes and misunderstandings, the world will realize that it was no mere Emersonian disciple, but a master-mind and heart who left that burning message to his fellow-men. ([1890] 1993, pp. 127–28)

18. Thoreau, as he himself acknowledged, was a Transcendentalist, and critics generally agree. The question is simply, What kind of Transcendentalist? For one must seek a common denominator, given the diversity of the movement. Walter Harding pithily offers the following: "Thoreau classified himself as a Transcendentalist. If we use the popular definition that a Transcendentalist is one who believes that one can (and should) go beyond Locke in believing that all knowledge is acquired through the senses, that in order to attain the ultimate in knowledge one must 'transcend' the senses, we can unquestionably clas-

sify Thoreau as a Transcendentalist" (1959, p. 134). For my purposes here, this assignment will do.

19. As Robert Richardson (1986) has discussed in detail, Thoreau brought together several tributaries from "Nature" that would remain as major currents of his mature project. Emerson's pivotal essay had posed questions concerning 1) the relation of ideas that correspond to material nature, 2) the role of intuition as a valid mode of knowing, and 3) the character of an individual's ethical standpoint. Each of these issues, according to Emerson's perspective, was grounded in man's relation to nature, as opposed to God, state, or society. As did the Stoics long before him, Emerson evoked a parallelism: nature's laws were fundamentally the same as the laws of human nature, and thus man could base a good life, a life of virtue, on nature. Emerson took the next step of his argument in his Phi Beta Kappa address at Harvard, delivered the day after Thoreau graduated—and which he probably did not hear—by asserting that the business of the American Scholar (the title of this famous lecture [1983b]) was to study nature and thus attain self-knowledge by the correspondence discovered in that examination. Further, in a Hegelian variant, Emerson maintained an idea of history as the record of a universal mind. On this view, the human mind is, and has been, essentially the same in all ages and places, and thus the similarities of different ages and cultures are more important than their differences.

Influential earlier critics concurred that Thoreau should be regarded as an expositor of Emerson's doctrines. For instance, James Russell Lowell accused Thoreau of having gathered his "strawberries" from Emerson's garden (1899, p. 369; quoted by Hansen 1990, p. 133), and Mark Van Doren saw Thoreau as "a specific Emerson," whose philosophical position was "almost identical with Emerson's" (1916, pp. 70, 91; quoted by Porte 1966, p. 4). Hicks saw Thoreau as in "agreement with the essential features of Emerson's attitude toward nature" (1925, p. 80) and as one who "exemplified . . . in his life and in his work, most of the doctrines of Emerson's *Nature*" (ibid., p. 98). In this reading, Thoreau's "most important contribution . . . is his expression of the Transcendental attitude toward nature, which . . . gave rise to the poetic and philosophic attitude as contrasted with the utilitarian or purely scientific (ibid.).

20. Emerson's key concept of Correspondence—the notion that nature is symbolic of spiritual truth, and indeed holds its highest and truest function as a handbook of moral truth—is derived from a complex constellation of eighteenth-century ideas that Thoreau found less conducive, and from this position Porte draws diverging philosophical lines (1966, pp. 11 ff. and 68 ff.). Scholarly opinion is sharply divided on this point: for instance, Hansen (1990, p. 6) agrees, while Paul (1958) draws exactly the opposite conclusion, seeing Transcendentalism as "rejecting most of the assumptions of the eighteenth century" (p. 3), but he accedes to the critical point upon which Porte will build his own argument:

> Intuitive apprehension (the capitalized Reason of the nineteenth century as opposed to the reason of the eighteenth) was man's creative power, the warrant of his freedom, and his key to the universe. Not only did its synthesizing powers account for the way in which experience becomes meaningful, but being an imaginative faculty as well, it

> could directly seize reality. And this apprehension of reality, though mystical in the epistemological sense of making the knower one with the thing known, was not the vaporous emotional state usually ascribed to mysticism; it was a cognitive experience, the liberating power of which came from possessing ideas—not the mere Lockean representative idea, but the idea in the mind of God, the idea in the Platonic sense of being the correlative of Reality itself. . . . [T]he ideas in the mind were the only reality one could know; the world outside the mind was phenomenal. . . . [O]ne never knew the reality outside of one's self." (Paul 1958, p. 5)

And with Ideas, "man can remake the world" (ibid., p. 6), so that interpreting nature, turning it into consciousness, was "a process of taking up the Not-me by the Me. Mind, ideas, consciousness were primary, and the external world existed to be assimilated as the stuff of thought" (ibid., p. 7). The solipsistic break is made through Correspondence: spirit resides behind nature, and we might, because of our own spark of divinity, know spirit. I concur with Porte that Thoreau rejected this thesis and sought another path.

21. Emersonian Transcendentalism stressed the correspondences one might discern in observing nature to enlighten and spiritually instruct us. Nature was thus to be mastered and read for human purpose, and because man is only dimly aware of his innate divine sources, the natural world remains "the present expositor of the divine mind" (Emerson 1983a, p. 42). Through correspondences we might "read" nature and thus decode her, for "every natural fact is a symbol of some spiritual fact" (ibid., p. 30), and conversely, "all spiritual facts are represented by natural symbols" (ibid., p. 22). This "radical correspondence between visible things and human thoughts" (ibid.) reflects the emblematic nature of the world, where "the whole of nature is a metaphor of the human mind" (ibid., p. 24). If one would discern that language, nature then holds "models for human art, metaphors for human growth, assurances of human stability," and thus one who studies nature is afforded a "means of recovering his 'power,' his charismatic capacity for the mastery of life" (McIntosh 1974, p. 28). The product is the reconstruction of human divinity in its various forms and, most pertinent to our present concerns, the making of a self-created world. The key is the creative element, where meaning is established between a contemplating individualized mind—the self—and the world (natural and divine) about him. Emerson's return to nature is to bring her under human dominion so that the universe, devoid of value in itself without man's survey and assignment, might become entirely spiritual, and thus morally informed. Porte summarizes previous analyses that explain Emerson's (and Coleridge's) misreading of Kant (ibid., pp. 85 ff.), who denied ontological idealism and its implications for moral law.

22. A concise picture of Thoreau's divergent empiricist approach to nature is captured in Emerson's own journal entry of May 21, 1856:

> Yesterday to the Sawmill Brook with Henry. He was in search of yellow violet (pubescens) and menyanthes which he [found] waded into the water for. & which he concluded, on examination, had been out five days. Having found his flowers, he drew out of his breast pocket his diary & read the names of all the plants that should bloom on this day, 20 May; whereof he keeps account as a banker when his notes fall due. rubus triflora, guerens, vaccinium, &c. The cyprop[ae]dium not due 'till tomorrow. Then

we diverged to the brook, where was viburnum dentatum, arrowhead. But his attention was drawn to the redstart which flew about with its *cheah cheah chevet*, & presently two fine grosbeaks[,] rosebreasted, whose brilliant scarlet "made the rash gazer wipe his eye," & which he brought nearer with his spy glass, [his pockets are full of twine &c. also,] [then to the note of a bird] & whose fine clear note he compares to that of a "tanager who has got rid of his hoarseness," then he heard a note which he calls that of the nightwarbler, a bird he has never [seen] identified, has been in search of for twelve years; which, always, when he sees, is in the act of diving down into a tree or bush, & which 'tis vain to seek; the only bird that sings indifferently by night & by day. I told him, he must beware of finding & booking him, lest life should have nothing more to show him. He said, "What you seek in vain for half your life, one day you come full upon all the family at dinner.—You seek him like a dream, and as soon as you find him, you become his prey." He thinks he could tell by the flowers what day of the month it is, within two days. . . . There came Henry with music-book under his arm, to press flowers in; with telescope in his pocket, to see the birds, & microscope to count stamens; with a diary, jacknife, & twine, in stout shoes, & strong grey [pantal] trowsers, ready to brave the shrub oaks & smilax, & to climb the tree for a hawk's nest. His strong legs when he wades were no insignificant part of his armour. (1978, 90–92)

Thoreau's Journal entries for May 20 and 21, 1856 (*Journal*, [1906] 1962, 8:349–50), make no mention of Emerson, and there are inconsistencies that are not easily resolved. Thoreau notes going to Saw Mill Brook on the 21st, not the 20th as in Emerson's note, but since there are two Saw Mill Brooks, it is possible that Thoreau indeed visited one or the other on the 20th with Emerson, although on that date Thoreau notes only that he went to "Beck Stows." The grosbeaks and *pubescens* are noted by Thoreau in the 21st entry (not the 20th), but there is no mention at all of the nightwarbler in either account. Thoreau makes frequent Journal references to nightwarblers, which, according to Emerson's relay of information from "Brewer," "is probably the Nashville warbler" (Thoreau, May 3, 1857, *Journal*, [1906] 1962, 9:355). But Thoreau persisted in calling this elusive bird a nightwarbler in later Journal entries (e.g., May 16, 1858, ibid., 10:426) and finally seems to make a definite identification as a "Maryland yellow-throat!!" (August 5, 1858, ibid., 11:74), although referring to the bird thereafter by its original designation, nightwarbler (May 8, 1860, ibid., 13:283, and August 28, 1860, ibid., 14:67).

Emerson's admiring account was, to be sure, ambivalent. He narrates another outing with Thoreau two years later, and while giving due credit to the intrepid naturalist, there is no doubt that Emerson distances himself. While noting Thoreau's talent ("The charm which Henry T. uses for bird & frog & mink, is patience. They will not come to him, or show him aught, until he comes a log among the logs, sitting still for hours in the same place; then they come around him & to him, & show themselves at home" [May 21, 1858, Emerson 1978, p. 203]), Emerson admonishes him: "I tell him that a man was not made to live in a swamp, but a frog" (ibid.), an observation he reiterates in two separate journal notes: "If God meant him to live in a swamp, he would have made him a frog" (ibid.), and in the form of a mock letter: "My dear Henry, A frog was made to live in a swamp, but a man was not made to live in a swamp. Yours ever, R." (ibid., p. 204). Emerson, apparently, was quite pleased with his reproof.

23. "We may believe it, but never do we live a quite free life, such as Adam's, but are enveloped in an invisible network of speculations– Our progress is only from one such speculation to another, and only at rare intervals do we perceive that it is no progress. – – Could we for a moment drop this by-play–and simply wonder–without reference or inference!" (Thoreau, December 7, 1838, *Journal* 1, 1981, p. 58).

24. As already remarked in n. 22 above.

25. On the central role of symbols, Emerson is closer to Goethe than to Thoreau. There is a long scholarly tradition that regards Goethe's historicism as largely guided by symbolic rendering, but even more broadly we see in Goethe's archetypal leaf the crucial function symbol plays in his epistemology more generally (Van Cromphout 1990, pp. 100–101). Thoreau too sees symbolically, but the symbol hardly serves the same central function it does for Emerson, where it is the nexus of his system. Thoreau is certainly happy to represent various spiritual and aesthetic insights or visions through symbols, both literary and cognitive, but such representations are only part of a varied lexicon of recording experience and certainly do not claim primacy in his thinking or artistic endeavors.

26. If one were to place Thoreau on some continuum of Transcendental orthodoxy, with Emerson holding the middle position, William Ellery Channing would be closer to Thoreau and Bronson Alcott would be furthest away. Alcott might appear to have mimicked Thoreau's own sentiments in writing for the first issue of *The Dial*,

> Nature is not separate from me. She is mine, alike with my body; and in moments of true life I feel my identity with her; I breathe, pulsate, feel, think, will through her members, and know of no duality of being. (Alcott, "Orphic Sayings," no. 35; quoted by Shepard 1937, p. 293)

But in fact Alcott was far removed from Thoreau's own views of nature and human wildness. For Alcott, the imperative of civilization was to conquer the wild so that all could be cultivated and placed under human control:

> These woods do not belong to art nor civility till they are brought into keeping with man's thoughts, nor may they encroach upon us by nearness. . . . Like unkempt savages nodding saucily at us, they need to be cropped and combed before they are fairly taken into our good graces as ornaments of our estates. (Quoted by Shepard 1937, p. 395)

Thus taming of the wild was an inner cultivation for Alcott, one radically different from Thoreau's own efforts both to celebrate and to develop what he regarded as the source of human vitality.

27. Emerson also had his mystical moments—e.g., the famous passage in "Nature," "I become a transparent eye-ball; I am nothing; I see all; the currents of the Universal Being circulate through me; I am part or particle of God" (Emerson 1983a, p. 10)—but the contrast to emphasize is the absence of any notion of dominance in Thoreau's view of nature. See McIntosh 1977, pp. 284–85 n. 4, and further discussion here in chapter 5.

28. But before we dismiss Emerson so cavalierly, it is clear that while Thoreau's entire project was, in some sense, fundamentally different from Emerson's, Thoreau nevertheless actively responded within the broad boundaries of a framework established by Emerson. The basic structure of their respective inquiries may be said to share strong affinities: self-reliance and individuality, the introspective self, divided and dialectical with reference to the world and its own voice; the existential status of man counterposed to nature; the spiritual quest for meaning in a world increasingly hostile to man. To be sure, each stamped these issues with his own characteristic approach and understanding, but these general questions outline a shared inquiry; and while Emerson and Thoreau staked out differing claims and led very different intellectual lives, it is inappropriate simply to conclude that Thoreau "rejected" Emerson. Considering the close relationship Thoreau enjoyed in his formative period, the ability to exercise his intellect against his mentor, and yes, even the opportunity to "rebel" against the Master Transcendentalist, seem to follow Harold Bloom's notion of revision or correction engaged in the creative reaction, where "strong poets" must "clear imaginative space for themselves" (1973, p. 16). That discussion would take us too far afield, but suffice it to note that influence is a matter of multiple determinative factors and cannot be reducible to a simple rejection of one organizing idea or another.

4. THOREAU AT THE CROSSROADS

1. Rossi quotes a letter written to Benjamin Austin in 1860 regarding an invitation to lecture:

> I shall be very happy to read to your association three lectures on the evenings named, but the question is about their character. They will not be scientific in the common, nor, perhaps, in any sense. . . . [T]hey will be *transcendental*, that is, to the mass of hearers, probably *moonshine*. Do you think that this will do? Or does your audience prefer lamplight, or total darkness these nights? I dare say, however, that they would interest those who are most interested in what is called nature. (Thoreau 1958, p. 584)

2. Positivism's influence affected all intellectual domains. It called for renewed vigor in scientific objectivism, and it was also manifest in application to human sciences and moral philosophy, where explanations of social behavior were sought in biology. As Leszek Kolakowski observed, "positivism . . . renounces the transcendental meaning of truth and reduces logical features to biological behavior. The rejection of the possibility of synthetic judgments a priori—the fundamental act constituting positivism as a doctrine—can be identified with the reduction of all knowledge to biological responses" (1968, p. 214).

3. Diana Postlethwaite (1984) and Peter Dale (1989) have cogently argued that positivism was the dominant nineteenth-century successor to the Romantics' efforts at totalization, that vast cultural project which sought a unifying basis for nature and society. Dale writes that, militantly realistic,

> the ground of its realism lay not in the historical structures of society so much as in the evolving structures of the natural world, to which it tended to reduce the histori-

cal. And although, like Marxism, it proposed ultimately to bring about the the union of the individual with society and within himself, it began by proposing to fit the structures of the mind to those of nature, not in Wordsworth's metaphysical manner of strong romanticism, but in the materialistic or naturalistic manner that seemed increasingly to be offered by natural science. The use of "scientific naturalism," as F. M. Turner has testified . . . was the single most important intellectual phenomenon of the post-romantic nineteenth century. (Pp. 6–7)

4. The battle was to be fought on philosophical—specifically, epistemological—grounds. The reductionists proceeded to reduce life to a problem of defining attractive and repulsive forces (very much in keeping with the Romantic preoccupation with polarities) in order to link the physical sciences to the biological, which indeed were connected "not empirically, not because the physical foundations of physiology had been experimentally determined, but *a priori*, independent of any scientific investigation at all[!]" (Galaty 1974).

5. Romantic holism, as a philosophical construct, grew out of seventeenth-century debate over the metaphysical structure of nature. Indeed, Spinozan pantheism was the direct antecedent of the Romantic notion of nature's unity (McFarland 1969), and Thoreau was, of course, a disciple of that orientation. Spinoza, in response to the dualistic construction of mind and body proposed by Descartes, endeavored to unify the schism by transcending the alternative primacy of either mind or body with a new concept, "substance": absolute, infinite, and unknowable. The finite expression of substance was the "mode," known only by our cognizing abilities as "thought" and "extension." Thus, body and mind are the only conceivable manifestations of substance as mediated through modes, and although each appears distinct, both, according to Spinoza, are in fact derivative of primal substance and thus complementary aspects of one and the same reality. The key issue was the unity of nature that undergirded all the variegated manifestations. This is an important example of an abiding theme in Western civilization, namely, "the need to reconcile, to bring to line, to unify within a single, all-embracing, coherent, and logical system of thought those divergent—and diverse—elements that threaten to disrupt an orderly world" (Smocovitis 1996, p. 4, citing Berlin 1977 and 1992). In this sense, as discussed in chapter 6, Thoreau regarded himself as pursuing a heroic endeavor. But this definition is incomplete, for Romanticism also embraced disruption, fragmentation, irony, and chaos. It required its own sustaining structure, one constructed from the rejection of any universals. For further discussion, see the Introduction.

6. Notwithstanding the deficiencies of such a position, it is fascinating to note the fecundity of Goethe's musings, which were later developed in twentieth-century phenomenological philosophy. This general orientation is again regarded as an important direction to explore in terms of the experiential quality of science. See Kohàk 1978.

7. Thomas Nagel (1986) argues that "absolute objectivity"—or all-embracing knowledge—is deeply paradoxical because such knowledge cannot adopt some particular view, that is, be inclusive of reality as we know it (the subjective), and is thus always partial and incomplete. Ideally the subjective and the objective sides of objectivity should be joined, but *because* of the limits imposed on abso-

lute objectivity, it can offer only "a view from nowhere"—that is, a knowledge which cannot be situated. In such a world, there is no perspective, context or voice, and knowledge has no *meaning*.

8. See n. 1 to Acknowledgments.

9. Interestingly, Goethe did not defend Romantic subjectivity to preserve a particular humane orientation to counter a scientific worldview (he predated the positivists and perhaps felt less defensive than Thoreau); rather he sought a fine balance between interpretative free play with observations and a mode of doing science which would allow the full play of human imagination in order to stimulate discovery. Goethe thus personifies the deep conflict in Romantic science—the search for some objectified nature filtered through the sanctity of human interpretation—a tension that was to plague his cohort until their eclipse by the positivists, who sought to minimize, if not eliminate, the human element in the gathering of facts.

10. See n. 7 above.

11. I hasten to add that Thoreau was hardly an anti-scientist and clearly understood the power of the scientific method and the importance of science for his own worldview and poetic appreciation. For instance, in discussing the important role of identifying and naming a natural object, he wrote:

> I have known a particular rush . . . for at least twenty years, but have been prevented from describing some [of] its peculiarities, because I did not know its name. . . . With the knowledge of the name comes a distincter recognition and knowledge of the thing. That shore is now more describable, and poetic even. My knowledge was cramped and confined before, and grew rusty because not used,—for it could not be used. My knowledge now becomes communicable and grows by communication. I can now learn what others know about the same thing. (August 29, 1858, *Journal*, [1906] 1962, 11:137)

12. At the other end of the philosophical spectrum from Whewell, John Stuart Mill advocated both a pragmatic (or utilitarian) understanding and a rigorously inductive explanation of scientific research and theory formation (*A System of Logic* [1843]). He maintained that all reasoning, even apparently deductive reasoning, is ultimately inductive. Methodologically opposed to Whewell's reliance on the verification of hypotheses as evidence of truth, Mill insisted that since various hypotheses could explain a group of facts, inductive proof required the affirmation of one hypothesis at the expense of the others. The crucial difference between Mill and Whewell perhaps may be reduced to the role of hypotheses in their respective philosophies. Whewell, in reading the history of science, saw that history as an illustration of the Hypothetical Method, where the truth of a hypothesis is attested from its ability to explain observed phenomena (so-called Inference to the Best Explanation). Mill argued for the undeterminedness of theory, where a body of data might be equally explained by more than one hypothesis.

13. In the letter declining membership (December 19, 1853), Thoreau included answers to a questionnaire:

> *Occupation (Professional or otherwise).* Literary and Scientific, combined with Land-surveying. . . . *Branches of science in which especial interest is felt* The manners and

customs of the Indians of the Alonquin Group previous to contact with the civilized man. *Remarks* I may add that I am an observer of nature generally, and the character of my observations, so far as they are scientific, may be inferred from the fact that I am especially attracted by such books of science as White's Selborne and Humboldt's "Aspects of Nature." (Thoreau 1958, p. 310)

14. This perspective on "the disenchantment of the world" has found adherents in our own century, the most eloquent perhaps being Max Weber ([1922] 1946). While acknowledging that successful science depends on a single-minded devotion to its own methods and its own conclusions, Weber believed that to be a specialist is not simply to be a calculator or tool in the scientific process but a vital, creative agent. To situate science in terms of its humane function rather than its epistemological standing or its technological application, Weber referred to the "inward calling for science"; that is, he addressed the possible meaning of the enterprise for its practitioners. He suggested that the defined scope of scientific disciplines provides an opportunity for specialization, and that the fragmentation of domains of knowledge in modern society entails the conclusion that genuine achievement is possible for the individual only within a narrow and confined domain of expertise. However, Weber rejected the notion that science "has become a problem in calculation." He was unwilling to accept that only a "factory" method of cold calculation and methodical computation can yield scientific results, and he strongly maintained the necessity of intuition and inspiration—of "ideas"—in science (as in art). And so he joined the Romantic tradition of finding human value in scientific practice.

15. Kuhn looked at the history of science and saw that the narratives bequeathed him in the 1950s were hardly rational or cumulative in the normal sense. As a novice physicist, he understood that scientific development hardly ever depended on knowing the history of what had preceded the particular narrow question at hand, and thus that the practicing scientist had little, if any, historical consciousness. As Kuhn wrote in *Structure*, "More historical detail, whether of science's present or of its past, or more responsibility to the historical details that are presented, could only give artificial status to human idiosyncrasy, error, and confusion. Why dignify what science's best and most persistent efforts have made it possible to discard? The depreciation of historical fact is deeply, and probably functionally, ingrained in the ideology of the scientific profession, the same profession that places the highest of all values upon factual details of other sorts" (1970, p. 138). This was an important insight that brought at least two ideas in train. The first was the fundamental question of how and why science proceeds without this self-conscious awareness of its own method. The second—and this was the one Kuhn himself, and later the entire discipline of history of science, pursued—was to what extent science might be characterized by some historical self-reflexiveness. In a sense, the first set of questions would in effect be answered as a shadow response to the second set. If science, to proceed, does not rely on understanding its own origins and tracing its historical evolution, then to what extent does it adhere to such rational categories of development? The answer offered by Kuhn—and later aggres-

sively pursued by the more radical Kuhnians whom he repudiated—was that science was hardly as rational as previously assumed.

16. These attacks, begun in the 1960s and 1970s, on the normative standing of science generated heated rebuttals (Holton 1993; Gross, Levitt, and Lewis 1996), and the so-called Science Wars of the 1990s pitted conservative defenders of science against those whom they regarded as attacking a bastion of Western civilization. The fundamental issue in the Science Wars is the degree to which scientific findings—from theory to elemental fact—are "constructed." The issue goes back, at least in its modern formulation, to Kant, who, in proposing that we know the world only insofar as our mental faculties allow, offered a philosophical constructivist theory of cognition: our manner of perceiving the world and acting in it depend on the particular character (i.e., biology) of our minds, *and* that world exists for us (i.e., can be known) as defined by those faculties of knowing. (Metaphysical realism was thus challenged, if not replaced, by the noumena/phenomena distinction.) We might concur that the degree of epistemological agreement between individual knowers must be very high (because of adaptive evolution, the commonality of language, and the overwhelming evidence of practice); yet because of the "other minds" problem and the uncertainty of noumena, doors to skepticism and relativism have been opened. Science has, of course, always made a privileged claim on objectivity, but if one extrapolates the Kantian position from individual perceptions to instruments, on the one hand, and social factors (including language, cultural values, political organization, etc.) on the other hand, then "constructivism" in science becomes a problem of degree. In short, the argument hinges on the degree to which science's privileged epistemological position protects its cognitive content from contamination by confounding elements not factored into the calculus of ideal objective knowing.

The constructivist quandary entered science studies through each of its three branches—history, philosophy, and sociology of science. When a logical structure for scientific discovery and verification seemed elusive at best (philosophy), and the history of science seemed similarly marked by nonprogressive, nonrational models of growth, students of science paid closer attention to the social variables that might account for scientific practice. While a comprehensive description was hardly forthcoming, one major result of these studies was that science exhibited a construction of its knowledge in a fashion analogous to other forms of knowledge formation. While there indeed was a privileged epistemological standing in the natural sciences, this was different in degree, not kind. Simply put, science is, in a trivial sense, "social," i.e., it is a human activity, which draws upon all those elements of our culture that support its enterprise. This is hardly contentious in itself, but the argument commences as to the degree of construction which would be allowed for scientific practice and discourse, and from there, the degree of relativism allowed for science's content.

17. See n. 16 above.

18. My own views and papers supporting what I would call a pragmatic realist's position may be found in the anthology *Science and the Quest for Reality*

(Tauber 1997), where references to the philosophical, historical, and sociological dimensions of this issue are given.

19. When discussing science and aesthetics, it is difficult to draw the line between psychology and philosophy. Geometric form and other visual metaphors generally fulfill criteria of form that we "perceive" as beautiful, but whether the appreciation of a phenomenon or form as beautiful is learned (i.e., culturally derived) or in fact fulfills some resonant cognitive function remains a vexing question (Rentschler et al. 1988). The literature concerned only with defining the beautiful *in* science is vast; see Tauber 1996b for a partial listing.

20. Indeed, a useful way of illustrating the elusive synthesis of scientific experience may be seen in the way the aesthetic has often served to span, in scientists' own accounts, the deep metaphysical schism (Tauber 1996b). For instance, when the physicist Paul Dirac said, " it is more important that a theory be beautiful than that it be true" (quoted by Charles Hartshorne [1982] as heard in a lecture), he did not proclaim qualitative equivalence, as did John Keats ("Beauty is truth, truth beauty"), but offered the sense of the beautiful as paramount. Dirac clearly emphasized a mathematical-aesthetic method at the expense of inductive empiricism: "A theory of mathematical beauty is more likely to be correct than an ugly one that fits some experimental data," and "there are occasions when mathematical beauty should take priority over agreement with experiment" (Kragh 1990, p. 284, quoting Dirac). Or again, "It is more important to have beauty in one's equations than to have them fit experiment" (Dirac 1963). This so-called Dirac-Weyl doctrine in fact can be traced in modern physics to Hermann Minkowski, but perhaps of greater influence on Dirac was Einstein, who was guided by principles of simplicity and exhibited legendary confidence in his equations of gravitation theory. Dirac and many other physicists of his time regarded Einstein's gravitation theory as created virtually without empirical reasoning, although Einstein himself was more circumspect in his trust in aesthetic parameters (Kragh 1990, pp. 286–87; see also McAllister 1990).

Dirac's pronouncement falls prey to the disjunction of the rational scientific from the emotive beautiful. In the very separation of beauty from truth we perhaps might be satisfied with Keats's assignment of equality, or at least complementarity, inasmuch as "truth" fulfills certain necessary criteria and "beauty" others. Dirac distinguishes them as different and hierarchical. In a most profound sense, by separating truth and beauty, we again admit a potentially debilitating dichotomy. Dirac's proclamation jolts as it challenges the usual perception of scientific inquiry, and yet it is neither a novel assessment nor a radical position. The entire issue of the subjectivity and changing standards of aesthetic criteria is beyond our concern, but there has been much discussion of this issue. (See Renscher 1990 and Tauber 1996b for introductions.)

21. See Henri Atlan's discussion of this issue (1993, p. 193), where he draws upon Gaston Bachelard's original insights concerning the psychological motivations of scientists (Bachelard [1934] 1984). See also the discussions of Holton (1994) and Torrance (1994) for other perspectives on the quest for universal, transcendent truths from religious and scientific orientations.

5. THOREAU'S PERSONALIZED FACTS

1. There is little doubt where Thoreau placed science in the hierarchy of knowledge, even in his mature period. Two examples will suffice:

> Even the facts of science may dust the mind by their dryness—unless they are in a sense effaced each morning or rather rendered fertile by the dews of fresh & living truth (July 7, 1851, *Journal* 3, 1990, p. 291)

> The scientific startling & successful as it is, is always some thing less than the vague poetic . . . it is the sun shorn of its beams a mere disk . . . Science applies a finite rule to the infinite.— & is what you can weigh & measure and bring away. Its sun no longer dazzles us and fills the universe with light. (January 5, 1850, ibid., p. 44)

Indeed, Thoreau fully recognized his discomforture when too committed to a "scientific" pursuit, e.g., writing his sister in 1852: "I am not on the trail of any elephants or mastodons, but have succeeded in trapping only a few ridiculous mice, which can not feed my imagination. I have become sadly scientific" (*Correspondence*, 1958, p. 283). But as this chapter will show, Thoreau *did* use science for his own purposes, seeking objective facts of nature to ground his own aesthetic and spiritual musings. An interesting contrast with Emerson is that Thoreau seems not to have operated within a particular scientific paradigm as his mentor apparently did. According to Eric Wilson (1999), Emerson's fascination with electromagnetism inspired the powerful metaphors of *Nature*. Translating organic life into electric force and Romantic symbols into electromagnetic circuits, the essay became "a linguistic version of the electrical cosmos." Nature as animated and charged drew Emerson to conceive the unity of nature in such terms and to deepen his appreciation of the sublime order of the cosmos. As discussed later in this chapter, the shared metaphysics of unity linked the scientific and Romantic-poetic worldviews; so in this context, Emerson's project is characteristic of the era. The interesting point, however, is that Emerson chose a particular scientific theory upon which to hang his idealism and ground his version of the sublime.

2. There are numerous testaments to Thoreau's jaundiced view of objectivism in the guise of scientific inquiry. For example:

> The astronomer is as blind to the significant phenomena—or the significance of phenomena as the wood-sawyer who wears glasses to defend his eyes from sawdust— The question is not what you look at—but how you look & whether you see. (Thoreau, August 5, 1851, *Journal* 3, 1990, pp. 354–55)

> Science is inhuman. Things seen with a microscope begin to be insignificant. So described, they are as monstrous as if they should be magnified a thousand diameters. Suppose I should see and describe men and houses and trees and birds as if they were a thousand times larger than they are! With our prying instruments we disturb the balance and harmony of nature. (May 1, 1859, *Journal*, [1906] 1962, 12:171)

3. A subtle venture to address this issue is offered by Daniel Peck, who has astutely argued that Thoreau wrestled with the "realness" of *phenomenon*, a

catchall class for what Peck maintains is a synthesis between Thoreau's obvious commitment to objective observation and his poetic faculty of aesthetic perception (1990, 1991). Peck interprets Thoreau as seeking to establish the relation among elements as signified by science without relinquishing the implications of philosophical idealism. Thus in Peck's scheme, the "phenomenon" captures the totality of experience, both objectively and aesthetically. Almost analogous to a "painting of the mind," the "phenomenon" stands out as a self-aware picture of the world (in the form of, say, a landscape or cluster of natural objects). Things remain "things," but imagination orders them in composition and for contemplation: birds, trees, clouds, and so on do indeed belong both to the real world of nature and to the domain of the mind. But how to understand that relation? The aesthetics of nineteenth-century art criticism à la Ruskin or Gilpin hardly sufficed (ibid.), and the ontological standing of "phenomena" remained problematic.

Thoreau was highly critical of Ruskin (e.g., October 6, 1857, *Journal*, [1906] 1962, 10:69; October 29, 1857, ibid., p. 147), but Peck notes that this criticism was largely unfair, inasmuch as Ruskin's writings certainly reinforced and refined Thoreau's own ideas on nature's symmetry, its "likeness of forms" (Peck 1990, p. 65). But according to Daniel Pick there might have been an even deeper resonance linking Thoreau to Ruskin:

> Ruskin understood, ahead of impressionism, that our knowledge of the visible world creates the difficulties of art. We do not simply see afresh as we look through our eyes; our vision today is slave to our experience. If we could forget what we already know, we would see differently, better, he declared in *The Elements of Drawing* (1857): "The perception of solid Form is entirely a matter of experience. We *see* nothing but flat colours; and it is only by a series of experiments that we find out that stain of black or grey indicates the dark side of a solid substance, or that a feint hue indicates that the object in which it appears is far away." . . . It was crucial to free oneself as far as possible from any presumption of knowledge. All great artists, Ruskin proposed, have a capacity to look anew at shapes and colours; to see the world with what he took to be a childlike innocence. (Pick 1997, pp. 197–98)

4. I am indebted to Philip Cafaro for alerting me to the significance of the bream episode, and whose unpublished paper "Thoreau on Science and System" has offered me important insights. See Cafaro 1997 for a reading different from my own of how Thoreau might be regarded from a virtue ethics perspective, discussed in chapter 6.

5. See n. 17 to chapter 2.

6. "We boast of our system of education, but why stop at schoolmasters and schoolhouses? We are all schoolmasters, and our schoolhouse is the universe. To attend chiefly to the desk or schoolhouse while we neglect the scenery in which it is placed is absurd. If we do not look out we shall find our fine schoolhouse standing in a cow-yard at last." (Thoreau 2000, p. 238)

7. *Origin* was published in 1859, and Thoreau read the book in early 1860. Thoreau first encountered the text when Charles Brace, a New York social worker and brother-in-law of Asa Gray (a Harvard botanist and correspondent of Dar-

win's), brought a copy of the newly published book to Concord. On January 1, 1860, Brace, Bronson Alcott, and Thoreau had dinner at Frank Sanborn's home and discussed the new book. Thoreau soon got his own copy, made extensive notes, and, as a Sanborn letter indicates, apparently told Sanborn that he liked *Origin* very much (Harding 1965, p. 429). There are other indications that Darwin might have counted Thoreau as an intellectual comrade based on disparaging remarks Thoreau made about Agassiz, a Darwin nemesis (ibid.), but there is little by which we might assess the extent of influence *Origin* had on Thoreau's thinking. Harding thought Darwin's theories had appeared too late to have any significant influence (ibid.), while Richardson misassigns a Journal entry, where Thoreau applauds himself for reading clues in the wild and comments on the receptivity of the mind for such decoding, as a comment on Thoreau's preparedness to accept Darwin's thesis (Richardson 1993, p. 12). But Thoreau's late scientific interests and style of work suggest that he did, indeed, comprehend well the significance of Darwin's work and was keen to perceive its manifestations in his own observations, particularly the dispersion of seeds project.

8. As discussed in chapter 4, it is apparent that some scientists of the high Victorian period were able to translate the Romantic sensibility of wholeness and harmony into a post-Darwinian construct. For instance, Thomas Huxley, "Darwin's Bulldog" and most celebrated British champion of Darwinism, emphasized how the theory offered both unifying explanation and a vision of harmony in nature. For Huxley, the primary import of Darwinism was the value of its description of evolution as an all-inclusive Law, connoting unity and regularity through its bringing man himself within the realm of an all-inclusive natural causation (Huxley 1869). The relations of the various species was thus no longer metaphorical but had a literal basis in the notion of common descent. All of nature is thereby connected by Darwin's great Tree of Life. Instead of competition, organic interrelatedness and cooperation could just as easily be singled out as representing the cardinal feature of the organic world as depicted by Darwin, and indeed Darwin himself so emphasized ([1859] 1964, pp. 485, 130, 109; Kohn 1996).

9. As Canby opined, "His objective was literary, philosophic, not really scientific.... Thoreau's science is always amateur. It is the science of the self-made student who labors excessively for small returns because he lacks frames of reference and good methods. And in Thoreau's case it remained amateur because he was really more interested in the literature to be made of it than in the facts themselves" ([1939] 1958, pp. 335–36). Hildebidle (1983, pp. 24 ff.) appropriately disallows Canby's distinctions between "scientific" and "philosophic," and even between "amateur" and "professional," but like most critics agrees with the final assessment: Thoreau was primarily, as he himself described, a man of letters, a view held from John Burroughs ("Thoreau was not a great philosopher, he was not a great naturalist, he was not a great poet, but as a nature-writer and an original character he is unique in our literature" [1920, p. 120]) to Lawrence Buell ("Thoreau is the patron saint of American environmental writing" [1995, p. 115]).

10. Frank Egerton and Laura Walls have recently reviewed the debate as to whether Thoreau fits the designation of America's first "ecologist" and, more

generally, as to how well (first or not) he fulfills the putative role of ecologist or, more circumspectly, proto-ecologist (1997). Indeed, some mid-twentieth-century ecologists like Edward S. Deevey, Jr., and Aldo Leopold have generously embraced Thoreau into their tribe, and other critics see Thoreau's tireless observations—beyond his late work on forest succession—as worthy of scientific notice. Two issues, easily mingled, need to be teased apart in this discussion: 1) the character of Thoreau's science, and 2) his influence in the persona of scientist. In the first case, as I have maintained, Thoreau offers an intriguing attempt to forge divergent attitudes, and for that effort he deserves careful study, not as a "scientist" but as some other kind of "knower." In this context, I am attempting to show how Thoreau's own self-evaluation as "scientist" should be respected and acknowledged as distinguishing him from the scientific practice of the day. However, in the second case, I believe Thoreau's ecologic *ethos* allows us to see him as a key expositor for an integrated, holistic vision of nature of which the science of ecology partakes. There are, no doubt, cogent reasons to place him within an "Arcadian" ecologic tradition (e.g., Worster 1994), but given his attitudes about science and the paramount importance he assigns to "personal knowing," I think we border on an anachronistic assignment in making Thoreau the patron saint of ecology as a *science*. So by this interpretation we could hardly deny his inspirational or prophetic influence, but his status within the science of ecology is problematical for the reasons already cited; furthermore, the scientific profession hardly glanced at his work as preliminary to later study. Rather, we should recognize Thoreau's general insights regarding the character of nature and our relation to it as contributing to the development of ecology as part of a more general cultural adjustment, of which the science is only one element and whose complex evolution is only beginning to be deciphered (see, e.g., Bramwell 1989). To argue over Thoreau's standing as "ecologist" displaces him from the broader forum in which he must be considered and risks the full appreciation of his contribution.

11. Laura Dassow Walls has thoroughly discussed Thoreau's standing as a scientist and argues that as his career developed, Thoreau became "scientific," especially in his work of the late 1850s (Thoreau 1993), but only understood in his unique fashion (Walls 1995, pp. 179 ff.). Following themes I have already outlined and will further develop, Walls similarly sees Thoreau as holding a complex attitude toward positivist science and objectivity, more generally:

> Thoreau tried to join the "Woodman" and the "man of science" into something new: literary science, perhaps; not literature-and-science but science seen as literature, in its fictive constructions of the world, and literature seen as science, in its operational effectiveness in the world. Thoreau's consilience of an Emersonian insistence on higher or spiritual ends with a Humboldtian, worldly empiricism resulted in not just a new "fact" or a new literary work but an experimental new genre, conceptually avant-garde even in our own time. (Ibid., pp. 178–79)

The points upon which Walls and I meet are numerous, but probably most important is the appreciation that "authority comes from individual involvement and experience" (ibid., p. 207), i.e., "it is finally *ourselves making* science" (ibid., p. 209), so that Thoreau "did not just see but *created* his world, even as he was created by it" (ibid., p. 176). But our readings radically diverge at this point. Thoreau becomes a postmodern in her reading; indebted to recent constructivist theories (e.g., Latour 1987), she builds her case on the breakdown of the subject/object dichotomy (Walls 1995, p. 169). It was, in my view, precisely his self-conscious awareness of the observer's scrutiny that marked his science and poesis and distinguished him from other scientific practitioners of the day. I believe Walls applies categories of contemporary criticism that are not easily adapted to Thoreau's venture; most importantly, she fails to identify the unifying ethos for the coherence of his thought.

Walls's theses are twofold: In a general sense, she maintains that "Thoreau strove to create . . . a new form of science, a *scientia* that would be relational rather than objective" (ibid., p. 147). More particularly, in her view, Thoreau sought to create a holistic science, drawn from Romantic roots, and she believes that as a result of his efforts in this regard, he should be credited with building a science of the biota where connections and relationships were regarded as paramount, to wit, a proto-ecology (1995, pp. 142 ff.). I would concur with this general characterization (see n. 10 above), but then the postmodern theme appears, where she attempts to argue that the subject-object split is to be overcome in some communal venture so that the scientific community becomes Thoreau's larger alter ego. In this broadened sense, "relationship" involves the larger scientific community itself, where not only was all of nature to be studied as interconnected and dialectical but also the knowers of the natural world would similarly engage in a relational ethic as the basis of their scientific approach, both in the study of their object of scrutiny and in the character of their endeavor: "True knowledge is generated and maintained by the community of knowers, a 'round robin' in which the center rotates, which includes all as subjects and all as objects. In this way Thoreau breaks down the dualism embedded in the foundation of 'rational' holism, which assumes that knowing can take place within the isolated, rational mind" (ibid., pp. 143–44).

Not to argue this postmodern notion here, while Thoreau's relational philosophy is an important element of his epistemology, it is individualistic, not community-oriented; more importantly, his effort cannot be translated into science, or even a *scientia* (by which I understand she means a new form of science). Thoreau might have used science, but he was not a scientist and had no aspiration to become one. While he might have engaged in some scientific studies, the very ethos of those efforts were antithetical to science as even he understood it. To make Thoreau a scientist is to place him into a period two or three generations before his own. He, and the culture he inhabited, had evolved into a different setting altogether, and what might have been a legitimate program for a Romantic natural philosopher became, by the 1850s, another program altogether.

12. The critical turn (between 1890 and 1910) in Thoreau's literary and philosophical standing is well summarized by Oehlschlaeger and Hendrick (1979), and a useful survey of Thoreauvian criticism may be found in Glick 1969.

13. As Walter Harding observes, Burroughs's assessment has been widely held:

Havelock Ellis (*The New Spirit*, p. 94) has perhaps been the most vehement in his denunciation of Thoreau's science: "He seems to have been absolutely deficient in scientific sense." Lowell, in his well-known 1865 essay on Thoreau, said, "He discovered nothing. He thought everything a discovery of his own." Bradford Torrey, the editor of Thoreau's *Journal*, thought that he "leaves the present-day reader wondering how so eager a scholar could have spent so many years in learning so comparatively little" (*Journal* 1, xliii), and the coeditor of the *Journal*, Francis Allen, in *Thoreau's Bird-Lore*, devoted much space to pointing out Thoreau's errors in ornithology. Fanny Hardy Eckstorm, in her essay on "Thoreau's 'Maine Woods,' " went to some length to emphasize his weakness as a naturalist. W. L. McAtee denounced him as naïve for accepting some of the theories of protective coloration. And even John Burroughs, who . . . realized that natural history was not Thoreau's major interest, delighted in disparaging his observations on nature. (1959, p. 137)

Foerster (1923, pp. 87–95), while generally more sympathetic, agrees with these critics, but salvages Thoreau by recognizing that his observations were in service to another purpose than scientific or even natural history as practiced by the knowledgeable amateur.

14. Interestingly, as Goethe had seen the primal leaf fulfilling the aesthetic and organizing principle in botany, Thoreau would pick up this same leaf as the trope to carry his own witness of the birth of life itself:

The lobes [of the sand rivulet] are the fingers of the leaf . . .
　–So it seemed as if this one hill side contained an epitome of all the operations in nature.
　So the stream is but a leaf[.] What is the river with all its branches–but a leaf divested of its pulp– – but its pulp is intervening earth–forests & fields & towns & cities– What is the river but a tree an oak or pine–& its leaves perchance are ponds & lakes & meadows innumerable as the springs which feed it. (*Journal* 2, 1984, p. 384)

15. This was a theme already clearly articulated seven years earlier in "Thomas Carlyle and His Works," albeit in the writing of history, and cited in the previous chapter (Thoreau 1975a, pp. 264–65; originally published in *Graham's Magazine* in March 1847).

16. This Thoreauvian fiction holds a profound poignancy: Unlike the staff maker, Thoreau is caught in time and cannot achieve the ideal. The artist's vision cannot be fully conveyed:

There was an artist in the city of Kouroo who was disposed to strive after perfection. One day it came into his mind to make a staff. Having considered that in an imperfect work time is an ingredient, but into a perfect work time does not enter, he said to himself, it shall be perfect in all respects, though I should do nothing else in my life. . . . As he made no compromise with Time, Time kept out of his way, and only sighed at a distance because he could not overcome him. . . . When the finishing stroke was put to his work, it suddenly expanded before the eyes of the astonished artist into the fairest of all the creations of Brahma. He had made a new system in making a staff, a world with full and fair proportions; in which, though the old cities and dynasties had passed away, fairer and more glorious ones had taken their places. And now he saw by the heap of shavings still fresh at his feet, that, for him and his work, the former lapse of time had been an illusion, and that no more time had elapsed than is required for a single scintillation from the brain of Brahma to fall on and inflame the tinder of a mortal brain.

The material was pure, and his art was pure; how could the result be other than won-
derful? (*Walden*, 1971, pp. 326–27)

17. "[H]e was satisfied with giving an exact description of things as they
appeared to him, and their effect upon him. . . . He speaks as an unconcerned
spectator, whose object is faithfully to describe what he sees, and that, for the
most part, in the order in which he sees it. Even his reflections do not interfere
with his descriptions." (*A Week*, 1980a, p. 326)

18. Although I have concentrated on Goethe's epistemology and how it
guided Thoreau's own efforts, I might just as easily have also focused on
Goethe's notions of history and time, which are uncannily similar to Thoreau's
own views, albeit derived from a different perspective. Goethe's view of history,
like Thoreau's, was "mythical, intuitive, and poetic, rather than scientific" (Van
Cromphout 1990, p. 98). More to the point, anticipating Thoreau (and Emerson
and Nietzsche), Goethe "protested against the 'burden' of history, against the
ever-accumulating legacy of the ages that threatens to prevent the present from
living a life authentically its own" (ibid., p. 102). The present is elevated to make
the past relevant to the contemporary muse, and indeed the past and present
are pressed together. (As Goethe wrote, "The present is the only goddess I
adore" [*Werke*] (1948–71), 22:232; quoted by Van Cromphout 1990, p. 101.)
"What matters concerning history, therefore, is its presentness, not its pastness" (ibid., p. 102), a theme reiterated by Emerson (ibid.) and absorbed in his
own fashion by Thoreau.

19. What Thoreau might have accomplished is one thing, what is possible is
another. In other words, the Romantic aspiration may be regarded as having an
intrinsic flaw at its very foundation. As Roger Cardinal observed,

> It is . . . quite possible that the very premises of the Romantic project contained the for-
> mula for its collapse. Novalis' celebrated equation of Romantic vision with a "qualita-
> tive involution" engineered by the sheer authority of the percipient subjectivity,
> secretes an implicit disavowal: "The world must be romanticized. . . . When I confer a
> higher meaning upon the commonplace, a mysterious aspect upon the ordinary, the
> dignity of the unknown upon what is known, or an appearance of infinity upon what
> is finite, I romanticize it." In drawing attention to the magisterial power of the creative
> subject to confer special qualities upon what lies outside itself, Novalis tacitly concedes
> that the world is *not* intrinsically Romantic, and must receive poetic treatment before
> it can fulfill itself. It follows that, if the Romantic self should ever lose its potency, the
> non-self in isolation will fall short of the mark. . . . [A]lmost from the outset, Roman-
> ticism was forced to incorporate into its idealism a tacit recognition of its incompati-
> bility with real life. . . . I suggest that in fact few Romantics were so naively entranced
> as to have ignored the discrepancy; indeed the lament for a lost ideal was itself a Roman-
> tic commonplace from early on. (1997, p. 150)

6. THOREAU'S MORAL UNIVERSE

1. "I sometimes despair of getting anything quite simple and honest done in
this world with the help of men. They would have to be passed through a powerful press first, to squeeze their old notions out of them." (*Walden*, 1971, p. 25)

2. See n. 14 to chapter 1.

3. The use of personal story to frame philosophical questions of moral knowledge is a tradition in Western letters stretching back at least as far as Augustine (354–430), whose own *Confessions*, through the appeal and power of his introspective narrative, still engage the modern reader. Those *Confessions* stand stylistically as a triptych: the autobiographical illustration of his philosophical principles forms the first panel (books 1–9); his contemplation of the moral, epistemological, and integrative life of memory, the second (book 10); the direct application of these earlier insights to his immediate imperative—knowing God through Creation—the third (books 11–13). His narrative is so compelling and immediate, however, that too often the modern reader's interest ends with book 9. We mistake his ingenious essay for "simple" autobiography, and so miss the specifically philosophical restatement of the questions by which he shaped his life story, and the answers he has to give. Surely the power of his personal narrative informs and enriches his more formal philosophy, which in itself is an interesting comment about the nature of his discourse. But the critical point to emphasize is that Augustine's *Confessions* are first and foremost not autobiography but philosophy.

4. For instance,

Virtue will be known ere long by her elastic tread.—When man is in harmony with nature. (September 27, 1840, *Journal 1*, 1981, p. 180)

Virtue is not virtue's face. (November 2, 1840, ibid., p. 193)

My virtue loves to take an airing of the winter's morning–it scents itself, and snuffs its own fragrance in the bracing atmosphere of the fields–more than in the sluggishness of the parlor. (January 2, 1841, ibid., p. 215)

We cannot well do without our sins, they are the highway of our virtue. (March 22, 1842, ibid., p. 385)

5. He continued:

Though the youth at last grows indifferent, the laws of the universe are not indifferent, but are forever on the side of the most sensitive. Listen to every zephyr for some reproof, for it is surely there, and he is unfortunate who does not hear it. We cannot touch a string or move a stop but the charming moral transfixes us. Many an irksome noise, go a long way off, is heard as music, a proud sweet satire on the meanness of our lives. (*Walden*, 1971, pp. 218–19)

This theme was to appear again and again in Thoreau's Journal in different guises, many of them poetic and lyrically evocative. I cite but one from his early period:

The future will no doubt be a more natural life than this. We shall be acquainted and shall use flowers and stars, and sun and moon, and occupy this nature which now stands over and around us. We shall reach up to the stars and pluck fruit from many parts of the universe. We shall purely use the earth and not abuse it– God is in the breeze and whispering leaves and we shall then hear him. We live in the midst of all the beauty and grandeur that was ever described or conceived.

> We have hardly entered the vestibule of Nature. It was here be assured under these heavens that the gods intended our immortal life should pass–these stars were set to adorn and light it–these flowers to carpet it[.] (August 26, 1843, *Journal* 1, 1981, p. 460)

6. See n. 15 to chapter 1.

7. Thoreau wrote frequently and passionately of mythic heroes, with whom he closely identified. For example, consider this early Journal entry:

> Virtue is the deed of the bravest. It is that art which demands the greatest confidence and fearlessness. Only some hardy soul ventures upon it–it deals in what it has no experience in. The virtuous soul possess a fortitude and hardihood which not the grenadier nor pioneer can match. It never shrunk.
>
> It goes singing to its work. Effort is its relaxation. The rude pioneer work of this world has been done by the most devoted worshippers of beauty. Their resolution has possessed a keener edge than the soldier's. In winter is their campaign, they never go into quarters. They are elastic under the heaviest burden–under the extremest physical suffering. (January 1, 1842, *Journal* 1, 1981, p. 354)

8. McIntosh (1974) discusses this passage in pp. 114 ff. Self-consciousness necessarily separates the Romantic observer from nature, but the character of that relationship is variegated. McIntosh accepts Thoreau's complex relationship to nature as a "programmed inconsistency" (ibid., p. 17), and I think this is a fair reading:

> [Thoreau] is trying to do justice to a single concept and a single reality that is itself full of contradiction and inconsistency. One purpose of Thoreau's programmed inconsistency is to make sense of nature as a whole, to comprehend the multiplicity of the entire natural world he lived in. The diverse meanings of "nature" shade into each other. . . . Taken together, they are to be regarded not as an array of concepts, to be separated from each other in the manner of Lovejoy, but as comprising a single beloved realm, a theatre of operation for Thoreau's psyche. (Ibid., p. 26)

9. Porte (1966, p. 30) quotes a passage from Emerson's Journal (1828) that offers some interesting insight into the later psychological dynamics between Thoreau and his mentor:

> "It is a peculiarity . . . of humour in me, my strong propensity for strolling. I deliberately shut up my books . . . put on my old clothes . . . and slink away to the whortleberry bushes and slip with the greatest satisfaction into a little cowpath where I am sure I can defy observation. This point gained, I solace myself for hours with picking blueberries and other trash of the woods, far from fame, behind the birch-trees. I seldom enjoy hours as I do these. I remember them in winter; I expect them in spring" (*J*, II, 244–45 [July 10, 1828, Emerson 1963, pp. 136–37]). . . . Emerson . . . had apparently ceased to remember his golden hours . . . by 1851, when he jotted down in his journal a notable sentence which, in enlarged form, was to serve as part of his funeral oration on Thoreau eleven years later: "Thoreau wants a little ambition in his mixture. Fault of this, instead of being the head of American engineers, he is captain of huckleberry party" (*J*, VIII, 228 [Journal CO, May-November 1851, Emerson 1975, p. 400]). . . . There is clearly a personal animus in the statement. [*J* in Porte's citations = *Journals of Ralph Waldo Emerson,* ed. E. W. Emerson and W. E. Forbes (Boston and New York: Houghton Mifflin; Cambridge: Riverside Press, 1909–14)]

10. As Leo Marx observed of this ethos, "What concerns him [Thoreau] is the hope of making the word one with the thing, the notion that the naked fact

of sensation, if described with sufficient precision, can be made to yield its secret—its absolute meaning. This is another way of talking about the capacity of nature to 'produce delight'—to supply value and meaning" (1964, p. 249). A useful compendium of what Thoreau himself wrote on writing has been compiled by Burkett and Steward (1989).

11. See n. 7 to chapter 3.

12. Respecting Kierkegaard's insight, Wittgenstein drew the full implications beyond spiritual discourse. Indeed, the limits of language defined Wittgenstein's philosophy, which, for better or for worse, dominated twentieth-century analytic philosophy. Wittgenstein urged that one should abandon the hopes of developing language suitable for experience that is in fact unsuitable for public discourse. According to him, there is no logical basis by which we might understand ordinary language, bequeathing a tradition of analysis that restricts the province of logic to logic; of knowledge (in a empirical positivist fashion) to science; and of ethics to the metaphysical, where philosophy's analytical tools were inapplicable. His major message was that we are on very tenuous ground when assessing the logical basis of our language, and for that matter in understanding our very thought (for language and thought are inseparable). Philosophy's role was then to "shew the fly the way out of the fly-bottle" (Wittgenstein 1953, p. 103e), or, in other words, to demonstrate our faulty thinking when we believe we have finalized a philosophical problem. On this view, philosophy's primary role is to disenchant us from thinking that we are offering logical or analytical "solutions." The narratives we weave around the classic philosophical issues are simply delusional if we expect some kind of logical formulation. In Wittgenstein's terminology, questions of this kind are "meaningless" because they are bereft of final adjudication. In contrast, such a question as, "Is it raining?" demands a meaningful response: "Yes" or "No." So for Wittgenstein, only certain questions were "meaningful," and he turned to science as a paragon of such inquiry. Scientists deal with meaningful questions, because the answers investigators glean from nature may be verified by objective means. This is the realm of "facts" as commonly understood. For other kinds of "facts"—personal, supernatural, ethical—language restricts and even distorts. Of course, we must attempt to communicate, but philosophy was dealt the responsibility of showing the faulty logic employed in such discussions, albeit without necessarily offering a better means to communicate. He thus offers us a rather "lonely" solution, one Thoreau—at least temperamentally—would have understood. We each live in a solipsistic and insulated world of our own making, but on the other hand, we now might at least comprehend the locks and chains in which language ensnares us. Insight must balance the existential quandary.

13. With this understanding of *writing*, Cavell presents a certain ontological condition of words:

> [T]he occurrence of a word is the occurrence of an object whose placement always has a point, and whose point always lies before and beyond it. "The volatile truth of our words should continually betray the inadequacy of the residual statement. Their truth is instantly *translated;* its literal monument alone remains" [*Walden*, 1971,

p. 325]. ((Wittgenstein in the *Investigations* (section 432) records a related perception: "Every sign *by itself* seems dead." [Wittgenstein 1953, p. 128e])) (Cavell 1981, p. 27)

14. See n. 12 above.

15. The strife which occurs within is an early theme for Thoreau: "A glorious strife seems waging within us, yet so noiselessly that we but just catch the sound of the clarion ringing of victory, borne to us on the breeze. – – There are in each the seeds of a heroic ardor, Seeds, there are seeds enough which need only to be stirred in with the *soil where they lie,* by an inspired voice or pen, to bear fruit of a divine flavor" (July 15, 1838, *Journal* 1, 1981, p. 49).

16. This theme appears in Thoreau's earliest notebooks and is evidence of a grandiose vision that remained a powerful self-image, one that no doubt has fed Thoreau's various psychological analysts (e.g., Bridgman 1982; Lebrieux 1977, 1984). I doubt that the imagery is solely metaphoric, and there is a messianic element which is difficult to ignore:

> Cease not thou drummer of the night, thou too shalt have thy reward. The stars and the firmament hear thee, and their aisles shall echo thy beat till its call is answered, and the forces are mustered. The universe is attentive as a little child to thy sound, and trembles as if each stroke bounded against an elastic vibrating firmament. I should be contented if the night never ended–for in the darkness heroism will not be deferred, and I see fields where no hero has couched his lance. (June 19, 1840, *Journal* 1, 1981, p. 132)

The requirement, anticipating Nietzsche, is will, and also like Nietzsche, only a prophet of great personal strength might be successful:

> Who knows how incessant a surveillance a strong man may maintain over himself–how far subject passion and appetite to reason, and lead the life his imagination paints? (Thoreau, May 21, 1839, *Journal* 1, 1981, p. 73)

17. Of the many biblical narratives of such strife, the story of Jacob's return to "the land" he fled as a result of usurping his brother, Esau's, inheritance is particularly illuminating to our theme:

> Jacob was left alone; and a man wrestled with him until daybreak. When the man saw that he did prevail against Jacob, he struck him on the hip socket; and Jacob's hip was put out of joint as he wrestled with him. Then he said, "Let me go, for the day is breaking." But Jacob said, "I will not let you go, unless you bless me." So he said to him, "What is your name?" And he said, "Jacob." Then the man said, "You shall no longer be called Jacob, but Israel, for you have striven with God and with humans, and have prevailed." (Genesis 32:24–28)

The "man" is an agent of the divine, and Jacob's nighttime fight is the stuff of dreams. The setting is the eve of the critical meeting to take place with Esau the next day—fraught with danger and even guilt anxiety. It is quite apparent that Jacob is wrestling with the complex interplay of his return with a new identity, rich with wives and children, to a land he had fled under the most suspicious of circumstances. He prevails in the wrestling match, despite suffering a grievous blow, and is able to extract a blessing. The form of this blessing is most interesting, for it takes the form of a new name, signifying a new self. No longer was he the Supplanter (25.26; 27.36) but Israel (35.10), which probably means "God rules" and is interpreted to mean "The one who strives with God" (Metzger and Murphy 1991, p. 43, note to Genesis 32:28). He may just as easily have struggled with himself and emerged with a new name, a new identity, and with it a new ethical mandate.

18. Lebeaux asserts that Thoreau wished to become his own father in naming himself as part of a developmental self-assertion (1984, p. 15; see also 1977, pp. 70–71); Bridgman considers Thoreau's attempts at "self-conquest . . . a fantasy" (1982, p. 26).

19. Cavell has drawn identifications with Jeremiah and Ezekiel (1981, pp. 17 ff.). Although he also sees Thoreau's writing assuming a heroic pose (ibid., p. 21), this persona is subordinated to the prophet or perhaps "poet-prophet" (ibid., p. 19). Cavell is certainly correct in drawing out *Walden*'s biblical parallels, but at the same time he does not pay due service to Thoreau's immediate identification with the Greek tradition and the frequent citations to those ancient heroes. (Another allusion—in a rather minor essay—to Thoreau as prophet is offered by Groff [1961].)

20. Walter Harding may have expressed the matter most succinctly: "Nowhere in the past or present could Thoreau find his ideal man. He could only hope that such a man would develop in the future. He concentrated therefore upon developing such a man. And consistent with his philosophy, he began with himself" (1959, p. 155). Joseph Wood Krutch draws a similar conclusion: "Thoreau's principal achievement was not the creation of system but the creation of himself, and his principal literary work was, therefore, the presentation of that self in the form of a self-portrait to which even those descriptions and expositions which seem most objective are in fact contributions" (1948, p. 11). The parallel with Nietzsche—in the guise of Zarathustra—is striking, but this theme, of course, is a dominant one in Romanticism more generally (see, e.g., Garber 1982; Porte 1991; Taylor 1989) and thus hardly unique to Thoreau. Indeed, one might easily argue that Thoreau identifies as a Romantic in large measure as he seeks his self-actualization, or as Joel Porte put it: "His great theme, of course, was renewal, the Romantic myth of infinite self-possibility and self extension" (1991, p. 164). Taylor notes that the "expressive" turn of Romanticism may be characterized as the newly discovered ability, and imperative, to explore and express the inexhaustible inner domain of the self: "To the extent that digging to the roots of our being takes us beyond ourselves, it is to the larger nature from which we emerge. But this we only gain access to through its voice in us. This nature, unlike Augustine's God, cannot offer us a higher view on ourselves beyond our own self-exploration" (1989, p. 390). And thus the individual must explore himself and nature with creative imagination to uncover the radical subjectivism and the internalization of moral sources. The virtuous life is then one of self-seeking, self-responsibility, in an ever-demanding quest for some moral ideal.

21. To make Thoreau's political posture attractive, Len Gougeon makes the salient point that what Thoreau "ultimately discovered in his dealings with soci-

ety is that the reform of individuals, through the development of virtuous self-culture, can only occur in an environment where personal freedom is guaranteed. Political, spiritual, and physical oppression, especially in the form of the institution of slavery, must be actively opposed" (1995, p. 196). As discussed at the end of this chapter, I regard this rationalization of Thoreau's political posture as generous and forgiving.

22. Thoreau was obviously outraged by this episode. "I have lived for the last month . . . with the sense of having suffered a vast and indefinite loss. I did not know at first what ailed me. At last it occurred to me that what I had lost was a country" (Thoreau, "Slavery in Massachusetts," 1973c, p. 106). The trial of Anthony Burns and the linked proceedings against those who attempted to forcibly free him from jail are detailed by von Frank (1998), who situates this episode within the broader political and intellectual contexts of the period. In particular, like Len Gougeon before him (1990), von Frank cites the Transcendentalists, Emerson in particular, as lending moral leadership to the abolitionist movement: "In the thought of the Transcendentalists . . . the concept of a law higher than any that space and time could show had been extensively explored, not as a tool for blocking the compromise of 1850, but in the broadest sense of freeing slaves or (what is the same thing) producing a free point of view. There is an implication in this that no point of view can be truly free that is also predominantly instrumental" (von Frank 1998, p. 282).

23. Thoreau can hardly be regarded as subscribing "to what have become the defining elements of the standard account of civil disobedience in contemporary political theory—elements designed to distinguish it from revolution—non-violence, the limited nature and purpose of actions in violation of the law, and voluntary acceptance of punishment" (Rosenblum 1996, p. xxiv). To engage in civil disobedience, to the contrary, was to exercise conscientious action; democratic authority was thus regarded as only conditional (ibid., p. xxvi).

7. THE SELF-POSITING I

1. This conception of "moral" follows from Nietzsche's notion of "beyond good and evil," where, in the aftermath of God's death, man is responsible for establishing his moral code, as opposed to the universal dictates of religions, most particularly Christianity. From Nietzsche's perspective, such revealed precepts are inadequate, or worse, in serving as an ethics, and are discarded as human constructions. "Morality" consequently becomes more than defining the good-evil axis, and now encompasses the entire project of constructing a moral code. To go beyond good and evil is to go to the foundations of what it means to be a moral agent, and thus the architecture of *how* we value becomes the philosophical problem. Nietzsche discarded a Kantian categorical imperative and Millian utilitarianism, and grounded his morality in the self-aggrandizing Will. (This biological metaphor celebrating the individuality of the striving organism was discussed in chapter 1 and is discussed further in n. 16 below.) In many respects, Nietzsche articulated Thoreau's own vision of morality, inasmuch as they both concur that

the formulation of morals is an individual responsibility and envelops the entire universe of an individual's experience. Thus, for example, the aestheticization of experience is a moral mandate in their scheme, for to search for the beautiful is a moral act, one imbued with value as determined by a free-willing individual. (See Young 1992.)

2. Thoreau goes on to write:

> When facts are seen superficially they are seen as they lie in relation to certain institution's perchance. But I would have them expressed as more deeply seen with deeper references.– so that the hearer or reader cannot recognize them or apprehend their significance from the platform of common life–but it will be necessary that he be in a sense translated in order to understand them. (November 1, 1851, *Journal* 4, 1992, p. 158)

3. It is useful to compare this prayer with one written eight months later, March 15, 1852 (*Journal* 4, 1992, p. 390), and quoted in the Introduction, pp. 11–12.

4. The mind for Kant consisted of distinctive cognitive functions that required synthesis: sensibility (sensations received in space/time), understanding (faculty of conceptualizing and synthesizing data into knowledge of objects), and reason (faculty of synthesizing knowledge of objects into systems, like laws of science), which was in turn divided into "theoretical" and "practical" domains. Theoretical reason was based on the transcendental categories which permitted the "translation" of the noumenal world (the unknowable Real) into the "phenomenal"— the world of human perception and "knowledge." This so-called "Copernican revolution" in philosophy, as Henry Allison succinctly describes it, "involves reversing the usual way of viewing cognition and instead of thinking of our knowledge as conforming to a realm of objects, we think of objects as conforming to our ways of knowing. The latter include 'forms of sensibility,' through which objects are given to the mind in sensory experience, and pure concepts or categories, through which they are thought. Since objects must appear to us in accordance with these sensible forms in order to be known, it follows that we can know them only as they appear, not as they may be in themselves" (1995, p. 436). Thus the world of experience was structured by the categories of understanding, which in and of themselves were insufficient to capture nature in terms of simple empirical laws that could then be combined into a system of natural science. Theoretical reason was responsible for such systematic knowledge. Morality required a different form of reason, "practical reason," which distinguished man's action in the world and allowed the work of culture to proceed.

5. Kant's *Third Critique* (*The Critique of Judgment* [1790]) was to show that it is legitimate to think of the natural realm both as universally governed by the principle of natural causality and as embodying the effects of a rational, nonmechanistic causality. The operation of teleology in the biological world was to serve as an example of this unity, a reflective judgment that must supply a transcendental principle by which we might understand the functioning of the organic. This transcendental faculty could not be derived from theoretical understanding nor from pure practical reason, but had its own standing, and thereby permitted human comprehension of function not explained by other forms of reason (McFarland 1970).

6. Spinozan determinism was recast in terms of Critical Philosophy by F. H. Jacobi (in *Letters on the Doctrine of Spinoza* [1785]), who maintained that human freedom was incompatible with the view of reality that reason seems to require us to accept. Specifically, he argued that according to "sufficent reason," "every existing state of affairs Y is grounded in some other set of conditions X such that the presence of X is sufficient to necessitate the existence of Y. . . . [Therefore] how is it possible to conceive of the human being as capable of free action, if his deeds are all necessary consequences of prior conditions external to himself?" (Neuhouser 1990, p. 4).

7. Given the complexity of drawing the configurations of Thoreau's experience as he reported it, Peck has correctly sought a broad designation for Thoreau's attempts to mark the boundaries of his structured perceptions; this he calls Thoreau's "categorical imagination" (1990, p. 81), and from here he draws the contours of "phenomenon." The critic is primarily interested in unraveling the structuring of Thoreau's experience in his writing, and to the extent that Thoreau is assessed by his literary product, Peck's analysis is cogent and highly useful. But I believe that we must probe between Thoreau's words and the lines of his writings to the source of his experience, where we finally come to a metaphysics of the self.

8. See n. 6 to Introduction.

9. This passage did not appear until the post-Romantic "D" version of *Walden* was written (Adams and Ross 1988, p. 182), and we see it virtually intact in the Journal (August 8, 1852, *Journal* 5, 1997, p. 290).

10. The paragraph ends with, "This doubleness may easily make us poor neighbors and friends sometimes." I think it no accident that Thoreau begins with asserting his "sanity" and ends with the admission that he is difficult, ascribing his misanthropy to this double character. A complex personality, Thoreau was acutely aware of his solitude, and while I eschew a psychological analysis, it is difficult to ignore the psychic manifestations of his philosophical introspection. See various commentators (e.g., Harding 1965; Lebrieux 1977, 1984; Bridgman 1982; Richardson 1986) for wide-ranging discussions and opposing opinion, and Taylor 1996 for a fair and measured appraisal in the context of Thoreau's political philosophy.

11. For instance, Thoreau read Coleridge's *Biographia Literaria* (1817), where Coleridge was both drawn to and ultimately dissuaded from Fichte's philosophy. The rejection, based on substituting the Logos as a divine attribute for the unifying principle (Coleridge 1983, pp. 157–60; Perkins 1994, pp. 165, 248–50), is of less interest than Coleridge's embrace of Fichte's principal tenet about personhood in action. Coleridge believed Fichte had achieved a significant step beyond Kant: "by commencing with an *act*, instead of a *thing* or substance, Fichte assuredly gave the first blow to Spinozism" (Coleridge 1983, p. 158). Coleridge goes on, however, to reject Fichte's "other" as simply a "not-I" as opposed to a divinely imbued nature. But Coleridge looked more favorably on a later Fichte, who, in *The Vocation of Man*, had described the act of faith by which the individual determines himself, his consciousness; this determination

of consciousness by conscience was characteristic of Coleridge's own conception of "person" (Perkins 1994, p. 248). Thoreau was exposed to Fichte through other secondary sources (Sattelmeyer 1988, p. 46), and he may even have read the original in Emerson's library, but the direct connection is not at issue.

12. Because of the fundamental unity of his conception of the self, both theoretical and practical reason must be contained therein, and upon this construction Fichte attempted to reconcile the Kantian challenge of synthesizing the various forms of reason under one unitary scheme. The unity of the self, what Fichte called the "immediate unity" of both intellectual and empirical intuitions, constitutes a single conscious state composed of two basic modes of awareness: When seeing an object, there is, at one level, a perception or appreciation of the object, as well as an implicit (which may become explicit) self-awareness that "I know that I am seeing X." Self-consciousness is fundamentally different from the consciousness of objects. This early phenomenological formulation makes self-constitution an underlying foundation of knowing, so that, as Fichte claimed, the subject is at all times present to itself within consciousness, implicitly if not explicitly (Neuhouser 1990, p. 69). Thus Fichte's early philosophy places practical reason as a precondition for theoretical reason, but that need not concern us here, except to note the continuity of Fichte's project with Kant's.

13. Perhaps better stated in the First Introduction of the *Wissenschaftslehre* of 1797/98:

The representation of the self-sufficiency of the I can certainly co-exist with a representation of the self-sufficiency of the thing, though the self-sufficiency of the I cannot co-exist with that of the thing. Only one of these two can come first; only one can be the starting point; only one can be independent. The one that comes second, just because it comes second, necessarily becomes dependent upon the one that comes first, with which it is supposed to be connected. Which of these should come first? (Fichte [1797/98] 1994, pp. 17–18)

Fichte adopts a radical idealism, whose "philosophy shows that there is no other type of reality at all" (p. 34).

14. We readily see the notion of the striving self, central to the philosophies of Emerson, Thoreau, and Nietzsche, in this Romantic mulch: Fichte's "absolute I with which the system seems to begin turns out to be only a practical ideal of total self-determination, an ideal toward which the finite I continuously strives but can never achieve" (Breazeale 1998, p. 642).

15. Fichte preceded Hegel's dialecticism: "To be aware of itself the I must limit itself . . . and this it can do only by positing something other than itself, a non-I. (Antithesis.) The I is now involved in another contradiction: it both posits and negates itself. This can be resolved only by a synthesis: the I posits a divisible I, limited by, and limiting, a divisible non-I; that is, the non-I, in part negates the I, and the I, in part negates the non-I" (Inwood 1995, p. 278).

16. Nineteenth-century biology discovered its own expression of dialecticism in the form of "adaptation," the cardinal feature of Darwin's theory of evolution. The ability of organisms, and species writ large, to adapt determined their

survival in the short term, and evolutionary stability in the long run. Thus after Darwin, species were appreciated not as static entities but as subject to change as a result of the vicissitudes of time and happenstance. The scientific agenda directed itself to explain how each life form responded to endless competition and collective adaptation. Here we see the ipseity-alterity scheme presented in its natural setting. Biologists pursued these issues with a very different understanding of the organism from that assumed in the pre-Darwinian era. By postulating an ever-changing biosphere, the organism was constantly challenged by its environment, engaged in a dialectical process where, on the one hand, the environment was modified to the extent the organism might effect utilitarian use from it, and on the other hand, the organism/species was also subject to change through adaptation and ultimately species evolution. In this setting, a new element of relational cause and effect was introduced. Moreover, Darwinism became a scientific expression of indeterminacy, extending from the problem of defining a species (a question still unresolved) to the individual organism. Indeed, species may be regarded as an "individual" (Ghiselin 1997), and the particular organism then becomes only a constituent of the collective whole. The same kind of analysis may be applied to the organism itself, which is composed of symbiotic and parasitic elements. So, beyond the role assigned to the organism as a unit of selection (a major problem in its own right), what is the relation of the individual to the collective? Moreover, how is the individual organism in this evolutionary context to be defined in its own individual life history? The developmental process was reexamined as a *process* of emergence. No longer viewed as a static entity, the process character of the organism was recognized as its dominant defining element. The organism's boundaries and mechanisms of self-actualization represented definitional problems analogous to that posed for the species at large. *What* was the organism that must always adapt and change? In the twentieth century the question was modified, but hardly resolved: To what degree did genetics program the life history of the individual? What was the adaptive capacity of the organism? In what sense could biological "potentiality" be understood? How did the organism protect itself in its environs? Thus the core issue of organismal identity for the first time became a problem (see Tauber and Chernyak 1991) and continues to be (Tauber 1994, 1999b).

17. Kierkegaard offered a "reflexive" definition of the self, which broadens James's self-conscious examination of consciousness as the very definition of the self attempting to "find" itself:

> The self is a relation which relates itself to its own self, or it is that in the relation which relates itself to its own self, or it is that in the relation [which accounts for it] that the relation relates itself to its own self. . . . Man is a synthesis of the infinite and the finite. . . . A synthesis is a relation between two factors. So regarded, man is not yet a self. . . . Such a relation which relates itself to its own self (that is to say, a self) must either have constituted itself or have been constituted by another. If this relation which relates itself to its own self is constituted by another, the relation doubtless is the third term, but this relation (the third term) is in turn a relation relating itself to that which constituted the whole relation. Such a derived, constituted, relation is the human self,

a relation which relates itself to its own self, and in relating itself to its own self relates itself to another. (Kierkegaard [1849] 1955, p. 146)

18. Fichte, Hegel, and Kierkegaard laid the foundation for later phenomeno-logical philosophical responses to the problem of personal identity by making alterity the descriptive focus of selfhood. The self, to the extent that it can be actualized, is, from this general perspective, defined by the other (e.g., Taylor 1987). Discussion has focused on whether, and how, in response to an encounter, the self articulates itself or is altered as a consequence of that engagement. Also considered is how the engaged self might alter its object and their shared world. In short, the phenomenological approach explores how the self lives in its world, essentially in a universe of others. The self alone either is alienated, that is, alien-ated in its selfness, or it actively engages the world and thereby becomes actu-alized. The debate revolves about the contingency of this process and its prob-lematic opportunities for success. But by and large the parties agree that the potential for self-aggrandizement must be realized *in* the world, and the self must ultimately actualize itself in the encounter with the other (Tauber 1994). But even the contingency of the self's construction has been attacked in more recent post-structuralist arguments. Structuralism understands meaning to be a function of the relations among the components of any cultural formation or our very consciousness. For instance, the pictures of our mind's world assume their meaning, value, and significance from their relationships, that is, their "place" in a structure. But the deconstructionists broadly argued that any struc-ture crumbles when we recognize that no part can assume participation outside its relation to other parts. In other words, there is no center, no organizing prin-ciple privileged over structure and thus able to dominate its structural domain. From this perspective, there is nothing "natural" about cultural structures (e.g., language, kinship systems, social and economic hierarchies, sexual norms, reli-gious beliefs), no transcendental significance to limit "meanings," and only power explains the hegemony of one view over another. Similarly, "the self" may be regarded as constructed by arbitrary criteria, and thus occupies no nat-ural habitat. In this scenario, the phenomenological insistence on the self's dependence on the other has been radically challenged: not only has the self's autonomy been rendered meaningless, *any* construction of the self is regarded as arbitrary.

19. See n. 18 above.

20. From a Wittgensteinian perspective, the self is a metaphysical category and thus inaccessible to philosophical discussion. The question as to the nature of the self is, according to the "early" Wittgenstein, a false question, i.e., it is not a question at all and therefore any "answer" is meaningless. So, not surprisingly, Wittgenstein had precious little explicitly to say about "the self." In his early notebooks, written in World War I trenches and military prison camps, he sighs about the self as "deeply mysterious" (1961, p. 80e). Consequently, Wittgen-stein's position has been actively debated. A distillation yields two primary con-cepts: Wittgenstein's views are severely solipsistic. In a fundamental sense, only the self exists; the world exists for the self; thus is "knowledge" coordinated.

And therefore it is nonsense even to attempt to define such a self, since there is no external Archimedean point by which a knowing entity might survey or characterize itself otherwise than in the totality of its experience: we cannot see ourselves from outside, and thus possess no coordinates for any discussion of these matters. James's influence here is obvious, and clearly Wittgenstein read James carefully and with respect. Wittgenstein's profoundly disturbing philosophical critique issued forth from what in the 1890s seemed to represent a sophisticated psychological description. Selfhood is a metaphysical construct that has been rendered meaningless and that cannot be analyzed or concretized in any fashion. To try to do so is to speak nonsense. We obviously do refer to "the self," but this is an expression in our language game, a particular social convenience that allows us to communicate, but it has no logical or scientific basis. As Henri Atlan writes, "Of this 'I' itself one can say nothing. It can only be manifested, and that in silence. Any discourse about this *subject* (about the subject of the subject) is merely speaking to say nothing: words that do not *mean* to say anything, that are there *in order* to say nothing, an isolated abracadabra without context. Just like someone outside a closed door who, to the question, 'Who's there?,' responds, 'It's me'; but we do not recognize his voice, and before we can open up he vanishes without a trace" (Atlan 1993, p. 401).

But in his later philosophy Wittgenstein offered a possible vehicle for at least understanding the appeal that such a construct might hold for us. The self, Wittgenstein presumably would have argued, if pressed, only "exists" as part of a "language game," a convention within which it possesses some explanatory value. But to define that value is a seemingly hopeless task and, more importantly, a vacuous hope. Neither logic nor science can establish a basis for defining the self, and any attempt to do so sinks into the ambiguities of other metaphysical constructs like "mind." We might want to discuss consciousness, but we can only examine neurological function, measure brain electrical activity, trace nerve networks, assess biochemical transmitters. We *are*, and that is that.

If the self only "exists" as part of a "language game," a convention from which it possesses some explanatory meaning, to define that meaning is a vain aspiration. Within this postanalytic context, the self is no longer decentered, it is dissolved. The very question of selfhood is rendered meaningless altogether. This is the extreme radicalism of a postphilosophical analysis: Beyond the self as a relational construction (phenomenologists) or a decentered subject defined by arbitrary cultural constructions (deconstructionists), the self as an *entity* simply does not *exist*. If Wittgenstein's position is taken seriously, the *philosophical* basis of an ethics evidently also dissolves. *Who* is the moral agent and how is he or she defined? How can we ask about responsibility if we cannot even define the moral agent? Wittgenstein's fascinating, nihilistic response: Ethics is known, morality is enacted, but to require a philosophical answer as to how and why is to give false answers and to invoke deceptive rationalities, distorted by prejudice supposedly buttressed by logical argument. Ethics derives from beyond rationality; its ground is metaphysical. And, said Wittgenstein, metaphysics cannot be analyzed.

21. As Jonathan Dollimore cogently observes, "what we might now call neurosis, anxiety and alienation with the subject in crisis are not so much the consequence of its recent breakdown as the very stuff of its creation, and of the culture—Western European culture—which it sustains" (1997, p. 254).

22. Theoreau's self-portrait drew upon the same dynamic operative so clearly in Wordsworth and Rousseau, which saw the psyche "in terms of the interplay between a hidden structure that was the source of human energy and imagination and a visible one that revealed only derivative powers of intellectual invention" (Hutton 1993, p. 62).

23. Buell's reading of Thoreau's environmentalism has been roundly attacked, for instance by Bob Taylor (see n. 5 to Introduction) and Leo Marx (1999). This debate over Thoreau's place in the development of American environmentalism is extended by the various essays assembled by Schneider (2000), a collection containing rich resource material and measured discussion, which came to my attention only after my own manuscript was completed.

EPILOGUE: MENDING THE WORLD

1. Much vexed, Thoreau confided to his Journal:

Fatal is the discovery that our friend is fallible–that he has prejudices. He is then only prejudiced in our favor. What is the value of his esteem who does not justly esteem another?

Alas! Alas! When my friend begins to deal in confessions–breaks silence–makes a theme of friendship–(which then is always something past) and descends to merely ' human relations . . .

I thought that friendship–that love was still possible between–I thought that we had not withdrawn very far asunder– But now that my friend rashly thoughtlessly-prophanely speaks *recognizing* the distance between us–that distance seems infinitely increased. (February 15, 1851, *Journal* 3, 1990, p. 193)

Later in the year, Thoreau continues to lament:

Ah I yearn toward thee my friend, but I have not confidence in thee. We do not believe in the same God. I am not thou– Thou art not I. We trust each other today but we distrust tomorrow. Even when I meet thee unexpectedly I part from thee with disappointment. Though I enjoy thee more than other men yet I am more disappointed with thee than with others. I know a noble man what is it hinders me from knowing him better? I know not how it is that our distrust our hate is stronger than our love. Here I have been on what the world would call friendly terms with one 14 years, have pleased my imagination sometimes with loving him–and yet our hate is stronger than our love. Why are we related–yet thus unsatisfactorily. We almost are a sore to one another.

. . . We do not know what hinders us from coming together. (October 10, 1851, *Journal* 4, 1992, p. 137; see also the Journal entry for January 22, 1852, *Journal* 4, 1992, pp. 276–77)

Indeed, he did not, at least not consciously.

2. "There is some advantage in being the humblest cheapest least dignified man in the village–so that the very stable boys shall damn-you. Methinks I enjoy the advantage to a unusual extent. There is a many a coarsely well meaning fel-

low, who knows only the skin of me who addresses me familiarly by my christian name—I get the whole good of him & lose nothing myself. . . . I am not above being used, aye abused, sometimes" (July 6, 1851, *Journal* 3, 1990, p. 287).

3. See n. 2 above.

4. The testimony of a fellow townsman, James Hosmer, is illustrative: "He stood in the doorway with hair which looked as if it had been dressed with a pine-cone, inattentive grey eyes, hazy with far-away musings, an empathetic nose and disheveled attire that bore signs of tramps in woods and swamps" (quoted by Harding 1965, p. 255).

5. In the domain of the everlasting spirit, Thoreau is only the product of his Maker: "*I* did not *make* this demand for a more thorough sympathy. This is not my idiosyncrasy or disease. He that made the demand will answer the demand" (*Journal* 3, 1990, pp. 313–14).

6. This post-Kantian theme was developed by later American philosophers, most prominently William James, who reduced the various philosophical systems to "just so many visions, modes of feeling the whole push, and seeing the whole drift of life, forced on one by one's total character and experience, and on the whole preferred—there is no other truthful word—as one's best working attitude" (James [1909] 1987, p. 639). Russell Goodman, in observing how James regarded the relationship of the intellect and feeling, also summarizes Thoreau's own project:

> James makes four different claims about the feeling intellect that he discerns: 1) the *phenomenological* claim that thoughts are inseparable from feelings, 2) the *causal* claim that feelings produce or determine our thoughts and beliefs, 3) the *epistemological* claim (so common in Romanticism) that we know the world as much through feeling as through thought or sensation, and 4) the *metaphysical* or *existential* claim that in certain circumstances our feelings produce not our thoughts but the objects that our thoughts or feelings posit, anticipate, or acknowledge. (1990, p. 70)

7. From another perspective altogether, Wittgenstein, in his later philosophy, focused upon the question of *praxis*, which in the form of "language games" and "forms of life" directed philosophical attention on how we know and act in the world as lived experience as opposed to the private (and inaccessible) domain of the mind. Thus language and other overt behavior became suitable subjects for analysis. Tying together Wittgenstein, Heidegger, and most directly the later pragmatists, especially John Dewey, the human knower, as removed from the objects and processes she observes, is set aside and replaced by another epistemological model: Instead of some private mental domain as the core of personal identity, hidden in an "internal" realm of the *sensorium* (à la Locke) and thus separated from the "external" world, the knower is constituted in interaction with that world. This represents a major shift in philosophy, as questions about language and thought, meaning and reason, are shifted from the private domain to the public arena of *praxis*—i.e., practical operations and overt procedures (Toulmin 1984, p. xix).

8. The phenomenologists formally attempted to address whether, and how, we might encounter nature as "uncaged experience," that is, before we for-

mally organize it (Harvey 1989). By "bracketing," Husserl ([1913] 1982) proposed that we might strip experience of its social, symbolical, and historical meanings, to achieve an unfashioned "rawness," a project Merleau-Ponty continued in the attempt to return to that world which precedes knowledge (Merleau-Ponty 1962).

9. "Unremittingly, skepticism insists on the validity of the factually experienced world, that of actual experience, and finds in it nothing of reason or its ideas. Reason itself and its [object], 'that which is,' become more and more enigmatic. . . . [W]e find ourselves in the greatest danger of drowning in the skeptical deluge and thereby losing our hold on our own truth" (Husserl [1935] 1970, pp. 13–14).

10. Edmund Husserl saw scientific rationality as usurping the wider project of philosophical Reason, assuming in its practical victories the place of a more comprehensive theoretical Reason. Herbert Marcuse offers a succinct description of Husserl's criticism:

> The new science does not elucidate the conditions and the limits of its evidence, validity, and method; it does not elucidate its inherent historical denominator. It remains unaware of its own foundation, and it is therefore unable to recognize its servitude. . . . What happens in the developing relation between science and the empirical reality is the abrogation of the transcendence of Reason. Reason loses its philosophical power and its scientific right to define and project ideas and modes of Being beyond and against those established by the prevailing reality. I say: "beyond" the empirical reality, not in any metaphysical but in a historical sense, namely, in the sense of projecting essentially different, historical alternatives. (Marcuse 1985, p. 23)

11. The most comprehensive account of Nietzsche's view on science may be found in the collected essays edited by Babette Babich and Robert Cohen (1999). A succinct summary is best offered by Nietzsche himself: "[P]recisely the most superficial and external existence . . . would be grasped first, and might even be the only thing that allowed itself to be grasped. A 'scientific' interpretation of the world . . . might therefore be one of the *most stupid* of all interpretations of the world, meaning that it would be one of the poorest in meaning" (Nietzsche [1882] 1974, p. 335; emphasis in original).

12. What began as Descartes's Dream, a philosophy that seeks to encompass in the unity of a theoretical system all meaningful questions in a rigorous scientific manner, has left science as "a residual concept" (Husserl [1935] 1970, p. 9). By this, Husserl notes that "metaphysical" or "philosophical" problems that should still be broadly linked to science under the rubric of rational inquiry are separated over the criterion of "fact." In a powerful sense, "positivism . . . decapitates philosophy" (ibid.) by legitimating one form of knowledge at the expense of another. For Husserl, the crisis was not limited to "science" or "philosophy" but reflected a fundamental challenge to European cultural life—indeed, to its total *Existenz*—and betokened the very collapse of a universal philosophy. He thus renewed the Romantic attempts by Wordsworth ([1800] 1965), Shelley ([1821] 1977), and their compatriots to unify poetry and science.

References

Abbey, E. 1968. *Desert Solitaire: A Season in the Wilderness.* New York: Ballantine.

Adams, H. 1920. *A Cycle of Adams Letters, 1861–1865.* Edited by W. C. Ford. 2 vols. Boston: Houghton Mifflin.

Adams, S., and D. Ross. 1988. *Revising Mythologies: The Composition of Thoreau's Major Works.* Charlottesville: University Press of Virginia.

Agamben, G. 1993. *Infancy and History: Essays on the Destruction of Experience.* Translated by L. Heron. London: Verso.

Allison, H. E. 1995. "Kant, Immanuel." In *The Oxford Companion to Philosophy,* pp. 435–38. Oxford and New York: Oxford University Press.

Amrine, F., F. J. Zucker, and H. Wheeler, eds. 1987. *Goethe and the Sciences: A Reappraisal.* Dordrecht: D. Reidel.

Anderson, C. 1968. *The Magic Circle of Walden.* New York: Holt, Rinehart and Winston.

Anderson, L. W. 1973. *Hannah Duston: Heroine of 1697 Massacre of Indian Captors on River Islet at Boscawen, N.H.* Concord: Evans Printing Co.

Angelo, R. 1983. "Thoreau as Botanist." *Thoreau Quarterly* 15:15–31.

Arner, R. D. 1973. "The Story of Hannah Duston: Cotton Mather to Thoreau." *American Transcendental Quarterly* 18:19–22.

Atlan, H. [1986] 1993. *Enlightenment to Enlightenment: Intercritique of Science and Myth.* Translated by L. J. Schramm. Albany: State University of New York Press.

Atwood, G. E., and R. D. Stolorow. 1993. *Faces in a Cloud: Subjectivity in Personality Theory.* 2d ed. Northvale, N.Y.: Jason Aronson.

Ayer, A. J., ed. 1959. *Logical Positivism.* Glencoe, Ill.: The Free Press.

Babich, B., and R. S. Cohen, eds. 1999. *Nietzsche, Epistemology, and Philosophy of Science.* Vol. 2 of *Nietzsche and the Sciences.* Dordrecht: Kluwer Academic Publishers.

Bachelard, G. [1934] 1984. *The New Scientific Spirit*. Translated by A. Gold-hammer. Boston: Beacon Press.

———. [1958] 1969. *The Poetics of Space*. Translated by M. Jolas. Boston: Beacon Press.

Barthes, R. [1957] 1972. *Mythologies*. Translated by A. Lavers. New York: Hill and Wang.

———. [1980] 1981. *Camera Lucida: Reflections on Photography*. Translated by R. Howard. New York: Hill and Wang.

Baym, N. 1965. "Thoreau's View of Science." *Journal of the History of Ideas* 26:221–34.

———. 1966. "From Metaphysics to Metaphor: The Image of Water in Emerson and Thoreau." *Studies in Romanticism* 5:231–243.

Bergland, B. 1994. "Postmodernism and the Autobiographical Subject: Reconstructing the 'Other'." In *Autobiography and Postmodernism*, edited by K. Ashley, L. Gilmore, and G. Peters, pp. 130–66. Amherst: University of Massachusetts Press.

Berlin, I. 1977. *The Hedgehog and the Fox: An Essay in Tolstoy's View of History*. New York: Simon and Schuster.

———. 1992. *The Crooked Timber of Humanity: Chapters in the History of Ideas*. Edited by Henry Hardy. New York: Vintage.

———. 1999. *The Roots of Romanticism*. Princeton: Princeton University Press.

Bernasconi, R., R. Critchley, and S. Critchley, eds. 1991. *Re-reading Levinas*. Bloomington: Indiana University Press.

Berry, W. 1983. "Poetry and Place." In *Standing by Words*. San Francisco: North Point.

———. 1987. *Home Economics*. San Francisco: North Point.

Bloom, H. 1971. "The Internalization of Quest Romance." In *The Ringers in the Tower: Studies in Romantic Tradition*, pp. 13–35. Chicago: University of Chicago Press.

———. 1973. *The Anxiety of Influence: A Theory of Poetry*. New York: Oxford University Press.

Bortoft, H. 1996. *The Wholeness of Nature: Goethe's Way toward a Science of Conscious Participation in Nature*. Hudson, N.Y.: Lindisfarne Press.

Bramwell, A. 1989. *Ecology in the Twentieth Century: A History*. New Haven: Yale University Press.

Breazeale, D. 1998. "Fichte, Johann Gottlieb." In *Routledge Encyclopedia of Philosophy*, edited by E. Craig, 3:642–53. London and New York: Routledge.

Bridgman, R. 1982. *Dark Thoreau*. Lincoln and London: University of Nebraska Press.

Bruce, R. V. 1987. *The Launching of Modern American Science, 1846–1876*. Ithaca: Cornell University Press.

Buell, L. 1973. *Literary Transcendentalism*. Ithaca: Cornell University Press.

———. 1986. *New England Literary Culture: From Revolution through Renaissance*. Cambridge: Cambridge University Press.

———. 1995. *The Environmental Imagination: Thoreau, Nature Writing, and the Formation of American Culture*. Cambridge: Harvard University Press.

Burbick, J. 1987. *Thoreau's Alternative History: Changing Perspectives on Nature, Culture, and Language*. Philadelphia: University of Pennsylvania Press.

Burkett, E. M., and J. S. Steward. 1989. *Thoreau on Writing*. Conway, Ark.: University of Central Arkansas Press.

Burroughs, J. 1904. "Henry D. Thoreau." In *Indoor Studies*, vol. 8 of *The Writings of John Burroughs*, pp. 3–47. Boston: Houghton Mifflin; Cambridge: Riverside Press.

———. 1922. *The Last Harvest*. Boston: Houghton Mifflin; Cambridge: Riverside Press.

Cafaro, P. 1997. "Thoreau's Vision of a Good Life in Nature." Ph.D. diss., Department of Philosophy, Boston University.

Cameron, S. 1985. *Writing Nature: Henry Thoreau's "Journal."* Oxford and New York: Oxford University Press.

Canby, H. S. [1939] 1958. *Thoreau*. Boston: Beacon Press.

Caputo, J. 1993. *Against Ethics*. Bloomington: Indiana University Press.

Cardinal, R. 1997. "Romantic Travel." In *Rewriting the Self: Histories from the Renaissance to the Present*, edited by R. Porter, pp. 135–55. London and New York: Routledge.

Caswell, H. 1974. "Predator-Mediated Coexistence: A Non-equilibrium Model." *American Naturalist* 112:127–54.

Cavell, S. 1981. *The Senses of Walden*, Chicago: University of Chicago Press.

Chadwick, H., ed. and trans. 1991. Notes in *Confessions*, by Augustine. Oxford and New York: Oxford University Press.

Channing, W. E. 1873. *Thoreau: Poet-Naturalist*. Boston: Roberts Brothers.

Chase, G. W. 1861. *The History of Haverhill, from Its First Settlement in 1640 to the Year 1860*. Haverhill: G. W. Chase.

Clapper, R. E. 1967. "The Development of *Walden:* A Genetic Text." Ph.D. diss., University of California, Los Angeles.

Clodd, E. 1888. *Story of Creation*. London: Longmans.

Cohen, R. A. 1986. *Face to Face with Levinas*. Albany: State University of New York Press.

Coleridge, S. T. [1848] 1970. *Hints towards the Formation of a More Comprehensive Theory of Life*. Edited by S. B. Watson. London: John Churchill. Reprint, Farnborough, England: Gregg International Publishers.

———. [1817] 1983. *Biographia Literaria*. Edited by J. Engell and W. J. Bate. Princeton: Princeton University Press.

Collingwood, R. G. 1940. *An Essay on Metaphysics*. Oxford: Clarendon Press.

Comte, A. [1825] 1974. "Philosophical Considerations on the Sciences and Savants." In *The Crisis of Industrial Civilization: The Early Essays of Auguste Comte*, pp. 182–213. New York: Crane, Russak and Co.

Conant, S. 1997. *Animal Appetite: A Dog Lover's Mystery*. New York: Doubleday.

Cosslett, T. 1982. The "Scientific Movement" and Victorian Literature. Sussex: Harvester Press; New York: St. Martin's Press.

Cunningham, A., and N. Jardine, eds. 1990. Romanticism and the Sciences. Cambridge: Cambridge University Press.

Dale, P. A. 1989. In Pursuit of a Scientific Culture: Science, Art, and Society in the Victorian Age. Madison: University of Wisconsin Press.

Darwin, C. [1859] 1964. On the Origin of Species by Means of Natural Selection; or, The Preservation of Favored Races in the Struggle for Life: A Facsimile Reprint of the First Edition. Cambridge: Harvard University Press.

Daston, L. 2000. "Wordless Objectivity." In Little Tools of Knowledge: Historical Essays on Academic and Bureaucratic Practices, edited by P. Becker and W. Clark. Ann Arbor: University of Michigan Press.

Daston, L., and P. Galison. 1992. "The Image of Objectivity." Representations 40:81–128.

Depew, D. J., and B. H. Weber. 1995. Darwinism Evolving: Systems Dynamics and the Genealogy of Natural Selection. Cambridge: MIT Press.

Dewey, J. [1929] 1984. The Quest for Certainty. Carbondale: Southern Illinois University Press.

Dirac, P. A. M. 1963. "The Evolution of the Physicist's Picture of Nature." Scientific American 208:45–53.

Dollimore, J. 1997. "Death and the Self." In Rewriting the Self: Histories from the Renaissance to the Present, edited by R. Porter, pp. 249–61. London and New York: Routledge.

Egerton, F. N., Jr., and L. D. Walls. 1997 "Rethinking Thoreau and the History of American Ecology." The Concord Saunterer, N.s. 5:5–20.

Eiseley, L. 1978. The Star Thrower. New York: Times Books.

Emerson, E. W. [1917] 1999. Henry Thoreau as Remembered by a Young Friend. Mineola, N.Y.: Dover Publications.

Emerson, R. W. 1904. "Memory." In Natural History of Intellect and Other Papers, vol. 12 of The Complete Works of Ralph Waldo Emerson, edited by E. W. Emerson. Boston and New York: Houghton Mifflin; Cambridge: Riverside Press.

———. 1963 The Journals and Miscellaneous Notebooks of Ralph Waldo Emerson. Vol. 3, 1826–1832, edited by W. H. Gilman and A. R. Ferguson. Cambridge: Harvard University Press.

———. 1969. The Journals and Miscellaneous Notebooks of Ralph Waldo Emerson. Vol. 7, 1838–1842, edited by A. W. Plumstead and H. Hayford. Cambridge: Harvard University Press.

———. 1970. The Journals and Miscellaneous Notebooks of Ralph Waldo Emerson. Vol. 8, 1841–1843, edited by W. H. Gilman and J. E. Parsons. Cambridge: Harvard University Press.

———. 1975. The Journals and Miscellaneous Notebooks of Ralph Waldo Emerson. Vol. 11, 1848–1851, edited by A. W. Plumstead, W. H. Gilman, and R. H. Bennett. Cambridge: Harvard University Press.

———. 1978. *The Journals and Miscellaneous Notebooks of Ralph Waldo Emerson*. Vol. 14, *1854–1861*, edited by S. S. Smith and H. Hayford. Cambridge: Harvard University Press.

———. 1982. *The Journals and Miscellaneous Notebooks of Ralph Waldo Emerson*. Vol. 15, *1860–1866*, edited by L. Allardt, D. W. Hill, and R. H. Bennett. Cambridge: Harvard University Press.

———. 1983a. *Nature*. In *Ralph Waldo Emerson, Essays and Lectures*, edited by J. Porte, pp. 5–49. New York: Library of America.

———. 1983b. "The American Scholar." In *Ralph Waldo Emerson, Essays and Lectures*, edited by J. Porte, pp. 51–71. New York: Library of America.

———. 1983c. "Self-Reliance." In *Ralph Waldo Emerson, Essays and Lectures*, edited by J. Porte, pp. 257–82. New York: Library of America.

———. 1983d. "Circles." In *Ralph Waldo Emerson, Essays and Lectures*, edited by J. Porte, pp. 403–13. New York: Library of America.

Evernden, N. 1993. *The Natural Alien: Humankind and Environment*. 2d ed. Toronto: University of Toronto Press.

———. 1992. *The Social Creation of Nature*. Baltimore: Johns Hopkins University Press.

Fay, B., P. Pomper, and R. T. Vann, eds. 1998. *History and Theory: Contemporary Readings*. Malden and Oxford: Blackwell Publishers.

Feyerabend, P. 1975. *Against Method*. London: Verso.

———. 1981a. *Realism, Rationalism, and Scientific Method*. Vol. 1 of *Philosophical Papers*. Cambridge: Cambridge University Press.

———. 1981b. *Problems of Empiricism*. Vol. 2 of *Philosophical Papers*. Cambridge: Cambridge University Press.

Fichte, J. G. [1792] 1988. "Review of *Aenesidemus*." In *Fichte, Early Philosophical Writings*, translated and edited by D. Breazeale, pp. 59–77. Ithaca: Cornell University Press.

———. [1797/98] 1994. "First Introduction" to *An Attempt at a New Presentation of the Wissenschaftslehre*, translated and edited by D. Breazeale, pp. 7–35. Indianapolis: Hackett Publishing Co.

Fisch, M. 1991. *William Whewell, Philosopher of Science*. Oxford: Clarendon Press.

———. 1998. "William Whewell." In *Routledge Encyclopedia of Philosophy*, edited by E. Craig, 9:709–11. London and New York: Routledge.

Foerster, N. 1923. *Nature in American Literature: Studies in the Modern View of Nature*. New York: Macmillan Co.

Foster, D. R. 1999. *Thoreau's Country: Journey through a Transformed Landscape*. Cambridge: Harvard University Press.

Fredriksen, P. L. 1986. "Paul and Augustine: Conversion Narratives, Orthodox Traditions, and the Retrospective Self." *Journal of Theological Studies* 37:3–34.

Friedlander, S., ed. 1992. *Probing the Limits of Representation: Nazism and the "Final Solution."* Cambridge: Harvard University Press.

Fritzell, P. 1990. *Nature Writing and America: Essays upon a Cultural Type.* Ames: State University of Iowa Press.

Fruton, J. S. 1999. *Proteins, Enzymes, Genes: The Interplay of Chemistry and Biology.* New Haven: Yale University Press.

Galaty, D. H. 1974. "The Philosophical Basis for Mid-nineteenth-Century German Reductionism." *Journal of the History of Medicine and Allied Sciences* 29:295–316.

Garber, F. 1977. *Thoreau's Redemptive Imagination.* New York: New York University Press.

———. 1991. *Thoreau's Fable of Inscribing.* Princeton: Princeton University Press.

Ghiselin, M. T. 1997. *Metaphysics and the Origin of Species.* Albany: State University Press of New York.

Giere, R. N., and A. W. Richardson, eds. 1996. *Origins of Logical Empiricism.* Minnesota Studies in the Philosophy of Science, vol. 16. Minneapolis: University of Minnesota Press.

Gifford, D. 1990. *The Farther Shore: A Natural History of Perception, 1798–1984.* New York: Atlantic Monthly Press.

Gilmore, L. 1994. "The Mark of Autobiography: Postmodernism, Autobiography, and Genre." In *Autobiography and Postmodernism,* edited by K. Ashley, L. Gilmore, and G. Peters, pp. 3–18. Amherst: University of Massachusetts Press.

Ginzburg, C. 1989. "Clues: Roots of an Evidential Paradigm." In *Clues, Myths and the Historical Method,* translated by J. Tedeschi and A. C. Tedeschi, pp. 96–125. Baltimore: Johns Hopkins University Press.

Glick, W., ed. 1969. *The Recognition of Henry David Thoreau: Selected Criticism since 1848.* Ann Arbor: University of Michigan Press.

Goethe, J. W. [1786–88] 1982. *Italian Journey (1786–1788).* Translated by W. H. Auden and E. Mayer. San Francisco: North Point Press.

———. [1790] 1989. "Metamorphosis of Plants." In *Goethe's Botanical Writings,* translated by B. Mueller, pp. 30–78. Woodbridge: Oxbow Press.

———. [1792] 1988. "The Experiment as Mediator between Object and Subject." In *Scientific Studies,* edited and translated by D. Miller, pp. 11–17. New York: Suhrkamp Publishers.

———. [1794] 1988. "Fortunate Encounter." In *Scientific Studies,* edited and translated by D. Miller, pp. 18–21. New York: Suhrkamp Publishers.

———. [1810] 1988. *A Theory of Colors.* In *Scientific Studies,* edited and translated by D. Miller, pp. 157–298. New York: Suhrkamp Publishers.

———. [1817] 1989. "History of the Printed Brochure." In *Goethe's Botanical Writings,* edited by B. Mueller, pp. 170–76. Woodbridge: Oxbow Press.

———. [1818] 1988. "Doubt and Resignation." In *Scientific Studies,* edited and translated by D. Miller, pp. 32–34. New York: Suhrkamp Publishers.

———. [1823] 1988. "Significant Help Given by an Ingenious Turn of Phrase." In *Scientific Studies,* edited and translated by D. Miller, pp. 39–41. New York: Suhrkamp Publishers.

Goodman, R. B. 1990. *American Philosophy and the Romantic Tradition*. Cambridge: Cambridge University Press.

Gougeon, L. 1990 *Virtue's Hero: Emerson, Antislavery, and Reform*. Athens: University of Georgia Press.

———. 1995. "Thoreau and Reform." In *The Cambridge Companion to Henry David Thoreau*, edited by J. Myerson, pp. 194–214. Cambridge: Cambridge University Press.

Groff, R. 1961. *Thoreau and the Prophetic Tradition*. Los Angeles: Manas Publishing Co.

Gross, P. R., N. Levitt, and M. W. Lewis, eds. 1996. *The Flight from Science and Reason*. New York: New York Academy of Sciences.

Hankins, T. L. 1985. *Science and the Enlightenment*. Cambridge: Cambridge University Press.

Hansen, O. 1990. *Aesthetic Individualism and Practical Intellect: American Allegory in Emerson, Thoreau, Adams, and James*. Princeton: Princeton University Press.

Hanson, N. R. 1958. *Patterns of Discovery*. Cambridge: Cambridge University Press.

Harding, W. 1959. *A Thoreau Handbook*. New York: New York University Press.

———. 1965. *The Days of Henry David Thoreau: A Biography*. New York: Alfred A. Knopf.

Hartshorne, C. 1982. "Science as the Search for the Hidden Beauty of the World." In *The Aesthetic Dimension of Science: 1980 Nobel Conference*, edited by D. W. Curtin, pp. 95–106. New York: Philosophical Library.

Harvey, C. W. 1989. *Husserl's Phenomenology and the Foundations of Natural Science*. Athens: Ohio University Press.

Heisenberg, W. 1979. "The Teachings of Goethe and Newton on Colour in the Light of Modem Physics." In *Philosophical Problems of Quantum Physics*, pp. 60–76. Woodbridge: Oxbow Press.

Hicks, P. M. 1925. *The Development of the Natural History Essay in American Literature*. Philadelphia: University of Pennsylvania Press.

Hildebidle, J. 1983. *Thoreau: A Naturalist's Liberty*. Cambridge: Harvard University Press.

Hollis, M., and S. Lukes, eds. 1982. *Rationality and Relativism*. Cambridge: MIT Press.

Holton, G. 1993. *Science and Anti-science*. Cambridge: Harvard University Press.

Hovey, A. B. 1966. *The Hidden Thoreau*. Beirut: n.p.

Howarth, W. 1982. *The Book of Concord: Thoreau's Life as a Writer*. New York: Viking Press.

Husserl, E. [1913] 1982. *Ideas Pertaining to a Pure Phenomenology and to a Phenomenological Philosophy: First Book*. Translated by F. Kersten. Dordrecht: Kluwer Academic Publishers.

———. [1935] 1970. *The Crisis of European Sciences and Transcendental Phenomenology*. Translated by D. Carr. Evanston: Northwestern University Press.

Hutton, P. H. 1993. *History as an Art of Memory*. Hanover and London: University Press of New England.

Huxley, T. H. 1869. "The Genealogy of Animals." In *Collected Essays*, vol. 2, *Darwiniana*. London: Macmillan, 1893–94.

———. 1886. "Science and Morals." In *Collected Essays*, vol. 9, *Evolution and Ethics*. London: Macmillan, 1893–94.

Inwood, M. J. 1995. "Fichte, Johann Gottlieb." In *The Oxford Companion to Philosophy*, pp. 277–79. Oxford and New York: Oxford University Press.

James, W. [1890] 1983. *The Principles of Psychology*. Cambridge: Harvard University Press.

———. [1904] 1987. "Does Consciousness Exist?" In *William James, Writings 1902–1910*, edited by B. Kuklick, pp. 1141–58. New York: Literary Classics of the United States.

———. [1909] 1987. *A Pluralistic Universe*. In *William James, Writings 1902–1910*, edited by B. Kuklick, pp. 625–819. New York: Literary Classics of the United States.

Jasanoff, S., G. E. Markle, J. C. Petersen, and T. Pinch. 1995. *Handbook of Science and Technology Studies*. Thousand Oaks, Calif.: Sage Publications.

Jay, P. 1994. "Posing: Autobiography and the Subject of Photography." In *Autobiography and Postmodernism*, edited by K. Ashley, L. Gilmore, and G. Peters, pp. 191–211. Amherst: University of Massachusetts Press.

Johnson, L. C. 1986. *Thoreau's Complex Weave: The Writing of "A Week on the Concord and Merrimack Rivers."* Charlottesville: University Press of Virginia.

Jonas, H. 1963. *The Gnostic Religion: The Message of the Alien God and the Beginnings of Christianity*. 2d ed. Boston: Beacon Press.

———. 1982. *The Phenomenon of Life: Toward a Philosophical Biology*. Chicago: University of Chicago Press.

Kant, I. [1788] 1993. *Critique of Practical Reason*. Translated by L. W. Beck. 3d ed. New York: Macmillan Publishing Co.

Kateb, G. 1995. *Emerson and Self-Reliance*. Thousand Oaks, Calif.: Sage Publications.

Keller, E. F. 1994. "The Paradox of Scientific Subjectivity." In *Rethinking Objectivity*, edited by A. Megill, pp. 313–31. Durham: Duke University Press. Also in *Science and the Quest for Reality*, edited by A. Tauber, pp. 182–200. New York: New York University Press; London: Macmillan, 1997.

Kierkegaard, S. [1843] 1985. *Fear and Trembling*. Translated by Alastair Hannay. New York: Penguin Books.

———. [1849] 1955. *The Sickness unto Death*. Translated by W. Lorrie. Garden City, N.Y.: Doubleday.

Kohàk, E. 1978. *Idea and Experience: Edmund Husserl's Project of Phenomenology in Ideas I*. Chicago: University of Chicago Press.

Kohlstedt, S. G. 1976. "The Nineteenth-Century Amateur Tradition: The Case of the Boston Society of Natural History." In *Science and Its Public: The*

Changing Relationship, edited by G. Holton and W. A. Blanpied, pp. 173–90. Dordrecht: D. Reidel.

Kohn, D. 1996. "The Aesthetic Construction of Darwin's Theory's." In *Aesthetics and Science: The Elusive Synthesis,* edited by A. I. Tauber, pp. 13–48. Dordrecht: Kluwer Academic Publishers.

Kolakowski, L. 1968. *The Alienation of Reason: A History of Positivist Thought.* Garden City, N.Y.: Doubleday.

Kopp, C. C. 1963. "The Mysticism of Henry David Thoreau." Ph.D. diss., Department of English, Pennsylvania State University. Ann Arbor: University Microfilms.

Kragh, H. 1987. *An Introduction to the Historiography of Science.* Cambridge: Cambridge University Press.

———. 1990. *Dirac: A Scientific Biography.* Cambridge: Cambridge University Press.

Krell, D. F. 1990. *Of Memory, Reminiscence, and Writing: On the Verge.* Bloomington and Indianapolis: Indiana University Press.

Krutch, J. W. 1948. *Henry David Thoreau.* New York: William Sloan Associates.

Kuhn, T. 1970. *The Structure of Scientific Revolutions.* 2d ed. Chicago: University of Chicago Press.

Latour, B. 1987. *Science in Action: How to Follow Scientists and Engineers through Society.* Cambridge: Cambridge University Press.

———. 1993. *We Have Never Been Modern.* Translated by C. Porter. Cambridge: Harvard University Press.

Lebeaux, R. 1977. *Young Man Thoreau.* Amherst: University of Massachusetts Press.

———. 1984. *Thoreau's Seasons.* Amherst: University of Massachusetts Press.

Lenoir, T. 1990. "Morphotypes and the Historical-Genetic Method in Romantic Biology." In *Romanticism and the Sciences,* edited by A. Cunningham and N. Jardine, pp. 119–29. Cambridge: Cambridge University Press.

Lepore, J. 1997. *The Name of the War: King Philip's War and the Origins of American Identity.* New York: Alfred A. Knopf.

Levere, T. H. 1981. *Poetry Realized in Nature: Samuel Taylor Coleridge and Early Nineteenth-Century Science.* Cambridge: Cambridge University Press.

Levinas, E. [1961] 1969. *Totality and Infinity.* Translated by A. Lingis. Pittsburgh: Duquesne University Press.

———. [1974] 1991. *Otherwise Than Being, or Beyond Essence.* Translated by A. Lingis. Dordrecht: Kluwer Academic Publishers.

Lowell, J. R. 1899. *Literary Essays.* Vol. 1. Cambridge: Harvard University Press.

Lyford, J. O., ed. 1903. *History of Concord, New Hampshire, from the Original Grant in Seventeen Hundred and Twenty-Five to the Opening of the Twentieth Century.* Concord, N. H.: Rumford Press.

Lyons, M. E. 1967. "Walden Pond as Symbol." *PMLA* 82:289–300.

MacIntyre, A. 1984. *After Virtue.* 2d ed. Notre Dame: Notre Dame University Press.

MacPherson, C. B. 1962. *The Political Theory of Possessive Individualism: Hobbes to Locke.* Oxford: Clarendon Press.

Marcuse, H. 1985. "On Science and Phenomenology." In *A Portrait of Twenty-Five Years: Boston Colloquium for the Philosophy of Science, 1960–1985,* pp. 19–30. Dordrecht: D. Reidel.

Marx, L. 1964. *The Machine in the Garden: Technology and the Pastoral Ideal in America.* New York and Oxford: Oxford University Press.

———. 1979. "Reflections on the Neo-romantic Critique of Science." In *Limits of Scientific Inquiry,* edited by G. Holton and R. S. Morison, pp. 61–74. New York: W. W. Norton.

———. 1999. "The Full Thoreau." *New York Review of Books* 46:44–48.

Mather, C. 1702. *Magnalia Christi Americana; or, The Ecclesiastical History of New-England, from Its First Planting in the Year 1620 unto the Year of Our Lord 1698, in Seven Books.* London: Thomas Parkhurst.

Matthiessen, F. 1941. *American Renaissance: Art and Expression in the Age of Emerson and Whitman.* Oxford: Oxford University Press.

McAllister, J. W. 1990. "Dirac and the Aesthetic Evaluation of Theories." *Methodology and Science* 23:87–102.

McClintock, J. N. 1889. *Colony, Province, State, 1623–1888: History of New Hampshire.* Boston: B. B. Russell.

McFarland, J. D. 1970. *Kant's Concept of Teleology.* Edinburgh: University of Edinburgh Press.

McFarland, T. 1969. *Coleridge and the Pantheist Tradition.* Oxford: Clarendon Press.

McGregor, R. H. 1997. *A Wider View of the Universe: Henry Thoreau's Study of Nature.* Urbana: University of Illinois Press.

McIntosh, J. 1974. *Thoreau as Romantic Naturalist: His Shifting Stance toward Nature.* Ithaca: Cornell University Press.

Megill, A. 1994. *Rethinking Objectivity.* Durham: Duke University Press.

Merleau-Ponty, M. [1945] 1962. *Phenomenology of Perception.* Translated by C. Smith. London: Routledge.

Metzger, B. M., and R. E. Murphy, eds. 1991. *The New Oxford Annotated Bible: New Revised Standard Version.* New York: Oxford University Press.

Milder, R. 1995. *Reimagining Thoreau.* Cambridge: Cambridge University Press.

Mirick, B. L. 1832. *The History of Haverhill, Massachusetts.* Haverhill: Thayer.

Morrissey, R. J. 1988. "Introduction: Jean Starobinski and Otherness." In *Jean-Jacques Rousseau: Transparency and Obstruction,* by J. Starobinski, translated by A. Goldhammer. Chicago: University of Chicago Press.

Moser, E. I. 1951. "Henry David Thoreau: The College Essays." M.A. thesis, New York University.

Nagel, T. 1986. *The View from Nowhere.* New York and Oxford: Oxford University Press.

Nash, R. 1967. *Wilderness and the American Mind.* New Haven: Yale University Press.

Nehamas, A. 1985. *Nietzsche: Life as Literature.* Cambridge: Harvard University Press.

Neuhouser, F. 1990. *Fichte's Theory of Subjectivity.* Cambridge: Cambridge University Press.

Nietzsche, F. [1874] 1980. *On the Advantage and Disadvantage of History for Life.* Indianapolis: Hackett Publishing Co.

———. [1882] 1974. *The Gay Science.* Translated by W. Kaufmann. New York: Random House.

———. [1886] 1966. *Beyond Good and Evil: Prelude to a Philosophy of the Future.* Translated by W. Kaufmann. New York: Random House.

———. [1904] 1967. *The Will to Power.* Translated by W. Kaufmann and R. J. Hollingdale. New York: Random House.

Nyhart, Lynn K. 1996. "Natural History and the 'New' Biology." In *Cultures of Natural History,* edited by N. Jardine, J. A. Secord, and E. C. Spary. Cambridge: Cambridge University Press.

Oehlschlaeger, F., and G. Hendrick. 1979. Introduction to *Toward the Making of Thoreau's Modern Reputation: Selected Correspondence of S. A. Jones, A. W. Hosmer, H. S. Salt, H. G. O. Blake, and D. Ricketson,* pp. 1–54. Urbana: University of Illinois Press.

Packer, B. L. 1995. "The Transcendentalists." In *The Cambridge History of American Literature,* edited by S. Bercovitch and C. R. K. Patell, vol. 2, *1820–1865.* Cambridge: Cambridge University Press.

Patôcka, J. 1989. "Edmund Husserl's Philosophy of the Crisis of the Sciences and His Conception of a Phenomenology of the Life-World." In *Philosophy and Selected Writings,* edited and translated by E. Kohàk, pp. 223–38. Chicago: University of Chicago Press.

Paul, S. 1958. *The Shores of America: Thoreau's Inward Exploration.* Urbana: University of Illinois Press.

———. 1992. "Three Reviews." In *For Love of the World: Essays on Nature Writers,* pp. 22–33. Iowa City: University of Iowa Press.

Peck, H. D. 1990. *Thoreau's Morning Work: Memory and Perception in "A Week on the Concord and Merrimack Rivers," the Journal, and "Walden."* New Haven and London: Yale University Press.

———. 1991. "Better Mythology: Perception and Emergence in Thoreau's Journal." *North Dakota Quarterly,* spring 1991, pp. 33–45.

Peperzak, A. 1993. *To the Other: An Introduction to the Philosophy of Emmanuel Levinas.* West Lafayette, Ind.: Purdue University Press.

Perkins, M. A. 1994. *Coleridge's Philosophy: The Logos as a Unifying Principle.* Oxford: Clarendon Press.

Petroski, H. 1989. *The Pencil: A History of Design and Circumstance.* New York: Alfred A. Knopf.

Pick, D. 1997. "Stories of the Eye." In *Rewriting the Self: Histories from the Renaissance to the Present,* edited by R. Porter, pp. 186–99. London and New York: Routledge.

Pillsbury, H. 1927. *New Hampshire: Resources, Attractions, and Its People*. Vol. 1. New York: Lewis Historical Publishing Co.

Polanyi, M. 1962. *Personal Knowledge: Towards a Post-critical Philosophy*. Corrected ed. Chicago: University of Chicago Press. Original edition published in 1958.

————. 1966. *The Tacit Dimension*. Garden City, N.Y.: Doubleday.

Porte, J. 1966. *Emerson and Thoreau: Transcendentalists in Conflict*. Middletown: Wesleyan University Press.

————. 1991. *In Respect to Egotism: Studies in American Romantic Writing*. Cambridge: Cambridge University Press.

Postlethwaite, D. 1984. *Making It Whole: A Victorian Circle and the Shape of Their World*. Columbus: Ohio State University Press.

Putnam, H. 1982. "Beyond the Fact/Value Dichotomy." *Critica* 14:3–12. Reprinted in *Realism with a Human Face*, edited by J. Conant, pp. 135–41. Cambridge: Harvard University Press, 1990. Also reprinted in *Science and the Quest for Reality*, edited by A. Tauber, pp. 363–69. New York: New York University Press; London: Macmillan, 1997.

Rescher, N. 1997. *Objectivity: The Obligations of Impersonal Reason*. Notre Dame, Ind.: University of Notre Dame Press.

————, ed. 1990. *Aesthetic Factors in Natural Science*. Lanham, Md.: University Press of America.

Richardson, R. D., Jr. 1986. *Thoreau: A Life of the Mind*. Berkeley, Los Angeles, London: University of California Press.

————. 1993. Introduction to *Faith in a Seed: The Dispersion of Seeds and Other Late Natural History Writings*, by H. D. Thoreau, edited by B. P. Dean, pp. 3–17. Washington, D.C., and Covela, Calif.: Island Press/Shearwater Books.

————. 1995. *Emerson: The Mind on Fire*. Berkeley, Los Angeles, London: University of California Press.

Rieff, P. 1959. *Freud: The Mind of the Moralist*. New York: Viking Press.

————. 1966. *The Triumph of the Therapeutic: Uses of Faith after Freud*. New York: Harper and Row.

Rosen, S. 1999. "The Lived Present." In *Metaphysics in Ordinary Language*, pp. 15–38. New Haven: Yale University Press.

Rosenblum, N. L. 1996. Introduction to *Thoreau: Political Writings*, pp. vii–xxxi. Cambridge: Cambridge University Press.

Ross, D. [1923] 1995. *Aristotle*. London and New York: Routledge.

Rossi, W., ed. 1992. *Walden and Resistance to Civil Government*, by H. D. Thoreau. 2d ed. A Norton Critical Edition. New York: W. W. Norton and Co.

————. 1993. "Thoreau as a Philosophical Naturalist-Writer." In *Thoreau's World and Ours: A Natural Legacy*, edited by E. A. Schofield and R. C. Baron, pp. 64–73. Golden, Colo.: North American Press.

Salt, H. S. [1890] 1993. *Life of Henry David Thoreau*. Edited by G. Hendrick, W. Hendrick, and F. Oehlschlaeger. Urbana and Chicago: University of Illinois Press.

Sattelmeyer, R. 1988. *Thoreau's Reading: A Study in Intellectual History with Bibliographical Catalogue.* Princeton: Princeton University Press.

———. 1990. "The Remaking of *Walden.*" In *Writing the American Classics,* edited by J. Barbour and T. Quirk, pp. 53–78. Chapel Hill: University of North Carolina Press.

Sattelmeyer, R., and R. A. Hocks. 1985. "Thoreau and Coleridge's *Theory of Life.*" In *Studies in the American Renaissance,* edited by J. Myerson, pp. 269–84. Charlottesville: University Press of Virginia.

Schneider, R. J., ed. 2000. *Thoreau's Sense of Place: Essays in American Environmental Writing.* Iowa City: University of Iowa Press.

Schofield, R. E. 1970. *Mechanism and Materialism: British Natural Philosophy in an Age of Reason.* Princeton: Princeton University Press.

Seamon, D., and A. Zajonc, eds. 1998. *Goethe's Way of Science.* Albany: State University of New York Press.

Sells, M. A. 1994. *Mystical Languages of Unsaying.* Chicago: University of Chicago Press.

Shanley, J. L. 1957. *The Making of Walden.* Chicago: University of Chicago Press.

Shelley, P. B. [1821] 1977. "A Defense of Poetry." In *Shelley's Poetry and Prose: Authoritative Texts and Criticism,* edited by D. H. Reiman and S. B. Powers, pp. 480–508. New York: W. W. Norton.

Shepard, O. 1937. *Pedlar's Progress: The Life of Bronson Alcott.* Boston: Little, Brown and Co.

Simon, W. M. 1963. *European Positivism in the Nineteenth Century.* Ithaca: Cornell University Press.

———. 1973. "Positivism in Europe to 1900." In *Dictionary of the History of Ideas,* edited by P. P. Wiener, 3:532–39. New York: Scribner's.

Slovic, S. 1992. *Seeking Awareness in American Nature Writing: Henry Thoreau, Annie Dillard, Edward Abbey, Wendell Berry, Barry Lopez.* Salt Lake City: University of Utah Press.

Smith, J. 1994. *Fact and Feeling: Baconian Science and the Nineteenth-Century Literary Imagination.* Madison: University of Wisconsin Press.

Smith, S. 1995. "Judging Hannah." *Yankee Magazine,* January 1995, pp. 52–55, 118–21.

Smocovitis, V. B. 1996. *Unifying Biology: The Evolutionary Synthesis and Evolutionary Biology.* Princeton: Princeton University Press.

Snow, C. P. 1959. *The Two Cultures.* Cambridge: Cambridge University Press.

Squires, J. D. 1956. *The Granite State of the United States: A History of New Hampshire from 1623 to the Present.* New York: American Historical Co.

Stack, G. J. 1992. *Nietzsche and Emerson: An Elective Affinity.* Athens: Ohio University Press.

Suppe, F. 1977. *The Structure of Scientific Theories.* 2d ed. Urbana: University of Illinois Press.

Tauber, A. I. 1992. "The Organismal Self: Its Philosophical Context." In *Selves, People, and Persons,* edited by L. Rouner, pp. 149–67. Notre Dame, Ind.: University of Notre Dame Press.

———. 1993. "Goethe's Philosophy of Science: Modern Resonances." *Perspectives in Biology and Medicine* 36:244–57.

———. 1994. *The Immune Self: Theory or Metaphor?* Cambridge and New York: Cambridge University Press.

———. 1995. "From the Self to the Other: Building a Philosophy of Medicine." In *Meta Medical Ethics: The Philosophical Foundations of Bioethics,* edited by M. A. Grodin, pp. 149–95. Dordrecht: Kluwer Academic Publishers.

———. 1996a. "From Descartes' Dream to Husserl's Nightmare." In *Aesthetics and Science: The Elusive Synthesis,* edited by A. I. Tauber, pp. 289–312. Dordrecht: Kluwer Academic Publishers.

———. 1998a. "Ecology and the Claims for a Science-Based Ethics." In *Philosophies of Nature: The Human Dimension,* edited by R. S. Cohen and A. I. Tauber, pp. 185–206. Dordrecht: Kluwer Academic Publishers.

———. 1998b. "Outside the Subject: Levinas's Jewish Perspective on Time." *Graduate Faculty Philosophy Journal* (New School for Social Research, N.Y.), 20/21:139–59.

———. 1999a. *Confessions of a Medicine Man: An Essay in Popular Philosophy.* Cambridge: MIT Press.

———. 1999b. Review of *The Historiography of Contemporary Science and Technology,* edited by T. Soderqvist (Amsterdam: Harwood Academic Publishers, 1997). *Science, Technology, and Human Values* 24:384–401.

———. 1999c. "The Elusive Immune Self: A Case of Category Errors." *Perspectives in Biology and Medicine* 42:459–74.

———, ed. 1996b. *Aesthetics and Science: The Elusive Synthesis.* Dordrecht: Kluwer Academic Publishers.

———, ed. 1997. *Science and the Quest for Reality.* New York: New York University Press; London: Macmillan.

Tauber, A. I., and L. Chernyak. 1991. *Metchnikoff and the Origins of Immunology: From Metaphor to Theory.* New York and Oxford: Oxford University Press.

Taylor, B. P. 1996. *America's Bachelor Uncle: Thoreau and the American Polity.* Lawrence: University Press of Kansas.

Taylor, C. 1989. *The Sources of the Self.* Cambridge: Harvard University Press.

Taylor, M. C. 1987. *Alterity.* Chicago: University of Chicago Press.

Teske, R. J. 1996. *Paradoxes of Time in Saint Augustine.* Milwaukee: Marquette University Press.

Thoreau, H. D. [1906] 1962. *The Journal of Henry David Thoreau.* Edited by B. Torrey and F. H. Allen. New York: Dover Books.

———. 1958. *The Correspondence of Henry David Thoreau.* Edited by W. Harding and C. Bode. New York: New York University Press.

———. 1971. *The Writings of Henry D. Thoreau: Walden.* Edited by J. L. Shanley. Princeton: Princeton University Press.

———. 1972. *The Writings of Henry D. Thoreau: The Maine Woods.* Edited by J. J. Moldenhauer. Princeton: Princeton University Press.

———. 1973a. *The Writings of Henry D. Thoreau: Reform Papers.* Edited by W. Glick. Princeton: Princeton University Press.

———. 1973b. "Resistance to Civil Government." In *The Writings of Henry D. Thoreau: Reform Papers,* edited by W. Glick, pp. 63–90. Princeton: Princeton University Press.

———. 1973c. "Slavery in Massachusetts." In *The Writings of Henry D. Thoreau: Reform Papers,* edited by W. Glick, pp. 91–109. Princeton: Princeton University Press.

———. 1975a. "Thomas Carlyle and His Works." In *The Writings of Henry D. Thoreau: Early Essays and Miscellanies,* edited by J. J. Moldenhauer, E. Moser, and A. Kern, pp. 219–67. Princeton: Princeton University Press.

———. 1975b. "Homer. Ossian. Chaucer." In *The Writings of Henry D. Thoreau: Early Essays and Miscellanies,* edited by J. J. Moldenhauer, E. Moser, and A. Kern, pp. 154–73. Princeton: Princeton University Press.

———. 1975c. "Dark Ages." In *The Writings of Henry D. Thoreau: Early Essays and Miscellanies,* edited by J. J. Moldenhauer, E. Moser, and A. Kern, pp. 143–46. Princeton: Princeton University Press. Originally published in *The Dial* 3, no. 4 (April 1843): 527–29.

———. 1980a. *The Writings of Henry D. Thoreau: A Week on the Concord and Merrimack Rivers.* Edited by C. F. Hovde, W. L. Howarth, and E. H. Witherell. Princeton: Princeton University Press.

———. 1980b. "Walking." In *The Natural History Essays,* introduction and notes by R. Sattelmeyer, pp. 93–136. Salt Lake City: Gibbs-Smith Publisher.

———. 1980c. "Natural History of Massachusetts." In *The Natural History Essays,* introduction and notes by R. Sattelmeyer, pp. 1–29. Salt Lake City: Gibbs-Smith Publisher.

———. 1980d. "Autumnal Tints." In *The Natural History Essays,* introduction and notes by R. Sattelmeyer, pp. 137–77. Salt Lake City: Gibbs-Smith Publisher.

———. 1980e. "A Winter Walk." In *The Natural History Essays,* introduction and notes by R. Sattelmeyer, pp. 51–71. Salt Lake City: Gibbs-Smith Publisher.

———. 1980f. "The Succession of Forest Trees." In *The Natural History Essays,* introduction and notes by R. Sattelmeyer, pp. 72–92. Salt Lake City: Gibbs-Smith Publisher.

———. 1981. *The Writings of Henry D. Thoreau: Journal.* Vol. 1, *1837–1844,* edited by E. H. Witherell, W. L. Howarth, R. Sattelmeyer, and T. Blanding. Princeton: Princeton University Press.

———. 1984. *The Writings of Henry D. Thoreau: Journal.* Vol. 2, *1842–1848,* edited by R. Sattelmeyer. Princeton: Princeton University Press.

———. 1988. *The Writings of Henry D. Thoreau: Cape Cod.* Edited by J. J. Moldenhauer. Princeton: Princeton University Press.

———. 1990. *The Writings of Henry D. Thoreau: Journal.* Vol. 3, *1848–1851,* edited by R. Sattelmeyer, M. R. Patterson, and W. Rossi. Princeton: Princeton University Press.

———. 1992. *The Writings of Henry D. Thoreau: Journal*. Vol. 4, *1851–1852*, edited by L. N. Neufeldt and N. C. Simmons. Princeton: Princeton University Press.

———. 1993. "The Dispersion of Seeds." In *Faith in a Seed: The Dispersion of Seeds and Other Late Natural History Writings*, edited by B. P. Dean, pp. 23–123. Washington, D.C., and Covela, Calif.: Island Press/Shearwater Books.

———. 1997. *The Writings of Henry D. Thoreau: Journal*. Vol. 5, *1852–1853*, edited by P. F. O'Connell. Princeton: Princeton University Press.

———. 2000. *Wild Fruits: Thoreau's Rediscovered Last Manuscript*. Edited and introduced by B. P. Dean. New York: W. W. Norton and Co.

Torrance, R. M. 1994. *The Spiritual Quest: Transcendence in Myth, Religion, and Science*. Berkeley, Los Angeles, London: University of California Press.

Toulmin, S. 1984. Introduction to Dewey [1929] 1984, pp. vii–xii.

Tuerk, R. 1975. *Central Still: Circle and Sphere in Thoreau's Prose*. The Hague and Paris: Mouton.

Tyndall, J. 1854. "On the Study of Physics." In *Fragments of Science*, 7th ed., 2 vols. London: Longmans, 1889.

———. 1865. "Vitality." In *Fragments of Science*, 7th ed., 2 vols. London: Longmans, 1889.

Ulrich, L. T. 1982. *Good Wives: Image and Reality in the Lives of Women in Northern New England, 1650–1750*. New York: Alfred A. Knopf.

Van Cromphout, G. 1990. *Emerson's Modernity and the Example of Goethe*. Columbia and London: University of Missouri Press.

Von Frank, A. J. 1998. *The Trials of Anthony Burns: Freedom and Slavery in Emerson's Boston*. Cambridge: Harvard University Press.

Walls, L. D. 1993. "Seeing New Worlds: Thoreau and Humboldtian Science." In *Thoreau's World and Ours: A Natural Legacy*, edited by E. A. Schofield and R. C. Baron, pp. 55–63. Golden, Colo.: North American Press.

———. 1995. *Seeing New Worlds: Henry David Thoreau and Nineteenth-Century Natural Science*. Madison: University of Wisconsin Press.

Weber, M. [1922] 1946. "Science as Vocation." In *From Max Weber: Essays in Sociology*, translated and edited by H. H. Gerth and C. W. Mills, pp. 137–56. New York: Oxford University Press.

Wells, G. 1971. "Goethe's Qualitative Optics." *Journal of the History of Ideas* 32:617–26.

Whitehead, A. N. 1925. *Science and the Modern World*. New York: Macmillan.

Williams, B. 1985. *Ethics and the Limits of Philosophy*. Cambridge: Harvard University Press.

Wilson, E. 1999. *Emerson's Sublime Science*. Houndsmills: Macmillan Press; New York: St. Martin's Press.

Wittgenstein, L. [1922] 1981. *Tractatus Logico-Philosophicus*. Translated by C. K. Ogden. London and New York: Routledge.

———. 1953. *Philosophical Investigations*. New York: Macmillan.

———. 1961. *Notebooks, 1914–1916*. Oxford: Blackwell.

Wordsworth, W. [1800] 1965. Preface to *Lyrical Ballads*, 2d ed. In *Selected Poems and Prefaces*, edited by J. Stillinger, pp. 445–64. Boston: Houghton Mifflin.

Worster, D. 1994. *Nature's Economy: A History of Ecological Ideas*. 2d ed. New York and Cambridge: Cambridge University Press.

Wyschogrod, E. 1974. *Emmanuel Levinas: The Problem of Ethical Metaphysics*. The Hague: Martinus Nijhoff.

Yeo, R. R. 1985. "An Idol of the Market-Place: Baconism in Nineteenth-Century Britain." *History of Science* 23:251–98.

———. 1993. *Defining Science: William Whewell, Natural Knowledge, and Public Debate in Early Victorian Britain*. Cambridge: Cambridge University Press.

Young, J. 1992. *Nietzsche's Philosophy of Art*. Cambridge: Cambridge University Press.

Zagzebski, L. T. 1996. *Virtues of the Mind: An Inquiry of Virtue and the Ethical Foundations of Knowledge*. Cambridge: Cambridge University Press.

Index

Compositor:	Impressions Book and Journal Services, Inc.
Text:	10/13 Aldus
Display:	Aldus
Printer and binder:	Haddon Craftsmen